THE AUTHENTIC MUSNAD OF

Reasons for the Decending of
REVELATION

ABRIDGED VERSION

By the Reviver of the Sunnah in the Land of Yemen
Ash-Sheikh Muqbil ibn Haadi al-Waadi'ee

© Authentic Statements Publishing, USA

All rights reserved. No part of this publication may be reproduced in any language, stored in any retrieval system or transmitted in any form or by any means, weather electronic, mechanic, photocopying, recording or otherwise, without express permission of the copyright owner.

ISBN : 978-1-4675-1821-5

First Edition : February 2012

Cover Design: Usul Design

E-mail: info@usuldesign.com

Abridged, translated and footnotes added by:
Abdullah MacPhee

Publisher's Information:
Authentic Statements Publishing
P.O.Box 15536
Phila,Pa. 19131
215.382-3382
215.382.3782-Fax

Store:
5000 Locust St.(Side Entrance)
Phila Pa 19139

Website:
authenticstatements.com

E-mail:
info@authenticstatements.com

Please visit our website for upcoming publications, audio/Dvd online catalog, and info on events and seminars, insha Allah.

Table of Contents:

Sooratul Baqarah	Pg.18
Sooratu Aali 'Imraan	Pg.58
Sooratun-Nisaa	Pg.82
Sooratul-Maa'idah	Pg.109
Sooratul-An'aam	Pg.123
Sooratul-A'raaf	Pg.126
Sooratul-Anfaal	Pg.128
Sooratut-Tawbah	Pg.141
Sooratu Hud	Pg.159
Sooratu Yoosuf	Pg.162
Sooratul-Ra'd	Pg.164
Sooratun-Nahl	Pg.167
Sooratul-Israa	Pg.174
Sooratu Maryam	Pg.181
Sooratul-Anbiyaa	Pg.183
Sooratul-Hajj	Pg.185
Sooratul-Mu'minoon	Pg.186
Sooratun-Noor	Pg.187
Sooratul-Qasas	Pg.209
Sooratul-Ankaboot	Pg.211
Sooratu Luqmaan	Pg.214
Sooratus-Sajdah	Pg.216
Sooratul-Ahzaab	Pg.217
Sooratu Yaa Seen	Pg.234
Sooratuz-Zumar	Pg.236
Sooratu Fussila	Pg.240
Sooratush-Shooraa	Pg.242
Sooratuz-Zukhruf	Pg.245
Sooratud-Dukhaan	Pg.247
Sooratul-Jaathiyah	Pg.249
Sooratul-Fath	Pg.251
Sooratul-Hujuraat	Pg.274
Sooratul-Qamar	Pg.278
Sooratul-Waaqi'ah	Pg.281
Sooratul-Mujaadilah	Pg.283
Sooratul-Hashr	Pg.287
Sooratul-Mumtahanah	Pg.292
Sooratus-Saff	Pg.294
Sooratul-Jumu'ah	Pg.296

Sooratul-Munaafiqoon	Pg.298
Sooratut-Tahreem	Pg.300
Sooratul-Jinn	Pg.307
Sooratul-Muzzammil	Pg.309
Sooratul-Muddath'thir	Pg.310
Sooratul-Qiyaamah	Pg.313
Sooratun-Naazi'aat	Pg.316
Sooratu 'Abasa	Pg.317
Sooratul-Mutaffifeen	Pg.318
Sooratud-Duhaa	Pg.319
Sooratul-'Alaq	Pg.321
Sooratul-Masad	Pg.324

بسم الله الرحمن الرحيم

Verily all praise[1] is due to Allaah. We praise Him, seek His aid, and ask for His forgiveness. We seek refuge in Allaah from the evil of our souls and from our evil deeds. Whoever Allaah guides, then he is truly guided; and whoever Allaah misguides, no one can guide him. I bear witness that there is no deity that has the right to be worshipped except Allaah, alone without any partner, and I bear witness that Muhammad is His slave and messenger.

O you who believe, fear Allaah as He should be feared and die not except as Muslims. O mankind, fear your Lord who created you from one soul and from that soul created its mate, and produced there from many men and women. And fear Allaah, He through whom you demand your mutual rights; and guard the ties of the wombs, indeed, Allaah is Ever-Watchful over you. O you who believe, fear Allaah and speak the truth; he will guide you to do righteous deeds and forgive you of your sins, and whoever obeys Allaah and His Messenger has indeed achieved a great achievement.

Of the books that Allaah has enabled me to compile is *As-Saheehul-Musnad Min Asbaab An-Nuzool* (The Authentic *Musnad*[2] of Reasons for the Descending of the Revelation). And indeed I praise Allaah ﷻ, who has made [the project] beneficial such that it it has become a source of reference for this subject. [I find that] I refer back to it during my research, writings and teachings! During its initial composition I mentioned some of the *ahaadeeth* (narrations on the Prophet ﷺ) pertaining to the main *hadeeth* of the chapter without their chains. In this print, however, I decided to mention the chains that I came across [during its compilation]. Similarly in the initial print, I only mentioned the highlighting point from some of the *ahaadeeth* but have now decided to mention the *hadeeth* in entirety because of the benefits related to doing so. As for mentioning the chain of narrators, this was done in an effort to imitate the practice of our scholars, may Allaah ﷻ have mercy upon them, who would refuse to accept a *hadeeth* without its chain?

---

[1] The Arabic word حمد (*hamd*) is translated into English as praise, however, in that translation some of the meaning is lost. The great scholar Ibnul-Qayyim ﷺ has defined *hamd* as: "Mentioning the beautiful attributes of the one being praised out of love, high-esteem and exaltation." Therefore, if praise is not accompanied by love and exaltation it is not called *hamd*, rather it is called مدح (*madh*). For more, refer to Ibnul-Qayyim's book *Badaa'i Al-Fawaa'id* volume 2, page 93.

[2] *Musnad* meaning the Sheikh ﷺ mentions the narrations with their chains. This practice, long abandoned, has been revived by the likes of our Sheikh Muqbil ﷺ. *Musnad* can also be used for a *hadeeth* that has a connected chain to the Prophet ﷺ, or it can be used for a book that mentions *ahaadeeth* arranged according to the names of the Companions who narrated them like the *Musnad* of Al-Imaam Ahmad for example. As-Suyootee mentioned these usages in his book *Al-Bahrul-ladhee Zakhar*, volume 1, pages 315-316.

Al-Haafidh Al-'Alaa'ee said in his book *Jaami' At-Tahseel*, page 58, "...also in *Saheeh Muslim* it has been narrated that Ibn Seereen stated, 'They (the scholars) did not used to ask about the chain but once the *fitnah*[3] (strife) occurred they starting saying to those who related narrations , 'Name for us your people.' So they would accept the narrations of followers of the Sunnah and would refuse narrations of the people of *bid'ah* (innovation)."[4] Similarly Sufyaan ibn 'Uyainah once stated, "Az-Zuhree narrated one narrated a *hadeeth* and I said to him, 'Quote it without a chain.' He replied, "Do you climb the roof without a ladder?"[5] Likewise Baqeeyah stated, "'Utbah ibn Abee Hakeem narrated to us that he was with Ishaaq ibn Abee Farwah in the presence of Az-Zuhree when Ibn Abee Farwah began saying, 'The Messenger of Allaah ﷺ said...'. So Az-Zuhree responded, '*Qaatalakallaah*![6] How bold you are! Why don't you mention the chain of your *hadeeth*? You narrate to us *ahaadeeth* that do not have any reins to hold on to."[7] Also, 'Abdus-Samad ibn Hassaan stated, "I heard Sufyaan Ath-Thawree say, 'The chain is the weapon of the believer; if he does not have a weapon, with what will he

---

[3] Al-Haafidh Abul-'Abbaas Ahmad ibn 'Umar Al-Qurtubee said in *Al-Mufhim*, volume 1, pages 122-123, "This *fitnah*, he intends by it, and Allaah knows best, the *fitnah* of the killing of 'Uthmaan ؓ and the *fitnah* of the uprising of the *khawaarij* against 'Ali and Mu'aawiyah, for verily they declared those two to be disbelievers and they considered lawful the blood and the wealth (of the Muslims). There is a difference of opinion over declaring these people (the *khawaarij*) to be disbelievers, and there is no doubt that the one who declares them to be disbelievers does not accept their *hadeeth*, and those who do not declare them to be disbelievers have differed over accepting their *hadeeth* as we have explained beforehand. So what he meant by that, and Allaah knows best, is that the killers of 'Uthmaan and the *khawaarij* since they are certainly evildoers and their narrations have been mixed with the narrations of those not amongst them it is incumbent to search for their narrations so they can be rejected and to search for the narrations of others from those who are not from them so they can be accepted. Then the rule applies likewise to those other than them from the people of innovations."

[4] This narration on Ibn Seereen has been transmitted by Muslim in the preface to his *Saheeh* (27) and others with an authentic chain.

[5] This narration on Az-Zuhree has been transmitted by Al-Baihaqee in his book *Manaaqib Ash-Shaafi'ee*, volume 2, page 34, with a chain that is extremely weak. In the chain is Abu 'Abdir-Rahmaan As-Sulamee who has been accused of forging *ahaadeeth* for the Soofees.

[6] This phrase literally means, "may Allaah kill you", however, the Arabs often use this phrase when they are surprised at someone for doing something they disapprove of not intending its literal meaning. Refer to the book *An-Nihaayah* by Ibn Al-Atheer, volume 4, page 12, for more detail.

[7] This narration on Az-Zuhree has been transmitted by Ibn Hibbaan in his book *Al-Majrooheen*, volume 1, pages 131-132, and At-Tirmidhee in *Al-'Ilal As-Sagheer*, and Al-Haakim in *Ma'rifah 'Uloom Al-Hadeeth*, page 6, and others. In the chain is 'Utbah ibn Abee Hakeem who has some weakness in narrating, however, here he is narrating a story that he himself witnessed strengthening the position that the narration is authentic, and Allaah knows best.

fight?'"[8] In this regard Shu'bah said, "Every *hadeeth* that does not read *haddathanaa* and *akhbaranaa*[9] is like vinegar and *baql*."[10][11] Also, in *Saheeh Muslim* 'Abdaan has mentioned, "I heard 'Abdullaah ibn Al-Mubaarak say, 'The chain, as far as I am concerned, is from the *deen* (religion). If it were not for the chain, anyone could say whatever he wanted." Similarly, Al-'Abbaas ibn Abee Rizmah said, "I heard 'Abdullaah ibn Al-Mubaarak say, 'Between us and them (the people) are the pillars (meaning the chain)." Also, Ibraaheem ibn 'Eesaa At-Taalaqaanee said, "I said to 'Abdullaah ibn Al-Mubaaraak, 'O Abaa 'Abdir-Rahmaan, [inform me about] the *hadeeth* which reads, "Indeed from righteousness after righteousness is to pray on behalf of your parents with your prayer, and to fast on their behalf with your fasting.' 'Abdullaah then said, "O Abaa Ishaaq, who narrated that [hadeeth]?" I said, 'This is one of the narrations of Shihaab ibn Khiraash.' He asked, "He is trustworthy. On whom did he narrate?" I said, "On Al-Hajjaaj ibn Deenaar." He said, "He is trustworthy. On whom did he narrate?" I said, "On the Messenger of Allaah ﷺ." He said, "O Abaa Ishaaq, verily between Al-Hajjaaj ibn Deenaar and the Prophet ﷺ is a long distance of deserts that the riding animals traverse,[12] however, there is no difference of opinion about giving charity on behalf of

---

[8] This narration on Sufyaan Ath-Thawree has been transmitted by Ibn Hibbaan in the preface of his book *Al-Majrooheen*, volume 1, page 27, and Al-Haakim in his book *Al-Madkhal ilal-Ikleel*, and Al-Harawee in his book *Dham Al-Kalaam* (891), and As-Sam'aanee in his book *Adab Al-Imlaa* page 8, and Al-Khateeb in his book *Sharaf Ashaab Al-Hadeeth*, page 42. In the chain of this narration is Al-Husain ibn Faraj who has been declared a liar, so this narration is extremely weak.

[9] *Haddathanaa* and *akhbarnaa* are from the phrases that the people of *hadeeth* use when narrating a *hadeeth*, meaning so and so narrated to us, and so and so reported to us.

[10] The word *baql* is commonly used for vegetation specifically consumed by humans without having to be cooked. For example: leeks, cress, radish tops, etc. Some linguists challenge this usage giving this word a different meaning. Refer to the book *Khizaanah Al-Adab*, volume 1, pages 49-50, for more.

[11] What is meant by this statement is just as vinegar and *baql* are not a prized commodity in the peoples' eyes, similar to that with Shu'bah is a *hadeeth* which its chain does not contain these phrases that clearly affirm the chain to be connected. If this is the case with a *hadeeth* that has a chain without these phrases, how much worse is the case of a *hadeeth* without a chain. This narration on Shu'bah has been transmitted by Al-Baghawee in *Al-Ja'diyaat* (32), and Ar-Raamahurmuzee in *Al-Muhaddith Al-Faasil* (649), and Abu Ya'laa in *Tabaqaat Al-Hanaabilah*, volume 1, page 300, and Abu Nu'aim in *Al-Hilyah*, volume 7, page 149, and Al-Haakim in *Al-Madkhal ilaa Al-Ikleel*, and others, and it is authentic.

[12] What is meant by this statement is there is no way that Al-Hajjaaj ibn Deenaar heard from the Messenger of Allaah ﷺ because Al-Hajjaaj is from the time period of the Successors of the *Taabi'een*. The *Taabi'een* are those who met some of the Companions of the Prophet ﷺ and died as a believers.

your parents."[13] (End quote from what Al-'Alaa'ee ﷺ mentioned in his book *Jaami' At-Tahseel*)[14]

And take, for example, the story of Shu'bah, how he traveled searching for a single *hadeeth*. Ibn Abee Haatim said in his book *Al-Jarh wat-Ta'deel*, volume 1, page 167, "'Ali ibn Al-Husain ibn Al-Junaid narrated to us that 'Ali ibn Al-Madeenee said, 'Bishr ibn Al-Mufaddal narrated to us saying, "Israa'eel came to us and narrated to us on Abu Ishaaq on 'Abdullaah ibn 'Ataa on 'Uqbah ibn 'Aamir two *hadeeth*. I then went to Shu'bah and said, "You are not doing anything, Israa'eel narrated to us on Abu Ishaaq on 'Abdullaah ibn 'Ataa on 'Uqbah such-and-such." He (Shu'bah) then said, "O insane one, Abu Ishaaq narrated this to us so I said to Abu Ishaaq, "Who is 'Abdullaah ibn 'Ataa?" He said, "A young man from the people of *Al-Basrah* who came here to us." So I went to *Al-Basrah* and asked about him and found out that he sits with so-and-so but he was not present. He then came, so I asked him and he narrated the hadeeth to me. I then said, "Who narrated it to you?" He said, "Ziyaad ibn Mikhraaq narrated it to me," and by doing so, he referred me to a person of *hadeeth*. I then met Ziyaad ibn Mikhraaq and asked him, so he narrated it to me and said, "Some of our companions narrated to me on Shahr ibn Hawshab."[15]

Abu 'Abdir-Rahmaan (Ash-Sheikh Muqbil) said, "So in light of this this, those who exclude the chains from the books and publish them devoid of their chains, they have dealt erroneously with the knowledge and with our righteous predecessors, those who exerted great effort in following the chains and likewise exerted great efforts in traveling for them. Because of this, our brothers for Allaah's sake are eager to mention the *ahaadeeth* with their chains, and, praise is to Allaah, I have found an approval and acceptance of this; and The researchers are pleased, and all praise is due to Allaah, Lord of all that exists."

THE REASON I CHOSE THIS TOPIC

Verily, all praise is due to Allaah. We praise him, seek His aid and ask for His forgiveness. We seek refuge in Allaah from the evils of our souls and from our evil deeds. Whoever Allaah guides, no one can misguide him, and whoever Allaah misguides, no one can guide him. I bear witness that there is no deity that has the right to be worshipped except Allaah alone without any partner, and I bear witness that Muhammad is His Slave and Messenger.

---

[13] These three previous narrations on 'Abdullaah ibn Al-Mubaarak have been transmitted by Muslim in the preface of his *Saheeh* (32) and by others, and they are authentic.

[14] As you see the Sheikh quoted from the book *Jaami' At-Tahseel* without researching the chains of these narrations himself. That is why I checked these narrations.

[15] In this story Shu'bah traveled for the chain of this one *hadeeth*. Then at the end he finds it to be on Shahr ibn Hawshab, someone whose narrations Shu'bah rejects.

O you who believe, fear Allaah as He should be feared and die not except as Muslims. O mankind, fear your Lord who created you from one soul and created from it its mate and spread forth from them many men and women. And fear Allaah, He through whom you demand your mutual rights, and guard the ties of the wombs. Indeed, Allaah is Ever-Watchful over you. O you who believe, fear Allaah and speak the truth, He will guide you to do righteous deeds and forgive you your sins.   And whoever obeys Allaah and His Messenger has indeed achieved a great achievement.

To proceed: The topic I chose for my research paper that I was to submit to the Islamic University was *As-Saheehul-Musnad Min Asbaab An-Nuzool* (The Authentic *Musnad* of Reasons for the Descending of the Revelation). I chose this topic for several reasons, amongst them:

1. It is linked to two great sciences: *Tafseer* (the explanation) of Allaah's book and the *Sunnah* of the Messenger of Allaah ﷺ which together serve as are the foundation of our religion.
2. Knowing the reason why a verse was revealed helps us to understand its meaning. Some verses were difficult for some of the Companions of the Prophet ﷺ and those after them to understand until they knew the reason behind their revelation. Of the things that which was difficult for them to understand was the verse:

$$وَلَا تُلْقُوا۟ بِأَيْدِيكُمْ إِلَى ٱلتَّهْلُكَةِ$$

"And do not throw yourselves into destruction" (*Al-Baqarah*: 195) until Abu Ayyoob ؓ informed them about its reason for revelation, then the meaning became clear to them as will later be mentioned, if Allaah ﷻ wills. Another verse that initially escaped their understanding was Allah's statement:

$$ٱلَّذِينَ ءَامَنُوا۟ وَلَمْ يَلْبِسُوٓا۟ إِيمَٰنَهُم بِظُلْمٍ$$

"Those who believe and mix not their faith with wrongdoing…" (*Al-An'aam*: 82) until, in according to one narration of the *hadeeth*, the following verse was revealed:

$$إِنَّ ٱلشِّرْكَ لَظُلْمٌ عَظِيمٌ$$

"Verily joining others in worship with Allaah is a tremendous wrong," (*Luqmaan*: 13)
this will later be mentioned, if Allaah □ wills. Also, It was also difficult for 'Urwah to understand His statement:

$$إِنَّ ٱلصَّفَا وَٱلْمَرْوَةَ مِن شَعَآئِرِ ٱللَّهِ$$

"Verily, As-Safaa and Al-Marwah are from the signs of Allaah..." (*Al-Baqarah*: 158) until 'Aishah ﷺ told him why it was revealed.

3. Another thing that prompted me to choose this topic is that false information has crept into the subject of "Reasons for the Descending of the Revelation," as has occurred in the other sciences. Al-Waahidee ﷺ said in the preface of his book *Asbaab An-Nuzool* after he mentioned the statement of 'Abeedah As-Salmaanee when he was asked about a verse in the Qur'aan and said, "Fear Allaah and speak the truth! The people who know why the Qur'aan was revealed are gone." Al-Waahidee said, "As for today, everyone makes stuff up and invents lies throwing himself into ignorance without contemplating the threat in store for the ignorant in relation to the verse. And that is what has compelled me to write this book which comprises the reasons for the revelation, so that those studying this topic as well as those who talk about why the Qur'aan was revealed can come to know the truth and do without the distortions and the lies, and they can strive to memorize it after hearing and studying it"—End quote from Al-Waahidee's book, page 5 ﷺ. As-Suyootee mentioned in his book *Al-Itqaan*, volume 2, page 190, after mentioning a group of those who mention *Tafseer* (explanation of the Qur'aan) with chains, like Ibn Jareer, Ibn Abee Haatim and others, "...Then people started writing about *Tafseer* without chains and started quoting the different opinions, one after another, and from here false information crept in and the authentic got mixed with the unauthentic. Then it got to the point where anyone who had an opinion come to his mind would mention it and would use that as a basis. Then those after them would quote that statement thinking it had a basis without turning to what has been recorded from our righteous predecessors and those who are referred to for *Tafseer*, to such an extent that I came across someone who quoted in the explanation of His ﷻ statement:

غَيْرِ ٱلْمَغْضُوبِ عَلَيْهِمْ وَلَا ٱلضَّآلِّينَ

"Not the path of those who earned your anger or those who went astray," (*Al-Faatihah*: 7) ten opinions despite the fact that its explanation to mean the Jews and Christians has been reported on the Prophet ﷺ and all of the *Taabi'een* (Successors of the Companions) and the Successors of the *Taabi'een*, to the point where Ibn Abee Haatim said, "I know of no difference of opinion about that among the people of *Tafseer*"—End quote from the book *Al-Itqaan*.

I say, this is the reason why I mentioned the chains that I was able to find despite the fact that there is hardship in doing so, which is well known to the people of this science. Take one example which shows the truthfulness of what these two Imaams have mentioned regarding the negligence that has occurred in relation to unauthentic quotes in the books of *Tafseer*. This example is the story of Tha'labah ibn Haatib which includes the statement, "Doing little and carrying out its merit is better than doing more than you are able to do." The people of *Tafseer* mention this story in the explanation of Allaah's statement:

$$\text{وَمِنْهُم مَّنْ عَـٰهَدَ ٱللَّهَ لَئِنْ ءَاتَىٰنَا مِن فَضْلِهِۦ لَنَصَّدَّقَنَّ وَلَنَكُونَنَّ مِنَ ٱلصَّـٰلِحِينَ ۝}$$

"And from them are those who made a covenant with Allaah (saying), 'If He bestows on us from His bounty, we will indeed give charity and we will indeed be among those who are righteous.'" (*At-Tawbah*: 75).

Perhaps there is not a single book of *Tafseer* except this story is mentioned in it while only few mention that it is not authentic. However, as for the major Scholars of *hadeeth* who are critical in the way they analyze narrations, consider what they say about this story: Al-Imaam Abu Muhammad ibn Hazm stated after mentioning it the narration from the chain of Miskeen ibn Bukair:

Ma'aan ibn Rifaa'ah As-Sulamee narrated to us on 'Ali ibn Yazeed, on Al-Qaasim ibn 'Abdir-Rahmaan, on Abu Umaamah that he said, "Tha'labah ibn Haatib brought charity to 'Umar of which he refused to accept and said, 'The Prophet did not accept it nor did Abu Bakr and I will not accept it.'" Abu Muhammad ibn Hazm said, "This *hadeeth* is false without any doubt because Allaah gave an order to collect the *zakaah* (obligatory charity) from the Muslim's wealth, and the Prophet commanded at the time of his death that there should not remain in the Arabian Peninsula two religions. So Tha'labah is either a Muslim making it incumbent on Abu Bakr and 'Umar to collect his *zakaah* and there is no way out of that, or if he was a disbeliever then he must not be allowed to reside in the Arabian Peninsula. So this narration is false, without doubt. Furthermore, Ma'aan ibn Rifaa'ah, Al-Qaasim ibn 'Abdir-Rahmaan, and 'Ali ibn Yazeed who is Abu 'Abdil-Maalik Al-Alhaanee, are in the chain of narrators and all of them are weak; and Miskeen ibn Bukair is not a strong narrator"—End quote from Ibn Hazm's book *Al-Muhallaa*, volume 11, page 208.

As-Suyootee said in his book *Lubaabun-Nuqool*, "Its chain is weak." Al-Haafidh said in his book *Takhreej Al-Kash'shaaf*, "In its chain is 'Ali ibn Yazeed Al-Alhaanee, and he is *waahin* (very weak)." He also said in his book *Fathul-Baaree*, volume 3, page 8, after mentioning a part of the story, "…but it is *da'eef* (unauthentic), it can not be used as a proof." Al-Haithamee said in his book *Majma' Az-Zawaa'id*, volume 7, page 32, "It has been transmitted by At-Tabaraanee and in its chain is 'Ali ibn Yazeed Al-Alhaanee and he is *matrook* (meaning his narrations are abandoned)." Adh-Dhahabee said about it in his book *Tajreed Asmaa As-Sahaabah*, "It is a rejected *hadeeth*." Al-Munaawee said in his book *Faid Al-Qadeer*, volume 4, page 527, "Al-Baihaqee said, 'In the chain of this *hadeeth* is a defect and it is popular with the people of *Tafseer*.'" Furthermore, he (Ibn Hajar) alluded to the unauthenticity of this *hadeeth* in his book *Al-Isaabah* where he mentioned this *hadeeth* in the biography of Tha'labah and then said, "…and regarding him being the person of this story, if it were authentic, which I doubt is the case, the issue of him being *Al-Badree* (from the people who fought at Badr) is something which needs to be examined"— End quote of Al-Munaawee. Al-Haafidh Al-'Iraaqee said in his book *Takhreej Al-Ihyaa*, volume 3, page 338, "Its chain is weak."

I only used this story as an example because of its popularity in the books of *Tafseer* and because many of our brothers who busy themselves with giving lectures and spreading guidance, may Allaah guide me and them, see it to be a good story so they relate it to the common people without paying attention to the fact that along with its chain being unauthentic, the meaning is not authentic because it contradicts a principle of the religion, a principle which holds that whenever a person repents, even if his sins were to reach the clouds of the sky, if he repents, Allaah accepts his repentance.

4. An additional impetus which urged me to choose this topic was the desire to get acquainted with the secrets of this great legislation and the lessons found in the reasons for revelation , specifically how it ameliorates the difficulties that weigh heavily on the people until the relief from Allaah ensues. Such as the story of the three whose case was deferred and the story of the slander which was responsible for the grief that the Prophet of guidance ﷺ suffered in consequence of its occurrence because of it and the grief that the Mother of the Believers suffered as she cried so much to such an extent that her parents thought her crying would cause her liver to tear. Ultimately, the relief came after that hardship. And like the story of Hilaal ibn Umaiyah when he accused his wife of committing adultery, so the Messenger of Allaah ﷺ said to him, "Provide proof or the legal punishment will be inflicted on your back." So he said, "By the one who has sent you with the truth, I am telling the truth and indeed Allaah will send down a vindication which will free my back from the legal punishment." The Messenger of Allaah ﷺ nearly ordered for him to be flogged when Allaah sent down the verse of *Al-li'aan* (*An-Noor*: 6-9) and substantiated his (Hilaal's) oath and provided the remedy after the illness had become critical. So may failure and loss be the plight of one who thinks he can do without this wise legislation.

5. Another point that influenced me to choose this topic was the hope that benefit will be gained from examining the different phases undergone by the legislation; we are in urgent need of regarding ourselves as revivers and starting the *da'wah* (call to Islaam) anew. In light of that, the reasons for the revelation offer an abundance of good in clarifying the phases of *da'wah* along with divine instructions from Allaah. Such as the verse about fighting; it was not revealed until after Allaah knew they had the capability to fight, as well as other examples which highlight the difference between *Al-Makkee* (that which descended before the *hijrah*) and *Al-Madanee* (that which descended after the *hijrah*) as is well known.

NOTE:

I tried my best to gather the different chains of the *hadeeth* because of the benefits associated with this endeavor, such as knowing whether or not the chain is fully connected, or not and knowing if the narration is authentic or weak due to a hidden defect, because at times a *hadeeth's* chain may appear to be authentic in one book while in another it reveals a hidden defect. Ibnus-Salaah said in his book *'Uloom Al-Hadeeth*, page 82, "It has been narrated that 'Ali ibn Al-Madeenee said, 'If the chains of the *hadeeth* are not juxtaposed, its defect will not become apparent.'"[16] For example, Al-Haakim said in his book *Al-Mustadrak*, volume 3, page 324, "Abul-'Abbaas Muhammad ibn Ya'qoob narrated to us that Ahmad ibn 'Abdil-Jabbaar narrated to us that Yoonus ibn Bukair narrated to us on Ibn Ishaaq that Yahyaa ibn 'Abbaad ibn 'Abdillaah ibn Az-Zubair narrated to us on his father, on 'Aishah that she said:

When the people of Makkah came to pay ransom for their prisoners of war, Zainab the daughter of the Messenger of Allaah sent the ransom money to free Abul-'Aas (her husband). In that ransom money was a necklace that Khadeejah gave her to wear for her wedding night with Abul-'Aas. When the Messenger of Allaah saw the necklace he became overwhelmed with sympathy and said (to his companions), 'If you see releasing her prisoner of war and returning to her what she sent to be a good idea, then do so.' They replied, 'Yes, O Messenger of Allaah,' and then proceeded accordingly and returned to her what she sent as ransom money. Al-'Abbaas said, 'O Messenger of Allaah, I was and still am a Muslim.'[17] The Messenger of Allaah replied, 'Allaah knows best about your Islaam. If what you say is true then Allaah will reward you. Pay ransom for yourself and the sons of

---

[16] Al-Khateeb has transmitted this narration on Ibn Al-Madeenee in his book *Al-Jaami' li Akhlaaq Ar-Raawee wa Aadaab As-Saami'*, volume 2, page 212. In the chain there is a narrator who was not named, so the chain is not authentic.

[17] This story took place after the battle of Badr. Al-'Abbaas fought on the side of the polytheists and was captured. This part of the story where he supposedly said, "I was and still am a Muslim," is not authentic as the Sheikh will mention.

your two brothers, Nawfal ibn Al-Haarith ibn 'Abdil-Muttalib and 'Aqeel ibn Abee Taalib ibn 'Abdil-Muttalib, and for your ally 'Utbah ibn 'Amr ibn Jahdam the brother of the tribe Banee Al-Haartih ibn Fihr.' He said, 'I do not have that, O Messenger of Allaah.' He ﷺ said, "Where is the money that you and Umm Al-Fadl buried together when you said to her, "if I die this money is for the children of Al-Fadl, and 'Abdullaah and Qutham"?" He said, 'I swear by Allaah, O Messenger of Allaah, I bear witness that you are Allah's Messenger. This matter, none but Umm Al-Fadl and I knew about it. Take from me as ransom twenty *uqeeyah*[18] from the money I had with me.' The Messenger of Allaah ﷺ said, "I agree to that." So Al-'Abbaas ransomed himself, the sons of his two brothers and his ally. And Allaah ﷻ sent down:

$$\text{يَٰٓأَيُّهَا ٱلنَّبِيُّ قُل لِّمَن فِىٓ أَيْدِيكُم مِّنَ ٱلْأَسْرَىٰٓ إِن يَعْلَمِ ٱللَّهُ فِى قُلُوبِكُمْ خَيْرًا يُؤْتِكُمْ خَيْرًا مِّمَّآ أُخِذَ مِنكُمْ وَيَغْفِرْ لَكُمْ ۗ وَٱللَّهُ غَفُورٌ رَّحِيمٌ ۝}$$

"O Prophet, say to the captives that are in your hands, "If Allaah knows any good in your hearts He will give you something better than what has been taken from you and He will forgive you, and Allaah is Oft-Forgiving Most Merciful." (*Al-Anfaal*: 70)

"Allaah then gave me in place of the twenty *uqeeyah* twenty slaves in Islaam all of them bringing in money for me along with what I hope for from Allaah's ﷻ forgiveness." Al-Haakim said, "This *hadeeth* is authentic according to the standards of Muslim, although they (Al-Bukhaaree and Muslim) did not transmit it." In regards to this view, Adh-Dhahabee remained silent (did not oppose that ruling). Al-Haithamee said in his book *Majma' Az-Zawaa'id*, volume 7, page 28, "At-Tabaraanee has transmitted the narration in *Al-Kabeer* and in *Al-Awsat*, and the men who comprise the chain in *Al-Awsat* are people of the *Saheeh* (Al-Bukhaaree and/or Muslim) with the exception of Ibn Ishaaq; however, he clarified that he heard the *hadeeth* from his Sheikh."

Then, when I came across what was mentioned in the book *As-Sunan Al-Kubraa* by Al-Baihaqee, volume 6, page 322, it became apparent that the story of Al-'Abbaas had been inserted into the *hadeeth* along with this chain although it is not actually a part of the *hadeeth*. Al-Baihaqee ﷺ said, "That is how our Sheikh Abu 'Abdillaah narrated it to us in his book *Al-Mustadrak*." Then Al-Haafidh Al-Baihaqee mentioned the *hadeeth* correctly and explained that the story of Al-'Abbaas has a different chain which is *mursal*.[19] Al-

---

[18] One *uqeeyah* is equivalent to forty dirhams. A *dirham* is a type of silver coin.
[19] *Mursal* is a type of *hadeeth* which has a broken chain because a *Taabi'ee* ascribes the *hadeeth* directly to the Prophet ﷺ without mentioning who he heard the *hadeeth* from. This type of *hadeeth* is weak because we do not know who the break in the chain is. It

Haafidh Ibn Hajar said in his book *Fathul-Baaree*, volume 9, page 382, after mentioning this story, "In the chain of 'Ataa is Muhammad ibn Ishaaq. This story is not connected in his chain, rather, it is *mu'dal*[20] while the arrangement of Ishaaq, meaning Ibn Raahawaih, and after him At-Tabaraanee and Ibn Mardawaih, demands that it is connected, and the knowledge [regarding what is corrects] is with Allaah." He also said in his book *Al-Mataalib Al-'Aaliyah*, volume 3, page 337, "I think that [the story of Al-'Abbaas] has been inserted into the *hadeeth* and is actually Ibn Ishaaq's statement. Consequently, the story of 'Abbaas on this position is *mu'dal*. As for what is outwardly apparent, at first glance the chain seems to be connected and Ishaaq acted upon that [outward appearance]." The examples of this are many.

APOLOGY:

I went out of my way to try and quote from the Imaams of *hadeeth* and their books, but at times I did not have enough time so I had to suffice with quoting from some of the authors who quoted from them; however, that was rare. Furthermore, on occasion it was difficult for me to find the chain of a *hadeeth* if it was in the books that have been lost or are rarely in circulation; so if an Imaam whose rulings on *hadeeth* we feel comfortable with declared the *hadeeth* to be authentic, I would write it without its chain, and if I did not find an Imaam who declared it to be authentic, I would abstain from mentioning it until Allaah facilitates a way for us to come across the chain. And I ask Allaah ﷻ to make my work sincerely for His beautiful face, and I ask Him to benefit Islaam and the Muslims by this literary work, Aameen.

PRINCIPLES CONCERNING THIS TOPIC

There are principles associated with the topic, "Reasons for the Descending of the Revelation,". We will mention some of these principles which have been outlined by our Sheikh Mahmood ibn 'Abdil-Wahhaab Faa'id, may Allaah protect him, while limiting ourselves to the most prominent and deserving ones for the sake of brevity.

1. <u>The definition of a reason for the descending of revelation</u>. A reason for the descending of revelation is confined to two matters. The first: an incident occurs then a portion of the Noble Qur'aan is revealed because of it. For example, the reason for the descending of the following revelation:

---

is possible that he is another *Taabi'ee*, and if so, we must know his status and who he heard from. Some of the early Scholars also use the word *mursal* for any *hadeeth* that has a break in the chain wherever that break may be. The later Scholars use the word *munqati'* for such a *hadeeth*.

[20] *Mu'dal* is a type of *hadeeth* where two or more people have been dropped from the chain in succession.

$$\text{تَبَّتْ يَدَا أَبِى لَهَبٍ}$$

"Perish the two hands of Abee Lahab…" (*Al-Masad*: 1), which will be discussed later, if Allaah wills. The second: the Messenger of Allaah ﷺ is asked about something, then a portion of the Qur'aan is revealed, clarifying the ruling of issue in question. An example of this is the reason why the verse of *Al-li'aan* was revealed as will be mentioned later, if Allaah wills.

2. <u>The method of pinpointing the reason for revelation.</u>   Regarding the method of pinpointing the reason for revelation the Scholars rely on what has been authentically narrated on the Messenger of Allaah ﷺ or on a *Sahaabee* (Companion of the Messenger of Allaah ﷺ) because the narration of a *Sahaabee* about a topic such as this has the ruling of a narration on the Messenger of Allaah ﷺ. Ibnus-Salaah ﷺ said in his book *'Uloom Al-Hadeeth*, page 46, "Thirdly, as for what has been said regarding the *Tafseer* (explanation of the Qur'aan) by a *Sahaabee* having the same ruling as a *hadeeth* on the Prophet ﷺ, that is only the case if the *Tafseer* is connected to the reason why the verse was revealed, such that the *Sahaabee* narrates that or something similar. Such as the statement of Jaabir ﷺ, "The Jews used to say, 'Whoever has sexual intercourse with his wife from behind, their baby will be born cross-eyed.' Then Allaah ﷻ sent down the following:

$$\text{نِسَآؤُكُمْ حَرْثٌ لَّكُمْ}$$

"Your wives are a tilth for you…" (*Al-Baqarah*: 223).
As for the rest of the *tafaaseer* of the Companions that do not include an ascription to the Messenger of Allaah ﷺ, then they are regarded as statements of the companions, and Allaah knows best." As for when a *Taabi'ee* states, "This verse was revealed because of such and such," this is referred to as *mursal*. If it has numerous chains, which make it stronger, it will be accepted; and if not, it will be rejected according to the stronger opinion of the people of *hadeeth*.

3. <u>The regard is for the generality of the verse's wording and not for the specificity of its reason for revelation.</u> The proof of this is the story of the *Ansaaree*[21] who was the reason for the following verse's revelation after he kissed a woman,

---

[21] *Ansaaree* meaning he is one of the *Ansaar* (the helpers). Ibn Hajar said in his book *Fathul-Baaree* in the explanation of *hadeeth* (17), "What is meant (by the *Ansaar*) is the tribes Al-Aws and Al-Khazraj. They used to be known before as the tribe Banee Qailah… (Qailah) is the maternal ancestor joining the two tribes. The Messenger of Allaah ﷺ then called them the *Ansaar*, so that became their name. It is also used for their children, their allies and their freed slaves. They were distinguished with this great virtue for what they achieved aside from the other tribes, from giving the Prophet

$$إِنَّ الْحَسَنَاتِ يُذْهِبْنَ السَّيِّئَاتِ$$

"Verily the good deeds remove the evil deeds…" (*Hud*: 114). He said to the Prophet ﷺ, "Is that for me alone, O Messenger of Allaah?" In other words, is the ruling from that verse specifically for me because I was the reason why it was revealed? So the Prophet replied in a way that clarified ﷺ that the regard is for the generality of the wording by saying, "[No] Rather for my entire nation." As for the overall gist of the reason, the majority of the people of *usool* (*fiqh* principles) take the position that it, without doubt, is generally worded and is therefore impermissible to be taken out of the general context. This is the correct position. While [on the other hand] it has been mentioned that Maalik takes the position that it is only assumed that this falls under the general wording as well as other statements assumed to be understood based on their generality. Refer to the book *Mudhakkirah Usool Al-Fiqh* by Muhammad Al-Ameen Ash-Shinqeetee, pages 209-210.

4. There can be more than one reason why a single verse was revealed, such as the verse of *Al-li'aan* and other verses as you will find, if Allaah wills, mentioned in their places throughout this work. Moreover, there can be more than one verse revealed for a single reason, as indicated in the *hadeeth* of Al-Musayyab ﷺ about the death of Abu Taalib wherein the Prophet stated ﷺ, "I will seek forgiveness for you so long as I am not prohibited from doing so." Then Allaah sent down:

$$مَا كَانَ لِلنَّبِيِّ وَالَّذِينَ ءَامَنُوٓا۟ أَن يَسْتَغْفِرُوا۟ لِلْمُشْرِكِينَ$$

"It is not proper for the Prophet and those who believe to ask Allaah's forgiveness for the polytheists…" (*At-Tawbah*: 113). Concerning Abu Taalib the following was revealed:

$$إِنَّكَ لَا تَهْدِى مَنْ أَحْبَبْتَ وَلَٰكِنَّ ٱللَّهَ يَهْدِى مَن يَشَآءُ$$

"Verily you guide not whom you love, but Allaah guides whom He wills…" (*Al-Qasas*: 56). In this respect there are many examples, as you will see, if Allaah wills.

5. The wording of the text surrounding a reason for revelation can either explicitly delineate that it is a reason, or it can indicate that it contains a degree of probability for being the reason for revelation. It is an explicit text if the narrator says, "The reason why this verse was revealed is such and such," or if the narrator attaches the letter *faa*

ﷺ and those with him refuge, taking care of them and supporting them with their lives and wealth. And how they gave them preference over themselves in many issues…"

which has the meaning of succession onto the phrase نزل (it descended) after mentioning an incident or question [that prompted the descending of revelation]. For example, if he says, "such and such happened," or, "the Messenger of Allaah ﷺ was asked about such and such and then verse such and such descended." These two forms are explicit in their indication that the text is a reason behind the revelation and examples of this will be seen throughout this work, if Allaah wills. Contrarily, a text can indicate a probability of being a reason for revelation while also suggesting an implication that what is intended is the general rulings that pertain to the verse, not necessarily that it is a reason for the revelation's descent. For example if the narrator says, "This verse was revealed في (concerning) such and such." At times that is said with the intention that the text is a reason for the revelation and at times it is said intending that the ruling of an issue is included in the general meaning of the verse. Likewise if the narrator says, "I think this verse was revealed because of such and such," or, "I do not think this verse was revealed for any other reason besides such and such," the narrator, when using this wording is uncertain that it is a reason. Therefore, these two forms of wording indicate the possibility of being reasons for revelation or something else. Examples of this will come, if Allaah wills. Refer to the book *Mabaahith fee 'Uloom Al-Qur'aan* by Mannaa' Al-Qattaan.

NOTE:

Some of the Qur'aan was revealed due to a reason while other parts were revealed without a specific reason establishing the doctrines of faith and the duties of Islaam as well as other aspects of the legislation. I mention this because once someone asked me to mention an additional reason as to why His ﷻ statement was revealed:

وَمِنْهُم مَّنْ عَٰهَدَ ٱللَّهَ

"And of them is he who made a covenant with Allaah…" (*At-Tawbah*: 75) once I told him the story of Tha'labah is inauthentic. A similar situation occurred regarding His ﷻ statement:

يُوفُونَ بِٱلنَّذْرِ وَيَخَافُونَ يَوْمًا كَانَ شَرُّهُۥ مُسْتَطِيرًا ۝

"They fulfill their vows and they fear a day whose evil will be wide spread," (*Al-Insaan*: 7) up to and including the last of those verses, when I said to some people that the report that indicates that these verses were revealed because of 'Ali and Faatimah is not authentic. Furthermore, Ibnul-Jawzee mentioned that it is a fabricated narration and As-Suyootee agreed with him. I wanted to make note of this so that one who is not familiar with the topic reasons for the descending of the revelation, will not think that every verse has a specific reason behind its descent.

The above mentioned is what was feasible for me to mention. If you want to know more about the principles of this topic then refer to the book *Al-Itqaan fee 'Uloom Al-Qur'aan* by Al-Haafidh As-Suyootee ﷺ. I ask Allaah to reward our Sheikh, who oversaw my work, for his good advice and for pointing out my mistakes. He, may Allaah protect him, troubled himself and supervised my work to the smallest detail. May Allaah reward him with good and bless him in his deeds, his children and his wealth, *Aameen*.[22]

---

[22] Note: From this point starts the abridged version of the Sheikh's book. I omitted the *ahaadeeth* that the Sheikh found defects in affecting their authenticity and at times I abbreviated the sources where the *hadeeth* is found and other portions so the book can be easier for the English reader to benefit from.

بسم الله الرحمن الرحيم

سورة البقرة

SOORATUL-BAQARAH

His, the Exalted One's statement:

فَوَيْلٌ لِّلَّذِينَ يَكْتُبُونَ ٱلْكِتَٰبَ بِأَيْدِيهِمْ ثُمَّ يَقُولُونَ هَٰذَا مِنْ عِندِ ٱللَّهِ لِيَشْتَرُوا۟ بِهِۦ ثَمَنًا قَلِيلًا ۖ فَوَيْلٌ لَّهُم مِّمَّا كَتَبَتْ أَيْدِيهِمْ وَوَيْلٌ لَّهُم مِّمَّا يَكْسِبُونَ ۝

"Then woe to those who write the book with their own hands and then say, 'This is from Allaah,' to purchase with it a small price. Woe to them for what their hands have written and woe to them for what they earn thereby." (verse: 79)

قال الإمام البخاري ﷺ في كتابه خلق أفعال العباد (ص:54): حدثنا يحيى ثنا وكيع عن سفيان عن عبد الرحمن بن علقمة عن ابن عباس ﷺ: (فَوَيْلٌ لِّلَّذِينَ يَكْتُبُونَ ٱلْكِتَٰبَ بِأَيْدِيهِمْ) قال: نزلت في أهل الكتاب.

Ibn 'Abbaas ﷺ said about the verse:

فَوَيْلٌ لِّلَّذِينَ يَكْتُبُونَ ٱلْكِتَٰبَ بِأَيْدِيهِمْ

"Then woe to those who write the book with their own hands…,"
"This verse descended because of the people of the book (the Jews and Christians)."

This *hadeeth* has been transmitted by Al-Bukhaaree in his book *Khalq Af'aal Al-'Ibaad*, page 54. Ash-Sheikh Muqbil ﷺ said, "The *hadeeth* in question, the people of its chain are people of the *Saheeh* (Al-Bukhaaree and/or Muslim) except for 'Abdur-Rahmaan ibn 'Alqamah, however, he has been declared trustworthy by An-Nasaa'ee, Ibn Hibbaan and Al-'Ijlee; and Ibn Shaaheen has mentioned that that Ibn Mahdee said, "He was one of the sound trustworthy narrators." Refer to the book *Tahdheeb At-Tahdheeb*.

His, the Exalted One's statement:

$$\text{وَلَمَّا جَآءَهُمْ كِتَٰبٌ مِّنْ عِندِ ٱللَّهِ مُصَدِّقٌ لِّمَا مَعَهُمْ وَكَانُوا۟ مِن قَبْلُ يَسْتَفْتِحُونَ عَلَى ٱلَّذِينَ كَفَرُوا۟}$$

"And when there came to them a book from Allaah confirming what they knew prior to its coming while aforetime they had invoked Allaah in order to gain victory over those who disbelieved…" (verse: 89)

قال ابن إسحاق: وحدثني عاصم بن عمر بن قتادة عن رجال من قومه قالوا: إن مما دعانا إلى الإسلام مع رحمة الله تعالى وهداه لنا لما كنا نسمع من رجال يهود وكنا أهل الشرك أصحاب أوثان وكانوا أهل كتاب عندهم علم ليس لنا وكانت لا تزال بيننا وبينهم شرور فإذا نلنا منهم بعض ما يكرهون قالوا لنا: إنه قد تقارب زمان نبي يبعث الآن نقتلكم معه قتل عاد وإرم فكنا نسمع ذلك منهم فلما بعث الله رسوله ﷺ أجبناه حين دعانا إلى الله تعالى وعرفنا ما كانوا يتوعدوننا به فبادرناهم إليه فآمنا به وكفروا به ففينا وفيهم نزلت هذه الآيات من البقرة: (وَلَمَّا جَآءَهُمْ كِتَٰبٌ مِّنْ عِندِ ٱللَّهِ مُصَدِّقٌ لِّمَا مَعَهُمْ وَكَانُوا۟ مِن قَبْلُ يَسْتَفْتِحُونَ عَلَى ٱلَّذِينَ كَفَرُوا۟ فَلَمَّا جَآءَهُم مَّا عَرَفُوا۟ كَفَرُوا۟ بِهِۦ ۚ فَلَعْنَةُ ٱللَّهِ عَلَى ٱلْكَٰفِرِينَ) اه من سيرة ابن هشام (ج: 1 / ص: 213)

'Aasim ibn 'Umar ibn Qataadah narrated from people his tribe that they said, "Verily of the things that prompted us to come to Islaam, along with the mercy of Allaah ﷻ and His guidance, is what we used to hear from some Jewish men. At that time we were polytheists worshipping idols and they were people of the book and thus, they had knowledge that we did not have. Bad relations were constant between us and them. So when we would do something to them that they did not like they would say to us, 'Indeed, the time has now approached that a Prophet will be sent, with him we will annihilate you the way 'Aad and Iram were annihilated.' We used to hear them say that a lot. Then when Allaah sent His Messenger ﷺ we responded to his invitation when he called us to Allaah ﷻ. We were aware of what they used to threaten us with so we rushed to him before them and we believed in him while they disbelieved in him. So these following verses from *Sooratul-Baqarah* descended because of the aforementioned:

$$\text{وَلَمَّا جَآءَهُمْ كِتَٰبٌ مِّنْ عِندِ ٱللَّهِ مُصَدِّقٌ لِّمَا مَعَهُمْ وَكَانُوا۟ مِن قَبْلُ يَسْتَفْتِحُونَ عَلَى ٱلَّذِينَ كَفَرُوا۟ فَلَمَّا جَآءَهُم مَّا عَرَفُوا۟ كَفَرُوا۟ بِهِۦ ۚ فَلَعْنَةُ ٱللَّهِ عَلَى ٱلْكَٰفِرِينَ}$$

"And when there came to them a book from Allaah confirming what they knew prior to its coming while aforetime they had invoked Allaah in order to gain victory over those who disbelieved; then when there came to them what they recognized they disbelieved in it. So let the curse of Allaah be upon the disbelievers."

This *hadeeth* has been transmitted by Ibn Hishaam in his *Seerah*, volume 1, page 213. Ash-Sheikh Muqbil ﷺ said, "It is a *hasan hadeeth*. Indeed Ibn Ishaaq made it clear that he heard from his Sheikh, so his *hadeeth* is *hasan* as Al-Haafidh Adh-Dhahabee mentioned in *Al-Meezaan*."

His, the Exalted One's statement:

$$\text{قُلْ مَن كَانَ عَدُوًّا لِّجِبْرِيلَ فَإِنَّهُ نَزَّلَهُ عَلَىٰ قَلْبِكَ بِإِذْنِ ٱللَّهِ مُصَدِّقًا لِّمَا بَيْنَ يَدَيْهِ وَهُدًى وَبُشْرَىٰ لِلْمُؤْمِنِينَ}$$

"Say: Whoever is an enemy to Jibreel [then let him die in his fury], for indeed he has brought it down to your heart by Allaah's permission confirming what came before it and as a guidance and glad tidings for the believers." (verse: 97)

قال الإمام أحمد (ج: 1 / ص: 274): حدثنا أبو أحمد حدثنا عبد الله بن الوليد العجلي وكانت له هيئة رأيناه عند حسن حدثنا بكير بن شهاب عن سعيد بن جبير عن ابن عباس ﷺ قال: أقبلت يهود إلى رسول الله ﷺ فقالوا: يا أبا القاسم إنا نسألك عن خمسة أشياء فإن أنبأتنا بهن عرفنا أنك نبي واتبعناك فأخذ عليهم ما أخذ إسرائيل على بنيه إذ قالوا: الله على ما نقول وكيل قال: هاتوا قالوا: أخبرنا عن علامة النبي قال: تنام عيناه ولا ينام قلبه قالوا: أخبرنا كيف تؤنث المرأة وكيف تذكر قال: يلتقي الماءان فإذا علا ماء الرجل ماء المرأة أذكرت وإذا علا ماء المرأة ماء الرجل أنثت قالوا: أخبرنا ما حرم إسرائيل على نفسه قال: كان يشتكي عرق النسا فلم يجد شيئا يلائمه إلا ألبان كذا وكذا قال عبد الله قال أبي: قال بعضهم: يعني الإبل، فحرم لحومها قالوا: صدقت قالوا: أخبرنا ما هذا الرعد قال: ملك من ملائكة الله عز وجل موكل بالسحاب بيده أو في يده مخراق من نار يزجر به السحاب يسوقه حيث أمر الله قالوا: فما هذا الصوت الذي يسمع قال: صوته قالوا: صدقت إنما بقيت واحدة وهي التي نبايعك إن أخبرتنا بها فإنه ليس من نبي إلا له ملك يأتيه بالخبر فأخبرنا من صاحبك قال: جبريل عليه السلام قالوا: جبريل ذاك الذي ينزل بالحرب والقتال والعذاب عدونا لو قلت ميكائيل الذي ينزل بالرحمة والنبات والقطر لكان فأنزل الله عز و جل: (مَن كَانَ عَدُوًّا لِّجِبْرِيلَ) إلى آخر الآية.

Ibn 'Abbaas ﷺ said, "Some Jews came to the Messenger of Allaah ﷺ and said, 'O Abal-Qaasim, we will ask you about five things. If you tell us about them we will know that you are a Prophet and we will follow you.' So he ﷺ enjoined upon them what Israa'eel enjoined upon his children when they said,

"Allaah is a witness to what we say." He said, 'Present the issues to me.' They said, "Tell us about the sign of a Prophet." He replied, 'His eyes sleep but his heart does not sleep.' They said, "What determines whether a baby is born female or male?" He said, 'The two fluids meet, so when the man's fluid overwhelms the woman's fluid the baby will be born male, and when the fluid of the woman overwhelms the fluid of the male it will be born female.'

They said, "Tell us what Israa'eel made forbidden upon himself." He said, 'He was suffering from Sciatica[23] and could not find anything other than the milk of such and such an animal to treat it, ('Abdullaah said, "My father Al-Imaam Ahmad said,' 'Some of the narrators mentioned that He means the camel'), so he made its meat forbidden." They said, "You have spoken the truth." They said, "Tell us about this thunder." He said, 'One of Allaah's angels is entrusted with the clouds and in his hand is a *mikhraaq*[24] made of fire used to drive the clouds and so he drives them to wherever Allaah commands.' They said, "So what is the sound about?" He said, '[It is] The sound from that instrument.' They replied, "You have spoken the truth.

Now only one more thing remains, if you tell us about it then we will pledge allegiance to you. There is not a Prophet except that he has an angel who brings the revelation to him, so tell us, who is your companion?" He answered, 'Jibreel, peace be upon him.' They said, "Jibreel! That is the one who descends with war, fighting and punishment, he is our enemy, if only you were to have said Mikaa'eel, the one who descends with mercy, vegetation and rain it would have happened." Then Allaah sent down:

$$\text{مَن كَانَ عَدُوًّا لِجِبْرِيل}$$

"Whoever is an enemy to Jibreel…".

Al-Imaam Ahmad transmitted this *hadeeth* in his *Musnad*, volume 1, page 274. Ash-Sheikh Muqbil said, "Bukair ibn Shihaab is in The chain of the *hadeeth*. Al-Haafidh said about him in his book *At-Taqreeb*, "He is *maqbool* [an acceptable narrator]," meaning if he is supported, but if not then he is weak as he mentioned in the preface of his book; however, the *hadeeth* has various chains on Ibn 'Abbaas as has been mentioned in *Tafseer Ibn Jareer*. Of those chains is what Al-Imaam Ahmad mentioned:

قال الإمام أحمد (ج: 1 / ص: 278): ثنا هاشم بن القاسم ثنا عبد الحميد ثنا شهر قال ابن عباس: حضرت عصابة من اليهود نبي الله يوما فقالوا: يا أبا القاسم حدثنا عن خلال نسألك عنهن لا يعلمهن إلا نبي قال: سلوني عما شئتم ولكن اجعلوا لي ذمة الله وما أخذ يعقوب عليه

---

[23] Sciatica is an illness that causes a pain that starts from the hip then descends to the back of the thigh, and at times descends all the way to the ankle. Refer to Ibnul-Qayyim's book *At-Tib An-Nabawee*, page 71 (the Arabic version), for more.

[24] Ibnul-Atheer explained the word *mikhraaq* in his book *An-Nihaayah* saying, "It is originally a piece of clothing that is wound up. The children hit one another with it, but it now means an instrument that the angels use to drive the clouds…"

السلام على بنيه لئن حدثتكم شيئا فعرفتموه لتتابعنّي على الإسلام قالوا: فذلك لك قال: فسلوني عما شئتم قالوا: أخبرنا عن أربع خلال نسألك عنهن أخبرنا أي الطعام حرم إسرائيل على نفسه من قبل أن تنزل التوراة وأخبرنا كيف ماء المرأة وماء الرجل كيف يكون الذكر منه وأخبرنا كيف هذا النبي الأمي في النوم ومن وليه من الملائكة قال: فعليكم عهد الله وميثاقه لئن أنا أخبرتكم لتتابعنّي قال: فأعطوه ما شاء من عهد وميثاق قال: فأنشدكم بالذي أنزل التوراة على موسى صلى الله عليه وسلم هل تعلمون أن إسرائيل يعقوب عليه السلام مرض مرضا شديدا وطال سقمه فنذر لله نذرا لئن شفاه الله تعالى من سقمه ليحرمنّ أحب الشراب إليه وأحب الطعام إليه وكان أحب الطعام إليه لحم الإبل وأحب الشراب إليه ألبانها قالوا: اللهم نعم قال: اللهم اشهد عليهم فأنشدهم بالله الذي لا إله إلا هو الذي أنزل التوراة على موسى هل تعلمون أن ماء الرجل أبيض وأن ماء المرأة أصفر رقيق فأيهما علا كان له الولد والشبه بإذن الله إن علا ماء الرجل على ماء المرأة كان ذكرا بإذن الله وإن علا ماء المرأة على ماء الرجل كان أنثى بإذن الله قالوا: اللهم نعم قال: اللهم اشهد عليهم فأنشدهم بالذي أنزل التوراة على موسى هل تعلمون أن هذا النبي الأمي تنام عيناه ولا ينام قلبه قالوا: اللهم نعم قال: اللهم اشهد قالوا: أنت الآن فحدثنا من وليك من الملائكة فعندها نجامعك أو نفارقك قال: فإن ولي جبريل عليه السلام ولم يبعث الله نبيا قط إلا وهو وليه قالوا: فعندها نفارقك لو كان وليك سواه من الملائكة لتابعناك وصدقناك قال: فما يمنعكم من أن تصدقوه قالوا: إنه عدونا قال: فعند ذلك قال الله عز وجل: (قُلْ مَن كَانَ عَدُوًّا لِّجِبْرِيلَ فَإِنَّهُ نَزَّلَهُ عَلَىٰ قَلْبِكَ بِإِذْنِ اللَّهِ) إلى قوله عز وجل: (كِتَابَ اللَّهِ وَرَاءَ ظُهُورِهِمْ كَأَنَّهُمْ لَا يَعْلَمُونَ) فعند ذلك باؤوا بغضب على غضب، الآية.

Ibn 'Abbaas ؓ said, "One day a group of Jews went to the Prophet of Allaah ﷺ and said, 'O Abal-Qaasim, tell us about these peculiarities that we will ask you about which no one except a Prophet knows about them.' He said, "Ask me whatever you wish but grant me what Ya'qoob enjoined upon his children, a promise to Allaah that if I inform you and you know it to be correct then you will follow me in Islaam." They said, 'We grant you that.' He said, "Ask me whatever you wish." They said, 'Tell us about these four peculiarities: Tell us what food Israa'eel made forbidden upon himself before the Tawraah was revealed. And tell us about the fluid of the woman and the fluid of the man; how does the male child come about from the two fluids? And tell us the state of this illiterate Prophet is in his sleep. And tell us what angel supports him.' He [Ibn Abbaas?] said, "You must make a promise and a covenant with Allaah that if I tell you, you will follow me."

They gave him the promise and covenant he requested. He said, 'I implore you [to acknowledge the truth] by the one who revealed the Tawraah to Moses ﷺ do you not know that Israa'eel, Ya'qoob, peace be upon him, became very sick? His illness lasted a long time so he made a vow to Allaah that if Allaah ﷻ were to heal him of his illness he would forbid himself from his most beloved drink and food. The most beloved food to him was camel's meat and the most beloved drink to him was camel's milk.' They said, "By Allaah, yes." He said, 'O Allaah bear witness against them. I implore you by Allaah, He whom there is no deity that has the right to be worshipped except Him, the one who revealed the Tawraah to Moses, do you not know that the fluid of the man is thick and white, and the fluid of the woman is thin and yellow, so whichever of the two overwhelms the other, the gender and the resemblance will be a product of the overwhelming fluid by Allaah's permission? If the fluid of the man overwhelms the fluid of the woman they will have a male child by Allaah's permission, and if the fluid of the woman overwhelms the fluid of the man they will have a female child by Allaah's permission.' They said, "By Allaah, yes." He said, 'O Allaah, bear witness against them. I implore you by the one who revealed the Tawraah to Moses, do you not know that this illiterate Prophet's eyes sleep but his heart does not sleep?' They said, "By Allaah, yes." He said, 'O Allaah, bear witness.' They said, "Now tell us who supports you from the angels, and with this we will either join you or depart from you." He said, 'My supporter is Jibreel, peace be upon him. Allaah has never sent a Prophet except that he has been his supporter.' They said, "With this we depart from you, if your supporter was any other angel besides him we would have followed you and believed in you." He said, 'And what prevents you from trusting him?' They said, "He is our enemy." At that point Allaah ﷻ revealed:

$$\text{قُلْ مَن كَانَ عَدُوًّا لِّجِبْرِيلَ فَإِنَّهُ نَزَّلَهُ عَلَىٰ قَلْبِكَ بِإِذْنِ ٱللَّهِ}$$

"Say: Whoever is an enemy to Jibreel [then let him die in his fury] for indeed he has brought it down to your heart by Allaah's permission ..."
up to His ﷻ statement:

$$\text{كِتَـٰبَ ٱللَّهِ وَرَآءَ ظُهُورِهِمْ كَأَنَّهُمْ لَا يَعْلَمُونَ}$$

"...Those who were given the scripture threw the Book of Allaah behind their backs as if they do not know." (Al-Baqarah: 101).
At that point they warranted anger on top of anger."

Ash-Sheikh Muqbil ﷺ mentioned," Shahr ibn Hawshab is in the *hadeeth's* chain and there is a difference of opinion about his status. The stronger position holds that he is weak because of his bad memory; however, he can be used in a supporting role." The Sheikh also said, "And Ibn Jareer mentioned that there is *ijmaa'* (unanimous agreement among the Scholars) that this verse was revealed in response to the Jews when they claimed that Jibreel is their enemy and Mikaa'eel is their supporter. So this *ijmaa'* strengthens the weakness in these two chains."

His, the Exalted One's statement:

$$\text{فَاعْفُواْ وَاصْفَحُواْ حَتَّىٰ يَأْتِيَ ٱللَّهُ بِأَمْرِهِۦٓ ۗ إِنَّ ٱللَّهَ عَلَىٰ كُلِّ شَىْءٍ قَدِيرٌ}$$

"But forgive and overlook until Allaah brings His command. Verily Allaah is able to do all things." (verse: 109)

قال أبو الشيخ في كتاب الأخلاق (74): أخبرنا ابن أبي عاصم ثنا عمرو بن عثمان عن بشر ابن شعيب عن أبيه عن الزهري عن عروة عن أسامة بن زيد ﷺ أنه أخبره أن رسول الله ﷺ ركب على حمار فقال لسعد: ألم تسمع ما قال أبو الحباب – يريد عبد الله بن أبي – قال كذا و كذا فقال سعد بن عبادة: اعف عنه واصفح فعفا عنه رسول الله ﷺ و كان رسول الله ﷺ وأصحابه يعفون عن أهل الكتاب والمشركين فأنزل الله عز وجل:

$$\text{(فَاعْفُواْ وَاصْفَحُواْ حَتَّىٰ يَأْتِيَ ٱللَّهُ بِأَمْرِهِۦٓ ۗ إِنَّ ٱللَّهَ عَلَىٰ كُلِّ شَىْءٍ قَدِيرٌ).}$$

Usaamah ibn Zaid ؓ narrated that the Messenger of Allaah ﷺ mounted a donkey and said, "O Sa'd, have you not heard what Abul-Hubaab, meaning 'Abdullaah ibn Ubay, said? He said such and such." Sa'd ibn 'Ubaadah said, 'Pardon and forgive him.' So the Messenger of Allaah ﷺ pardoned him. The Messenger of Allaah ﷺ and his Companions used to pardon the people of the book as well as the polytheists. Then Allaah ﷻ sent down:

$$\text{فَاعْفُواْ وَاصْفَحُواْ حَتَّىٰ يَأْتِيَ ٱللَّهُ بِأَمْرِهِۦٓ ۗ إِنَّ ٱللَّهَ عَلَىٰ كُلِّ شَىْءٍ قَدِيرٌ}$$

"But forgive and overlook until Allaah brings His command. Verily Allaah is able to do all things."

This *hadeeth*, Abush-Sheikh transmitted it in his book *Akhlaaq An-Nabee*, *hadeeth* (74). Ash-Sheikh Muqbil ؒ said, " [in regards to]The *hadeeth*, the people of its chain are trustworthy narrators; Ibn Abee 'Aasim is a major *haafidh* and his biography is mentioned in the book *Tadhkirah Al-Huffaadh*, volume 2, page 640.The rest of the narrators can be found in *Tahdheeb At-Tahdheeb*. Furthermore, the *hadeeth* is in the *Saheeh* (Al-Bukhaaree: 4290 and 5854), emanating from the chain of Shu'aib ibn Abee Hamzah with this same chain; however; the reason for the verse's revelation is not mentioned in the *Saheeh* (Al-Bukhaaree), nor is it mentioned in the *Tafseer* of Ibn Abee Haatim, as stated in *Tafseer Ibn Katheer*, volume 1, page 135."

His, the Exalted One's statement:

$$\text{وَلِلَّهِ ٱلْمَشْرِقُ وَٱلْمَغْرِبُ ۚ فَأَيْنَمَا تُوَلُّواْ فَثَمَّ وَجْهُ ٱللَّهِ}$$

"And to Allaah belongs the East and the West, so wherever you turn, there is the face of Allaah." (verse: 115)

قال الإمام مسلم ﷺ في صحيحه (700 / 33): حدثنا عبيد الله بن عمر القواريري حدثنا يحيى بن سعيد عن عبد الملك بن أبي سليمان قال حدثنا سعيد بن جبير عن ابن عمر ﷺ قال: كان رسول الله ﷺ يصلي وهو مقبل من مكة إلى المدينة على راحلته حيث كان وجهه وفيه نزلت: (فَأَيْنَمَا تُوَلُّواْ فَثَمَّ وَجْهُ ٱللَّهِ).

Ibn 'Umar ﷺ narrated that while the Messenger of Allaah ﷺ was heading from Makkah to Madeenah he prayed on his riding animal facing whatever direction he faced; consequently, the following descended:

فَأَيْنَمَا تُوَلُّواْ فَثَمَّ وَجْهُ ٱللَّهِ

"So wherever you turn there is the face of Allaah."

[As for] This *hadeeth*, Muslim transmitted it in his *Saheeh* (700 / 33).

His, the Exalted One's statement:

وَٱتَّخِذُواْ مِن مَّقَامِ إِبْرَٰهِۦمَ مُصَلًّى

"And take the station of Ibraaheem as a place of prayer…" (verse: 125)

قال الإمام البخاري ﷺ في صحيحه (4486): حدثنا عمرو بن عون حدثنا هشيم عن حميد عن أنس ﷺ قال عمر ﷺ: وافقت ربي في ثلاث فقلت: يا رسول الله لو اتخذنا من مقام إبراهيم مصلى فنزلت: (وَٱتَّخِذُواْ مِن مَّقَامِ إِبْرَٰهِۦمَ مُصَلًّى) وآية الحجاب قلت:

يا رسول الله لو أمرت نساءك أن يحتجبن فإنه يكلمهن البر والفاجر فنزلت آية الحجاب واجتمع نساء النبي ﷺ في الغيرة عليه فقلت لهن: عسى ربه إن طلقكن أن يبدله أزواجا خيرا منكن فنزلت هذه الآية.

'Umar ﷺ said, "I [concurred and] was in agreement with my Lord in three instances. I once said, 'O Messenger of Allaah, if only you took the station of Ibraaheem as a place of prayer.' Thereafter this verse descended:

وَٱتَّخِذُواْ مِن مَّقَامِ إِبْرَٰهِۦمَ مُصَلًّى

"And take the station of Ibraaheem as a place of prayer…"

Similarly, regarding the verse of the veil, I said, "O Messenger of Allaah, if only you ordered your wives to wear the veil, because verily the righteous and the unrighteous speak to them." Consequently the verse of the veil descended. Lastly, the wives of the Prophet ﷺ took a unified stance against him out of their jealousy so I said to them, "Perhaps his Lord, if he were to divorce you, will give him better wives than you…" Thereupon this verse descended" (Tahreem, verse: 5).

This *hadeeth* has been transmitted by Al-Bukhaaree it in his *Saheeh* (4486).

<u>His, the Exalted One's statement:</u>

﴿سَيَقُولُ ٱلسُّفَهَآءُ مِنَ ٱلنَّاسِ مَا وَلَّىٰهُمْ عَن قِبْلَتِهِمُ ٱلَّتِى كَانُوا۟ عَلَيْهَا﴾

"The imbeciles amongst the people will say: 'What has diverted them from their direction of prayer which they used to face (verse: 142)?'

قال ابن إسحاق كما في لباب النقول في أسباب النزول للحافظ السيوطي وفي تفسير الحافظ ابن كثير: حدثني إسماعيل بن أبي خالد عن أبي إسحاق عن البراء قال: كان رسول الله ﷺ يصلي نحو بيت المقدس ويكثر النظر إلى السماء ينتظر أمر الله فأنزل الله: (قَدْ نَرَىٰ تَقَلُّبَ وَجْهِكَ فِى ٱلسَّمَآءِ فَلَنُوَلِّيَنَّكَ قِبْلَةً تَرْضَىٰهَا ۚ فَوَلِّ وَجْهَكَ شَطْرَ ٱلْمَسْجِدِ ٱلْحَرَامِ) فقال رجال من المسلمين: وددنا لو علمنا علم من مات قبل أن نصرف إلى القبلة فأنزل الله: (وَمَا كَانَ ٱللَّهُ لِيُضِيعَ إِيمَـٰنَكُمْ) وقال السفهاء من الناس: ما ولاهم عن قبلتهم التي كانوا عليها فأنزل الله: (سَيَقُولُ ٱلسُّفَهَآءُ مِنَ ٱلنَّاسِ) إلى آخر الآية.

Al-Baraa ؓ narrated that the Messenger of Allaah ﷺ used to pray facing Bait Al-Maqdis (in Jerusalem). He would often look toward the heavens awaiting Allaah's command. Subsequently Allaah sent down the following:

﴿قَدْ نَرَىٰ تَقَلُّبَ وَجْهِكَ فِى ٱلسَّمَآءِ ۖ فَلَنُوَلِّيَنَّكَ قِبْلَةً تَرْضَىٰهَا ۚ فَوَلِّ وَجْهَكَ شَطْرَ ٱلْمَسْجِدِ ٱلْحَرَامِ﴾

"Verily We have seen the turning of your face towards the heavens. Surely We shall turn you to a prayer direction that shall please you, so turn your face in the direction of *Al-Masjid Al-Haraam* (in Makkah)." (*Al-Baqarah*: 144).

Then a group of Muslim men said, "We would like to know about those who died before we changed our prayer direction to the *qiblah* (in Makkah)." In consequence Allaah sent down,

$$\text{وَمَا كَانَ ٱللَّهُ لِيُضِيعَ إِيمَـٰنَكُمْ}$$

"And Allaah would never let your faith (prayer) be lost." (*Al-Baqarah*: 143).

The fools among the people said, "What has diverted them from their direction of prayer which they used to face?" Then Allaah sent down:

$$\text{سَيَقُولُ ٱلسُّفَهَآءُ مِنَ ٱلنَّاسِ}$$

"The imbeciles amongst the people will say…".

Ibn Ishaaq transmitted this *hadeeth*, and it can be found in the book *Lubaab An-Nuqool fee Asbaab An-Nuzool* by Al-Haafidh As-Suyootee and in the *Tafseer* of Al-Haafidh Ibn Katheer.

His, the Exalted One's statement:

$$\text{وَمَا كَانَ ٱللَّهُ لِيُضِيعَ إِيمَـٰنَكُمْ}$$

"And Allaah would never let your faith (prayer) be lost." (verse: 143)

قال الإمام البخاري رحمه الله (4486): حدثنا أبو نعيم سمع زهيرا عن أبي إسحاق عن البراء رضي الله عنه أن النبي ﷺ صلى إلى بيت المقدس ستة عشر شهرا أو سبعة عشر شهرا وكان يعجبه أن تكون قبلته قبل البيت وأنه صلى أو صلاها صلاة العصر وصلى معه قوم فخرج رجل ممن كان صلى معه فمر على أهل المسجد وهم راكعون قال: أشهد بالله لقد صليت مع النبي ﷺ قبل مكة فداروا كما هم قبل البيت وكان الذي مات على القبلة قبل أن تحول قبل البيت رجال قتلوا فلم ندر ما نقول فيهم فأنزل الله: (وَمَا كَانَ ٱللَّهُ لِيُضِيعَ إِيمَـٰنَكُمْ إِنَّ ٱللَّهَ بِٱلنَّاسِ لَرَءُوفٌ رَّحِيمٌ).

Al-Baraa narrated that the Prophet ﷺ prayed towards Bait Al-Maqdis (in Jerusalem) for sixteen months or seventeen months. He used to be delighted by the idea of his prayer direction changing to the Sacred House (in Makkah). [One the revelation descended] He prayed the *'Asr* prayer (towards the Sacred House) and a group of people prayed with him. Thereafter one of the men who prayed with him left and passed by people praying in another *masjid* while they were in the bowing position. He said, "By Allaah, I bear witness that I prayed with the Prophet ﷺ towards Makkah." They then turned around in their places and faced the Sacred House. There was a group of men who were killed before the prayer direction was changed to the Sacred House and thus we did not know what to say about them. Then Allaah sent down:

$$\text{وَمَا كَانَ ٱللَّهُ لِيُضِيعَ إِيمَٰنَكُمْ إِنَّ ٱللَّهَ بِٱلنَّاسِ لَرَءُوفٌ رَّحِيمٌ}$$

"And Allaah would never let your faith (prayer) be lost. Truly Allaah is Kind, Most Merciful towards mankind."

Al-Bukhaaree transmitted this *hadeeth* in his *Saheeh* (4486).

<u>His, the Exalted One's statement:</u>

$$\text{قَدْ نَرَىٰ تَقَلُّبَ وَجْهِكَ فِى ٱلسَّمَآءِ}$$

"Verily We have seen the turning of your face towards the heavens…" (verse: 144)

قال الإمام البخاري رحمه الله (399): حدثنا عبد الله بن رجاء قال حدثنا إسرائيل عن أبي إسحاق عن البراء بن عازب رضي الله عنه قال: كان رسول الله ﷺ صلى نحو بيت المقدس ستة عشر شهرا أو سبعة عشر شهرا وكان رسول الله ﷺ يحب أن يوجه إلى الكعبة فأنزل الله عز وجل: (قَدْ نَرَىٰ تَقَلُّبَ وَجْهِكَ فِى ٱلسَّمَآءِ) فتوجه نحو الكعبة وقال السفهاء من الناس وهم اليهود: ما ولاهم عن قبلتهم التي كانوا عليها (قُل لِّلَّهِ ٱلْمَشْرِقُ وَٱلْمَغْرِبُ يَهْدِى مَن يَشَآءُ إِلَىٰ صِرَٰطٍ مُّسْتَقِيمٍ) فصلى مع النبي ﷺ رجل ثم خرج بعدما صلى فمر على قوم من الأنصار في صلاة العصر نحو بيت المقدس فقال هو يشهد أنه صلى مع رسول الله ﷺ وأنه توجه نحو الكعبة فتحرف القوم حتى توجهوا نحو الكعبة.

Al-Baraa ؓ narrated that the Messenger of Allaah ﷺ prayed towards Bait Al-Maqdis for sixteen months or seventeen months. The Messenger of Allaah ﷺ loved [the idea] of his prayer direction being changed to the *Ka'bah*. Then Allaah ﷻ sent down:

$$\text{قَدْ نَرَىٰ تَقَلُّبَ وَجْهِكَ فِى ٱلسَّمَآءِ}$$

"Verily We have seen the turning of your face towards the heavens…"
He then faced the *Ka'bah* and the fools among the people—the Jews, said, "What has diverted them from their direction of prayer which they used to face?"

$$\text{قُل لِّلَّهِ ٱلْمَشْرِقُ وَٱلْمَغْرِبُ يَهْدِى مَن يَشَآءُ إِلَىٰ صِرَٰطٍ مُّسْتَقِيمٍ}$$

"Say: To Allaah belongs the East and the West, He guides whom He wills to a straight way." (*Al-Baqarah*: 142).

A man prayed with the Prophet ﷺ and then he left after the prayer and passed by a group of the *Ansaar* praying the *'Asr* prayer facing *Bait Al-Maqdis*. So he testified that he prayed with the Messenger of Allaah ﷺ facing the *Ka'bah*. The people then turned around and faced the *Ka'bah*.

Al-Bukhaaree transmitted this *hadeeth*, it in his *Saheeh* (399) as well as Muslim in his *Saheeh* (525).

<u>His, the Exalted One's statement:</u>

$$\text{إِنَّ ٱلصَّفَا وَٱلْمَرْوَةَ مِن شَعَآئِرِ ٱللَّهِ}$$

"Verily As-Safaa and Al-Marwah are from the signs of Allaah…" (verse: 158)

قال الإمام البخاري رحمه الله (1643): حدثنا أبو اليمان أخبرنا شعيب عن الزهري قال عروة: سألت عائشة رضي الله عنها فقلت لها: أرأيت قول الله تعالى:(إِنَّ ٱلصَّفَا وَٱلْمَرْوَةَ مِن شَعَآئِرِ ٱللَّهِ فَمَنْ حَجَّ ٱلْبَيْتَ أَوِ ٱعْتَمَرَ فَلَا جُنَاحَ عَلَيْهِ أَن يَطَّوَّفَ بِهِمَا) فوالله ما على أحد جناح ألا يطوف بالصفا والمروة فقالت: بئس ما قلت يابن أختي إن هذه الآية لو كانت كما أولتها عليه كانت لا جناح عليه ألا يطوف بهما ولكنها أنزلت في الأنصار كانوا قبل أن يسلموا يهلون لمناة الطاغية التي كانوا يعبدونها بالمشلل فكان من أهل يتحرج أن يطوف بالصفا والمروة فلما أسلموا سألوا رسول الله ﷺ عن ذلك قالوا: يا رسول الله إنا كنا نتحرج أن نطوف بالصفا والمروة فأنزل الله تعالى: (إِنَّ ٱلصَّفَا وَٱلْمَرْوَةَ مِن شَعَآئِرِ ٱللَّهِ) الآية. قالت عائشة رضي الله عنها: وقد سن رسول الله ﷺ الطواف بينهما فليس لأحد أن يترك الطواف بينهما ثم أخبرت أبا بكر بن عبد الرحمن فقال: إن هذا العلم ما كنت سمعته ولقد سمعت رجالا من أهل العلم يذكرون أن الناس إلا من ذكرت عائشة ممن كان يهل بمناة كانوا يطوفون كلهم بالصفا والمروة فلما ذكر الله تعالى الطواف بالبيت ولم يذكر الصفا والمروة في القرآن قالوا: يا رسول الله كنا نطوف بالصفا والمروة وإن الله أنزل الطواف بالبيت فلم يذكر الصفا والمروة فهل علينا من حرج أن نطوف بالصفا والمروة فأنزل الله تعالى: (إِنَّ ٱلصَّفَا وَٱلْمَرْوَةَ مِن شَعَآئِرِ ٱللَّهِ) الآية. قال أبو بكر: فأسمع هذه الآية نزلت في الفريقين كليهما في الذين كانوا يتحرجون أن يطوفوا بالجاهلية بالصفا والمروة والذين يطوفون ثم تحرجوا أن يطوفوا بهما في الإسلام من أجل أن الله تعالى أمر بالطواف بالبيت ولم يذكر الصفا حتى ذكر ذلك بعد ما ذكر الطواف بالبيت.

'Urwah narrated that he asked 'Aishah (about the verse) ﷺ saying, "Inform me about the statement of Allaah ﷻ:

$$\text{إِنَّ ٱلصَّفَا وَٱلْمَرْوَةَ مِن شَعَآئِرِ ٱللَّهِ ۖ فَمَنْ حَجَّ ٱلْبَيْتَ أَوِ ٱعْتَمَرَ فَلَا جُنَاحَ عَلَيْهِ أَن يَطَّوَّفَ بِهِمَا}$$

'Verily As-Safaa and Al-Marwah are from the signs of Allaah so whoever performs *hajj* or *'umrah*, there is no sin on one who performs *tawaaf*[25] between them...'

For by Allaah, there is no sin on one who does not perform *tawaaf* between As-Safaa and Al-Marwah." She said, "What a terrible thing you said, O son of my sister. Verily this verse [would mean], if it were to be as you explained, that there would be no sin on one who does not perform *tawaaf* between them; however, this verse was revealed because of the *Ansaar*. Before they embraced Islaam they used to make pilgrimage for their false god, Manaah, which they used to worship at Al-Mushallal.[26] So the one who made pilgrimage would avoid making *tawaaf* between As-Safaa and Al-Marwah out of fear of sin. Then when they embraced Islaam they asked the Messenger of Allaah ﷺ about that. They said, "O Messenger of Allaah, we used to avoid making *tawaaf* between As-Safaa and Al-Marwah out of fear of sin." Then Allaah ﷻ sent down:

$$\text{إِنَّ ٱلصَّفَا وَٱلْمَرْوَةَ مِن شَعَآئِرِ ٱللَّهِ}$$

"Verily As-Safaa and Al-Marwah are from the signs of Allaah...".

'Aishah said, "And the Messenger of Allaah ﷺ has prescribed the *tawaaf* between them through his *sunnah*, so it is not [appropriate] for anyone to leave off the *tawaaf* between them." Then I (Az-Zuhree one of the narrators in the chain) informed Abu Bakr ibn 'Abdir-Rahmaan, so he said, "Indeed this is the knowledge that I did not hear about. Instead, I heard men from the people of knowledge mention that all of the people, except those who 'Aishah mentioned who used to make pilgrimage to Manaah, used to make *tawaaf* between As-Safaa and Al-Marwah. Then when Allaah ﷻ mentioned the *tawaaf* of the Sacred House without mentioning As-Safaa and Al-Marwah in the Qur'aan they said, 'O Messenger of Allaah, we used to make *tawaaf* between As-Safaa and Al-Marwah and indeed Allaah has revealed the *tawaaf* of the Sacred House and He did not mention As-Safaa and Al-Marwah. So is

---

[25] As-Safaa and Al-Marwah are two small mountains located adjacent to the *Ka'bah*. The pilgrim makes *tawaaf* between them, meaning he goes from one mountain to the other seven times.

[26] Al-Mushallal is a mountain pass located close to Qadeed, a village between Makkah and Madeenah.

there any sin on us if we perform *tawaaf* between As-Safaa and Al-Marwah?" Allaah ﷻ then sent down:

$$إِنَّ ٱلصَّفَا وَٱلْمَرْوَةَ مِن شَعَآئِرِ ٱللَّهِ$$

"Verily As-Safaa and Al-Marwah are from the signs of Allaah…".

Abu Bakr (ibn 'Abdir-Rahmaan) said, "So I have now heard that this verse was revealed because of two groups, those who used to avoid making *tawaaf* in *Jaahiliyah*[27] between As-Safaa and Al-Marwah out of fear of sin, and because of those who used to make *tawaaf*, then avoided it after [embracing] Islaam out of fear of sin, because Allaah ﷻ prescribed the *tawaaf* of the Sacred House without mentioning As-Safaa. They avoided making tawaaf until He (Allaah) mentioned it after mentioning the *tawaaf* of the Sacred House."

This *hadeeth* has been transmitted by Al-Bukhaaree in his *Saheeh* (1643) as well as Muslim in his *Saheeh* (1277).

قال الإمام البخاري ﵀ (4496): حدثنا محمد بن يوسف حدثنا سفيان عن عاصم بن سليمان قال: سألت أنس بن مالك ﵁ عن الصفا والمروة فقال: كنا نرى أنهما من أمر الجاهلية فلما كان الإسلام أمسكنا عنهما فأنزل الله تعالى: (إِنَّ ٱلصَّفَا وَٱلْمَرْوَةَ مِن شَعَآئِرِ ٱللَّهِ فَمَنْ حَجَّ ٱلْبَيْتَ أَوِ ٱعْتَمَرَ فَلَا جُنَاحَ عَلَيْهِ) الآية.

'Aasim ibn Sulaimaan said, "I asked Anas ibn Maalik ﵁ about As-Safaa and Al-Marwah so he said, "We used to consider them to be from the affairs of *Jaahiliyah* so when Islaam came we avoided them. Then Allaah ﷻ sent down:

$$إِنَّ ٱلصَّفَا وَٱلْمَرْوَةَ مِن شَعَآئِرِ ٱللَّهِ فَمَنْ حَجَّ ٱلْبَيْتَ أَوِ ٱعْتَمَرَ فَلَا جُنَاحَ عَلَيْهِ$$

"Verily As-Safaa and Al-Marwah are from the signs of Allaah, so whoever performs *hajj* or *'umrah* there is no sin on one …".

Al-Bukhaaree transmitted this *hadeeth* it in his *Saheeh* (4496) and Muslim in his *Saheeh* (1278). Ash-Sheikh Muqbil ﵀ said, "There is nothing which prevents the verse from being revealed because of both groups."

His, the Exalted One's statement:

$$أُحِلَّ لَكُمْ لَيْلَةَ ٱلصِّيَامِ ٱلرَّفَثُ إِلَىٰ نِسَآئِكُمْ$$

---

[27] *Jaahiliyah* is the time of ignorance before the Messenger of Allaah ﷺ was sent.

"It is made lawful for you to have sexual relations with your wives during the night of fasting…"
including His statement:

$$\text{وَكُلُواْ وَٱشْرَبُواْ حَتَّىٰ يَتَبَيَّنَ لَكُمُ ٱلْخَيْطُ ٱلْأَبْيَضُ مِنَ ٱلْخَيْطِ ٱلْأَسْوَدِ}$$

"…And eat and drink until the white thread of dawn appears distinct to you from the black thread (of night)." (verse: 187)

قال الإمام البخاري ﷺ (1915): حدثنا عبيد الله بن موسى عن إسرائيل عن أبي إسحاق عن البراء ﷺ قال: كان أصحاب محمد ﷺ إذا كان الرجل صائما فحضر الإفطار فنام قبل أن يفطر لم يأكل ليلته ولا يومه حتى يمسي وإن قيس بن صِرْمة الأنصاري كان صائما فلما حضر الإفطار أتى امرأته فقال لها: أعندك طعام قالت: لا ولكن أنطلق فأطلب لك وكان يعمل يومه فغلبته عيناه فقالت: خيبة لك فلما انتصف النهار غشي عليه فذكر ذلك للنبي ﷺ فنزلت هذه الآية: (أُحِلَّ لَكُمْ لَيْلَةَ ٱلصِّيَامِ ٱلرَّفَثُ إِلَىٰ نِسَآئِكُمْ) ففرحوا بها فرحا شديدا ونزلت: (وَكُلُواْ وَٱشْرَبُواْ حَتَّىٰ يَتَبَيَّنَ لَكُمُ ٱلْخَيْطُ ٱلْأَبْيَضُ مِنَ ٱلْخَيْطِ ٱلْأَسْوَدِ).

Al-Baraa ﷺ said, "[Regarding]The Companions of Muhammad ﷺ, when a man [from amongst them] was fasting and the time for breaking the fast came and he slept before breaking the fast, he would not eat for the rest of the night and the next day until the time for breaking the fast came again. [One time] Qais ibn Sirmah Al-Ansaaree was fasting. When the time for breaking the fast came he went to his wife and, 'Do you have any food?' She said, "No, but I will go and look for you." He used to work during the day so [the heaviness of] his eyes overwhelmed him and he fell asleep. she then said to him, 'You lost out,' and by midday of the following day he passed out. That [story] was mentioned to the Prophet ﷺ and this verse descended:

$$\text{أُحِلَّ لَكُمْ لَيْلَةَ ٱلصِّيَامِ ٱلرَّفَثُ إِلَىٰ نِسَآئِكُمْ}$$

"It has been made lawful for you to have sexual relations with your wives during the night of fasting…". Consequently they became ecstatic by its revelation and in addition, the following descended:

$$\text{وَكُلُواْ وَٱشْرَبُواْ حَتَّىٰ يَتَبَيَّنَ لَكُمُ ٱلْخَيْطُ ٱلْأَبْيَضُ مِنَ ٱلْخَيْطِ ٱلْأَسْوَدِ}$$

"And eat and drink until the white thread of dawn appears distinct to you from the black thread (of night)."

[Concerning] this *hadeeth*, Al-Bukhaaree transmitted it in his *Saheeh* (1915) and Ash-Sheikh Muqbil ﷺ commented, ", Al-Bukhaaree mentioned the *hadeeth* once more in the book of *Tafseer* (4508) with some alteration in the chain, wherein Abu Ishaaq clarified that he heard the *hadeeth* from Al-Baraa. The text of the *hadeeth* reads,

لما نزل صوم رمضان كانوا لا يقربون النساء رمضان كله وكان رجال يخونون أنفسهم فأنزل الله تعالى: (عَلِمَ ٱللَّهُ أَنَّكُمْ كُنتُمْ تَخْتَانُونَ أَنفُسَكُمْ فَتَابَ عَلَيْكُمْ) الآية.

"When [the verse mandating] the fast of Ramadaan descended revealed, they would not approach their wives for the entire month of Ramadaan. [However] There were some men who deceived themselves (by having sexual relations with their wives at night). In this regard Allaah ﷻ sent down:

عَلِمَ ٱللَّهُ أَنَّكُمْ كُنتُمْ تَخْتَانُونَ أَنفُسَكُمْ فَتَابَ عَلَيْكُمْ

"Allaah knows that you used to deceive yourselves, so He has forgiven you…" (*Al-Baqarah*: 187).

Ash-Sheikh Muqbil ﷺ said, "It appears that these two texts are different; however, there is nothing which prevents [accepting that] the verse descended regarding the plight of both groups of people."

His, the Exalted One's statement:

مِنَ ٱلْفَجْرِ

"… of the dawn." (verse: 187)

قال الإمام البخاري ﷺ (1917): حدثنا سعيد بن أبي مريم حدثنا ابن أبي حازم عن أبيه عن سهل بن سعد ح وحدثني سعيد بن أبي مريم حدثنا أبو غسان محمد بن مطرف قال حدثني أبو حازم عن سهل بن سعد ﷺ قال: أنزلت: (وَكُلُوا۟ وَٱشْرَبُوا۟ حَتَّىٰ يَتَبَيَّنَ لَكُمُ ٱلْخَيْطُ ٱلْأَبْيَضُ مِنَ ٱلْخَيْطِ ٱلْأَسْوَدِ) ولم ينزل: (مِنَ ٱلْفَجْرِ) فكان رجال إذا أرادوا الصوم ربط أحدهم في رجله الخيط الأبيض والخيط الأسود ولم يزل يأكل حتى يتبين له رؤيتهما فأنزل الله بعد: (مِنَ ٱلْفَجْرِ) فعلموا أنه إنما يعني الليل والنهار.

Sahl ibn Sa'd ﷺ said, "The following verse descended:

$$\text{وَكُلُواْ وَٱشْرَبُواْ حَتَّىٰ يَتَبَيَّنَ لَكُمُ ٱلْخَيْطُ ٱلْأَبْيَضُ مِنَ ٱلْخَيْطِ ٱلْأَسْوَدِ}$$

'And eat and drink until the white thread appears to you distinct from the black thread…'
while

$$\text{مِنَ ٱلْفَجْرِ}$$

"of the dawn"

had not yet descended. So some men, when they intended to fast, would tie a white thread and a black thread to his leg and would continue to eat until he could see the distinction between the two. At that point Allaah revealed,

$$\text{مِنَ ٱلْفَجْرِ}$$

'of the dawn'

so they knew that He only meant the night and the day."

This *hadeeth* has been transmitted by Al-Bukhaaree in his *Saheeh* (1917) and Muslim in his *Saheeh* (1091).

His, the Exalted One's statement:

$$\text{وَأْتُواْ ٱلْبُيُوتَ مِنْ أَبْوَٰبِهَا}$$

"So enter the houses by their doors." (verse: 189)

قال الإمام البخاري ﵀ (1803): حدثنا أبو الوليد حدثنا شعبة عن أبي إسحاق قال سمعت البراء ﵁ يقول: نزلت هذه الآية فينا كانت الأنصار إذا حجوا فجاءوا ولم يدخلوا من قبل أبواب بيوتهم ولكن من ظهورها فجاء رجل من الأنصار فدخل من قبل بابه فكأنه عُيِّر بذلك فنزلت: (وَلَيْسَ ٱلْبِرُّ بِأَن تَأْتُواْ ٱلْبُيُوتَ مِن ظُهُورِهَا وَلَٰكِنَّ ٱلْبِرَّ مَنِ ٱتَّقَىٰ ۗ وَأْتُواْ ٱلْبُيُوتَ مِنْ أَبْوَٰبِهَا).

Al-Baraa ﵁ said, "This verse was revealed because of us. The *Ansaar*, when they used to return from *hajj*, would not enter their houses by their doors; instead, they would enter [their houses] by climbing over the wall. Then a man from the *Ansaar* returned from *hajj* and entered his house by its door and it was as if he was condemned for doing that. Then the verse descended:

$$\text{وَلَيْسَ ٱلْبِرُّ بِأَن تَأْتُوا۟ ٱلْبُيُوتَ مِن ظُهُورِهَا وَلَٰكِنَّ ٱلْبِرَّ مَنِ ٱتَّقَىٰ ۗ وَأْتُوا۟ ٱلْبُيُوتَ مِنْ أَبْوَٰبِهَا}$$

"It is not righteousness that you enter the houses from above; rather, righteousness is he who fears Allaah. So enter the houses by their doors."

Al-Bukhaaree transmitted this *hadeeth* it in his *Saheeh* (1803) and Muslim in his *Saheeh* (3026).

His, the Exalted One's statement:

$$\text{وَأَنفِقُوا۟ فِى سَبِيلِ ٱللَّهِ وَلَا تُلْقُوا۟ بِأَيْدِيكُمْ إِلَى ٱلتَّهْلُكَةِ}$$

"And spend in the cause of Allaah and do not throw yourselves into destruction." (verse: 195)

قال الإمام البخاري رحمه الله (4516): حدثنا إسحاق حدثنا النضر حدثنا شعبة عن سليمان قال سمعت أبا وائل عن حذيفة رضي الله عنه: (وَأَنفِقُوا۟ فِى سَبِيلِ ٱللَّهِ وَلَا تُلْقُوا۟ بِأَيْدِيكُمْ إِلَى ٱلتَّهْلُكَةِ) قال: نزلت في النفقة.

Hudhaifah stated,

$$\text{وَأَنفِقُوا۟ فِى سَبِيلِ ٱللَّهِ وَلَا تُلْقُوا۟ بِأَيْدِيكُمْ إِلَى ٱلتَّهْلُكَةِ}$$

"And spend in the cause of Allaah and do not throw yourselves into destruction…, descended because of spending."[28]

Al-Bukhaaree transmitted this *hadeeth* in his *Saheeh* (4516).

قال الترمذي رحمه الله (2972): حدثنا عبد بن حميد نا أبو عاصم النبيل عن حيوة بن شريح عن يزيد بن أبي حبيب عن أسلم أبي عمران التجيبي قال: كنا بمدينة الروم فأخرجوا إلينا صفا عظيما من الروم فخرج إليهم من المسلمين مثلهم أو أكثر وعلى أهل مصر عقبة بن عامر وعلى الجماعة فضالة بن عبيد فحمل رجل من المسلمين على صف الروم حتى دخل عليهم فصاح الناس وقالوا: سبحان الله يلقي بيديه إلى التهلكة فقام أبو أيوب الأنصاري رضي الله عنه فقال: يأيها الناس إنكم لتأولون هذه الآية هذا التأويل وإنما نزلت هذه الآية فينا معشر الأنصار لما أعز الله الإسلام وكثر ناصروه فقال بعضنا لبعض سرا دون رسول الله ﷺ: إن أموالنا قد ضاعت وإن الله قد أعز الإسلام وكثر

---

[28] Meaning, do not throw yourselves into destruction by not spending in the cause of Allaah.

ناصروه فلو أقمنا في أموالنا فأصلحنا ما ضاع منها فأنزل الله تبارك وتعالى على نبيه ﷺ يرد علينا ما قلنا: (وَأَنفِقُوا۟ فِى سَبِيلِ ٱللَّهِ وَلَا تُلْقُوا۟ بِأَيْدِيكُمْ إِلَى ٱلتَّهْلُكَةِ) فكانت التهلكة الإقامة على الأموال وإصلاحها وتركنا الغزو فما زال أبو أيوب شاخصا في سبيل الله حتى دفن بأرض الروم.

Aslam Abu 'Imraan At-Tujeebee said, "We were in the city of the Romans (The Constantine Empire) when they dispatched in our direction large group of soldiers and in such manner the Muslims dispatched towards them the same amount or greater. [At that time] 'Uqbah ibn 'Aamir was the *ameer* (leader) in charge of Misr (Egypt) and Fudaalah ibn 'Ubaid was the *ameer* in charge of the army. A man from the Muslims then attacked the Roman army. When he reached the battalion the people shouted, "*SubhaanAllaah*! (Glorified be Allaah) He throws himself into destruction!" Abu Ayyoob Al-Ansaaree ﷺ then stood up and said, "O people, verily you interpret this verse with this explanation while it was only revealed because of us, the *Ansaar*. When Allaah made Islaam mighty and its supporters became many, we said to one another secretly without the Messenger of Allaah ﷺ knowing, 'Certainly we have lost our wealth and indeed Allaah has made Islaam mighty and its supporters have become many. Now if only we were to stick to our wealth so we can regain what has been lost.' Then Allaah ﷻ sent down to His Prophet ﷺ the following, refuting what we said:

$$\text{وَأَنفِقُوا۟ فِى سَبِيلِ ٱللَّهِ وَلَا تُلْقُوا۟ بِأَيْدِيكُمْ إِلَى ٱلتَّهْلُكَةِ}$$

"And spend in the cause of Allaah and do not throw yourselves into destruction."

Therefore, what was meant by destruction was our preoccupation with wealth and regaining it, and how we abandoned fighting." After that Abu Ayyoob did not cease fighting for Allaah's cause until he was [martyred and] buried in the land of the Romans."

This *hadeeth* has been transmitted by At-Tirmidhee in his *Jaami'* (2972) where he classified it to be *hasan ghareeb saheeh*.

قال الطبراني ﷺ في الأوسط (5668): حدثنا محمد بن عبد الله الحضرمي قال حدثنا هدبة ابن خالد قال حدثنا حماد بن سلمة عن سماك بن حرب عن النعمان بن بشير ﷺ في قوله: (وَلَا تُلْقُوا۟ بِأَيْدِيكُمْ إِلَى ٱلتَّهْلُكَةِ) قال: كان الرجل يذنب فيقول: لا يغفر الله لي فأنزل الله تعالى: (وَلَا تُلْقُوا۟ بِأَيْدِيكُمْ إِلَى ٱلتَّهْلُكَةِ وَأَحْسِنُوٓا۟ إِنَّ ٱللَّهَ يُحِبُّ ٱلْمُحْسِنِينَ).

An-Nu'maan ibn Basheer ﷺ said pertaining to His statement:

$$\text{وَلَا تُلْقُوا بِأَيْدِيكُمْ إِلَى التَّهْلُكَةِ}$$

"And do not throw yourselves into destruction"
"A man would commit a sin and then say, "Allaah will not forgive me." Then Allaah ﷻ sent down:

$$\text{وَلَا تُلْقُوا بِأَيْدِيكُمْ إِلَى التَّهْلُكَةِ وَأَحْسِنُوا إِنَّ اللَّهَ يُحِبُّ الْمُحْسِنِينَ}$$

"…And do not throw yourselves into destruction, and do good, indeed Allaah loves the doers of good."

At-Tabaraanee transmitted this *hadeeth* in *Al-Mu'jam Al-Awsat* (5668) as well as his book *Al-Mu'jam Al-Kabeer*. Al-Haithamee mentioned in his book *Majma' Az-Zawaa'id* volume 6, page 317, "And the people in the two chains are the people of the *Saheeh* (Al-Bukhaaree and/or Muslim)." Al-Haafidh Ibn Hajar mentioned in *Fathul-Baaree* in the explanation of *hadeeth* (4516) that this *hadeeth* has also been narrated by Al-Baraa and its chain is *saheeh*. He then said, "And the first *hadeeth* is more apparent since the verse began by mentioning spending; therefore, it is the basis for why the verse was revealed." Ash-Sheikh Muqbil ﷺ said, "I say, there is no cause for nullifying the two narrations, meaning the narrations of An-Nu'maan and Al-Baraa, since they are authentic because the verse encompasses the one who leaves off *jihaad* and becomes stingy as well as the one who sinned and thought that Allaah will not forgive him. There is nothing which prevents the verse from being revealed in regards to both cases, and Allaah knows best."

His, the Exalted One's statement:

$$\text{فَمَن كَانَ مِنكُم مَّرِيضًا أَوْ بِهِ أَذًى مِّن رَّأْسِهِ فَفِدْيَةٌ مِّن صِيَامٍ أَوْ صَدَقَةٍ أَوْ نُسُكٍ}$$

"And whoever among you is ill or has an ailment in his scalp he must pay a *fidyah* (redemption) by fasting, or giving charity, or offering sacrifice." (verse: 196)

قال الإمام البخاري ﷺ (1815): حدثنا أبو نعيم حدثنا سيف قال حدثني مجاهد قال سمعت عبد الرحمن بن أبي ليلى أن كعب بن عجرة ﷺ حدثه قال: وقف عليّ رسول الله ﷺ بالحديبية ورأسي يتهافت قملا فقال: يؤذيك هوامك قلت: نعم قال: فاحلق رأسك أو احلق قال: فيّ نزلت هذه الآية: (فَمَن كَانَ مِنكُم مَّرِيضًا أَوْ بِهِ أَذًى مِّن رَّأْسِهِ) إلى آخرها فقال النبي ﷺ: صم ثلاثة أيام أو تصدق بفرق بين ستة أو انسك مما تيسر.

Ka'b ibn 'Ujrah ؓ said, "The Messenger of Allaah ﷺ stood over me at Al-Hudaibiyah while my head suffered severely from lice. He asked, 'Are your vermin annoying you?' I replied, "Yes." He said, 'Shave your head.' He (Ka'b) said, "And because of me this verse descended,

$$\text{فَمَن كَانَ مِنكُم مَّرِيضًا أَوْ بِهِۦٓ أَذًى مِّن رَّأْسِهِۦ}$$

'And whoever among you is ill or has an ailment in his scalp…'.

So the Prophet ﷺ said, "Fast three days, or give a *faraq*[29] in charity to six people, or slaughter a sacrificial animal that you are able to afford.'"

Al-Bukhaaree transmitted this *hadeeth* in his *Saheeh* (1815) as well as Muslim in his *Saheeh* (1201/82).

His, the Exalted One's statement:

$$\text{وَتَزَوَّدُواْ فَإِنَّ خَيْرَ ٱلزَّادِ ٱلتَّقْوَىٰ}$$

"And take provision, for indeed the best provision is piety." (verse: 197)

قال الإمام البخاري ؒ (1523): حدثنا يحيى بن بشر حدثنا شبابة عن ورقاء عن عمرو بن دينار عن عكرمة عن ابن عباس ؓ قال: كان أهل اليمن يحجون ولا يتزودون ويقولون: نحن المتوكلون فإذا قدموا مكة سألوا الناس فأنزل الله تعالى: (وَتَزَوَّدُواْ فَإِنَّ خَيْرَ ٱلزَّادِ ٱلتَّقْوَىٰ).

Ibn 'Abbaas ؓ said, "The people of Yemen used to make *hajj* without taking provisions for the journey. They used to say, 'We are a people who trust in Allaah.' Then when they would arrive in Makkah they would beg the people. Then Allaah ﷻ sent down:

$$\text{وَتَزَوَّدُواْ فَإِنَّ خَيْرَ ٱلزَّادِ ٱلتَّقْوَىٰ}$$

"And take provision for indeed the best provision is piety."

(Regarding) This *hadeeth*, Al-Bukhaaree transmitted it in his *Saheeh* (1523).

His, the Exalted One's statement:

$$\text{لَيْسَ عَلَيْكُمْ جُنَاحٌ أَن تَبْتَغُواْ فَضْلًا مِّن رَّبِّكُمْ}$$

---

[29] A *faraq* is a measurement well known in Madeenah explained in another narration of this *hadeeth*: "give three Saa's." A *Saa'* is a dry measurement roughly equivalent to four double handfuls of a person with medium sized hands.

"There is no sin on you for seeking the bounty of your Lord." (verse: 198)

قال الإمام البخاري ﵀ (2098): حدثنا علي بن عبد الله حدثنا سفيان عن عمرو عن ابن عباس ﵄ قال: كانت عكاظ ومجنة وذو المجاز أسواقا في الجاهلية فلما كان الإسلام تأثموا من التجارة فيها فأنزل الله تعالى: (ليس عليكم جناح ... في مواسم الحج) قرأ ابن عباس كذا.

Ibn 'Abbaas said, "'Ukaadh and Majannah and Dhul-Majaaz were markets during the time *Jaahiliyah*. Then when Islaam came they abandoned trading in these markets out of fear of sin. Then Allaah sent down:

ليس عليكم جناح أن تبتغوا فضلا من ربكم في مواسم الحج

'There is no sin on you for seeking the bounty of your Lord in the seasons of *hajj*.' Ibn 'Abbaas recited the verse like that.[30]

Al-Bukhaaree transmitted this *hadeeth* in his *Saheeh* (2098). The complete recitation of Ibn 'Abbaas was taken from *hadeeth* number 2,050.

قال الإمام أبو داود ﵀ (1733): حدثنا مسدد نا عبد الواحد بن زياد نا العلاء بن المسيب نا أبو أمامة التيمي قال: كنت رجلا أكري في هذا الوجه وكان ناس يقولون: إنه ليس لك حج فلقيت ابن عمر فقلت: يا أبا عبد الرحمن إني رجل أكري في هذا الوجه وإن ناسا يقولون: إنه ليس لك حج فقال ابن عمر ﵄: أليس تحرم وتلبي وتطوف بالبيت وتفيض من عرفات وترمي الجمار قال قلت: بلى قال: فإن لك حجا جاء رجل إلى النبي ﷺ فسأله عن مثل ما سألتني عنه فسكت عنه رسول الله ﷺ ولم يجبه حتى نزلت هذه الآية: (لَيْسَ عَلَيْكُمْ جُنَاحٌ أَن تَبْتَغُوا فَضْلًا مِّن رَّبِّكُمْ) فأرسل إليه رسول الله ﷺ وقرأ عليه هذه الآية وقال: لك حج.

Abu Umaamah At-Taimee said, "I was a man who rented out riding animals for the *hajj* journey and some people used to say, 'You do not have a *hajj*.'[31] I then met Ibn 'Umar and said, "O Abaa 'Abdir-Rahmaan, verily I am a man who rents out riding animals for the *hajj* and people say to me, 'You do not have a *hajj*.'" Ibn 'Umar said, "Do you not enter the state of *ihraam* (that of a pilgrim) and make *talbiyah* (the chant of the pilgrim) and make *tawaaf* (circumbulation) of the Sacred House and depart from 'Arafah and throw the stones?" I said, 'Certainly.' He said, "Then you have a *hajj*. A man came to

---

[30] Ibn Hajar said in *Fathul-Baaree* in the explanation of *hadeeth* (2050), "The recitation of Ibn 'Abbaas: (في مواسم الحج) "...in the seasons of *hajj*" is from the singular recitations whose chain is authentic so it is a proof, but it is not Qur'aan."

[31] Meaning your *hajj* will not be accepted because you do business during it.

the Prophet ﷺ and asked him something similar to what you asked me. He ﷺ then remained silent and did not answer him until this verse descended,

$$\text{لَيْسَ عَلَيْكُمْ جُنَاحٌ أَن تَبْتَغُواْ فَضْلًا مِّن رَّبِّكُمْ}$$

'There is no sin on you for seeking the bounty of your Lord.'
The Messenger of Allaah ﷺ then sent for him and recited to him this verse and said, "You have a *hajj*."'

This *hadeeth* has been transmitted by Abu Daawud in *As-Sunan* (1733) and Ash-Sheikh Muqbil ﷺ said, "This is a *saheeh hadeeth*."

His, the Exalted One's statement:

$$\text{ثُمَّ أَفِيضُواْ مِنْ حَيْثُ أَفَاضَ ٱلنَّاسُ}$$

"Then depart from the place where the people depart." (verse: 199)

قال الإمام البخاري رَحِمَهُ اللهُ (1665): حدثنا فروة بن أبي المَغْراء حدثنا علي بن مسهر عن هشام ابن عروة قال: كان الناس يطوفون في الجاهلية عراة إلا الحمس والحمس قريش وما ولدت وكانت الحمس يحتسبون على الناس يعطي الرجل الرجل الثياب يطوف فيها وتعطي المرأة المرأة الثياب تطوف فيها فمن لم يعطه الحمس طاف بالبيت عريانا وكان يفيض جماعة الناس من عرفات ويفيض الحمس من جمع قال: وأخبرني أبي عن عائشة ﷺ أن هذه الآية نزلت في الحمس: (ثُمَّ أَفِيضُواْ مِنْ حَيْثُ أَفَاضَ ٱلنَّاسُ) قال: كانوا يفيضون من جمع فدفعوا إلى عرفات.

Hishaam ibn 'Urwah stated, "'Urwah narrated that the people used to make *tawaaf* in *Jaahiliyah* naked except for the *hums*, which is the tribe of Quraish and its descendents. The *hums* used to charge the people so a man would give another man clothes to make *tawaaf* with and a woman would give another woman clothes to make *tawaaf* with, and whoever the *hums* did not give [clothes to] then he would make *tawaaf* naked. Majority of the people would depart from 'Arafaat while the *hums* would depart from Jam' (Al-Muzdalifah)." My father narrated to me by way of 'Aishah ﷺ that this verse descended because of the *hums*,

$$\text{ثُمَّ أَفِيضُواْ مِنْ حَيْثُ أَفَاضَ ٱلنَّاسُ}$$

"Then depart from the place where the people depart," because they used to depart from Jam'. Thus, they were moved to 'Arafaat.

Al-Bukhaaree transmitted this *hadeeth* it in his *Saheeh* (1665).

قال الإمام البخاري رَحِمَهُ اللهُ (4520): حدثنا علي بن عبد الله حدثنا محمد بن حازم حدثنا هشام عن أبيه عن عائشة رَضِيَ اللهُ عَنْهَا كانت قريش ومن دان دينها يقفون بالمزدلفة وكانوا يسمون الحمس وكان سائر العرب يقفون بعرفات فلما جاء الإسلام أمر الله نبيه ﷺ أن يأتي عرفات ثم يقف بها ثم يفيض منها فذلك قوله تعالى: (ثُمَّ أَفِيضُوا۟ مِنْ حَيْثُ أَفَاضَ ٱلنَّاسُ).

'Aishah said, "Quraish along with whoever practiced their religion used to stop at Al-Muzdalifah (in *hajj*). They used to be referred to as the *hums*. Contrarily, the rest of the Arabs used to stop at 'Arafaat. Then when Islaam came, Allaah ordered His Prophet ﷺ to go to 'Arafaat, stop there, and then depart from there. That is the meaning of His statement:

$$\text{ثُمَّ أَفِيضُوا۟ مِنْ حَيْثُ أَفَاضَ ٱلنَّاسُ}$$

"Then depart from the place where the people depart."

This *hadeeth* has been transmitted by Al-Bukhaaree in his *Saheeh* (4520) and Muslim in his *Saheeh* (1219).

His, the Exalted One's statement:

$$\text{وَمِنَ ٱلنَّاسِ مَن يَشْرِى نَفْسَهُ ٱبْتِغَآءَ مَرْضَاتِ ٱللَّهِ}$$

"And of mankind is he who would sell himself seeking the pleasure of Allaah." (verse: 207)

قال الإمام أبو عبد الله الحاكم رَحِمَهُ اللهُ في مستدركه (ج 3 ص 398): حدثنا أبو عبد الله محمد بن عبد الله الزاهد حدثنا إسماعيل بن إسحاق القاضي ثنا سليمان بن حرب حدثنا حماد بن زيد عن أيوب عن عكرمة قال: لما خرج صهيب مهاجرا تبعه أهل مكة فنثل كنانته فأخرج منها أربعين سهما فقال: لا تصلون إليّ حتى أضع في كل رجل منكم سهما ثم أصير بعده إلى السيف فتعلمون أني رجل وقد خلفت بمكة قينتين فهما لكم قال: وحدثنا حماد بن سلمة عن ثابت عن أنس نحوه ونزلت على النبي ﷺ: (وَمِنَ ٱلنَّاسِ مَن يَشْرِى نَفْسَهُ ٱبْتِغَآءَ مَرْضَاتِ ٱللَّهِ) الآية فلما رآه النبي ﷺ قال: أبا يحيى ربح البيع قال: وتلا هذه الآية.

'Ikrimah said, "When Suhaib left to make *hijrah* (migration to Madeenah) some of the people of Makkah pursued him. So he pulled out his quiver of arrows and removed forty arrows from it and said, 'You all will not reach me until I put an arrow in every one of you, and then after that I will use my sword. [You can choose that] or, as you know, I am a man who has left behind in Makkah two female slaves so take them (and let me go).'" Hammaad ibn Salamah narrated on Thaabit, by way of Anas ﷺ saying that he mentioned the story of Suhaib in a similar fashion and the verse descended to the Prophet ﷺ,

$$\text{وَمِنَ ٱلنَّاسِ مَن يَشْرِي نَفْسَهُ ٱبْتِغَآءَ مَرْضَاتِ ٱللَّهِ}$$

"And of mankind is he who would sell himself seeking the pleasure of Allaah."

When the Prophet ﷺ saw him he said, "O Abaa Yahyaa,[32] the sale was profitable." Then he recited the verse to him.

Al-Haakim transmitted This *hadeeth* in *Al-Mustadrak*, volume 3, page 398. Ash-Sheikh Muqbil ﷺ said, "The *hadeeth* has other chains, most of them are *mursal* as can be found in the book *Al-Isaabah* volume 2, page 162 and 163, in the first section. These chains, when combined, strengthen the *hadeeth* and prove it to be authentic."

His, the Exalted One's statement:

$$\text{يَسْـَٔلُونَكَ عَنِ ٱلْخَمْرِ وَٱلْمَيْسِرِ}$$

"They ask you concerning alcoholic drinks and gambling…" (verse: 219)

قال الإمام أحمد ﷺ (ج 1 ص 53): حدثنا خلف بن الوليد حدثنا إسرائيل عن أبي إسحاق عن أبي ميسرة عن عمر بن الخطاب ﷺ قال لما نزل تحريم الخمر قال: اللهم بين لنا في الخمر بيانا شافيا فنزلت هذه الآية التي في سورة البقرة: (يَسْـَٔلُونَكَ عَنِ ٱلْخَمْرِ وَٱلْمَيْسِرِ قُلْ فِيهِمَآ إِثْمٌ كَبِيرٌ) قال فدعي عمر ﷺ فقرئت عليه فقال: اللهم بين لنا في الخمر بيانا شافيا فنزلت الآية التي في سورة النساء: (يَـٰٓأَيُّهَا ٱلَّذِينَ ءَامَنُوا۟ لَا تَقْرَبُوا۟ ٱلصَّلَوٰةَ وَأَنتُمْ سُكَـٰرَىٰ) فكان منادي رسول الله ﷺ إذا أقام الصلاة نادى أن لا يقربن الصلاة سكران فدعي عمر ﷺ فقرئت عليه فقال: اللهم بين لنا في الخمر بيانا شافيا فنزلت الآية التي في المائدة فدعي عمر ﷺ فقرئت عليه فلما بلغ: (فَهَلْ أَنتُم مُّنتَهُونَ) قال فقال عمر ﷺ: انتهينا انتهينا.

---

[32] Abu Yahyaa is the *kunyah* of Suhaib.

It has been narrated on 'Umar that when the prohibition of alcoholic drinks had drawn near he ('Umar) said, "O Allaah, articulate for us a clear declaration on alcoholic drinks." Then the verse in *Sooratul-Baqarah* descended:

$$يَسْـَٔلُونَكَ عَنِ ٱلْخَمْرِ وَٱلْمَيْسِرِ ۖ قُلْ فِيهِمَآ إِثْمٌ كَبِيرٌ$$

"They ask you concerning alcoholic drink and gambling. Say: In them is great sin…"

'Umar was called and the verse was read to him so he said, "O Allaah, articulate for us a clear declaration on alcoholic drinks." Thereafter the verse in *Sooratun-Nisaa* descended:

$$يَـٰٓأَيُّهَا ٱلَّذِينَ ءَامَنُوا۟ لَا تَقْرَبُوا۟ ٱلصَّلَوٰةَ وَأَنتُمْ سُكَـٰرَىٰ$$

"O you who believe, do not approach the prayer while you are in a drunken state…" (verse: 43).

Consequently when The caller to the prayer for the Messenger of Allaah would call the *Iqaamah* (second call to prayer) he would say, "The drunken person does not approach the prayer." Again 'Umar was called and the verse was read to him so he said, "O Allaah, articulate for us a clear declaration on alcoholic drinks." Then the verse in *Sooratul-Maa'idah* descended and 'Umar was called and the verse was read to him up until the point where it reads,

$$فَهَلْ أَنتُم مُّنتَهُونَ$$

"So will you not then cease!?" (verse: 91)
'Umar said, "We cease! We cease!"

This *hadeeth* has been transmitted by Al-Imaam Ahmad in his *Musnad* volume 1, page 53. Ash-Sheikh Muqbil omitted this *hadeeth* from the earlier editions of this book because in its chain Abu Maisarah 'Amr ibn Shurahbeel narrates on 'Umar ibn Al-Khattaab and the Imaam Abu Zur'ah has stated, "'Amr ibn Shurahbeel did not hear from 'Umar." Then Ash-Sheikh Muqbil came across the statements of Al-Bukhaaree and Abu Haatim affirming that 'Amr ibn Shurahbeel did hear from 'Umar. In this regard Ash-Sheikh Muqbil said, "And the one who affirms is given precedence over the one who negates, all praise is due to Allaah alone."

His, the Exalted One's statement:

$$وَيَسْـَٔلُونَكَ عَنِ ٱلْمَحِيضِ ۖ قُلْ هُوَ أَذًى فَٱعْتَزِلُوا۟ ٱلنِّسَآءَ فِى ٱلْمَحِيضِ$$

"And they ask you about menstruation. Say: It is a harmful thing so keep away from the women during their menses…" (verse: 222)

قال الإمام مسلم ﵀ (302): وحدثني زهير بن حرب حدثنا عبد الرحمن بن مهدي حدثنا حماد بن سلمة حدثنا ثابت عن أنس ﵁ أن اليهود كانوا إذا حاضت المرأة فيهم لم يؤاكلوها ولم يجامعوهن في البيوت فسأل أصحاب النبي ﷺ النبي ﷺ فأنزل الله تعالى: (وَيَسْـَٔلُونَكَ عَنِ ٱلْمَحِيضِۖ قُلْ هُوَ أَذًى فَٱعْتَزِلُوا۟ ٱلنِّسَآءَ فِى ٱلْمَحِيضِۖ) إلى آخر الآية فقال رسول الله ﷺ: اصنعوا كل شيء إلا النكاح فبلغ ذلك اليهود فقالوا: ما يريد هذا الرجل أن يدع من أمرنا شيئا إلا خالفنا فيه فجاء أسيد بن حضير وعباد بن بشر فقالا: يا رسول الله إن اليهود تقول كذا وكذا فلا نجامعهن فتغير وجه رسول الله ﷺ حتى ظننا أن قد وجد عليهما فخرجا فاستقبلهما هدية من لبن إلى النبي ﷺ فأرسل في آثارهما فسقاهما فعرفا أن لم يجد عليهما.

Anas ﵁ narrated about the Jews: if one of their women was menstruating they would not dine with her nor would they intermingle with their women in the houses. So the Companions of the Prophet ﷺ asked the Prophet ﷺ about that. Then Allaah ﷻ sent down:

$$\text{وَيَسْـَٔلُونَكَ عَنِ ٱلْمَحِيضِۖ قُلْ هُوَ أَذًى فَٱعْتَزِلُوا۟ ٱلنِّسَآءَ فِى ٱلْمَحِيضِ}$$

"And they ask you about menstruation. Say: It is a harmful thing so keep away from the women during their menses…".

The Messenger of Allaah clarified saying ﷺ, "Do everything with them except sexual intercourse." This verdict reached the Jews so they said, "This man does not want to leave a single part of our religion spared from his opposition." Similarly, Usaid ibn Hudair and 'Abbaad ibn Bishr came to the Prophet and said, "O Messenger of Allaah, verily the Jews say such-and-such so should we stop intermingling with them (the women during their menstrual cycles)?" At that point the facial expression of the Messenger of Allaah ﷺ changed in a way that led us to think he was mad at them. They then began to leave and as they were leaving a gift of milk was being sent to the Prophet ﷺ. He ﷺ then sent someone after them to give them milk to drink and by this gesture they knew he was not mad at them.

This *hadeeth* has been transmitted by Muslim in his *Saheeh* (302).

His, the Exalted One's statement:

$$\text{نِسَآؤُكُمْ حَرْثٌ لَّكُمْ فَأْتُوا۟ حَرْثَكُمْ أَنَّىٰ شِئْتُمْ}$$

"Your wives are a tilth for you so go to your tilth however you wish." (verse: 223)

قال الإمام البخاري رَحِمَهُ اللهُ (4528): حدثنا أبو نعيم حدثنا سفيان عن ابن المنكدر سمعت جابر ابن عبد الله ﷺ قال: كانت اليهود تقول إذا جامعها من ورائها جاء الولد أحول فنزلت: (نِسَآؤُكُمْ حَرْثٌ لَّكُمْ فَأْتُواْ حَرْثَكُمْ أَنَّىٰ شِئْتُمْ).

Jaabir ibn 'Abdillaah ﷺ narrated that the Jews used to say, "If a man has sexual intercourse with (his wife) from behind, the baby will be born cross-eyed." Then the following descended,

نِسَآؤُكُمْ حَرْثٌ لَّكُمْ فَأْتُواْ حَرْثَكُمْ أَنَّىٰ شِئْتُمْ

'Your wives are a tilth for you so go to your tilth however you wish.'"

Al-Bukhaaree transmitted this *hadeeth* in his *Saheeh* (4528) and likewise Muslim in his *Saheeh* (1435/117). In Muslim (1435/119) there is a *ziyaadah* (additional wording) which reads, "If he wills, while she is lying on her stomach and if he wills while she is not lying on her stomach; however, that is only in one opening (the vagina)." Ash-Sheikh Muqbil ﷺ commented, "This additional wording is not authentic because the narrator is An-Nu'maan ibn Raashid and he is weak. Al-Haafidh said in *Fathul-Baaree*, "This additional wording looks as if it is from the explanation of Az-Zuhree because the other narrators on Ibn Al-Munkadir have not mentioned it." I add, its meaning is taken from other proofs as is mentioned in *Fathul-Baaree*.

Ash-Sheikh Muqbil ﷺ then said, "As for what has been mentioned on Ibn 'Umar, that the verse was revealed because of having sex with women in their anuses as is alluded to in Al-Bukhaaree (4527) and in *Fathul-Baaree* (the explanation of *hadeeth* 4527), the scholars, and at the head of them *Habrul-Ummah* (Ibn 'Abbaas), have refuted that claim as mentioned in *Fathul-Baaree*. Abu Ja'far ibn Jareer said in his *Tafseer*, volume 4, page 416, after mentioning his refutation against that notion, "And it has become clear from what we have explained that the correct meaning from what has been narrated on Jaabir and Ibn 'Abbaas is that this verse was revealed because the Jews used to say to the Muslims, "If a man has sexual intercourse with his wife from behind in her vagina, the baby will be born cross-eyed." Ibn Jareer also said before this, "And what type of planting ground (tilth) is the anus that it could be said, have sexual relations in it!?" The great Scholar Ash-Shawkaanee said after mentioning some of those who say it is permissible (anal sex with your wife), "There is no proof in the statements of those people whatsoever, and it is not permissible for anyone to act according to their statements since they did not bring a single proof which shows it to be permissible. Furthermore, whichever of them claims that he discerned its permissibility from the verse then he is mistaken in his understanding, whoever he may be. And whichever of them claims that the reason why the verse was revealed was that a man had sex with his wife in her anus, contrarily, there is nothing that indicates that the verse makes that permissible. And whoever claims that is mistaken; conflictingly, the verse shows that to be *haraam* (forbidden). And being the reason behind its revelation does not necessitate that the verse was revealed to make that act permissible. In fact, the verses that were revealed because of particular circumstances sometimes descend to make something permissible and sometimes to make something forbidden." As for Al-Haafidh Ibn Katheer's position on this issue, ﷺ after he mentioned the statement of Ibn 'Umar pertaining to why the verse was revealed he stated, "This should be interpreted with what has preceded. In other words, he has sex with her, in her vagina, from behind because of what An-Nasaa'ee narrated on 'Ali ibn 'Uthmaan An-Nufailee, on Sa'eed ibn 'Eisaa, on Al-Fadl ibn Fudaalah, on 'Abdullaah ibn Sulaimaan At-Taweel, on Ka'b ibn 'Alqamah, on Abun-Nadr that he narrated to him that he said to Naafi' Mawlaa ibn 'Umar, 'The word has spread that you say that Ibn 'Umar gives the ruling that it is permissible to have anal sex with the women.' He said, "They lied on me, however, I will tell you what happened. Ibn 'Umar reviewed the *mushaf* (The Qur'aan written down in book form) one day while I was with him. When he reached,

$$نِسَاؤُكُمْ حَرْثٌ لَكُمْ فَأْتُوا حَرْثَكُمْ أَنَّىٰ شِئْتُمْ$$

'Your wives are a tilth for you so go to your tilth however you wish.'

He said, "O Naafi', do you know about this verse?" I said, 'No.' He said, "We, the Quraish, used to make our wives lay down on their stomachs [during sexual intercourse]; however, once we entered Madeenah and married women from the *Ansaar*, we wanted to do the same to them but that bothered them. In fact they detested it and considered it to be a grave thing. The women from the *Ansaar* were accustomed to doing like the Jews do; they would only have sex lying down on their sides. Then Allaah sent down this verse,

$$نِسَاؤُكُمْ حَرْثٌ لَكُمْ فَأْتُوا حَرْثَكُمْ أَنَّىٰ شِئْتُمْ$$

"Your wives are a tilth for you, so go to your tilth however you wish," And this chain is *saheeh*."

Then he (Ibn Katheer) quoted a number of *ahaadeeth* proving that anal sex with the women is forbidden. In this regard he mentioned, "And the statements of Ibn Mas'ood, Abud-Dardaa, Abu Hurairah, Ibn 'Abbaas and 'Abdullaah ibn 'Amr have already been mentioned declaring anal sex to be forbidden and that [ruling], without doubt, is what has been authentically reported by way of Ibn 'Umar. In other words, he also sees anal sex to be forbidden. Furthermore, Abu Muhammad ibn 'Abdir-Rahmaan Ad-Daarimee said in his *Musnad*, "'Abdullaah ibn Saalih narrated to us that Al-Laith narrated on Al-Haarith ibn Ya'qoob, on Sa'eed ibn Yasaar Abee Al-Hubaab that he said, "I said to Ibn 'Umar, 'What do you say about making *tahmeed* with the women?'" He said, "And what is *tahmeed*?" He then mentioned [that he was referring to sex in] the anus so he (Ibn 'Umar) asked in astonishment, "Does anyone from the Muslims do that!?" Lastly Ibn Wahb and Qutaibah narrated the same story from the chain of Al-Laith. This chain is *saheeh* and it is a clear and explicit text from him declaring that act be forbidden. Therefore, everything that has been narrated on him that bears the possibility of carrying this meaning must be juxtaposed against this clear text."

His, the Exalted One's statement:

لَّا يُؤَاخِذُكُمُ ٱللَّهُ بِٱللَّغْوِ فِىٓ أَيْمَٰنِكُمْ

"Allaah will not call you to account for what is unintentional in your oaths…" (verse: 225)

قال الإمام البخاري رحمه الله (6663): حدثنا محمد بن المثنى حدثنا يحيى عن هشام قال أخبرني أبي عن عائشة رضي الله عنها: (لَّا يُؤَاخِذُكُمُ ٱللَّهُ بِٱللَّغْوِ فِىٓ أَيْمَٰنِكُمْ) قال: قالت: أنزلت في قوله: لا والله وبلى والله.

'Aishah said,

لَّا يُؤَاخِذُكُمُ ٱللَّهُ بِٱللَّغْوِ فِىٓ أَيْمَٰنِكُمْ

"Allaah will not call you to account for what is unintentional in your oaths…" was sent down in relation to one who, while making an oath says, 'No, by Allaah,' and, Certainly, by Allaah."

This *hadeeth* has been transmitted by Al-Bukhaaree in his *Saheeh* (6663).

His, the Exalted One's statement:

وَإِذَا طَلَّقْتُمُ ٱلنِّسَآءَ فَبَلَغْنَ أَجَلَهُنَّ فَلَا تَعْضُلُوهُنَّ أَن يَنكِحْنَ أَزْوَٰجَهُنَّ إِذَا تَرَٰضَوْاْ بَيْنَهُم بِٱلْمَعْرُوفِ

"And when you divorce women and they fulfill the term of their prescribed period, do not prevent them from marrying their former husbands if they mutually agree on a reasonable basis." (verse: 232)

قال الإمام البخاري رحمه الله (4529): حدثنا عبيد الله بن سعيد حدثنا أبو عامر العقدي حدثنا عباد ابن راشد حدثنا الحسن حدثني معقل بن يسار رضي الله عنه قال: كانت لي أخت تخطب إليّ. وقال إبراهيم عن يونس عن الحسن حدثني معقل بن يسار ، حدثنا أبو معمر حدثنا عبد الوارث حدثنا يونس عن

الحسن أن أخت معقل بن يسار طلقها زوجها فتركها حتى انقضت عدتها فخطبها فأبى معقل فنزلت:

(فَلَا تَعْضُلُوهُنَّ أَن يَنكِحْنَ أَزْوَٰجَهُنَّ).

Al-Hasan narrated that the sister of Ma'qil ibn Yasaar was divorced by her husband and he did not reinstate the marriage before the *'iddah*[33] had expired. He then asked to re-marry her, however, Ma'qil refused. Then the following descended,

فَلَا تَعْضُلُوهُنَّ أَن يَنكِحْنَ أَزْوَٰجَهُنَّ

"Do not prevent them from marrying their former husbands…"

Al-Bukhaaree transmitted this *hadeeth* in his *Saheeh* (4529).

His, the Exalted One's statement:

حَٰفِظُوا۟ عَلَى ٱلصَّلَوَٰتِ وَٱلصَّلَوٰةِ ٱلْوُسْطَىٰ

"Guard strictly the prayers, and the middle[34] prayer…" (verse: 238)

قال الإمام أحمد ﷺ في مسنده (ج 5 ص 183): حدثنا محمد بن جعفر حدثنا شعبة حدثني عمرو بن أبي حكيم قال سمعت الزبرقان يحدث عن عروة بن الزبير عن زيد بن ثابت ﷺ قال: كان رسول الله ﷺ يصلي الظهر بالهاجرة ولم يكن يصلي صلاة أشد على أصحاب النبي ﷺ منها قال: فنزلت: (حَٰفِظُوا۟ عَلَى ٱلصَّلَوَٰتِ وَٱلصَّلَوٰةِ ٱلْوُسْطَىٰ) وقال: إن قبلها صلاتين وبعدها صلاتين.

Zaid ibn Thaabit narrated that the Messenger of Allaah ﷺ used to pray the *Dhuhr* prayer at midday and there was no prayer that he used to pray which was harder on the Companions of the Prophet ﷺ than it. Subsequently, the verse descended,

حَٰفِظُوا۟ عَلَى ٱلصَّلَوَٰتِ وَٱلصَّلَوٰةِ ٱلْوُسْطَىٰ

"Guard strictly the prayers and the middle prayer."

---

[33] The *'iddah* is the prescribed waiting period for the separation to be finalized.
[34] الوسطى (the middle) can also mean "the superior" as Ibn Hajar mentioned in *Fathul-Baaree* explanation of *hadeeth* (4533) and Ash-Shawkaanee in *Fathul-Qadeer*.

He (Zaid) commented, "There are two prayers before it and two prayers after it."

Al-Imaam Ahmad transmitted this *hadeeth* in his *Musnad*, volume 5, page 183. Ash-Sheikh Muqbil ؓ mentioned some of the inconsistencies in the chains of this *hadeeth* then added, "The strongest position about the middle prayer is that it is *Al-'Asr* as is mentioned in the *Saheehain*." (Al-Bukhaaree (4533) and Muslim (627/205).

His, the Exalted One's statement:

وَقُومُواْ لِلَّهِ قَٰنِتِينَ

"And stand before Allaah in silence." (verse: 238)

قال الإمام البخاري ؓ (4534): حدثنا مسدد حدثنا يحيى عن إسماعيل بن أبي خالد عن الحارث بن شبل عن أبي عمرو الشيباني عن زيد بن أرقم ؓ قال: كنا نتكلم في الصلاة يكلم أحدنا أخاه في حاجته حتى نزلت هذه الآية: (حَٰفِظُواْ عَلَى ٱلصَّلَوَٰتِ وَٱلصَّلَوٰةِ ٱلْوُسْطَىٰ وَقُومُواْ لِلَّهِ قَٰنِتِينَ)

فأمرنا بالسكوت.

Zaid ibn Arqam ؓ said, "We used to talk during prayer. One of us would talk to his brother about his needs until this verse descended,

حَٰفِظُواْ عَلَى ٱلصَّلَوَٰتِ وَٱلصَّلَوٰةِ ٱلْوُسْطَىٰ وَقُومُواْ لِلَّهِ قَٰنِتِينَ

'Guard strictly the prayers and the middle prayer, and stand before Allaah in silence,' thus we were ordered to be silent."[35] Al-Bukhaaree transmitted this *hadeeth* in his *Saheeh* (4534) and Muslim in his *Saheeh* (539).

NOTE: Al-Haafidh Ibn Katheer ؓ said in his *Tafseer*, volume 1, page 294, "This *hadeeth* poses a problem for a group of Scholars because according to them, it has been established that the prohibition of talking in prayer occurred in Makkah, before the migration to Madeenah and after the migration to the land of the Habashah (Abyssinians) as substantiated by the *hadeeth* of Ibn Mas'ood in the *Saheeh*.[36] He explicated, 'We used to give the Prophet ﷺ

---

[35] Ibn Hajar noted in *Fathul-Baaree* in the explanation of this *hadeeth*, "What is intended by that is to leave off talking to people, not that you stand in complete silence because the prayer, there is no complete silence in it, rather it is filled with recitation of the Qur'aan and supplication, and Allaah knows best."

[36] Al-Bukhaaree (1199 and 1216 and 3875) and Muslim (538) with a different wording. As for the wording that Ibn Katheer mentioned, I found a similar wording to it in the *Sunan* of Abu Daawud (924) and in the *Musnad* of Al-Imaam Ahmad, volume 1, page 377. Al-Bukhaaree mentioned a portion of this wording *mu'allaqan* (*mu'allaq* is a

greetings while he prayed before we migrated to *Habashah*, and he would return our greetings. Then when we returned [from Habashah] I greeted him as he prayed but he did not return the greeting and thus I was overwhelmed by sadness.[37] Finally, when he made *tasleem* [finishing the prayer] he said, "I did not return your greeting because I was in prayer and indeed Allaah reveals what He wills from His command, and verily what He has revealed is that you do not speak in prayer.'"

Ibn Mas'ood was of those who accepted Islaam early and migrated to Habashah, and later returned to Makkah When he migrated to Madeenah, this verse,

وَقُومُواْ لِلَّهِ قَـٰنِتِينَ

"And stand before Allaah in silence,"

was revealed in Madeenah without any dispute in this regard. Some say that Zaid ibn Arqam only meant by, 'One of us would talk to his brother about his needs in prayer,' to convey the type of speech, and he used this verse to prove its prohibition according to his understanding of the verse, and Allaah knows best. Others say he only meant to impart that this occurred in Madeenah after the migration, thus, speaking in prayer was made permissible twice and then forbidden twice, as a group of our contemporaries and others have chosen; however, the first opinion is more apparent, and Allaah knows best."

Ash-Sheikh Muqbil ﷺ added, "I say, what is readily apparent, and Allaah knows best, is that speaking [in prayer] was forbidden in Makkah by the authentic Sunnah as mentioned in the *hadeeth* of Ibn Mas'ood. Then when he ﷺ arrived at Madeenah some of the people whom the prohibition did not reach continued to speak in prayer such as Mu'aawiyah ibn Al-Hakam and subsequently the verse descended, and Allaah knows best. If you would like to read more on this issue refer to the book *Nail Al-Awtaar* volume 2, page 329-330, and the book *Fathul-Baaree*. In addition, I have quoted what Al-Haafidh said in *Fathul-Baaree* in my book *Riyaad Al-Jannah*."

---

hadeeth in which some or all of the chain is dropped starting from the author's end of the chain) in his *Saheeh* in the book of *Tawheed*, chapter 42.

[37] I came across two different explanations for this statement (فأخذني ما قرب وما بعد). The first being all of his past grief returned and overwhelmed him. The second being he started to contemplate searching for something he might have done in the past which may have caused the Prophet ﷺ not to return his salaams. Refer to the book *'Awn Al-Ma'bood* volume 3, page 193.

His, the Exalted One's statement:

$$\text{لَآ إِكْرَاهَ فِى ٱلدِّينِ ۖ قَد تَّبَيَّنَ ٱلرُّشْدُ مِنَ ٱلْغَىِّ}$$

"There is no compulsion in the religion. Verily the right path has become distinct from the wrong path…" (verse: 256)

قال الإمام أبو جعفر بن جرير ﵀ في تفسيره (ج 5 ص 407): حدثنا محمد بن بشار حدثنا ابن أبي عدي عن شعبة عن أبي بشر عن سعيد بن جبير عن ابن عباس ﵁ قال: كانت المرأة تكون مقلاتا فتجعل على نفسها إن عاش لها ولد أن تهوده فلما أجليت بنو النضير كان فيهم من أبناء الأنصار فقالوا: لا ندع أبناءنا فأنزل الله تعالى ذكره: (لَآ إِكْرَاهَ فِى ٱلدِّينِ ۖ قَد تَّبَيَّنَ ٱلرُّشْدُ مِنَ ٱلْغَىِّ).

Ibn 'Abbaas ﵁ narrated that a woman would be bereaved of children so she would take a vow [swearing] that if a baby of hers lived she would send it to become a Jew. When the Jews of the tribe Banu An-Nadeer were ousted they had some children from the *Ansaar* with them. So they (the *Ansaar*) said, "We cannot let our children go!" Then Allaah ﷻ sent down:

$$\text{لَآ إِكْرَاهَ فِى ٱلدِّينِ ۖ قَد تَّبَيَّنَ ٱلرُّشْدُ مِنَ ٱلْغَىِّ}$$

"There is no compulsion in the religion. Verily the right path has become distinct from the wrong path…"

This *hadeeth*, Ibn Jareer has transmitted it in his *Tafseer*, volume 5, page 407. Ash-Sheikh Muqbil ﵀ said, "[In regards to the]The *hadeeth*, the people of its chain are people of the *Saheeh* (Al-Bukhaaree and/or Muslim)."

His, the Exalted One's statement:

$$\text{يَٰٓأَيُّهَا ٱلَّذِينَ ءَامَنُوٓا۟ أَنفِقُوا۟ مِن طَيِّبَٰتِ مَا كَسَبْتُمْ وَمِمَّآ أَخْرَجْنَا لَكُم مِّنَ ٱلْأَرْضِ ۖ وَلَا تَيَمَّمُوا۟ ٱلْخَبِيثَ مِنْهُ تُنفِقُونَ وَلَسْتُم بِـَٔاخِذِيهِ إِلَّآ أَن تُغْمِضُوا۟ فِيهِ}$$

"O you who believe, spend of the good things you have earned and of what We have produced for you from the earth. And do not aim to spend what is bad from it while you yourselves would not accept it unless you were to overlook and tolerate [the degeneracy of what you are being given]." (verse: 267)

قال الإمام الترمذي ﵀ (2987): حدثنا عبد الله بن عبد الرحمن أنا عبيد الله بن موسى عن إسرائيل عن السدي عن أبي مالك عن البراء ﷺ (وَلَا تَيَمَّمُوا۟ ٱلْخَبِيثَ مِنْهُ تُنفِقُونَ) قال: نزلت فينا معشر الأنصار كنا أصحاب نخل فكان الرجل يأتي من نخله على قدر كثرته وقلته وكان الرجل يأتي بالقنو والقنوين فيعلقه في المسجد وكان أهل الصفة ليس لهم طعام فكان أحدهم إذا جاع قد أتى القنو فضربه بعصاه فيسقط البسر والتمر فيأكل وكان ناس ممن لا يرغب في الخير يأتي الرجل بالقنو فيه الشيص والحشف وبالقنو قد انكسر فيعلقه فأنزل الله تبارك وتعالى: (يَـٰٓأَيُّهَا ٱلَّذِينَ ءَامَنُوٓا۟ أَنفِقُوا۟ مِن طَيِّبَـٰتِ مَا كَسَبْتُمْ وَمِمَّآ أَخْرَجْنَا لَكُم مِّنَ ٱلْأَرْضِ ۖ وَلَا تَيَمَّمُوا۟ ٱلْخَبِيثَ مِنْهُ تُنفِقُونَ وَلَسْتُم بِـَٔاخِذِيهِ إِلَّآ أَن تُغْمِضُوا۟ فِيهِ) قال: لو أن أحدكم أهدي إليه مثل ما أعطى لم يأخذه إلا على إغماض أو حياء. قال: فكنا بعد ذلك يأتي أحدنا بصالح ما عنده.

Al-Baraa ﷺ said,

وَلَا تَيَمَّمُوا۟ ٱلْخَبِيثَ مِنْهُ تُنفِقُونَ

"And do not aim to spend what is bad from it…"

was revealed because of us, the *Ansaar*. We used to own date palms and a man would give from his date palm an amount proportionate to its size. A man would bring one or two bunches of dates and hang it in the *masjid*. Meanwhile, the people of the *suffah* (the area of the *masjid* where the poor would stay) did not have any food so when one of them would get hungry he would go to the bunch of dates and hit it with his stick causing some of the dates to fall and he would eat. Moreover, there were some people who did not strive to do good. Such a person would bring a bunch of dates of bad quality and hang them [in the masjid] regarding which Allaah ﷻ sent down:

يَـٰٓأَيُّهَا ٱلَّذِينَ ءَامَنُوٓا۟ أَنفِقُوا۟ مِن طَيِّبَـٰتِ مَا كَسَبْتُمْ وَمِمَّآ أَخْرَجْنَا لَكُم مِّنَ ٱلْأَرْضِ ۖ وَلَا تَيَمَّمُوا۟ ٱلْخَبِيثَ مِنْهُ تُنفِقُونَ وَلَسْتُم بِـَٔاخِذِيهِ إِلَّآ أَن تُغْمِضُوا۟ فِيهِ

"O you who believe, spend of the good things you have earned and of what We have produced for you from the earth. And do not aim to spend what is bad from it while you yourselves would not accept it unless you were to overlook and tolerate [the degeneracy of what you are being given]."

He explained, "If one of you was given similar to what he gave, he would not accept it unless he were to overlook or accept it out of embarrassment." He then concluded, "So from that point on, one of us would [only] bring [dates] of good quality."

At-Tirmidhee transmitted this *hadeeth* it in his *Jaami'* (2987) and classified it to be *hasan saheeh ghareeb*.

قال الحاكم ﷺ (ج 2 ص 284): حدثنا أبو بكر أحمد بن إسحاق الفقيه أنبأ محمد بن غالب الضبي ومحمد بن سنان قالا ثنا سعيد بن سليمان الواسطي ثنا عباد وهو ابن العوام عن سفيان ابن حسين عن الزهري عن أبي أمامة بن سهل بن حنيف عن أبيه ﷺ قال: أمر رسول الله ﷺ بصدقة فجاء رجل من هذا السحل قال سفيان: يعني الشيص فقال رسول الله ﷺ: من جاء بهذا وكان لا يجيء أحد بشيء إلا نسب إلى الذي جاء به فنزلت: (وَلَا تَيَمَّمُوا۟ ٱلْخَبِيثَ مِنْهُ تُنفِقُونَ وَلَسْتُم بِـَٔاخِذِيهِ إِلَّآ أَن تُغْمِضُوا۟ فِيهِ) ونهى رسول الله ﷺ عن لونين من التمر أن يؤخذا في الصدقة الجعرور ولون الحبيق.

قال الزهري: واللونين من تمر المدينة تابعه سليمان بن كثير عن الزهري.

Sahl ibn Hunaif ؓ narrated that the Messenger of Allaah ﷺ ordered to give charity and a man then brought dates of bad quality.[38] The Messenger of Allaah ﷺ then said, "Who brought this?" The norm for those times was that no one would bring something without it being attributed to its bringer. Thereafter the verse descended,

وَلَا تَيَمَّمُوا۟ ٱلْخَبِيثَ مِنْهُ تُنفِقُونَ وَلَسْتُم بِـَٔاخِذِيهِ إِلَّآ أَن تُغْمِضُوا۟ فِيهِ

"And do not aim to spend what is bad from it while you yourselves would not accept it unless you were to overlook and tolerate [the degeneracy of what you are being given]."

The Messenger of Allaah ﷺ prohibited that two types of dates be taken for charity, *Al-Ju'roor* and *Al-Hubaiq* (which are two types of dates of very bad quality).

Regarding this *hadeeth*, Al-Haakim transmitted it in *Al-Mustadrak*, volume 2, page 284. In its chain Sufyaan ibn Husain narrates on Az-Zuhree and Sufyaan's narrations on Az-Zuhree are weak; however, he has been supported by Sulaimaan ibn Katheer, whose narrations on Az-Zuhree are also weak. Ash-Sheik Muqbil ؓ concluded that, "The *hadeeth* of Sahl ibn Hunaif is *hasan* because the narrations of Sufyaan ibn Husain and Sulaimaan ibn Katheer on Az-Zuhree have some weakness in them."

His, the Exalted One's statement:

لَّيْسَ عَلَيْكَ هُدَىٰهُمْ وَلَـٰكِنَّ ٱللَّهَ يَهْدِى مَن يَشَآءُ

---

[38] The type of date which its pit has not fully developed or there is no pit in it at all.

"You are not entrusted with their guidance, but Allaah guides whom He wills." (verse: 272)

قال الإمام أبو جعفر بن جرير ﵀ (ج 5 ص 587): حدثنا أبو كريب قال حدثنا أبو داود عن سفيان عن الأعمش عن جعفر بن إياس عن سعيد بن جبير عن ابن عباس ﵄ قال: كانوا لا يرضخون لقراباتهم من المشركين فنزلت: (لَّيْسَ عَلَيْكَ هُدَىٰهُمْ وَلَٰكِنَّ ٱللَّهَ يَهْدِى مَن يَشَآءُ).

Ibn 'Abbaas ﵁ narrated that they would not give gifts to their relatives who were polytheists. Then the following descended,

$$\text{لَّيْسَ عَلَيْكَ هُدَىٰهُمْ وَلَٰكِنَّ ٱللَّهَ يَهْدِى مَن يَشَآءُ}$$

"You are not entrusted with their guidance, but Allaah guides whom He wills."[39]

This *hadeeth*, Ibn Jareer transmitted it in his *Tafseer*, volume 5, page 587. Ash-Sheikh Muqbil ﵀ said about it, " This *hadeeth*, the people of its chain are the people of the *Saheeh* (Al-Bukhaaree and/or Muslim)."

His, the Exalted One's statement:

$$\text{ءَامَنَ ٱلرَّسُولُ بِمَآ أُنزِلَ إِلَيْهِ مِن رَّبِّهِۦ وَٱلْمُؤْمِنُونَ}$$

"The Messenger believes in what has been sent down to him from his Lord and so do the believers…" (verses: 285-286)

قال الإمام مسلم ﵀ (125): حدثني محمد بن منهال الضرير وأمية بن بسطام العيشي واللفظ لأمية قالا حدثنا يزيد بن زريع حدثنا روح وهو ابن القاسم عن العلاء عن أبيه عن أبي هريرة ﵁ قال: لما نزلت على رسول الله ﷺ: (لِّلَّهِ مَا فِى ٱلسَّمَٰوَٰتِ وَمَا فِى ٱلْأَرْضِ وَإِن تُبْدُوا۟ مَا فِىٓ أَنفُسِكُمْ أَوْ تُخْفُوهُ يُحَاسِبْكُم بِهِ ٱللَّهُ فَيَغْفِرُ لِمَن يَشَآءُ وَيُعَذِّبُ مَن يَشَآءُ وَٱللَّهُ عَلَىٰ كُلِّ شَىْءٍ قَدِيرٌ) قال: فاشتد ذلك على أصحاب رسول الله ﷺ فأتوا رسول الله ﷺ ثم بركوا على الركب فقالوا: أي رسول الله كلفنا من الأعمال ما نطيق الصلاة والصيام والجهاد والصدقة وقد أنزلت عليك هذه الآية ولا نطيقها قال رسول الله ﷺ: أتريدون أن تقولوا كما قال أهل الكتابين من قبلكم سمعنا

---

[39] In another narration of this *hadeeth* it was added: "Then it was made permissible for them," meaning to give gifts to their relatives who were polytheists. Refer to *Tafseer Ibn Jareer*, volume 5, page 588, *hadeeth* (6204).

وعصينا بل قولوا سمعنا وأطعنا غفرانك ربنا وإليك المصير قالوا: سمعنا وأطعنا غفرانك ربنا وإليك المصير فلما اقترأها القوم ذلت بها ألسنتهم فأنزل الله في أثرها: (ءَامَنَ ٱلرَّسُولُ بِمَآ أُنزِلَ إِلَيْهِ مِن رَّبِّهِۦ وَٱلْمُؤْمِنُونَ ۚ كُلٌّ ءَامَنَ بِٱللَّهِ وَمَلَٰٓئِكَتِهِۦ وَكُتُبِهِۦ وَرُسُلِهِۦ لَا نُفَرِّقُ بَيْنَ أَحَدٍ مِّن رُّسُلِهِۦ ۚ وَقَالُوا۟ سَمِعْنَا وَأَطَعْنَا ۖ غُفْرَانَكَ رَبَّنَا وَإِلَيْكَ ٱلْمَصِيرُ) فلما فعلوا ذلك نسخها الله تعالى فأنزل: (لَا يُكَلِّفُ ٱللَّهُ نَفْسًا إِلَّا وُسْعَهَا ۚ لَهَا مَا كَسَبَتْ وَعَلَيْهَا مَا ٱكْتَسَبَتْ ۗ رَبَّنَا لَا تُؤَاخِذْنَآ إِن نَّسِينَآ أَوْ أَخْطَأْنَا) قال: نعم (رَبَّنَا وَلَا تَحْمِلْ عَلَيْنَآ إِصْرًا كَمَا حَمَلْتَهُۥ عَلَى ٱلَّذِينَ مِن قَبْلِنَا) قال: نعم (رَبَّنَا وَلَا تُحَمِّلْنَا مَا لَا طَاقَةَ لَنَا بِهِۦ) قال: نعم (وَٱعْفُ عَنَّا وَٱغْفِرْ لَنَا وَٱرْحَمْنَآ ۚ أَنتَ مَوْلَىٰنَا فَٱنصُرْنَا عَلَى ٱلْقَوْمِ ٱلْكَٰفِرِينَ) قال: نعم.

Abu Hurairah ﷺ narrated that when the following verse descended to the Messenger of Allaah ﷺ:

لِّلَّهِ مَا فِى ٱلسَّمَٰوَٰتِ وَمَا فِى ٱلْأَرْضِ ۗ وَإِن تُبْدُوا۟ مَا فِىٓ أَنفُسِكُمْ أَوْ تُخْفُوهُ يُحَاسِبْكُم بِهِ ٱللَّهُ ۖ فَيَغْفِرُ لِمَن يَشَآءُ وَيُعَذِّبُ مَن يَشَآءُ ۗ وَٱللَّهُ عَلَىٰ كُلِّ شَىْءٍ قَدِيرٌ

"To Allaah belongs all that is in the heavens and all that is on the earth, and whether you disclose what is in yourselves or conceal it, Allaah will call you to account for it. Then He forgives whom He wills and punishes whom He wills, and Allaah is able to do all things," (Al-Baqarah: 284)

it was hard for the Companions of the Messenger of Allaah ﷺ to handle. So they went to the Messenger of Allaah ﷺ and kneeled down before him and saying, "O Messenger of Allaah, we have been entrusted with what we are able to carry out in regards to prayer, fasting, *jihaad* and charity; however, this verse has been sent down to you and we cannot execute it." The Messenger of Allaah ﷺ said, "Do you want to say as the people of the two books before you said, 'We hear and we disobey'? Instead say, "We hear and we obey. O our Lord, we seek your forgiveness and to You is the return." When the people said that, it flowed from their tongues. Then right after that Allaah sent down:

ءَامَنَ ٱلرَّسُولُ بِمَآ أُنزِلَ إِلَيْهِ مِن رَّبِّهِۦ وَٱلْمُؤْمِنُونَ ۚ كُلٌّ ءَامَنَ بِٱللَّهِ وَمَلَـٰٓئِكَتِهِۦ وَكُتُبِهِۦ وَرُسُلِهِۦ لَا نُفَرِّقُ بَيْنَ أَحَدٍ مِّن رُّسُلِهِۦ ۚ وَقَالُوا۟ سَمِعْنَا وَأَطَعْنَا ۖ غُفْرَانَكَ رَبَّنَا وَإِلَيْكَ ٱلْمَصِيرُ

"The Messenger believes in what has been sent down to him from his Lord and so do the believers. Each one believes in Allaah, and His angels, and His books, and His Messengers. (They say) 'We make no distinction between any of His Messengers.' And they say, 'We hear and we obey. We seek your forgiveness, O our Lord and to You is the return.'"

Then, once they did that Allaah ﷻ abrogated the verse and sent down:

لَا يُكَلِّفُ ٱللَّهُ نَفْسًا إِلَّا وُسْعَهَا ۚ لَهَا مَا كَسَبَتْ وَعَلَيْهَا مَا ٱكْتَسَبَتْ ۗ رَبَّنَا لَا تُؤَاخِذْنَآ إِن نَّسِينَآ أَوْ أَخْطَأْنَا

"Allaah burdens not a soul beyond its capacity. For it is (the good) it has earned and against it is (the evil) it has earned. 'Our Lord, punish us not if we forget or fall into error.'"
He (Allaah) replied, "Yes."

رَبَّنَا وَلَا تَحْمِلْ عَلَيْنَآ إِصْرًا كَمَا حَمَلْتَهُۥ عَلَى ٱلَّذِينَ مِن قَبْلِنَا

"Our Lord, lay not on us a burden like that which you laid on those before us."
He (Allaah) replied, "Yes."

رَبَّنَا وَلَا تُحَمِّلْنَا مَا لَا طَاقَةَ لَنَا بِهِۦ

"Our Lord, put not on us a burden greater than we have strength to bear."
He (Allaah) replied, "Yes."

وَٱعْفُ عَنَّا وَٱغْفِرْ لَنَا وَٱرْحَمْنَآ ۚ أَنتَ مَوْلَىٰنَا فَٱنصُرْنَا عَلَى ٱلْقَوْمِ ٱلْكَـٰفِرِينَ

"And pardon us and grant us forgiveness and have mercy on us. You are our helper so give us victory over the disbelieving people."
He (Allaah) replied, "Yes."

This *hadeeth* has been transmitted by Muslim in his *Saheeh* (125).

قال الإمام مسلم ﷺ (126): حدثنا أبو بكر بن أبي شيبة وأبو كريب وإسحاق بن إبراهيم واللفظ لأبي بكر قال إسحاق أخبرنا وقال الآخران حدثنا وكيع عن سفيان عن آدم بن سليمان مولى خالد قال سمعت سعيد بن جبير يحدث عن ابن عباس ﷺ قال: لما نزلت هذه الآية: (وَإِن تُبْدُوا۟ مَا فِى

أَنفُسِكُمْ أَوْ تُخْفُوهُ يُحَاسِبْكُم بِهِ ٱللَّهُ) قال: دخل قلوبهم منها شيء لم يدخل قلوبهم من شيء فقال النبي ﷺ: قولوا سمعنا وأطعنا وسلمنا قال: فألقى الله الإيمان في قلوبهم فأنزل الله تعالى: (لَا يُكَلِّفُ ٱللَّهُ نَفْسًا إِلَّا وُسْعَهَا ۚ لَهَا مَا كَسَبَتْ وَعَلَيْهَا مَا ٱكْتَسَبَتْ ۗ رَبَّنَا لَا تُؤَاخِذْنَآ إِن نَّسِينَآ أَوْ أَخْطَأْنَا) قال: قد فعلت (رَبَّنَا وَلَا تَحْمِلْ عَلَيْنَآ إِصْرًا كَمَا حَمَلْتَهُۥ عَلَى ٱلَّذِينَ مِن قَبْلِنَا) قال: قد فعلت (وَٱعْفُ عَنَّا وَٱغْفِرْ لَنَا وَٱرْحَمْنَآ ۚ أَنتَ مَوْلَىٰنَا) قال: قد فعلت.

Ibn 'Abbaas ؓ narrated that when this verse descended,

$$\text{وَإِن تُبْدُوا۟ مَا فِىٓ أَنفُسِكُمْ أَوْ تُخْفُوهُ يُحَاسِبْكُم بِهِ ٱللَّهُ}$$

"And whether you disclose what is in yourselves or conceal it, Allaah will call you to account for it,"

Something entered their hearts because of it that had never entered before. So the Messenger of Allaah ﷺ said, "Say: We hear and we obey and we submit." Then Allaah caused faith to enter their hearts, after which Allaah ﷻ sent down:

$$\text{لَا يُكَلِّفُ ٱللَّهُ نَفْسًا إِلَّا وُسْعَهَا ۚ لَهَا مَا كَسَبَتْ وَعَلَيْهَا مَا ٱكْتَسَبَتْ ۗ رَبَّنَا لَا تُؤَاخِذْنَآ إِن نَّسِينَآ أَوْ أَخْطَأْنَا}$$

"Allaah burdens not a soul beyond its capacity. For it is (the good) it has earned and against it is (the evil) it has earned. 'Our Lord, punish us not if we forget or fall into error.'
He (Allaah) replied, "I have done that."

$$\text{رَبَّنَا وَلَا تَحْمِلْ عَلَيْنَآ إِصْرًا كَمَا حَمَلْتَهُۥ عَلَى ٱلَّذِينَ مِن قَبْلِنَا}$$

'Our Lord, lay not on us a burden comparable to what you have laid on those before us.'
He (Allaah) replied, "I have done that."

$$\text{وَٱغْفِرْ لَنَا وَٱرْحَمْنَآ ۚ أَنتَ مَوْلَىٰنَا}$$

'And grant us forgiveness and have mercy on us, You are our patron.' He (Allaah) replied, "I have done that."

Muslim transmitted this *hadeeth* in his *Saheeh* (126).

سورة آل عمران

Sooratu Aali 'Imraan

His, the Exalted One's statement:

إِنَّ ٱلَّذِينَ يَشْتَرُونَ بِعَهْدِ ٱللَّهِ وَأَيْمَٰنِهِمْ ثَمَنًا قَلِيلًا أُوْلَٰٓئِكَ لَا خَلَٰقَ لَهُمْ فِى ٱلْءَاخِرَةِ وَلَا يُكَلِّمُهُمُ ٱللَّهُ وَلَا يَنظُرُ إِلَيْهِمْ يَوْمَ ٱلْقِيَٰمَةِ وَلَا يُزَكِّيهِمْ وَلَهُمْ عَذَابٌ أَلِيمٌ ۝

"Verily, those who purchase a small gain at the cost of Allaah's covenant and their oaths, will have no portion in the hereafter, nor will Allaah speak to them or look at them on the day of resurrection, nor will He purify them, and they will have a painful punishment." (verse: 77)

قال الإمام البخاري ﷺ (2356 و2357): حدثنا عبدان عن أبي حمزة عن الأعمش عن شقيق عن عبد الله ﷺ عن النبي ﷺ قال: من حلف على يمين يقتطع بها مال امرئ هو عليها فاجر لقي الله وهو عليه غضبان فأنزل الله تعالى: (إِنَّ ٱلَّذِينَ يَشْتَرُونَ بِعَهْدِ ٱللَّهِ وَأَيْمَٰنِهِمْ ثَمَنًا قَلِيلًا) الآية.

فجاء الأشعث فقال: ما حدثكم أبو عبد الرحمن فيّ أنزلت هذه الآية كانت لي بئر في أرض ابن عم لي فقال لي: شهودك قلت: ما لي شهود قال: فيمينك قلت: يا رسول الله إذاً يحلف فذكر النبي ﷺ هذا الحديث فأنزل الله ذلك تصديقا له.

'Abdullaah ibn Mas'ood ﷺ narrated that the Prophet ﷺ said, "Whoever takes an oath only to take a person's money while he is really lying in his oath will meet Allaah while He (Allaah) is angry at him." Then Allaah تعالى revealed:

إِنَّ ٱلَّذِينَ يَشْتَرُونَ بِعَهْدِ ٱللَّهِ وَأَيْمَٰنِهِمْ ثَمَنًا قَلِيلًا

"Verily, those who purchase a small gain at the cost of Allaah's covenant and their oaths…".

Subsequently Al-Ash'ath came and asked, "What did Abu 'Abdir-Rahmaan (Ibn Mas'ood) narrate to you? This verse was sent down because of me. I owned a well in the land of one of my cousins [and my cousin and I had a dispute over who owned it].[40] So he (the Prophet ﷺ) said to me, 'Present your witnesses.' I responded, "I do not have any witnesses." He then said, 'Take an oath.' I said, "O Messenger of Allaah, [if I take an oath] he will then take a [false] oath." The Prophet ﷺ then mentioned the aforementioned

---

[40] What is between the parentheses was taken from another narration of the same *hadeeth* in Al-Bukhaaree.

statement and Allaah sent down this [verse] confirming that [statement of the Prophet ﷺ].”

This *hadeeth* has been transmitted by Al-Bukhaaree in his *Saheeh* (2356 and 2357) as well as Muslim in his *Saheeh* (138).

قال الإمام البخاري رَحِمَهُ اللهُ (4551): حدثنا علي هو ابن أبي هاشم سمع هشيما أخبرنا العوام بن حوشب عن إبراهيم بن عبد الرحمن عن عبد الله بن أبي أوفى ﷺ أن رجلا أقام سلعة في السوق فحلف فيها لقد أعطى بها ما لم يعطه ليوقع فيها رجلا من المسلمين فنزلت: (إِنَّ ٱلَّذِينَ يَشْتَرُونَ بِعَهْدِ ٱللَّهِ وَأَيْمَـٰنِهِمْ ثَمَنًا قَلِيلًا) إلى آخر الآية.

'Abdullaah ibn Abee Awfaa ﷺ narrated that a man put a product in the market and swore that he bought it for a price that he really did not so he could trick one of the Muslims into buying it. Then following verse descended:

$$\text{إِنَّ ٱلَّذِينَ يَشْتَرُونَ بِعَهْدِ ٱللَّهِ وَأَيْمَـٰنِهِمْ ثَمَنًا قَلِيلًا}$$

"Verily, those who purchase a small gain at the cost of Allaah's covenant and their oaths…".

Al-Bukhaaree transmitted This *hadeeth* in his *Saheeh* (4551). Ash-Sheikh Muqbil رَحِمَهُ اللهُ commented in its regard, "There is no contradiction between the two (*hadeeth*). It could be that the verse was revealed because of both reasons since the wording of the verse is general; however the *hadeeth* of 'Abdullaah ibn Mas'ood is stronger because the *hadeeth* of 'Abdullaah ibn Abee Awfaa has Ibraaheem ibn 'Abdir-Rahmaan As-Saksa'kee in its chain. Al-Haafidh Adh-Dhahabee said about him in his book *Al-Meezaan*, "Shu'bah and An-Nasaa'ee saw in him some weakness, however he was not rejected."

His, the Exalted One's statement:

$$\text{كَيْفَ يَهْدِى ٱللَّهُ قَوْمًا كَفَرُواْ بَعْدَ إِيمَـٰنِهِمْ}$$

"How shall Allaah guide a people who disbelieved after their belief…?"
Up to His ﷻ statement:

$$\text{إِلَّا ٱلَّذِينَ تَابُواْ مِنۢ بَعْدِ ذَٰلِكَ وَأَصْلَحُواْ فَإِنَّ ٱللَّهَ غَفُورٌ رَّحِيمٌ}$$

"Except for those who repent and thereafter do righteous deeds. Verily Allaah is Oft-Forgiving, Most Merciful." (verses: 86-89)

قال الإمام أبو جعفر بن جرير ﷺ (ج 6 ص 572): حدثنا محمد بن عبد الله بن بَزيع البصري قال حدثنا يزيد بن زريع قال حدثنا داود بن أبي هند عن عكرمة عن ابن عباس ﷺ قال: كان رجل من الأنصار أسلم ثم ارتد ولحق بالشرك ثم ندم فأرسل إلى قومه: أرسلوا إلى رسول الله هل لي من توبة قال: فنزلت: (كَيْفَ يَهْدِى ٱللَّهُ قَوْمًا كَفَرُوا بَعْدَ إِيمَٰنِهِمْ) إلى قوله: (وَجَاءَهُمُ ٱلْبَيِّنَٰتُ وَٱللَّهُ لَا يَهْدِى ٱلْقَوْمَ ٱلظَّٰلِمِينَ) (إِلَّا ٱلَّذِينَ تَابُوا مِنْ بَعْدِ ذَٰلِكَ وَأَصْلَحُوا فَإِنَّ ٱللَّهَ غَفُورٌ رَّحِيمٌ) فأرسل إليه قومه فأسلم.

Ibn 'Abbaas ﷺ narrated that a man from the *Ansaar* embraced Islaam, then later became a polytheist. He then felt regret and told his people to send a message to the Messenger of Allaah ﷺ asking if there was any chance for him to repent. Thereafter the verse descended:

$$\text{كَيْفَ يَهْدِى ٱللَّهُ قَوْمًا كَفَرُوا بَعْدَ إِيمَٰنِهِمْ}$$

"How shall Allaah guide a people who disbelieved after their belief…

$$\text{وَجَاءَهُمُ ٱلْبَيِّنَٰتُ وَٱللَّهُ لَا يَهْدِى ٱلْقَوْمَ ٱلظَّٰلِمِينَ}$$

…And after clear proofs had come to them, and Allaah guides not the people who are wrongdoers."
The revelation continued up to His statement:

$$\text{إِلَّا ٱلَّذِينَ تَابُوا مِنْ بَعْدِ ذَٰلِكَ وَأَصْلَحُوا فَإِنَّ ٱللَّهَ غَفُورٌ رَّحِيمٌ}$$

"Except for those who repent thereafter and do righteous deeds. Verily Allaah is Oft-Forgiving, Most Merciful."
His people then returned and delivered this message to him and he embraced Islaam.

Regarding this *hadeeth*, Ibn Jareer transmitted it in his *Tafseer*, volume 6, page 572. Ash-Sheikh Muqbil ﷺ said, "Concerning the *hadeeth*, the people of its chain are people of the *Saheeh* (Al-Bukhaaree and/or Muslim)."

His, the Exalted One's statement:

$$\text{إِنَّ ٱلَّذِينَ كَفَرُوا بَعْدَ إِيمَٰنِهِمْ ثُمَّ ٱزْدَادُوا كُفْرًا لَّن تُقْبَلَ تَوْبَتُهُمْ وَأُوْلَٰٓئِكَ هُمُ ٱلضَّآلُّونَ}$$

"Verily those who disbelieved after their belief and then went on increasing in disbelief, their repentance will not be accepted and they are those who are astray." (verse: 90)

قال الحافظ ابن كثير ﷺ في تفسيره (ج 1 ص 380): قال الحافظ أبو بكر البزار حدثنا محمد ابن عبد الله بن بزيع حدثنا يزيد بن زريع حدثنا داود بن أبي هند عن عكرمة عن ابن عباس ﷺ أن قوما أسلموا ثم ارتدوا ثم أسلموا ثم ارتدوا فأرسلوا إلى قومهم يسألون لهم فذكروا ذلك لرسول الله ﷺ فنزلت هذه الآية: (إِنَّ ٱلَّذِينَ كَفَرُوا۟ بَعْدَ إِيمَـٰنِهِمْ ثُمَّ ٱزْدَادُوا۟ كُفْرًا لَّن تُقْبَلَ تَوْبَتُهُمْ).

هكذا رواه وإسناده جيد. اه

Ibn 'Abbaas ﷺ narrated that a group of people embraced Islaam, disbelieved, then embraced Islaam again and thereafter disbelieved a second time. They then sent a message to their people requesting that they ask (about their situation) for them. Their people then mentioned their plight to the Messenger of Allaah ﷺ and this verse descended:

إِنَّ ٱلَّذِينَ كَفَرُوا۟ بَعْدَ إِيمَـٰنِهِمْ ثُمَّ ٱزْدَادُوا۟ كُفْرًا لَّن تُقْبَلَ تَوْبَتُهُمْ

"Verily those who disbelieved after their belief and then went on increasing in disbelief, their repentance will not be accepted…"

Al-Bazzaar transmitted this *hadeeth* in his *Musnad* as Ibn Katheer mentioned in his *Tafseer*, volume 1, page 380. Ibn Katheer said, "That is how he narrated it, and its chain is *jayyid*."

His, the Exalted One's statement:

لَيْسُوا۟ سَوَآءً مِّنْ أَهْلِ ٱلْكِتَـٰبِ أُمَّةٌ قَآئِمَةٌ يَتْلُونَ ءَايَـٰتِ ٱللَّهِ ءَانَآءَ ٱلَّيْلِ وَهُمْ يَسْجُدُونَ

"They are not all alike. A group of the people of the book stand for what right, [while] reciting the verses of Allaah during the hours of the night [and] prostrating themselves in prayer,"
up to His statement:

وَمَا يَفْعَلُوا۟ مِنْ خَيْرٍ فَلَن يُكْفَرُوهُ وَٱللَّهُ عَلِيمٌۢ بِٱلْمُتَّقِينَ

"And whatever good they do they will not be overlooked (deprived of its reward), and Allaah knows those who are the pious." (verses: 113-115)

قال الإمام أحمد ﷺ (ج 1 ص 396): حدثنا أبو النضر وحسن بن موسى قالا حدثنا شيبان عن عاصم عن زر عن ابن مسعود ﷺ قال: أخر رسول الله ﷺ صلاة العشاء ثم خرج إلى المسجد فإذا الناس ينتظرون الصلاة قال: أما إنه ليس من أهل هذه الأديان أحد يذكر الله هذه الساعة غيركم قال: فأنزل الله هؤلاء الآيات: (لَيْسُوا۟ سَوَآءً مِّنْ أَهْلِ ٱلْكِتَـٰبِ) حتى بلغ (وَمَا يَفْعَلُوا۟ مِنْ خَيْرٍ فَلَن يُكْفَرُوهُ وَٱللَّهُ عَلِيمٌۢ بِٱلْمُتَّقِينَ).

Ibn Mas'ood ﷺ narrated that the Messenger of Allaah ﷺ once delayed the *'Ishaa* prayer and went to the *masjid* he found the people waiting for the prayer. He then said, "Verily there is no one from the people of these religions who remembers Allaah at this hour other than you." He (Ibn Mas'ood) said, "Then Allaah sent down these verses:

لَيْسُوا۟ سَوَآءً مِّنْ أَهْلِ ٱلْكِتَـٰبِ

"They are not all alike. A group of the people of the book…"
up to,

وَمَا يَفْعَلُوا۟ مِنْ خَيْرٍ فَلَن يُكْفَرُوهُ وَٱللَّهُ عَلِيمٌۢ بِٱلْمُتَّقِينَ

"And whatever good they do they will not be overlooked (deprived of its reward), and Allaah knows those who are the pious."

This *hadeeth* has been transmitted by Al-Imaam Ahmad in his *Musnad*, volume 1, page 396. Ash-Sheikh Muqbil ﷺ commented, "The *hadeeth* is *hasan* as Ash-Shawkaanee said quoting from As-Suyootee, because there is something [wrong] with 'Aasim's memory."

His, the Exalted One's statement:

إِذْ هَمَّت طَّآئِفَتَانِ مِنكُمْ أَن تَفْشَلَا وَٱللَّهُ وَلِيُّهُمَا

"(Remember) when two groups among you were about to lose heart, but Allaah was their helper…" (verse: 122)

قال الإمام البخاري ﷺ (4051): حدثنا محمد بن يوسف عن ابن عيينة عن عمرو عن جابر ﷺ قال: نزلت هذه الآية فينا: (إِذْ هَمَّت طَّآئِفَتَانِ مِنكُمْ أَن تَفْشَلَا وَٱللَّهُ وَلِيُّهُمَا) بني سلمة وبني حارثة وما أحب أنها لم تنزل والله يقول: (وَٱللَّهُ وَلِيُّهُمَا).

Jaabir ﷺ said, "This verse descended because of us,

62

$$\text{إِذْ هَمَّت طَّآئِفَتَانِ مِنكُمْ أَن تَفْشَلَا وَٱللَّهُ وَلِيُّهُمَا}$$

'(Remember) when two groups among you were about to lose heart, but Allaah was their helper.'

Because of the tribe Banee Salimah and Banee Haarithah, and I do not regret its descension because Allaah says:

$$\text{وَٱللَّهُ وَلِيُّهُمَا}$$

'But Allaah was their helper.'"[41]

Al-Bukhaaree transmitted this *hadeeth* in his *Saheeh* (4051) and Muslim in his *Saheeh* (2505).

His, the Exalted One's statement:

$$\text{لَيْسَ لَكَ مِنَ ٱلْأَمْرِ شَيْءٌ أَوْ يَتُوبَ عَلَيْهِمْ أَوْ يُعَذِّبَهُمْ فَإِنَّهُمْ ظَالِمُونَ ۝}$$

"It is not for you to decide whether He pardons them or punishes them, for indeed they are wrongdoers." (verse:128)

قال الإمام البخاري رحمه الله (4069 و4070): حدثنا يحيى بن عبد الله السلمي أخبرنا عبد الله أخبرنا معمر عن الزهري حدثني سالم عن أبيه ﷺ سمع رسول الله ﷺ إذا رفع رأسه من الركوع من الركعة الأخيرة من الفجر يقول: اللهم العن فلانا وفلانا بعدما يقول: سمع الله لمن حمده ربنا لك الحمد فأنزل الله عز وجل: (لَيْسَ لَكَ مِنَ ٱلْأَمْرِ شَيْءٌ) إلى قوله: (فَإِنَّهُمْ ظَالِمُونَ). وعن حنظلة بن أبي سفيان قال سمعت سالم بن عبد الله يقول: كان رسول الله ﷺ يدعوا على صفوان بن أمية وسهيل بن عمرو والحارث بن هشام فنزلت: (لَيْسَ لَكَ مِنَ ٱلْأَمْرِ شَيْءٌ) إلى قوله: (فَإِنَّهُمْ ظَالِمُونَ).

Ibn 'Umar ؓ heard the Messenger of Allaah ﷺ, when he raised his head from the *rukoo'* (the bowing position) in the second *rak'ah* of the *Fajr* prayer say, "O Allaah, curse so-and-so and so-and-so," and afterward he said, "Allaah responds to he who praises Him. O our Lord, to you the praise is due." Then Allaah ﷻ sent down:

$$\text{لَيْسَ لَكَ مِنَ ٱلْأَمْرِ شَيْءٌ}$$

"It is not for you to decide …"
up to His statement:

---

[41] This *hadeeth* pertains to what occurred at the battle of Uhud.

$$\text{فَإِنَّهُمْ ظَالِمُونَ}$$

"For indeed they are wrongdoers."

Furthermore, Handhalah ibn Abee Sufyaan said, "I heard Saalim ibn 'Abdillaah say, 'The Messenger of Allaah ﷺ supplicated against Safwaan ibn Umaiyah, and Suhail ibn 'Amr, and Al-Haarith ibn Hishaam. Then this verse descended:

$$\text{لَيْسَ لَكَ مِنَ ٱلْأَمْرِ شَيْءٌ}$$

"It is not for you to decide …"

up to His statement,

$$\text{فَإِنَّهُمْ ظَالِمُونَ}$$

"For indeed they are wrongdoers."

This *hadeeth* has been transmitted by Al-Bukhaaree in his *Saheeh* (4069 and 4070).

قال الإمام مسلم رحمه الله (1791): حدثنا عبد الله بن مسلمة بن قعنب حدثنا حماد بن سلمة عن ثابت عن أنس ﷺ أن رسول الله ﷺ كسرت رباعيته يوم أحد وشج في رأسه فجعل يسلت الدم عنه ويقول: كيف يفلح قوم شجوا نبيهم وكسروا رباعيته وهو يدعوهم إلى الله فأنزل الله عز وجل: (لَيْسَ لَكَ مِنَ ٱلْأَمْرِ شَيْءٌ).

Anas ﷺ narrated that one of the Messenger of Allaah's ﷺ teeth[42] was broken on the day of the battle of Uhud and he suffered a head wound so he said while wiping away the blood, "How can a people who cut open the head of their Prophet and broke his tooth while he is calling them to Allaah be successful!" Then Allaah ﷻ sent down:

$$\text{لَيْسَ لَكَ مِنَ ٱلْأَمْرِ شَيْءٌ}$$

"It is not fore you to decide …"

Muslim transmitted this *hadeeth*, in his *Saheeh* (1791).

قال الإمام البخاري رحمه الله (4560): حدثنا موسى بن إسماعيل حدثنا إبراهيم بن سعد حدثنا ابن شهاب عن سعيد بن المسيب وأبي سلمة بن عبد الرحمن عن أبي هريرة ﷺ أن رسول الله ﷺ كان إذا أراد أن يدعو على أحد أو يدعو لأحد قنت بعد الركوع فربما قال إذا قال: سمع الله لمن حمده اللهم ربنا

---

[42] The tooth located between the fang-tooth and the two front teeth.

لك الحمد: اللهم انج الوليد بن الوليد وسلمة بن هشام وعياش بن أبي ربيعة اللهم اشدد وطأك على مضر واجعلها سنين كسني يوسف يجهر بذلك وكان يقول في بعض صلاته في صلاة الفجر: اللهم العن فلانا وفلانا لأحياء من العرب حتى أنزل الله: (لَيْسَ لَكَ مِنَ ٱلْأَمْرِ شَىْءٌ).

Abu Hurairah narrated that the Messenger of Allaah whenever he wanted to supplicate against someone or supplicate for someone he would make *qunoot*[43] after the *rukoo'* (bowing position). At times he would say after saying, "Allaah responds to he who praises Him. O Allaah, our Lord, to you the praise is due," "O Allaah, save Al-Waleed ibn Al-Waleed, and Salamah ibn Hishaam and 'Ayyaash ibn Abee Rabee'ah. O Allaah, send your punishment on the tribe Mudar. Give them years of drought like the years of the drought during the time of Yoosuf." He used to say that audibly, and he used to say in a portion of the *Fajr* prayer, " O Allaah, curse so-and-so and so-and-so," from the tribes of the Arabs, until Allaah sent down:

لَيْسَ لَكَ مِنَ ٱلْأَمْرِ شَىْءٌ

"It is not for you to decide …".

This *hadeeth* has been transmitted by Al-Bukhaaree in his *Saheeh* (4560) and Muslim in his *Saheeh* (675). In the narration of Yoonus on Az-Zuhree in Muslim (675), the tribes were named, "O Allaah, curse Lihyaan, and Ri'l, and Dhakwaan and 'Usaiyah." Al-Haafidh Ibn Hajar commented on this narration in *Fathul-Baaree* in the explanation of *hadeeth* (4560) saying, "…and it was already mentioned in the chapters about the battle of Uhud that this causes a problem because the story of Ri'l and Dhakwaan occurred after Uhud and the revelation of the verse:

لَيْسَ لَكَ مِنَ ٱلْأَمْرِ شَىْءٌ

'It is not for you to decide …'

occurred because of the story of Uhud. So how can the reason for revelation take place after the verse had already been revealed! Then the defect of the *hadeeth* became apparent to me. There is *idraaj*[44] in the narration and his statement, 'until Allaah sent down,' is *munqati'* (its chain is broken) from the narration of Az-Zuhree on whoever[45] informed him.

---

[43] What is meant by *qunoot* is a special supplication made in the prayer in times of calamity.
[44] *Idraaj*: meaning a statement of one of the narrators which is not a part of the *hadeeth* has been inserted into the *hadeeth* by one of the narrators.
[45] That 'whoever' is not known so the chain is broken.

Muslim demonstrated that in the above mentioned narration of Yoonus. He said at this portion of the *hadeeth*, "He -meaning Az-Zuhree- said, 'Then it had reached us that he left that when it descended...'. This *balaagh*[46] is not authentic because of what was mentioned previously." Then Al-Haafidh Ibn Hajar said, "And the way to harmonize between it (the *hadeeth* of Anas) and the *hadeeth* of Ibn 'Umar is to say that he ﷺ made supplication against the previous mentioned people (those mentioned in the *hadeeth* of Ibn 'Umar) in his prayer after that had occurred. Consequently, the verse descended due to both incidents,. The two incidents being what happened to him (when he was wounded and said what he said) and what he did by supplicating against them (those mentioned in the *hadeeth* of Ibn 'Umar). And all of that occurred because of the battle of Uhud in contrast to the story of Ri'l and Dhakwaan, it had nothing to do with the battle of Uhud. It is possible to say that their story took place after Uhud and the revelation of the verse was delayed a short while after its reason had already taken place and then the verse descended because of all of those reasons, and Allaah knows best."

His, the Exalted One's statement:

$$\text{ثُمَّ أَنزَلَ عَلَيْكُم مِّنۢ بَعْدِ ٱلْغَمِّ أَمَنَةً نُّعَاسًا يَغْشَىٰ طَآئِفَةً مِّنكُمْ}$$

"Then after the distress He sent down security for you, drowsiness overwhelming a group of you..." (verse: 154)

قال الإمام الترمذي رحمه الله (3007): حدثنا عبد بن حميد ثنا روح بن عبادة عن حماد بن سلمة عن ثابت عن أنس ﷺ عن أبي طلحة ﷺ قال: رفعت رأسي يوم أحد فجعلت أنظر وما منهم يومئذ أحد إلا يميد تحت حَجَفته من النعاس فذلك قول الله تعالى: (ثُمَّ أَنزَلَ عَلَيْكُم مِّنۢ بَعْدِ ٱلْغَمِّ أَمَنَةً نُّعَاسًا) قال أبو عيسى: هذا حديث حسن صحيح.

Abu Talhah ﷺ said, "I lifted my head on the day of Uhud and began to look around. There was no one that day except that he was swaying under his shield because of drowsiness. That is the meaning of the statement of Allaah تعالى:

$$\text{ثُمَّ أَنزَلَ عَلَيْكُم مِّنۢ بَعْدِ ٱلْغَمِّ أَمَنَةً نُّعَاسًا}$$

"Then after the distress He sent down security for you, drowsiness..."

At-Tirmidhee transmitted this *hadeeth* in his *Jaami'* (3007) and he classified it to be *hasan saheeh*.

---

[46] *Balaagh*: meaning the portion of the *hadeeth* where Az-Zuhree said, "It had reached us," without mentioning who informed him.

قال الإمام إسحاق بن راهويه ﵀ كما في إتحاف الخيرة المهرة (6245): وأبنا يحيى بن آدم ثنا ابن أبي زائدة عن محمد بن إسحاق عن يحيى بن عباد عن أبيه عن عبد الله بن الزبير ﵄ عن أبيه ﵁ قال: لقد رأيتني مع رسول الله ﷺ يوم أحد حين اشتد علينا الخوف فأرسل علينا النوم فما منا أحد إلا وذقنه أو قال ذقنه في صدره فوالله إني لأسمع كالحلم قول معتب بن قشير: لو كان لنا من الأمر شيء ما قتلنا ههنا فحفظتها فأنزل الله تبارك وتعالى في ذلك: (ثُمَّ أَنزَلَ عَلَيْكُم مِّن بَعْدِ ٱلْغَمِّ أَمَنَةً نُّعَاسًا) إلى قوله: (مَّا قُتِلْنَا هَٰهُنَا) لقول معتب بن قشير قال: (لَوْ كُنتُمْ فِى بُيُوتِكُمْ) حتى بلغ: (عَلِيمٌۢ بِذَاتِ ٱلصُّدُورِ).

Az-Zubair ﵁ said, "I saw myself with the Messenger of Allaah ﷺ on the day of Uhud when the fright became intense. Then sleep was cast upon us and thus, there was not one of us except that his chin was in his chest. By Allaah, I can hear, as if it is like a dream, the statement of Mu'attib ibn Qushair, 'If we had anything to do with the affair, none of us would have been killed here.' I memorized this statement. Then Allaah ﷻ sent down the following in its regard:

$$\text{ثُمَّ أَنزَلَ عَلَيْكُم مِّن بَعْدِ ٱلْغَمِّ أَمَنَةً نُّعَاسًا}$$

'Then after the distress He sent down security for you, drowsiness…' to His statement,

$$\text{مَّا قُتِلْنَا هَٰهُنَا}$$

'… none of us would have been killed here;' and because of the statement of Muattib ibn Qushair He said,

$$\text{لَوْ كُنتُمْ فِى بُيُوتِكُمْ}$$

'Even if you had remained in your houses…'

Continuing to His statement,:

$$\text{عَلِيمٌۢ بِذَاتِ ٱلصُّدُورِ}$$

'Allaah is the all-knower of what is in the breasts.'"

Ishaaq ibn Raahawaih transmitted this *hadeeth* as Al-Buseeree mentioned in his book *Ithaaf Al-Khiyarah Al-Maharah* (6245) and Ibn Abee Haatim in his *Tafseer* (4373). In the chain of Ibn Abee Haatim, Muhammad ibn Ishaaq explicitly conveyed that he heard from his Sheikh clearing himself of *tadlees*. Ash-Sheikh Muqbil ﵀ said in his footnotes on *Tafseer Ibn Katheer*, "Its chain is *hasan*."

His, the Exalted One's statement:

$$وَمَا كَانَ لِنَبِيٍّ أَن يَغُلَّ$$

"It is not [befitting] for any prophet to take illegally a part of the war booty…" (verse:161)

قال الخطيب ﷺ في تاريخ بغداد (ج 1 ص 372–373): أخبرنا محمد بن عبد الله بن شهريار قال أنبأنا سليمان بن أحمد بن أيوب الطبراني قال نبأنا محمد بن أحمد بن يزيد النرسي البغدادي قال نبأنا أبو عمر حفص بن عمر الدوري المقرئ عن أبي محمد اليزيدي عن أبي عمرو بن العلاء عن مجاهد عن ابن عباس ﷺ أنه كان ينكر على من يقرأ: (وما كان لنبي أن يُغَل) ويقول: كيف لا يكون له أن يُغَل وقد كان له أن يقتل قال الله تعالى: (وَيَقْتُلُونَ ٱلْأَنۢبِيَآءَ بِغَيْرِ حَقٍّ) ولكن المنافقين اتهموا النبي ﷺ في شيء من الغنيمة فأنزل الله: (وَمَا كَانَ لِنَبِيٍّ أَن يَغُلَّ). قال سليمان: لم يروه عن أبي عمرو إلا اليزيدي تفرد به أبو عمر الدوري.

Ibn 'Abbaas ﷺ used to censure whoever recited and intended by its recitation:

وما كان لنبي أن يُغَل

"It is not for any Prophet to be betrayed."[47]

He would say, "How can it not be for him that he be betrayed while it is possible for him to be killed! Allaah ﷻ said:

$$وَيَقْتُلُونَ ٱلْأَنۢبِيَآءَ بِغَيْرِ حَقٍّ$$

"And they kill the Prophets without right." (Aal 'Imraan: 112)

However, the hypocrites accused the Prophet ﷺ of illegally taking some of the war booty. In response Allaah sent down:

$$وَمَا كَانَ لِنَبِيٍّ أَن يَغُلَّ$$

"It is not [befitting] for any prophet to take illegally a part of the war booty…"

---

[47] In this recitation the *yaa* has a *dammah* on it and the *ghain* has a *fathah* on it. Ibn Jareer said in his *Tafseer*, volume 7, page 353-354, "It is the recitation of most of the people of Madeenah and Koofah. The reciters of this recitation also differ in its meaning. Some of them say its meaning is: "It is not for any Prophet that his companions betray him"…Others amongst them say the meaning of that is: "It is not for any Prophet to be accused of taking illegally a part of the war booty being accused of betrayal and theft."

At-Tabaraanee transmitted this *hadeeth* in *Al-Mu'jam Al-Kabeer* volume 11, page 101, *hadeeth* (11174) and Al-Khateeb in *Taareekh Baghdaad* volume 1, page 372-373, with the chain of At-Tabaraanee.[48] Ash-Sheikh Muqbil commented, "[Regarding] The *hadeeth*, the people of its chain are sound trustworthy narrators with the exception of the Sheikh of At-Tabaraanee; I could not find a biography of him besides what is mentioned in the book *Taareekh Baghdaad* volume 1, page 372. Al-Khateeb said, 'Abul-Qaasim At-Tabaraanee narrated on him' and Al-Khateeb did not mention any criticism about him nor did he declare him to be trustworthy. In addition, Abu Daawud (3971) and At-Tirmidhee (3009) have transmitted [a *hadeet*h] similar to this, however, it is from the chain of Khusaif ibn 'Abdir-Rahmaan. Al-Haafidh said in his checking of *Al-Kash'shaaf*, "Ibn 'Adee found it to be a defected *hadeeth* because of Khusaif." Abu 'Abdir-Rahmaan (Ash-Sheikh Muqbil) said: [As for] Khusaif, the majority have declared him to be *da'eef* and he was not consistent in this *hadeeth*. At times he narrated it *mursal* and at times he narrated it connected. At times he says, 'On Miqsam,' and at times he says, "On 'Ikrimah," or on someone else. Refer to *Tafseer Ibn Jareer*, volume 4, page 155.[49]

Then I found an authentic chain for the hadeeth which read as follows:

قال الإمام البزار رحمه الله كما في كشف الأستار (ج 3 ص 43): حدثنا محمد بن عبد الرحيم ثنا عبد الوهاب بن عطاء ثنا هارون القارئ عن الزبير بن الخريت عن عكرمة عن ابن عباس رضي الله عنهما (وَمَا كَانَ لِنَبِيٍّ أَن يَغُلَّ) ما كان لنبي أن يتهمه أصحابه.

On Ibn 'Abbaas:

وَمَا كَانَ لِنَبِيٍّ أَن يَغُلَّ

"It is not [befitting] for any Prophet to take illegally a part of the war booty." (Ibn 'Abbaas said), "It is not befitting for any Prophet that his companions accuse him."[50]

---

[48] I quoted the *hadeeth* from *Taareekh Baghdaad* by Al-Khateeb because the wording is clearer.

[49] The Sheikh quotes from the old printed version of *Tafseer ibn Jareer* which is different from the version checked by Mahmood Shaakir which I used when quoting the *ahaadeeth*. I used his version because he placed emphasis on making sure the text matches what is in the manuscripts.

[50] In the verse Allaah negated that a Prophet would take illegally a part of the war booty. This negation is an indication that it is not proper to suspect him of that, nor is it proper to accuse him of something like that as Ibn 'Abbaas mentioned in the above explanation of this verse.

This *hadeeth* has been transmitted by Al-Bazzaar as mentioned in *Kashf Al-Astaar*, volume 3, page 43. Ash-Sheikh Muqbil ﷺ commented saying, "This narration, although there was not mentioned in it a reason for revelation, supports the reason for revelation which was previously mentioned on Ibn 'Abbaas, and Allaah knows best."

His, the Exalted One's statement:

$$أَوَلَمَّا أَصَابَتْكُم مُّصِيبَةٌ قَدْ أَصَبْتُم مِّثْلَيْهَا قُلْتُمْ أَنَّىٰ هَـٰذَا ۖ قُلْ هُوَ مِنْ عِندِ أَنفُسِكُمْ$$

"(What is the matter with you?) When a single disaster befalls you although you inflicted (your enemies) with one twice as great, you say, "From where does this come to us?" Say: It is from yourselves…"
(verse: 165)

قال الإمام أحمد ﷺ (ج 1 ص 30): حدثنا أبو نوح قراد أنبأنا عكرمة بن عمار حدثنا سماك الحنفي أبو زميل حدثني ابن عباس حدثني عمر بن الخطاب ﷺ قال: لما كان يوم بدر قال: نظر النبي ﷺ إلى أصحابه وهم ثلاثمائة ونيف ونظر إلى المشركين فإذا هم ألف وزيادة فاستقبل النبي ﷺ القبلة ثم مد يديه وعليه رداؤه وإزاره ثم قال: اللهم أين ما وعدتني اللهم أنجز لي ما وعدتني اللهم إنك إن تهلك هذه العصابة من أهل الإسلام فلا تعبد في الأرض أبدا قال: فما زال يستغيث ربه عز وجل ويدعوه حتى سقط رداؤه فأتاه أبو بكر فأخذ رداءه فردّاه ثم التزمه من ورائه ثم قال: يا نبي الله كفاك مناشدتك ربك فإنه سينجز لك ما وعدك وأنزل الله عز وجل: (إِذْ تَسْتَغِيثُونَ رَبَّكُمْ فَاسْتَجَابَ لَكُمْ أَنِّي مُمِدُّكُم بِأَلْفٍ مِّنَ الْمَلَائِكَةِ مُرْدِفِينَ) فلما كان يومئذ والتقوا فهزم الله عز وجل المشركين فقتل منهم سبعون رجلا وأسر منهم سبعون رجلا فاستشار رسول الله ﷺ أبا بكر وعليا وعمر فقال أبو بكر: يا رسول الله هؤلاء بنو العم والعشيرة والإخوان فإني أرى أن تأخذ منهم الفدية فيكون ما أخذنا منهم قوة لنا على الكفار وعسى الله أن يهديهم فيكونون لنا عضدا فقال رسول الله ﷺ: ما ترى يابن الخطاب قلت: والله ما أرى ما رأى أبو بكر ولكني أرى أن تمكنني من فلان قريبا لعمر فأضرب عنقه وتمكن عليا من عقيل فيضرب عنقه وتمكن حمزة من فلان أخيه فيضرب عنقه حتى يعلم الله أنه ليست في قلوبنا هوادة للمشركين هؤلاء صناديدهم وأئمتهم وقادتهم فهوى رسول الله ﷺ ما قال أبو بكر ولم يهو ما قلت فأخذ منهم الفداء فلما أن كان من الغد قال عمر: غدوت إلى رسول الله ﷺ فإذا هو قاعد وأبو بكر وإذا هما يبكيان فقلت: يا رسول الله أخبرني ماذا يبكيك أنت وصاحبك فإن وجدت بكاء بكيت وإن لم أجد تباكيت لبكائكما قال: فقال النبي ﷺ: الذي عرض عليَّ أصحابك من الفداء لقد عرض عليَّ عذابكم أدنى من هذه الشجرة لشجرة قريبة وأنزل الله عز وجل: (مَا كَانَ لِنَبِيٍّ أَن يَكُونَ لَهُ أَسْرَىٰ حَتَّىٰ يُثْخِنَ فِي الْأَرْضِ) إلى قوله: (لَّوْلَا كِتَابٌ مِّنَ اللَّهِ

سَبَقَ لَمَسَّكُمْ فِيمَآ أَخَذْتُمْ) من الفداء ثم أحل الله لهم الغنائم فلما كان يوم أحد من العام المقبل عوقبوا بما صنعوا يوم بدر من أخذهم الفداء فقتل منهم سبعون وفر أصحاب النبي ﷺ عن النبي ﷺ وكسرت رَبَاعيته وهشمت البيضة على رأسه وسال الدم على وجهه وأنزل الله عز وجل: (أَوَلَمَّآ أَصَبَتْكُم مُّصِيبَةٌ قَدْ أَصَبْتُم مِّثْلَيْهَا) بأخذكم الفداء.

'Umar ibn Al-Khattaab ؓ said, "On the day of Badr the Prophet ﷺ looked towards his Companions who numbered just over three hundred. Then he looked towards the polytheists and found them to be over a thousand. The Prophet ﷺ then faced the *qiblah* (the direction for prayer) and extended his arms while wearing his *izaar* (lower garment) and his *ridaa* (upper garment) then he said, 'O Allaah, where is what you promised me! O Allaah, fulfill for me what you promised me! O Allaah, if you allow this small group of Muslims to be destroyed you will never be worshipped on earth!' He continued to seek the aid of his Lord ﷻ and supplicate to Him to the extent that his upper garment fell off. So Abu Bakr came to him and picked up his upper garment and put it back on him and stood behind him saying, "O Prophet of Allaah, your imploration of your Lord is sufficient, for verily He will fulfill what He promised you." Allaah ﷻ then sent down:

إِذْ تَسْتَغِيثُونَ رَبَّكُمْ فَٱسْتَجَابَ لَكُمْ أَنِّى مُمِدُّكُم بِأَلْفٍ مِّنَ ٱلْمَلَـٰٓئِكَةِ مُرْدِفِينَ

'(Remember) when you sought help from your Lord so He answered you (saying): "I will help you with a thousand angels one behind the other in succession.' (*Al-Anfaal*: 9)

When that day came and they met in battle, Allaah ﷻ defeated the polytheists. Seventy of their men were killed and seventy more were taken prisoner. The Messenger of Allaah ﷺ then sought the advice of Abu Bakr, 'Ali, and 'Umar, may Allaah be pleased with them. Abu Bakr ؓ said, "They are our cousins, relatives and brothers. It is my opinion that you take the ransom money from them so that what we take from them will give us strength against the disbelievers, and perhaps Allaah will guide them and they will become our supporters." The Messenger of Allaah ﷺ then said, 'What is your opinion, O son of Al-Khattaab?' I said, "By Allaah, I do not agree with Abu Bakr's opinion. Rather, my opinion is that you let me have so-and-so, the relative of 'Umar, then let me strike his neck (chopping off his head), and that you let 'Ali have 'Aqeel (his brother) then let him strike his neck, and that you let Hamzah have his brother so-and-so then let him strike his neck. So Allaah will know there is no favoritism in our hearts for the polytheists. These people are their leaders, rulers and commanders." The Messenger of Allaah ﷺ favored what Abu Bakr said and did not favor what I said and so he took from them the ransom money."

'Umar said, "The next day I went to the Messenger of Allaah ﷺ and found him and Abu Bakr sitting down crying. I said, 'O Messenger of Allaah, tell me what makes you and your companion cry so if I find tears I can cry and if I do not find tears I will fake crying because of your crying.' The Prophet ﷺ said, "what your companions presented to me about taking the ransom money. It was shown to me your punishment, which will soon occur (in period of time) closer than this tree." It was a tree close by. And Allaah ﷻ sent down:

$$\text{مَا كَانَ لِنَبِيٍّ أَن يَكُونَ لَهُۥ أَسْرَىٰ حَتَّىٰ يُثْخِنَ فِى ٱلْأَرْضِ}$$

'It is not [befitting] for a prophet to have prisoners of war until he has made a great slaughter (amongst his enemies gaining the upper-hand) in the land,' (*Al-Anfaal*: 67)
up to His statement:

$$\text{لَّوْلَا كِتَٰبٌ مِّنَ ٱللَّهِ سَبَقَ لَمَسَّكُمْ فِيمَآ أَخَذْتُمْ}$$

"Were it not for a previous ordainment from Allaah, a severe torment would have touched you because of what you took [from the ransom money]" (*Al-Anfaal*: 68).

Then Allaah made the war booty permissible for them. When the day of the battle of Uhud arrived the following year, they were punished for what they did on the day of Badr when they took the ransom money. Seventy of them were killed and The Companions of the Prophet ﷺ deserted him ﷺ. His tooth was broken and his helmet on his head was smashed. Blood poured down onto his face and Allaah ﷻ sent down:

$$\text{أَوَلَمَّآ أَصَٰبَتْكُم مُّصِيبَةٌ قَدْ أَصَبْتُم مِّثْلَيْهَا}$$

'What is the matter with you?) When a single disaster befalls you, although you inflicted (your enemies) with one twice as great,...'
That was because they took the ransom money."

Al-Imaam Ahmad transmitted this *hadeeth* in his *Musnad*, volume 1, page 30. Ash-Sheikh Muqbil said, ", the people of the *hadeeth's* chain are people of the *Saheeh* (Al-Bukhaaree and/or Muslim)."

His, the Exalted One's statement:

$$\text{وَلَا تَحْسَبَنَّ ٱلَّذِينَ قُتِلُوا۟ فِى سَبِيلِ ٱللَّهِ أَمْوَٰتًۢا ۚ بَلْ أَحْيَآءٌ عِندَ رَبِّهِمْ يُرْزَقُونَ}$$

"Think not of those who are killed in the path of Allaah as dead. Rather they are alive with their Lord being provided for." (verse: 169)

قال الإمام أحمد ﷺ (ج 1 ص 265): ثنا يعقوب ثنا أبي عن ابن إسحاق حدثني إسماعيل بن أمية بن عمرو بن سعيد عن أبي الزبير المكي عن ابن عباس ﷺ قال: قال رسول الله ﷺ: لما أصيب إخوانكم بأحد جعل الله عز وجل أرواحهم في أجواف طير خضر ترد أنهار الجنة تأكل من ثمارها وتأوي إلى قناديل من ذهب في ظل العرش فلما وجدوا طيب شربهم ومأكلهم وحسن منقلبهم قالوا: يا ليت إخواننا يعلمون بما صنع الله لنا لئلا يزهدوا في الجهاد ولا ينكلوا عن الحرب فقال الله عز وجل: أنا أبلغهم عنكم فأنزل الله عز وجل هؤلاء الآيات على رسوله: (وَلَا تَحْسَبَنَّ ٱلَّذِينَ قُتِلُوا۟ فِى سَبِيلِ ٱللَّهِ أَمْوَٰتًۢا ۚ بَلْ أَحْيَآءٌ).

وقال الإمام أحمد ﷺ (ج 1 ص 266): ثنا عثمان بن أبي شيبة ثنا عبد الله بن إدريس عن محمد بن إسحاق عن إسماعيل بن أمية عن أبي الزبير عن سعيد بن جبير عن ابن عباس ﷺ عن النبي ﷺ نحوه.

قال الحافظ ابن كثير: وهذا أثبت. يعني الذي فيه واسطة بين أبي الزبير وابن عباس.

Ibn 'Abbaas ﷺ narrated that the Messenger of Allaah ﷺ said, "When your brothers were killed at Uhud, Allaah ﷻ placed their souls into the bellies of green birds. They drink from the rivers of paradise and eat from its fruits. They take shelter at lamps of gold in the shade of the throne. When they found the delight of their food and drink, and their exquisite place of destiny they said, 'O if only our brothers knew what Allaah did to us so they will not leave off *jihaad* or withdraw from battle.' Allaah ﷻ replied said, "I will inform them for you." Then Allaah ﷻ sent down these verses to His Messenger:

وَلَا تَحْسَبَنَّ ٱلَّذِينَ قُتِلُوا۟ فِى سَبِيلِ ٱللَّهِ أَمْوَٰتًۢا ۚ بَلْ أَحْيَآءٌ

"Think not of those who are killed in the path of Allaah as dead. Rather they are alive…"

As for this *hadeeth*, Al-Imaam Ahmad transmitted it in his *Musnad*, volume 1, page 265-266) and Ash-Sheikh Muqbil ﷺ classified it to be *saheeh li ghairihi*.

قال الإمام الترمذي ﷺ (3010): حدثنا يحيى بن حبيب بن عربي نا موسى بن إبراهيم بن كثير الأنصاري قال سمعت طلحة بن خراش قال سمعت جابر بن عبد الله ﷺ يقول: لقيني رسول الله ﷺ فقال لي: يا جابر ما لي أراك منكسرا قلت: يا رسول الله استشهد أبي وترك عيالا ودينا قال: ألا أبشرك بما لقي الله به أباك قال: بلى يا رسول الله قال: ما كلم الله أحدا قط إلا من وراء حجابه وأحيى أباك فكلمه كفاحا فقال: تمنَّ عليَّ أعطك قال: يا رب تحييني فأقتل فيك ثانية قال الرب تبارك وتعالى:

73

إنه قد سبق مني أنهم لا يرجعون قال: وأنزلت هذه الآية: (وَلَا تَحْسَبَنَّ ٱلَّذِينَ قُتِلُوا۟ فِى سَبِيلِ ٱللَّهِ أَمْوَٰتًۢا) الآية.

Jaabir ibn 'Abdillaah ﷺ said, "I was encountered by the Messenger of Allaah ﷺ encountered me and he said, 'O Jaabir, why is it that I see you downhearted?' I said, "O Messenger of Allaah, my father was martyred and he left behind dependants and debts." He said, 'Do you want me to announce to you the good news of what Allaah met your father with?' He (Jaabir) said, "Certainly, O Messenger of Allaah." He said, 'Allaah has never spoken to anyone except from behind His veil, but Allaah brought your father back to life and spoke to him face to face and said, "Request from me and I will give you." He said, 'O my Lord, will you bring me back to life so I can be killed for your sake a second time?' The Lord ﷻ said, "It has already preceded from Me that they will not return." He (Jaabir) said, 'And this verse was sent down:

وَلَا تَحْسَبَنَّ ٱلَّذِينَ قُتِلُوا۟ فِى سَبِيلِ ٱللَّهِ أَمْوَٰتًۢا

"Think not of those who are killed in the path of Allaah as dead...'"

At-Tirmidhee transmitted this *hadeeth* in his *Jaami'* (3010). Ash-Sheikh Muqbil ﷺ comments, "It (the chain of the *hadeeth*) centers around Moosaa ibn Ibraaheem ibn Katheer whose status is not known; however, the *hadeeth* has other *ahaadeeth* which support it thus it becomes *hasan* as At-Tirmidhee said."

قال الإمام ابن جرير ﷺ (ج 7 ص 392): حدثنا محمد بن مرزوق قال ثنا عمر بن يونس قال ثنا إسحاق بن أبي طلحة قال ثنا أنس بن مالك ﷺ في أصحاب النبي ﷺ الذين أرسلهم نبي الله ﷺ إلى أهل بئر معونة قال: لا أدري أربعين أو سبعين قال: وعلى ذلك الماء عامر ابن الطفيل الجعفري فخرج أولئك النفر من أصحاب النبي ﷺ حتى أتوا غارا مشرفا على الماء قعدوا فيه ثم قال بعضهم لبعض: أيكم يبلغ رسالة رسول الله ﷺ إلى أهل هذا الماء فقال أراه أبو ملحان الأنصاري: أنا أبلغ رسالة رسول الله ﷺ فخرج حتى أتى حيا منهم فاحتبى أمام البيوت ثم قال: يأهل بئر معونة إني رسول رسول الله ﷺ إني أشهد أن لا إله إلا الله وأن محمدا عبده ورسوله فآمنوا بالله ورسوله فخرج إليه رجل من كسر البيت برمح فضربه في جنبه حتى خرج من الشق الآخر فقال: الله أكبر فزت ورب الكعبة فاتبعوا أثره حتى أتوا أصحابه فقتلهم أجمعين عامر بن الطفيل. قال: قال إسحاق: حدثني أنس بن مالك أن الله تعالى أنزل فيهم قرآنا رفع بعدما قرأناه زمانا وأنزل الله: (وَلَا تَحْسَبَنَّ ٱلَّذِينَ قُتِلُوا۟ فِى سَبِيلِ ٱللَّهِ أَمْوَٰتًۢا بَلْ أَحْيَآءٌ عِندَ رَبِّهِمْ يُرْزَقُونَ).

Anas ibn Maalik ؓ narrated about the Companions of the Prophet ﷺ whom the Prophet of Allaah ﷺ sent to the people of Bi'r Ma'oonah (a place between Makkah and 'Asfaan). He said, "I can not remember if they numbered forty or seventy. 'Aamir ibn At-Tufail Al-Ja'faree was in charge of that village (Bi'r Ma'oonah). Those individuals from the Companions of the Prophet ﷺ departed to go to them until they reached a cave overlooking the village and sat in it. Then one of them said to the others, 'Which one of you will convey the message of the Messenger of Allaah ﷺ to the people of this village?' He, I think he was Abu Milhaan Al-Ansaaree,[51] said, "I will convey the message of the Messenger of Allaah ﷺ." So he went in their direction until he reached one of their sub-clans where he sat down in front of their houses and said, 'O people of Bi'r Ma'oonah, I am the messenger of the Messenger of Allaah ﷺ sent to you. I bear witness that there is no deity who deserves to be worshipped except Allaah and that Muhammad is His Slave and Messenger, so believe in Allaah and His Messenger." A man then came towards him from the side of the house with a spear and thrusted it into his side so hard that it came out his other side. He (Haraam) said, "*Allaahu Akbar* (Allaah is the greatest)! I succeeded, by the Lord of the *Ka'bah*!"[52] Then they (the people of Bi'r Ma'oonah) followed his trail until they reached his companions (in the cave) and 'Aamir ibn At-Tufail had all of them killed." Ishaaq (a narrator in the chain) said, 'Anas ibn Maalik narrated to me that Allaah ﷻ sent down Qur'aan about them; however, its recitation was abrogated after we had recited it for a while. Allaah also sent down:

$$ \text{وَلَا تَحْسَبَنَّ ٱلَّذِينَ قُتِلُواْ فِى سَبِيلِ ٱللَّهِ أَمْوَٰتًا ۚ بَلْ أَحْيَآءٌ عِندَ رَبِّهِمْ يُرْزَقُونَ} $$

"Think not of those who are killed in the path of Allaah as dead. Rather they are alive with their Lord being provided for."'

Ibn Jareer transmitted this *hadeeth* in his *Tafseer*, volume 7, page 392. Ash-Sheikh Muqbil ؓ said, "In it (the hadeeth), the reason why the verse was revealed was because of those who were killed at Bi'r Ma'oonah. The great Scholar Ash-Shawkaanee said in his *Tafseer*, "Whatever the case may be, the verse, when we look at its general wording includes every martyr."

قال الإمام مسلم ؓ (677): وحدثنا يحيى بن يحيى قال قرأت على مالك عن إسحاق بن عبد الله بن أبي طلحة عن أنس بن مالك ﷺ قال: دعا رسول الله ﷺ على الذين قتلوا أصحاب بئر معونة ثلاثين صباحا يدعو على رِعل وذكوان ولحيان وعصيّة عصت الله ورسوله قال أنس: أنزل الله

---

[51] This doubt is from one of the narrators in the chain. He was named in Al-Bukhaaree (4092): "Haraam ibn Milhaan," the maternal uncle of Anas ؓ.
[52] Meaning: I succeeded in being martyred in the path of Allaah. Refer to *Fathul-Baaree* in the explanation of *hadeeth* (4091).

عز وجل في الذين قتلوا ببئر معونة قرآنا قرأناه حتى نسخ بعد: (ألا بلغوا قومنا أن قد لقينا ربنا فرضي عنا ورضينا عنه).

Anas ibn Maalik ؓ narrated that the Messenger of Allaah ﷺ supplicated thirty mornings against those who killed the companions of Bi'r Ma'oonah (those he sent to Bi'r Ma'oonah). He supplicated against Ri'l, and Dhakwaan, and Lihyaan, and 'Usaiyah who disobeyed Allaah and His Messenger. Anas said, "Allaah ﷻ sent down Qur'aan about those who were killed at Bi'r Ma'oonah. We used to recite it until it was abrogated:

ألا بلغوا قومنا أن قد لقينا ربنا فرضي عنا ورضينا عنه

"Convey to our people that we have met our Lord, He is pleased with us and we are pleased with Him."

Muslim transmitted this *hadeeth* in his *Saheeh* (677) and Al-Bukhaaree in his *Saheeh* (4095).

<u>His, the Exalted One's statement:</u>

ٱلَّذِينَ ٱسْتَجَابُوا۟ لِلَّهِ وَٱلرَّسُولِ مِنۢ بَعْدِ مَآ أَصَابَهُمُ ٱلْقَرْحُ ۚ لِلَّذِينَ أَحْسَنُوا۟ مِنْهُمْ وَٱتَّقَوْا۟ أَجْرٌ عَظِيمٌ ۝

"Those who answered (the call of) Allaah and the Messenger after being wounded, for those of them who do good deeds and fear Allaah there is a great reward." (verse: 172)[53]

---

[53] Ash-Sheikh Muqbil ؓ in the latest edition of his book declared the *hadeeth* he mentioned here in the earlier editions to be *mursal*. However, I came across a different *hadeeth* which contains the reason why this verse was revealed, so I mentioned it here for the benefit of the readers.

قال الإمام البخاري ؒ (4077): حدثنا محمد حدثنا أبو معاوية عن هشام عن أبيه عن عائشة ؓ: (ٱلَّذِينَ ٱسْتَجَابُوا۟ لِلَّهِ وَٱلرَّسُولِ مِنۢ بَعْدِ مَآ أَصَابَهُمُ ٱلْقَرْحُ ۚ لِلَّذِينَ أَحْسَنُوا۟ مِنْهُمْ وَٱتَّقَوْا۟ أَجْرٌ عَظِيمٌ) قالت لعروة: يابن أختي كان من أبواك منهم الزبير وأبو بكر لما أصاب رسول الله ﷺ ما أصاب يوم أحد وانصرف عنه المشركون خاف أن يرجعوا قال: من يذهب في أثرهم فانتدب منهم سبعون رجلا قال: كان فيهم أبو بكر والزبير.

'Urwah narrated on 'Aishah ؓ:

ٱلَّذِينَ ٱسْتَجَابُوا۟ لِلَّهِ وَٱلرَّسُولِ مِنۢ بَعْدِ مَآ أَصَابَهُمُ ٱلْقَرْحُ ۚ لِلَّذِينَ أَحْسَنُوا۟ مِنْهُمْ وَٱتَّقَوْا۟ أَجْرٌ عَظِيمٌ

"Those who answered (the call of) Allaah and the Messenger after being wounded, for those of them who do good deeds and fear Allaah there is a great reward."
She said to 'Urwah, "O son of my sister, your two fathers, Az-Zubair and Abu Bakr, were amongst them. When that which afflicted the Messenger of Allaah ﷺ occurred on the day of Uhud and the polytheists departed turning away from him, he was afraid

His, the Exalted One's statement:

$$\text{وَلَتَسْمَعُنَّ مِنَ ٱلَّذِينَ أُوتُوا۟ ٱلْكِتَٰبَ مِن قَبْلِكُمْ وَمِنَ ٱلَّذِينَ أَشْرَكُوٓا۟ أَذًى كَثِيرًا}$$

"And you shall certainly hear much that will offend you from those who received the book before you and from those who ascribe partners to Allaah…" (verse: 186)

قال الإمام أبو داود ﵀ (3000): حدثنا محمد بن يحيى بن فارس أن الحكم بن نافع حدثهم نا شعيب عن الزهري عن عبد الرحمن بن عبد الله بن كعب بن مالك عن أبيه ﵁ وكان أحد الثلاثة الذين تيب عليهم: وكان كعب بن الأشرف يهجو النبي ﷺ ويحرّض عليه كفار قريش وكان النبي ﷺ حين قدم المدينة وأهلها أخلاط منهم المسلمون والمشركون يعبدون الأوثان واليهود وكانوا يؤذون النبي ﷺ وأصحابه فأمر الله عز وجل نبيه ﷺ بالصبر والعفو ففيهم أنزل الله تعالى: (وَلَتَسْمَعُنَّ مِنَ ٱلَّذِينَ أُوتُوا۟ ٱلْكِتَٰبَ مِن قَبْلِكُمْ) الآية فلما أبى كعب بن الأشرف أن ينزع عن أذى النبي ﷺ أمر النبي ﷺ سعد بن معاذ أن يبعث رهطا يقتلونه فبعث محمد بن مسلمة ، وذكر قصة قتله ، فلما قتلوه فزعت اليهود والمشركون فغدوا على النبي ﷺ فقالوا: طرق صاحبنا فقتل فذكر لهم النبي ﷺ الذي كان يقول ودعاهم النبي ﷺ إلى أن يكتب بينه وبينهم كتابا ينتهون إلى ما فيه فكتب النبي ﷺ بينه وبينهم وبين المسلمين عامة صحيفة. اه

قال المنذري : قوله: عن أبيه فيه نظر فإن أباه عبد الله بن كعب ليست له صحبة ولا هو أحد الثلاثة الذين تيب عليهم ويكون الحديث على هذا مرسلا ويحتمل أن يكون أراد بأبيه جده وهو كعب بن مالك فيكون الحديث على هذا مسندا إذ قد سمع عبد الرحمن من جده كعب بن مالك وكعب هو أحد الثلاثة

---

that they might turn back so he said, "Who will follow their trail?" Seventy men then volunteered. Abu Bakr and Az-Zubair were amongst them."

This *hadeeth*, Al-Bukhaaree transmitted it in his *Saheeh* (4077). Al-Haafidh Ibn Hajar said in *Fathul-Baaree* in the explanation of this *hadeeth*, "His (Al-Bukhaaree's) statement: "Chapter:

$$\text{ٱلَّذِينَ ٱسْتَجَابُوا۟ لِلَّهِ وَٱلرَّسُولِ}$$

"Those who answered (the call of) Allaah and the Messenger…"
Meaning: The reason why it was revealed and that it pertains to Uhud." Also, Al-Waahidee mentioned this *hadeeth* in his book *Asbaab An-Nuzool* (Reasons for the Descending of the Revelation) page 111, and Al-Haafidh Ibn Hajar in his book *Al-'Ujaab fee Bayaan Al-Asbaab*, volume 2, page 790.

الذين تيب عليهم وقد وقع مثل هذا في الأسانيد في غير موضع.اه من عون المعبود بتصرف وذكره الواحدي في أسباب النزول بهذا السند وبهذا اللفظ.

Ka'b ibn Maalik ﷺ one of the three who were forgiven (after staying behind the battle of *Tabook*) narrated that Ka'b ibn Al-Ashraf (a Jew) used to ridicule the Prophet ﷺ and incite the disbelievers of Quraish against him. The Prophet ﷺ arrived at Madeenah at a time when its people were mixed. They included the Muslims, the polytheists who worshipped the idols, and the Jews. They (the polytheists and the Jews) used to harm the Prophet ﷺ and his Companions. Allaah ﷻ ordered His Prophet ﷺ to be patient and pardon, and because of them Allaah ﷻ sent down:

$$وَلَتَسْمَعُنَّ مِنَ ٱلَّذِينَ أُوتُواْ ٱلْكِتَٰبَ مِن قَبْلِكُمْ$$

"And you shall certainly hear much that will offend you from those who received the book before you…".

Then, when Ka'b ibn Al-Ashraf refused to stop offending the Prophet ﷺ, the Prophet ﷺ ordered Sa'd ibn Mu'aadh to dispatch a group to kill him. So he sent Muhammad ibn Maslamah. He (the narrator) mentioned the story of how he was killed explaining that when they killed him, the Jews and the polytheists were frightened so they went to the Prophet ﷺ and said, "Our companion was struck and killed!" The Prophet ﷺ then mentioned to them what he used to say and he invited them to write a treaty between himself and them, and that they adhere to it. The Prophet ﷺ then had a treaty written between himself and them and the Muslims in general.

Abu Daawud transmitted this *hadeeth* in his *Sunan* (3000).

His, the Exalted One's statement:

$$لَا تَحْسَبَنَّ ٱلَّذِينَ يَفْرَحُونَ بِمَآ أَتَواْ وَّيُحِبُّونَ أَن يُحْمَدُواْ بِمَا لَمْ يَفْعَلُواْ فَلَا تَحْسَبَنَّهُم بِمَفَازَةٍ مِّنَ ٱلْعَذَابِ ۖ وَلَهُمْ عَذَابٌ أَلِيمٌ$$

"Think not that those who rejoice in what they have done and love to be praised for what they have not done, think not that they are safe from the punishment. For them is a painful punishment." (verse: 188)

قال الإمام البخاري رحمه الله (4567): حدثنا سعيد بن أبي مريم حدثنا محمد بن جعفر قال حدثني زيد بن أسلم عن عطاء بن يسار عن أبي سعيد الخدري ﷺ أن رجالا من المنافقين على عهد رسول الله ﷺ كان إذا خرج رسول الله ﷺ إلى الغزو تخلفوا عنه وفرحوا بمقعدهم خلاف رسول الله ﷺ فإذا

قدم رسول الله ﷺ اعتذروا إليه وحلفوا وأحبوا أن يحمدوا بما لم يفعلوا فنزلت: (لَا تَحْسَبَنَّ ٱلَّذِينَ يَفْرَحُونَ بِمَآ أَتَوا۟ وَّيُحِبُّونَ أَن يُحْمَدُوا۟ بِمَا لَمْ يَفْعَلُوا۟).

Abu Sa'eed Al-Khudree ؓ narrated that a group of men from the hypocrites during the time of the Messenger of Allaah ﷺ, when the Messenger of Allaah ﷺ would set out for a battle, would stay behind and they would be happy with staying behind the Messenger of Allaah ﷺ. When the Messenger of Allaah ﷺ would return they would give him their excuses and swear and they loved to be praised for what they did not do. Then the verse descended:

لَا تَحْسَبَنَّ ٱلَّذِينَ يَفْرَحُونَ بِمَآ أَتَوا۟ وَّيُحِبُّونَ أَن يُحْمَدُوا۟ بِمَا لَمْ يَفْعَلُوا۟

"Think not that those who rejoice in what they have done and love to be praised for what they have not done…"

Al-Bukhaaree transmitted this *hadeeth* in his *Saheeh* (4567) and Muslim in his *Saheeh* (2777).

قال الإمام البخاري ﷺ (4568): حدثني إبراهيم بن موسى أخبرنا هشام أن ابن جريج أخبرهم عن بن أبي مليكة أن علقمة بن وقاص أخبره أن مروان قال لبوابه: اذهب يا رافع إلى ابن عباس فقل له: لئن كان كل امرئ فرح بما أوتي وأحب أن يحمد بما لم يفعل معذبا لنعذبن أجمعون فقال ابن عباس ؓ: ما لكم ولهذه الآية إنما دعا النبي ﷺ يهودا وسألهم عن شيء فكتموه إياه وأخبروه بغيره فأروه أن قد استحمدوا إليه بما أخبروه عنه فيما سألهم وفرحوا بما أتوا من كتمانهم ثم قرأ ابن عباس: (وَإِذْ أَخَذَ ٱللَّهُ مِيثَـٰقَ ٱلَّذِينَ أُوتُوا۟ ٱلْكِتَـٰبَ) كذلك حتى قوله: (يَفْرَحُونَ بِمَآ أَتَوا۟ وَّيُحِبُّونَ أَن يُحْمَدُوا۟ بِمَا لَمْ يَفْعَلُوا۟).

تابعه عبد الرزاق عن ابن جريج.

حدثنا ابن مقاتل أخبرنا الحجاج عن ابن جريج أخبرني ابن أبي مليكة عن حميد بن عبد الرحمن بن عوف أنه أخبره مروان بهذا.

Marwaan said to his door man, "O Raafi', go to Ibn 'Abbaas and say to him, 'If every person who gets happy with what he brought forth and loves to be praised for what he did not do is to be punished, we will all be punished!' Ibn 'Abbaas ؓ said, "What is with you and this verse? (Verily this verse was only revealed because of the people of the book.)[54] The Prophet ﷺ called some Jews and asked them about something. So they concealed from him what he asked about and told him something else. They thought they earned his praise for what they told him in response to what he asked and they were happy about what they did in terms of concealing what he asked about." Then Ibn 'Abbaas recited:

$$وَإِذْ أَخَذَ ٱللَّهُ مِيثَٰقَ ٱلَّذِينَ أُوتُواْ ٱلْكِتَٰبَ$$

"And (mention) when Allaah took a covenant from those who were given the book…" (*Aal 'Imraan*: 187) up to His statement:

$$يَفْرَحُونَ بِمَآ أَتَواْ وَّيُحِبُّونَ أَن يُحْمَدُواْ بِمَا لَمْ يَفْعَلُواْ$$

"…those who rejoice in what they have done and love to be praised for what they have not done…"

This *hadeeth* has been transmitted by Al-Bukhaaree in his *Saheeh* (4568) and Muslim in his *Saheeh* (2778). Ash-Sheikh Muqbil ﷺ said, "It is possible to harmonize between the two *hadeeth* by saying the verse was revealed because of the two groups. That is what Al-Haafidh said in *Fathul-Baaree* (explanation of *hadeeth* 4567). I say, it would be better to give preference to the *hadeeth* of Abu Sa'eed because the *hadeeth* of Ibn 'Abbaas is one of the *ahaadeeth* in the two Saheehs which has been criticized as mentioned in the preface of *Fathul-Baaree*, volume 2, page 132. Also, it is meaningless to say that the verse is limited to the people of the book. Al-Haafidh said in *Fathul-Baaree* (explanation of hadeeth 4567), 'And its general wording includes everyone who does a good deed then gets happy because of that, the type of happiness that is accompanied by conceit and vanity; and he loves that people praise him for what he did not do.'

Also, of those things which support what I said about giving preference (to the *hadeeth* of Abu Sa'eed) is that Al-Haafidh ﷺ in *Fathul-Baaree* said about Raafi', the messenger sent to Ibn 'Abbaas whom the *hadeeth* centers around, "I did not find him mentioned in the books about the narrators. (I only found him) mentioned in the *hadeeth* and it appears to me from the wording of the *hadeeth* that he went to Ibn 'Abbaas and gave him the message then returned to Marwaan with the answer, and if he was not trustworthy with Marwaan then he would not be content with sending him…" may Allaah have mercy upon him. So based upon this, Raafi's status is unknown."

---

[54] What is between parentheses was taken from the narration of this *hadeeth* in Muslim (2778).

His, the Exalted One's statement:

$$وَإِنَّ مِنْ أَهْلِ ٱلْكِتَٰبِ لَمَن يُؤْمِنُ بِٱللَّهِ وَمَآ أُنزِلَ إِلَيْكُمْ وَمَآ أُنزِلَ إِلَيْهِمْ$$

"And verily there are some of the people of the book who believe in Allaah and in what has been revealed to you and in what has been revealed to them…" (verse: 199)

قال الإمام أبو بكر البزار رحمه الله كما في كشف الأستار (ج 1 ص 392): حدثنا محمد بن عبد الرحمن بن المفضل الحراني ثنا عثمان بن عبد الرحمن ثنا عبد الرحمن بن ثابت بن ثوبان عن حميد عن أنس رضي الله عنه عن النبي ﷺ (ح) وحدثنا أحمد بن بكار الباهلي ثنا المعتمر ابن سليمان ثنا حميد الطويل عن أنس رضي الله عنه أن النبي ﷺ صلى على النجاشي حين نُعي فقيل: يا رسول الله تصلي على عبد حبشي فأنزل الله عز وجل: (وَإِنَّ مِنْ أَهْلِ ٱلْكِتَٰبِ) الآية.

Anas narrated that the Prophet ﷺ prayed the *Janaazah* (funeral prayer) for An-Najaashee when his death was announced. It was said, "O Messenger of Allaah, do you pray for an Abyssinian slave?" Then Allaah sent down:

$$وَإِنَّ مِنْ أَهْلِ ٱلْكِتَٰبِ$$

"And verily there are some of the people of the book…".

Al-Bazzaar transmitted this *hadeeth* as mentioned in the book *Kashful-Astaar*, volume 1, page 392. Ash-Sheikh Muqbil commented, "I mentioned in my *hadeeth* checking of *Tafseer Ibn Katheer*, volume 2, page 226, 'The *hadeeth* has numerous chains and because of them it rises the level of being authentic although the *hadeeth* has a basis in the two Saheehs, *Al-Bukhaaree* (chapter), "The Virtues of the *Ansaar*", volume 5, pages 64-65 and the chapter, "The Funeral Prayers", volume 2, pages 108-109, and *Muslim* in the book, "The Funeral Prayers", volume 3, pages 54-55.

سورة النساء

Sooratun-Nisaa

<u>His, the Exalted One's statement:</u>

وَإِنْ خِفْتُمْ أَلَّا تُقْسِطُوا۟ فِى ٱلْيَتَـٰمَىٰ

"And if you fear that you will not be able to deal justly with the orphan girls…" (verse: 3)

قال الإمام البخاري رحمه الله (4573): حدثني إبراهيم بن موسى أخبرنا هشام عن ابن جريج قال أخبرني هشام بن عروة عن أبيه عن عائشة رضي الله عنها أن رجلا كانت له يتيمة فنكحها وكان لها عذق وكان يمسكها عليه ولم يكن لها من نفسه شيء فنزلت فيه: (وَإِنْ خِفْتُمْ أَلَّا تُقْسِطُوا۟ فِى ٱلْيَتَـٰمَىٰ) أحسبه قال: كانت شريكته في ذلك العذق وفي ماله.

'Aishah narrated that a man was in charge of an orphan girl and then he married her. She owned a date palm-tree and he used to keep her as a wife because of it although he had no desire for her. Then the verse descended because of him,

وَإِنْ خِفْتُمْ أَلَّا تُقْسِطُوا۟ فِى ٱلْيَتَـٰمَىٰ

"And if you fear that you will not be able to deal justly with the orphan girls…"

I[55] think he said, "She was his partner in regards to the date palm-tree and his wealth."[56]

Al-Bukhaaree transmitted this *hadeeth* in his *Saheeh* (4573) and Muslim in his *Saheeh* (3018).

---

[55] This doubt is from Hishaam ibn Yoosuf one of the narrators in the chain as Al-Haafidh Ibn Hajar mentioned in *Fathul-Baaree*.

[56] Al-Haafidh Ibn Hajar said in the explanation of this *hadeeth* in *Fathul-Baaree*, "His statement: "A man was in charge of an orphan girl. Then he married her." That is how Hishaam (ibn Yoosuf) mentioned (the *hadeeth*) on Ibn Juraij. He made it as if it (the verse) was revealed because of a specific person while it is well known from the narrations on Hishaam ibn 'Urwah that it is general, and that is how Al-Ismaa'eelee narrated it from the chain of Hajjaaj ibn Muhammad on Ibn Juraij, and its text is: "It was revealed because of the man who is in charge of an orphan girl…"

His, the Exalted One's statement:

$$\text{وَمَن كَانَ غَنِيًّا فَلْيَسْتَعْفِفْ وَمَن كَانَ فَقِيرًا فَلْيَأْكُلْ بِٱلْمَعْرُوفِ}$$

"And whoever (amongst the guardians) is rich he should refrain (from taking wages), and whoever is poor let him take what is just and reasonable…" (verse: 6)

قال الإمام البخاري رَحِمَهُ اللهُ (4575): حدثني إسحاق أخبرنا عبد الله بن نمير حدثنا هشام عن أبيه عن عائشة رَضِيَ اللهُ عَنْهَا في قوله تعالى: (وَمَن كَانَ غَنِيًّا فَلْيَسْتَعْفِفْ وَمَن كَانَ فَقِيرًا فَلْيَأْكُلْ بِٱلْمَعْرُوفِ) أنها نزلت في مال اليتيم إذا كان فقيرا فإنه يأكل منه مكان قيامه عليه بمعروف.

'Aishah said about His statement:

$$\text{وَمَن كَانَ غَنِيًّا فَلْيَسْتَعْفِفْ وَمَن كَانَ فَقِيرًا فَلْيَأْكُلْ بِٱلْمَعْرُوفِ}$$

"And whoever (amongst the guardians) is rich he should refrain (from taking wages), and whoever is poor let him take what is just and reasonable…"
"This verse descended pertaining to the wealth of the orphan. If he (the guardian) is poor, he is allowed to take what is just and reasonable in exchange for his administration of the wealth."

Al-Bukhaaree transmitted This *hadeeth* in his *Saheeh* (4575) and Muslim in his *Saheeh* (3019).

His, the Exalted One's statement:

$$\text{يُوصِيكُمُ ٱللَّهُ فِي أَوْلَٰدِكُمْ}$$

"Allaah commands you concerning your children['s] (inheritance)…" (verse: 11)

قال الإمام البخاري رَحِمَهُ اللهُ (4577): حدثني إبراهيم بن موسى أخبرنا هشام أن ابن جريج قال أخبرني ابن المنكدر عن جابر رَضِيَ اللهُ عَنْهُ قال: عادني رسول الله ﷺ وأبو بكر في بني سلمة ماشيين فوجدني النبي ﷺ لا أعقل فدعا بماء فتوضأ منه ثم رش عليّ فأفقت فقلت: ما تأمرني أن أصنع في مالي يا رسول الله فنزلت: (يُوصِيكُمُ ٱللَّهُ فِي أَوْلَٰدِكُمْ).

Jaabir said, "The Prophet ﷺ and Abu Bakr walked over to visit me while I was sick at (the area of) the tribe Banee Salimah (Jaabir's tribe). The Prophet ﷺ entered and found me passed out. He called for water and made ablution from it and then he sprinkled some of the water on me. I then regained consciousness and said, "What do you order me to do with my wealth, O Messenger of Allaah?" Then the verse descended:

$$يُوصِيكُمُ ٱللَّهُ فِىٓ أَوْلَٰدِكُمْ$$

"Allaah commands you concerning your children…"

As for this *hadeeth*, Al-Bukhaaree transmitted it in his *Saheeh* (4577) and Muslim in his *Saheeh* (1616/6).

His, the Exalted One's statement:

$$يَٰٓأَيُّهَا ٱلَّذِينَ ءَامَنُوا۟ لَا يَحِلُّ لَكُمْ أَن تَرِثُوا۟ ٱلنِّسَآءَ كَرْهًا$$

"O you who believe, it is not permissible for you to inherit women against their will…" (verse: 19)

قال الإمام البخاري ﷺ (4579): حدثنا محمد بن مقاتل أخبرنا أسباط بن محمد حدثنا الشيباني عن عكرمة عن ابن عباس ، قال الشيباني: وذكره أبو الحسن السوائي ولا أظنه ذكره إلا عن ابن عباس ﷺ (يَٰٓأَيُّهَا ٱلَّذِينَ ءَامَنُوا۟ لَا يَحِلُّ لَكُمْ أَن تَرِثُوا۟ ٱلنِّسَآءَ كَرْهًا وَلَا تَعْضُلُوهُنَّ لِتَذْهَبُوا۟ بِبَعْضِ مَآ ءَاتَيْتُمُوهُنَّ) قال: كانوا إذا مات الرجل كان أولياؤه أحق بامرأته إن شاء بعضهم تزوجها وإن شاءوا زوجوها وإن شاءوا لم يزوجوها وهم أحق بها من أهلها فنزلت هذه الآية في ذلك.

On Ibn 'Abbaas ﷺ:

$$يَٰٓأَيُّهَا ٱلَّذِينَ ءَامَنُوا۟ لَا يَحِلُّ لَكُمْ أَن تَرِثُوا۟ ٱلنِّسَآءَ كَرْهًا وَلَا تَعْضُلُوهُنَّ لِتَذْهَبُوا۟ بِبَعْضِ مَآ ءَاتَيْتُمُوهُنَّ$$

"O you who believe, it is not permissible for you to inherit women against their will, and do not treat them with harshness that you may take off with a portion of what you have given them…"

He (Ibn 'Abbaas) said, "When a man would die, they used to give his relatives more right to his wife (than her relatives). If one of them wished he would marry her, and if they wished they would marry her off (to someone), and if they wished they would not marry her off. They had more right to her than her own family. Then this verse descended because of that."

Al-Bukhaaree transmitted this *hadeeth* in his *Saheeh* (4579).

قال الحافظ ابن كثير ﷺ (ج 1 ص 465): وروى وكيع عن سفيان عن علي بن بَذيمة عن مقسم عن ابن عباس ﷺ : كانت المرأة في الجاهلية إذا توفي عنها زوجها فجاء رجل فألقى عليها ثوبا كان أحق بها فنزلت: (يَٰٓأَيُّهَا ٱلَّذِينَ ءَامَنُوا۟ لَا يَحِلُّ لَكُمْ أَن تَرِثُوا۟ ٱلنِّسَآءَ كَرْهًا).

Ibn 'Abbaas ﷺ narrated that in the days of *Jaahiliyah* that if a woman's husband were to die and a man came to her and threw a piece of clothing on her, he would have more right to her. Then the verse descended:

$$\text{يَٰٓأَيُّهَا ٱلَّذِينَ ءَامَنُوا۟ لَا يَحِلُّ لَكُمْ أَن تَرِثُوا۟ ٱلنِّسَآءَ كَرْهًا}$$

"O you who believe, it is not permissible for you to inherit women against their will…"

Regarding this *hadeeth*, Al-Haafidh Ibn Katheer mentioned it with its chain in his *Tafseer*, volume 1, page 465. Ash-Sheikh Muqbil ﷺ said, "Ali ibn Badheemah, the authors of *As-Sunan*, transmitted his narrations and he is a trustworthy narrator. The rest of the people of the chain are people of the *Saheeh* (Al-Bukhaaree and/or Muslim)."

His, the Exalted One's statement:

$$\text{وَلَا تَنكِحُوا۟ مَا نَكَحَ ءَابَآؤُكُم}$$

"And do not marry women whom your fathers married…" (verses: 22-23)

قال الإمام ابن جرير ﷺ (ج 8 ص 132): حدثني محمد بن عبد الله المخرمي قال حدثنا قراد قال حدثنا ابن عيينة عن عمرو عن عكرمة عن ابن عباس ﷺ قال: كان أهل الجاهلية يحرمون ما يحرم إلا امرأة الأب والجمع بين الأختين قال: فأنزل الله: (وَلَا تَنكِحُوا۟ مَا نَكَحَ ءَابَآؤُكُم مِّنَ ٱلنِّسَآءِ إِلَّا مَا قَدْ سَلَفَ) إلى قوله: (وَأَن تَجْمَعُوا۟ بَيْنَ ٱلْأُخْتَيْنِ).

Ibn 'Abbaas ﷺ said, "The people of *Jaahiliyah* used to forbid marrying those forbidden from marriage except the father's wife and having two sisters in wedlock at the same time. So Allaah sent down:

$$\text{وَلَا تَنكِحُوا۟ مَا نَكَحَ ءَابَآؤُكُم مِّنَ ٱلنِّسَآءِ إِلَّا مَا قَدْ سَلَفَ}$$

"And do not marry women whom your fathers married except what has already passed…"
up to His statement:

$$\text{وَأَن تَجْمَعُوا۟ بَيْنَ ٱلْأُخْتَيْنِ}$$

"…and two sisters in wedlock at the same time…"

As for this *hadeeth*, Ibn Jareer transmitted it in his *Tafseer*, volume 8, page 132. Ash-Sheikh Muqbil ﷺ said, "The people of the *hadeeth*'s chain are people of the *Saheeh* (Al-Bukhaaree and/or Muslim) except for Muhammad ibn 'Abdillaah Al-Makhramee, but he is a *haafidh* and trustworthy."

His, the Exalted One's statement:

$$\text{وَٱلْمُحْصَنَٰتُ مِنَ ٱلنِّسَآءِ إِلَّا مَا مَلَكَتْ أَيْمَٰنُكُمْ}$$

"Also (forbidden are) women already married except those (captives) whom your right hands possess…" (verse: 24)

قال الإمام مسلم ﷺ (1456): حدثني عبيد الله بن عمر بن ميسرة القواريري حدثنا يزيد بن زريع حدثنا سعيد بن أبي عروبة عن قتادة عن صالح أبي الخليل عن أبي علقمة الهاشمي عن أبي سعيد الخدري ﷺ أن رسول الله ﷺ يوم حنين بعث جيشا إلى أوطاس فلقوا عدوا فقاتلوهم فظهروا عليهم وأصابوا لهم سبايا فكأن ناسا من أصحاب رسول الله ﷺ تحرجوا من غشيانهن من أجل أزواجهن من المشركين فأنزل الله عز وجل في ذلك: (وَٱلْمُحْصَنَٰتُ مِنَ ٱلنِّسَآءِ إِلَّا مَا مَلَكَتْ أَيْمَٰنُكُمْ) أي فهن لكم حلال إذا انقضت عدتهن.

Abu Sa'eed Al-Khudree ﷺ narrated that on the day of Hunain the Messenger of Allaah ﷺ sent an army to Awtaas (a place in At-Taa'if). They encountered an enemy and fought them, were victorious and captured some female prisoners of war. Then it was as if some of the Companions of the Messenger of Allaah ﷺ avoided having sex with them out of fear of sin because they were married to polytheists. Then Allaah ﷻ sent down because of that:

$$\text{وَٱلْمُحْصَنَٰتُ مِنَ ٱلنِّسَآءِ إِلَّا مَا مَلَكَتْ أَيْمَٰنُكُمْ}$$

"Also (forbidden are) women already married except those (captives) whom your right hands possess…"

Meaning they are permissible for you when their waiting period[57] has expired.

Muslim transmitted this *hadeeth* in his *Saheeh* (1456).

---

[57] The waiting period for the pregnant captive woman is until she gives birth and the waiting period for the non-pregnant captive woman is one menstrual cycle as An-Nawawee mentioned in his explanation of *Saheeh Muslim*.

His, the Exalted One's statement:

$$\text{يَٰٓأَيُّهَا ٱلَّذِينَ ءَامَنُوٓاْ أَطِيعُواْ ٱللَّهَ وَأَطِيعُواْ ٱلرَّسُولَ وَأُوْلِى ٱلْأَمْرِ مِنكُمْ}$$

"O you who believe, obey Allaah and obey the Messenger and those in authority amongst you…" (verse: 59)

قال الإمام البخاري رَحِمَهُ اللهُ (4584): حدثنا صدقة بن الفضل أخبرنا حجاج بن محمد عن ابن جريج عن يعلى بن مسلم عن سعيد بن جبير عن ابن عباس رَضِيَ اللهُ عَنْهُ: (يَٰٓأَيُّهَا ٱلَّذِينَ ءَامَنُوٓاْ أَطِيعُواْ ٱللَّهَ وَأَطِيعُواْ ٱلرَّسُولَ وَأُوْلِى ٱلْأَمْرِ مِنكُمْ) قال: نزلت في عبد الله بن حذافة بن قيس إذ بعثه النبي ﷺ في سرية.

On Ibn 'Abbaas رضي الله عنه:

$$\text{يَٰٓأَيُّهَا ٱلَّذِينَ ءَامَنُوٓاْ أَطِيعُواْ ٱللَّهَ وَأَطِيعُواْ ٱلرَّسُولَ وَأُوْلِى ٱلْأَمْرِ مِنكُمْ}$$

"O you who believe, obey Allaah and obey the Messenger and those in authority amongst you…"
He said, "The verse descended because of 'Abdullaah ibn Hudhaafah ibn Qais when the Prophet ﷺ sent him on a raiding party."

Al-Bukhaaree transmitted this *hadeeth* in his *Saheeh* (4584) and is clarified by the following *hadeeth*:

قال الإمام البخاري رَحِمَهُ اللهُ (4340): حدثنا مسدد حدثنا عبد الواحد حدثنا الأعمش حدثني سعد بن عبيدة عن أبي عبد الرحمن عن علي رَضِيَ اللهُ عَنْهُ قال: بعث النبي ﷺ سرية واستعمل عليها رجلا من الأنصار وأمرهم أن يطيعوه فغضب فقال: أليس أمركم النبي ﷺ أن تطيعوني قالوا: بلى قال: فاجمعوا لي حطبا فجمعوا له فقال: أوقدوا نارا فأوقدوها فقال: ادخلوها فهموا وجعل بعضهم يمسك بعضا ويقولون: فررنا إلى النبي ﷺ من النار فما زالوا حتى خمدت النار فسكن غضبه فبلغ النبي ﷺ فقال: لو دخلوها ما خرجوا منها إلى يوم القيامة الطاعة في المعروف.

'Ali رضي الله عنه said, "The Prophet ﷺ dispatched a raiding party and put a man from the *Ansaar* in charge of them and ordered them to obey him. Then (while out with the raiding party) the man got angry and said, 'Did not the Prophet ﷺ order you all to obey me?' They said, "Certainly!" He said, "In that case, gather for me some firewood." So they gathered it. He said, "Light a fire." So they lit a fire. He then said, "Enter it." They contemplated and they held on to one another and said, 'We fled to the Prophet ﷺ fleeing from the fire.' They remained in that state until the fire died out and his anger ceased. News of that reached the Prophet ﷺ so he said, "If they were to have entered it they would not have left it until the day of resurrection. Obedience is only in righteousness."

As for this *hadeeth*, Al-Bukhaaree transmitted it in his *Saheeh* (4340).

His, the Exalted One's statement:

$$\text{أَلَمْ تَرَ إِلَى ٱلَّذِينَ يَزْعُمُونَ أَنَّهُمْ ءَامَنُوا۟ بِمَآ أُنزِلَ إِلَيْكَ وَمَآ أُنزِلَ مِن قَبْلِكَ يُرِيدُونَ أَن يَتَحَاكَمُوٓا۟ إِلَى ٱلطَّـٰغُوتِ وَقَدْ أُمِرُوٓا۟ أَن يَكْفُرُوا۟ بِهِۦ وَيُرِيدُ ٱلشَّيْطَـٰنُ أَن يُضِلَّهُمْ ضَلَـٰلًۢا بَعِيدًا ۝}$$

"Have you not seen those who claim that they believe in what has been sent down to you and in what has been sent down before you? They want to go for judgment (in their disputes) to the *Taaghoot* (the one who judges with falsehood from other sources than the Book and the Sunnah) while they have been ordered to reject it. And the Shaytaan wants to lead them far astray." (verse: 60)

قال الحافظ ابن كثير ﷺ في التفسير (ج 1 ص 519): قال الطبراني: حدثنا أبو زيد أحمد بن يزيد الحوطي حدثنا أبو اليمان حدثنا صفوان بن عمرو عن عكرمة عن ابن عباس ﷺ قال: كان أبو برزة الأسلمي كاهنا يقضي بين اليهود فيما يتنافرون فيه فتنافر إليه ناس من المسلمين فأنزل الله عز وجل: (أَلَمْ تَرَ إِلَى ٱلَّذِينَ يَزْعُمُونَ أَنَّهُمْ ءَامَنُوا۟ بِمَآ أُنزِلَ إِلَيْكَ وَمَآ أُنزِلَ مِن قَبْلِكَ) إلى قوله: (إِنْ أَرَدْنَآ إِلَّآ إِحْسَـٰنًا وَتَوْفِيقًا).

Ibn 'Abbaas ﷺ narrated that Abu Barzah Al-Aslamee was a fortune-teller who used to judge between the Jews in their disputes and some Muslims went to him for judgment in their dispute. Then Allaah ﷻ sent down:

$$\text{أَلَمْ تَرَ إِلَى ٱلَّذِينَ يَزْعُمُونَ أَنَّهُمْ ءَامَنُوا۟ بِمَآ أُنزِلَ إِلَيْكَ وَمَآ أُنزِلَ مِن قَبْلِكَ}$$

"Have you not seen those who claim that they believe what has been sent down to you and in what has been sent down before you..."
up to His statement:

$$\text{إِنْ أَرَدْنَآ إِلَّآ إِحْسَـٰنًا وَتَوْفِيقًا}$$

"We only intended to do good and make reconciliation." (verse: 62).

At-Tabaraanee transmitted this *hadeeth*, as Ibn Katheer mentioned in his *Tafseer*, volume 1, page 519. Ash-Sheikh Muqbil ﷺ mentioned that Ibnul-Qattaan said about Abu Zaid Ahmad ibn Yazeed Al-Hootee, the Sheikh of At-Tabaraanee in this chain, "His status is not known." However, he has been supported by Ibraaheem ibn Sa'eed Al-Jawharee in the chain that Al-Waahidee transmitted in his book *Asbaab An-Nuzool*.

His, the Exalted One's statement:

فَلَا وَرَبِّكَ لَا يُؤْمِنُونَ حَتَّىٰ يُحَكِّمُوكَ فِيمَا شَجَرَ بَيْنَهُمْ

"But no, by your Lord, they do not have faith until they make you the judge in the disputes between them…" (verse: 65)

قال الإمام البخاري ﷺ (4585): حدثنا علي بن عبد الله حدثنا محمد بن جعفر أخبرنا معمر عن الزهري عن عروة قال: خاصم الزبير رجلا من الأنصار في شَرِيج من الحرة فقال النبي ﷺ : اسق يا زبير ثم أرسل الماء إلى جارك فقال الأنصاري: يا رسول الله أن كان ابن عمتك فتلون وجهه ثم قال: اسق يا زبير ثم احبس الماء حتى يرجع إلى الجدر ثم أرسل الماء إلى جارك واستوعى النبي ﷺ للزبير حقه في صريح الحكم حين أحفظه الأنصاري وكان أشار عليهما بأمر لهما فيه سعة قال الزبير: فما أحسب هذه الآية إلا نزلت في ذلك: (فَلَا وَرَبِّكَ لَا يُؤْمِنُونَ حَتَّىٰ يُحَكِّمُوكَ فِيمَا شَجَرَ بَيْنَهُمْ).

'Urwah said, "Az-Zubair had a dispute with a man from the *Ansaar* over an irrigation canal at Al-Harrah. The Prophet ﷺ said, 'O Zubair, irrigate first then send the water to your neighbor.' The *Ansaaree* man said, "O Messenger of Allaah, is that because he is the son of your aunt?" His ﷺ face changed, then he said, 'O Zubair, irrigate then hold the water until the irrigation ditches (around the trunks of the date palm trees) are filled then send the water to your neighbor.' The Prophet ﷺ gave Az-Zubair his full right in the judgment after the *Ansaaree* man made him angry while before that he suggested to them something they could both feel comfortable with. Az-Zubair said, "I do not think the following verse descended for any other reason,

فَلَا وَرَبِّكَ لَا يُؤْمِنُونَ حَتَّىٰ يُحَكِّمُوكَ فِيمَا شَجَرَ بَيْنَهُمْ

"But no, by your Lord, they do not have faith until they make you the judge in the disputes between them…"

Al-Bukhaaree transmitted this *hadeeth* in his *Saheeh* (4585) and Muslim in his *Saheeh* (2357).

<u>His, the Exalted One's statement:</u>

وَمَن يُطِعِ ٱللَّهَ وَٱلرَّسُولَ فَأُو۟لَـٰٓئِكَ مَعَ ٱلَّذِينَ أَنْعَمَ ٱللَّهُ عَلَيْهِم مِّنَ ٱلنَّبِيِّـۧنَ وَٱلصِّدِّيقِينَ وَٱلشُّهَدَآءِ وَٱلصَّـٰلِحِينَ ۚ وَحَسُنَ أُو۟لَـٰٓئِكَ رَفِيقًا ۝

"And whoever obeys Allaah and the Messenger they will be in the company of those on whom Allaah has bestowed His grace, from the Prophets, the *Siddeeqeen* (the truthful ones foremost in faith), the martyrs and the righteous, and how excellent are those as companions!"
(verse: 69)

قال الإمام الطبراني ﵀ في الصغير (ج 1 ص 26): حدثنا أحمد بن عمرو الخلال المكي أبو عبد الله حدثنا عبد الله بن عمران العابدي حدثنا فضيل بن عياض عن منصور عن إبراهيم عن الأسود عن عائشة ﵂ قالت: جاء رجل إلى النبي ﷺ فقال: يا رسول الله إنك لأحب إليّ من نفسي وإنك لأحب إليّ من أهلي ومالي وأحب إليّ من ولدي لأكون في البيت فأذكرك فما أصبر حتى آتيك فأنظر إليك وإذا ذكرت موتي وموتك عرفت أنك إذا دخلت الجنة رفعت مع النبيين وإني إذا دخلت الجنة خشيت ألا أراك فلم يرد عليه النبي ﷺ حتى نزل جبريل عليه السلام بهذه الآية: (وَمَن يُطِعِ ٱللَّهَ وَٱلرَّسُولَ فَأُو۟لَـٰٓئِكَ مَعَ ٱلَّذِينَ أَنْعَمَ ٱللَّهُ عَلَيْهِم مِّنَ ٱلنَّبِيِّـۧنَ وَٱلصِّدِّيقِينَ وَٱلشُّهَدَآءِ وَٱلصَّـٰلِحِينَ) الآية.

لم يروه عن منصور عن إبراهيم عن الأسود عن عائشة إلا فضيل تفرد به عبد الله بن عمران.

'Aishah ﵂ said, "A man came to the Prophet ﷺ and said, 'O Messenger of Allaah, indeed you are more beloved to me than myself. Indeed you are more beloved to me than my wife and my wealth, and you are more beloved to me than my children. Indeed, when I am in my house then and I remember you, and I can not bear it until I must come and see you. When I contemplate my death and your death, I know that when you enter paradise you will be raised with the Prophets, and when I enter paradise, I fear I will not see you.' The Prophet ﷺ did not respond until Jibreel ﵇ came down with this verse:

وَمَن يُطِعِ ٱللَّهَ وَٱلرَّسُولَ فَأُو۟لَـٰٓئِكَ مَعَ ٱلَّذِينَ أَنْعَمَ ٱللَّهُ عَلَيْهِم مِّنَ ٱلنَّبِيِّـۧنَ وَٱلصِّدِّيقِينَ وَٱلشُّهَدَآءِ وَٱلصَّـٰلِحِينَ

"And whoever obeys Allaah and the Messenger they will be in the company of those on whom Allaah has bestowed His grace, from the Prophets, the *Siddeeqeen* (the truthful ones foremost in faith), the martyrs and the righteous…".

At-Tabaraanee transmitted this *hadeeth* in *Al-Mu'jam As-Sagheer*, volume 1, page 26. Ash-Sheikh Muqbil ﷺ said, "…and Ash-Shawkaanee said that Al-Maqdisee declared it to be *hasan*, and it has supporting *ahaadeeth* which strengthen it as mentioned in the *Tafseer* of Ibn Katheer, volume 1, page 523."

His, the Exalted One's statement:

أَلَمْ تَرَ إِلَى ٱلَّذِينَ قِيلَ لَهُمْ كُفُّوٓاْ أَيْدِيَكُمْ وَأَقِيمُواْ ٱلصَّلَوٰةَ

"Have you not seen those who were told to hold back their hands (from fighting) and establish the prayer…" (verse: 77)

قال الإمام النسائي رحمه الله في المجتبى (ج 6 ص 2-3): أخبرنا محمد بن علي بن الحسن بن شقيق قال أنبأنا أبي قال أنبأنا الحسين بن واقد عن عمرو بن دينار عن عكرمة عن ابن عباس رضي الله عنهما أن عبد الرحمن بن عوف وأصحابا له أتوا النبي ﷺ بمكة فقالوا: يا رسول الله إنا كنا في عزة ونحن مشركون فلما آمنا صرنا أذلة فقال: إني أمرت بالعفو فلا تقاتلوا فلما حولنا الله إلى المدينة أمرنا بالقتال فكفوا فأنزل الله عز وجل: (أَلَمْ تَرَ إِلَى ٱلَّذِينَ قِيلَ لَهُمْ كُفُّوٓاْ أَيْدِيَكُمْ وَأَقِيمُواْ ٱلصَّلَوٰةَ).

Ibn 'Abbaas ﷺ narrated that 'Abdur-Rahmaan ibn 'Awf and some of his companions went to the Prophet ﷺ in Makkah and said, "O Messenger of Allaah, when we were polytheists we were in a powerful state. Then when we believed we became weak." He ﷺ said, "I have been ordered to pardon, so do not fight." Then when Allaah moved us to Madeenah we were ordered to fight and they refrained from fighting. Then Allaah ﷻ sent down:

أَلَمْ تَرَ إِلَى ٱلَّذِينَ قِيلَ لَهُمْ كُفُّوٓاْ أَيْدِيَكُمْ وَأَقِيمُواْ ٱلصَّلَوٰةَ

"Have you not seen those who were told to hold back their hands (from fighting) and establish the prayer…"

An-Nasaa'ee has transmitted this *hadeeth* in *Al-Mujtabaa*, volume 6, pages 2-3. Ash-Sheikh Muqbil ﷺ said, "Regarding the *hadeeth*, Al-Haakim has transmitted it in volume 2, page 66 and 307, and he said in both places, "Authentic according the standards of Al-Bukhaaree although they (Al-Bukhaaree and Muslim) did not transmit it." Adh-Dhahabee was silent in that regard (he did not oppose that ruling). what they said is a problematic because Husain ibn Waaqid is not from the people of Al-Bukhaaree so it is more appropriate to say its people are people of the *Saheeh* (Al-Bukhaaree and/or Muslim) because Husain is from the people of Muslim and 'Ikrimah is from the people of Al-Bukhaaree and from the people of Muslim when he is accompanied with someone else…"

His, the Exalted One's statement:

$$\text{وَإِذَا جَاءَهُمْ أَمْرٌ مِّنَ ٱلْأَمْنِ أَوِ ٱلْخَوْفِ أَذَاعُوا۟ بِهِۦ}$$

"And when there comes to them a matter concerning safety or fear they publicize it…" (verse: 83)

قال الإمام مسلم ﵀ (30/1479): حدثني زهير بن حرب حدثنا عمر بن يونس الحنفي حدثنا عكرمة بن عمار عن سماك أبي زُميل حدثني عبد الله بن عباس ﵁ حدثني عمر بن الخطاب ﵁ قال: لما اعتزل نبي الله ﷺ نساءه قال: دخلت المسجد فإذا الناس ينكتون بالحصى ويقولون: طلق رسول الله ﷺ نساءه وذلك قبل أن يُؤمرن بالحجاب فقال عمر: فقلت: لأعلمن ذلك اليوم قال: فدخلت على عائشة فقلت: يا بنت أبي بكر أقد بلغ من شأنك أن تؤذي رسول الله ﷺ فقالت: ما لي وما لك يابن الخطاب عليك بعيبتك قال: فدخلت على حفصة بنت عمر فقلت لها: يا حفصة أقد بلغ من شأنك أن تؤذي رسول الله ﷺ والله لقد علمت أن رسول الله ﷺ لا يحبك ولولا أنا لطلقك رسول الله ﷺ فبكت أشد البكاء فقلت لها: أين رسول الله ﷺ قالت: هو في خزانته في المشربة فدخلت فإذا أنا برباح غلام رسول الله ﷺ قاعدا على أسكُفّة المشربة مدلٍّ رجليه على نقير من خشب وهو جذع يرقى عليه

رسول الله ﷺ وينحدر فناديت: يا رباح استأذن لي عندك على رسول الله ﷺ فنظر رباح إلى الغرفة ثم نظر إليَّ فلم يقل شيئا ثم قلت: يا رباح استأذن لي عندك على رسول الله ﷺ فنظر رباح إلى الغرفة ثم نظر إليَّ فلم يقل شيئا ثم رفعت صوتي فقلت: يا رباح استأذن لي عندك على رسول الله ﷺ فإني أظن أن رسول الله ﷺ ظن أني جئت من أجل حفصة والله لئن أمرني رسول الله ﷺ بضرب عنقها لأضربن عنقها ورفعت صوتي فأومأ إليَّ أن ارقه فدخلت على رسول الله ﷺ وهو مضطجع على حصير فجلست فأدنى عليه إزاره وليس عليه غيره وإذا الحصير قد أثر في جنبه فنظرت ببصري في خزانة رسول الله ﷺ فإذا أنا بقبضة نحو الصاع من شعير ومثلها قرظا في ناحية الغرفة وإذا أفيق معلق قال: فابتدرت عينايَ قال: ما يبكيك يابن الخطاب قلت يا نبي الله وما لي لا أبكي وهذا الحصير قد أثر في جنبك وهذه خزانتك لا أرى فيها إلا ما أرى وذاك قيصر وكسرى في الثمار والأنهار وأنت رسول الله ﷺ وصفوته وهذه خزانتك فقال: يابن الخطاب ألا ترضى أن تكون لنا الآخرة ولهم الدنيا قلت: بلى قال: ودخلت عليه حين دخلت وأنا أرى الغضب في وجهه فقلت: يا رسول الله ما يشق عليك من شأن النساء فإن كنت طلقتهن فإن الله تعالى معك وملائكته وجبريل وميكائيل وأنا وأبو بكر والمؤمنون معك وقلما تكلمت وأحمد الله بكلام إلا رجوت أن يكون الله يُصدّق قولي الذي أقول ونزلت هذه الآية آية التخيير: (عَسَىٰ رَبُّهُۥ إِن طَلَّقَكُنَّ أَن يُبْدِلَهُۥٓ أَزْوَٰجًا خَيْرًا مِّنكُنَّ) (وَإِن تَظَٰهَرَا عَلَيْهِ فَإِنَّ ٱللَّهَ هُوَ مَوْلَىٰهُ وَجِبْرِيلُ وَصَٰلِحُ ٱلْمُؤْمِنِينَ ۖ وَٱلْمَلَٰٓئِكَةُ بَعْدَ ذَٰلِكَ ظَهِيرٌ) وكانت عائشة بنت أبي بكر وحفصة تظاهران على سائر نساء النبي ﷺ فقلت: يا رسول الله أطلقتهن قال:

لا قلت: يا رسول الله إني دخلت المسجد والمسلمون ينكتون بالحصى يقولون طلق رسول الله ﷺ نساءه أفأنزل فأخبرهم أنك لم تطلقهن قال: نعم إن شئت فلم أزل أحدثه حتى تحسر الغضب عن وجهه وحتى كشر فضحك وكان من أحسن الناس ثغرا ثم نزل نبي الله ﷺ ونزلت ونزلت ونزلت أتشبث بالجذع ونزل رسول الله ﷺ كأنما يمشي على الأرض ما يمسه بيده فقلت: يا رسول الله إنما كنت في الغرفة تسعة وعشرين قال: إن الشهر يكون تسعا وعشرين فقمت على باب المسجد فناديت بأعلى صوتي: لم يطلق رسول الله ﷺ نساءه ونزلت هذه الآية: (وَإِذَا جَآءَهُمۡ أَمۡرٌ مِّنَ ٱلۡأَمۡنِ أَوِ ٱلۡخَوۡفِ أَذَاعُواْ بِهِۦۖ وَلَوۡ رَدُّوهُ إِلَى ٱلرَّسُولِ وَإِلَىٰٓ أُوْلِي ٱلۡأَمۡرِ مِنۡهُمۡ لَعَلِمَهُ ٱلَّذِينَ يَسۡتَنۢبِطُونَهُۥ مِنۡهُمۡۗ) فكنت أنا استنبطت ذلك الأمر وأنزل الله عز وجل آية التخيير.

'Umar ibn Al-Khattaab ؓ narrated about when the Prophet of Allaah ﷺ cut off relations with his wives saying, "I entered the *masjid* and found the people scratching up the ground with pebbles (out of grief), and they were saying, 'The Messenger of Allaah ﷺ divorced his wives.' This was before they were ordered to wear the veil.[58] 'Umar said, "I will come to know today what happened." So I entered upon 'Aishah and said, "O daughter of Abu Bakr, have you gone so far as to annoy the Messenger of Allaah ﷺ!" She said, 'What business do I have with you, O son of Al-Khattaab? Go advise your daughter.' So I entered upon Hafsah bint 'Umar and said to her, "O Hafsah, have you gone so far as to annoy the Messenger of Allaah ﷺ! By Allaah, you know well that the Messenger of Allaah ﷺ does not love you and if it were not for me the Messenger of Allaah ﷺ would have divorced you." She then cried very intensely. I said to her, 'Where is the Messenger of Allaah ﷺ?' She said, "He is in his storage room in the attic."

I then went to enter and found Rabaah, the boy servant of the Messenger of Allaah ﷺ, sitting at the doorstep of the attic with his legs hanging down from wooden stairs made from a tree trunk that the Messenger of Allaah ﷺ used in order to climb up and down. I called out, 'O Rabaah, ask permission for me to enter upon the Messenger of Allaah ﷺ!' Rabaah then looked towards the room. Then he looked towards me and did not say anything so I said, "O Rabaah, ask permission for me to enter upon the Messenger of Allaah

---

[58] Ibn Hajar said in *Fathul-Baaree* in the explanation of *hadeeth* (5191), "That is how it came in this narration and it is a clear mistake because the revelation of the veil took place in the beginning of the marriage of the Prophet ﷺ to Zainab bint Jahsh…and this story was the reason for the revelation of the verse of the choice and Zainab bint Jahsh was amongst those who were given the choice…The best explanation of this to me is that the narrator, when he saw the statement of 'Umar that he entered upon 'Aishah, he thought that was before the veil and he asserted that. However the response to that is entering does not necessitate raising the veil because it is possible for him to enter the door while she talks to him from behind the veil. Likewise a mistake by a narrator in a phrase of the *hadeeth* does not necessitate that the entire *hadeeth* be discarded."

ﷺ!" Rabaah then looked towards the room. Then he looked towards me and did not say anything so I raised my voice saying, "O Rabaah, ask permission for me to enter upon the Messenger of Allaah ﷺ, for verily I think that the Messenger of Allaah ﷺ thinks that I came because of Hafsah! By Allaah, if the Messenger of Allaah ﷺ orders me to strike her neck (chopping off her head), I will indeed strike her neck!"

He then signaled for me to come up. I entered upon the Messenger of Allaah ﷺ while he was lying down on his side on a mat. I sat down. He tucked in his *Izaar* (lower garment). He was not wearing anything else. Then to my surprise, I found that the mat had left an imprint in his side. I began to look around at the storage room of the Messenger of Allaah ﷺ. I saw some barley that measured about one *Saa'* (four double handfuls) and the same measurement of pods of the sant tree in the corner. And I saw a poor quality water-skin hanging. My eyes then began to flow with tears. He said, "What makes you cry, O son of Al-Khattaab?" I said, "O Prophet of Allaah, why should I not cry while this mat has left an imprint in your side and this is your storage room; I do not see anything but this in it while Caesar (the emperor of Rome) and Kisraa (the emperor of Persia) have fruits and rivers, and you are the Messenger of Allaah ﷺ and His chosen one, and this is your storage room." He said, 'O son of Al-Khattaab, are you not pleased that we have the hereafter and they have this life?' I said, "Certainly!" He ('Umar) said, "When I entered upon him I saw the anger in his face so I said, "O Messenger of Allaah, what, pertaining to the women, has distressed you? For verily if you have divorced them then indeed Allaah ﷻ is with you, and His angels, and Jibreel and Mikaa'eel, and I and Abu Bakr and the believers are with you." Rarely, and I praise Allaah, did I make a statement except that I hoped that Allaah approves of what I say, and this verse, the verse of the choice, descended:

عَسَىٰ رَبُّهُۥٓ إِن طَلَّقَكُنَّ أَن يُبْدِلَهُۥٓ أَزْوَٰجًا خَيْرًا مِّنكُنَّ

'Perhaps his Lord, if he were to divorce you, will give him instead of you, wives better than you…' (*At-Tahreem*: 5)

وَإِن تَظَٰهَرَا عَلَيْهِ فَإِنَّ ٱللَّهَ هُوَ مَوْلَىٰهُ وَجِبْرِيلُ وَصَٰلِحُ ٱلْمُؤْمِنِينَ ۖ وَٱلْمَلَٰٓئِكَةُ بَعْدَ ذَٰلِكَ ظَهِيرٌ

'And if you help one another against him then verily Allaah is his protector and Jibreel and the righteous among the believers, and furthermore, the angels are his helpers.' (*At-Tahreem*: 4)

'Aishah, the daughter of Abu Bakr, and Hafsah were helping one another against the rest of the wives of the Prophet ﷺ. So I said, "O Messenger of Allaah, did you divorce them?" He said, 'No.' I said, "O Messenger of Allaah, verily I had entered the *masjid* and found the Muslims scratching up the ground with pebbles saying, 'The Messenger of Allaah ﷺ divorced his wives.' Should I go down and tell them that you have not divorced them?" He said, "Yes, if you wish." I continued to talk with him to the point where the signs of anger disappeared from his face and he began to smile and laugh. He had a gap between his two front teeth from the best looking that I have seen anyone with. The Prophet of Allaah ﷺ then went down and I went down as well. I descended hanging on to the trunk while the Messenger of Allaah ﷺ descended without touching it as if he were walking on the ground. I then said to him, "O Messenger of Allaah, you were only in the room for twenty nine days." He said, "A month can be twenty nine days." I went and stood at the door of the *masjid* and shouted with my loudest voice, "The Messenger of Allaah ﷺ did not divorce his wives!" And this verse descended:

$$\text{وَإِذَا جَاءَهُمْ أَمْرٌ مِّنَ ٱلْأَمْنِ أَوِ ٱلْخَوْفِ أَذَاعُوا بِهِ ۖ وَلَوْ رَدُّوهُ إِلَى ٱلرَّسُولِ وَإِلَىٰ أُولِي ٱلْأَمْرِ مِنْهُمْ لَعَلِمَهُ ٱلَّذِينَ يَسْتَنبِطُونَهُ مِنْهُمْ}$$

"And when there comes to them a matter concerning safety or fear they publicize it. And if only they had referred it to the Messenger or to those of authority amongst them, those who investigate it would come to know about it directly from them."

I investigated that matter, and Allaah ﷻ sent down the verse of the choice."

This *hadeeth* has been transmitted by Muslim in his *Saheeh* (1479/30).

His, the Exalted One's statement:

$$\text{فَمَا لَكُمْ فِي ٱلْمُنَٰفِقِينَ فِئَتَيْنِ}$$

"What is the matter with you that you are divided into two groups over the hypocrites…" (verse: 88)

قال الإمام البخاري رَحِمَهُ اللهُ (4050): حدثنا أبو الوليد حدثنا شعبة عن عدي بن ثابت سمعت عبد الله بن يزيد يحدث عن زيد بن ثابت رَضِيَ اللهُ عَنهُ قال: لما خرج رسول الله ﷺ إلى غزوة أحد رجع ناس ممن خرج معه وكان أصحاب النبي ﷺ فرقتين فرقة تقول نقاتلهم وفرقة تقول لا نقاتلهم فنزلت: (فَمَا لَكُمْ فِي ٱلْمُنَٰفِقِينَ فِئَتَيْنِ وَٱللَّهُ أَرْكَسَهُم بِمَا كَسَبُوٓا۟) وقال: إنها طيبة تنفي الذنوب كما تنفي النار خبث الفضة.

Zaid ibn Thaabit ؓ said, "When the Messenger of Allaah ﷺ set out for the battle of Uhud, some of the people who went out with him turned back. The Companions of the Prophet ﷺ split into two groups over them, one group saying, "We must fight them," another group saying, "We should not fight them." Then the verse descended:

$$\text{فَمَا لَكُمْ فِي ٱلْمُنَٰفِقِينَ فِئَتَيْنِ وَٱللَّهُ أَرْكَسَهُم بِمَا كَسَبُوٓاْ}$$

"What is the matter with you that you are divided into two groups over the hypocrites while Allaah has turned them back because of what they have earned."

He ﷺ said, "Verily it (the city of Madeenah) is Taibah.[59] It rejects the sins like fire rejects the dirty refuse of silver."

Al-Bukhaaree transmitted this *hadeeth* in his *Saheeh* (4050) as well as Muslim in his *Saheeh* (2776).

His, the Exalted One's statement:

$$\text{يَٰٓأَيُّهَا ٱلَّذِينَ ءَامَنُوٓاْ إِذَا ضَرَبْتُمْ فِي سَبِيلِ ٱللَّهِ فَتَبَيَّنُواْ وَلَا تَقُولُواْ لِمَنْ أَلْقَىٰٓ إِلَيْكُمُ ٱلسَّلَٰمَ لَسْتَ مُؤْمِنًا تَبْتَغُونَ عَرَضَ ٱلْحَيَوٰةِ ٱلدُّنْيَا}$$

"O you who believe, when you go out in the path of Allaah (to fight) verify (the truth) and say not to anyone who gives you the (the Muslim greeting of) peace, 'You are not a believer,' seeking by that the goods of the worldly life…" (verse: 94)

قال الإمام البخاري ﵀ (4591): حدثني علي بن عبد الله حدثنا سفيان عن عمرو عن عطاء عن ابن عباس ﵄: (وَلَا تَقُولُواْ لِمَنْ أَلْقَىٰٓ إِلَيْكُمُ ٱلسَّلَٰمَ لَسْتَ مُؤْمِنًا) قال: قال ابن عباس: كان رجل في غنيمة له فلحقه المسلمون فقال: السلام عليكم فقتلوه وأخذوا غنيمته فأنزل الله في ذلك إلى قوله: (عَرَضَ ٱلْحَيَوٰةِ ٱلدُّنْيَا) تلك الغنيمة. قال: قرأ ابن عباس: السلام.

On Ibn 'Abbaas ﵄:

$$\text{وَلَا تَقُولُواْ لِمَنْ أَلْقَىٰٓ إِلَيْكُمُ ٱلسَّلَٰمَ لَسْتَ مُؤْمِنًا}$$

"And say not to anyone who gives you the (the Muslim greeting of) peace, "You are not a believer."

Ibn 'Abbaas ﵄ said, "A man was tending a small flock of his sheep when some Muslims caught up with him. So he said, '*As-Salaamu 'Alaikum.*' They then killed him and took his small flock of sheep. Because of that Allaah then sent down the verse up to His statement,

---

[59] Taibah is one of the names of Madeenah. Refer to *Fathul-Baaree* in the explanation of *hadeeth* (1872) for more on the different names of Madeenah.

$$\text{عَرَضَ ٱلْحَيَوٰةِ ٱلدُّنْيَا}$$

'The goods of the worldly life…'

(Meaning), that small flock of sheep." He ('Ataa the narrator on Ibn 'Abbaas) said, "Ibn 'Abbaas recited: السلام."

Al-Bukhaaree transmitted this *hadeeth* in his *Saheeh* (4591) as well as Muslim in his *Saheeh* (3025).

قال الإمام أحمد ﷺ (ج 6 ص 11): ثنا يعقوب ثنا أبي عن ابن إسحاق حدثني يزيد بن عبد الله بن قسيط عن القعقاع بن عبد الله بن أبي حدرد عن أبيه عبد الله بن أبي حدرد ﷺ قال: بعثنا رسول الله ﷺ إلى إضم فخرجت في نفر من المسلمين فيهم أبو قتادة الحارث ابن ربعي ومُحلِّم بن جثامة بن قيس فخرجنا حتى إذا كنا ببطن إضم مر بنا عامر الأشجعي على قعود له متيع ووطب من لبن فلما مر بنا سلم علينا فأمسكنا عنه وحمل عليه محلم بن جثامة فقتله بشيء كان بينه وبينه وأخذ بعيره ومتيعه فلما قدمنا على رسول الله ﷺ وأخبرناه الخبر نزل فينا القرآن: (يَا أَيُّهَا ٱلَّذِينَ ءَامَنُوٓا۟ إِذَا ضَرَبْتُمْ فِى سَبِيلِ ٱللَّهِ فَتَبَيَّنُوا۟ وَلَا تَقُولُوا۟ لِمَنْ أَلْقَىٰٓ إِلَيْكُمُ ٱلسَّلَٰمَ لَسْتَ مُؤْمِنًا تَبْتَغُونَ عَرَضَ ٱلْحَيَوٰةِ ٱلدُّنْيَا فَعِندَ ٱللَّهِ مَغَانِمُ كَثِيرَةٌ كَذَٰلِكَ كُنتُم مِّن قَبْلُ فَمَنَّ ٱللَّهُ عَلَيْكُمْ فَتَبَيَّنُوٓا۟ إِنَّ ٱللَّهَ كَانَ بِمَا تَعْمَلُونَ خَبِيرًا).

'Abdullaah ibn Abee Hadrad ﷺ said, "The Messenger of Allaah ﷺ sent us to Idam.[60] I set out with a group of the Muslims, amongst them was Abu Qataadah Al-Haarith ibn Rib'ee and Muhallim ibn Jath'thaamah ibn Qais. Then when we reached Idam, 'Aamir Al-Ashja'ee passed by us riding a small camel with a milk-skin and some small provisions. While passing by he gave us the greeting of *salaam* but we refrained from (returning the greeting to him). Muhallim ibn Jath'thaamah then attacked him and killed him because of something personal between them. He took his camel and his provisions. When we returned to the Messenger of Allaah ﷺ and told him what happened, we found that Qur'aan had descended because of us:

يَا أَيُّهَا ٱلَّذِينَ ءَامَنُوٓا۟ إِذَا ضَرَبْتُمْ فِى سَبِيلِ ٱللَّهِ فَتَبَيَّنُوا۟ وَلَا تَقُولُوا۟ لِمَنْ أَلْقَىٰٓ إِلَيْكُمُ ٱلسَّلَٰمَ لَسْتَ مُؤْمِنًا تَبْتَغُونَ عَرَضَ ٱلْحَيَوٰةِ ٱلدُّنْيَا فَعِندَ ٱللَّهِ مَغَانِمُ كَثِيرَةٌ

---

[60] Idam is a place north of Madeenah behind the mountain Uhud where the valleys of Madeenah meet.

$$\text{كَذَٰلِكَ كُنتُم مِّن قَبْلُ فَمَنَّ ٱللَّهُ عَلَيْكُمْ فَتَبَيَّنُوٓا۟ ۚ إِنَّ ٱللَّهَ كَانَ بِمَا تَعْمَلُونَ خَبِيرًا}$$

"O you who believe, when you go out in the path of Allaah (to fight), verify (the truth) and say not to anyone who gives you the (the Muslim greeting of) peace, "You are not a believer," seeking by that the goods of the worldly life for there are many spoils with Allaah. The way he is now so were you yourselves beforehand, then Allaah conferred His favor upon you. Therefore, verify. Indeed Allaah is aware of what you do."

Regarding this *hadeeth*, Al-Imaam Ahmad transmitted it in his *Musnad*, volume 6, page 11. Ash-Sheikh Muqbil said about it, "The *hadeeth* is *hasan li ghairihi*…" Al-Haafidh Ibn Hajar said in *Fathul-Baaree* in the explanation of *hadeeth* (4591), "This to me is a different story, however, there is nothing which prevents the verse from being revealed because of both stories."

His, the Exalted One's statement:

$$\text{لَّا يَسْتَوِى ٱلْقَٰعِدُونَ مِنَ ٱلْمُؤْمِنِينَ غَيْرُ أُو۟لِى ٱلضَّرَرِ وَٱلْمُجَٰهِدُونَ فِى سَبِيلِ ٱللَّهِ بِأَمْوَٰلِهِمْ وَأَنفُسِهِمْ ۚ فَضَّلَ ٱللَّهُ ٱلْمُجَٰهِدِينَ بِأَمْوَٰلِهِمْ وَأَنفُسِهِمْ عَلَى ٱلْقَٰعِدِينَ دَرَجَةً}$$

"Not equal are those of the believers who remain (at home), except those who are disabled, and those who fight in the cause of Allaah with their wealth and their lives. Allaah has preferred in grades those who fight with their wealth and their lives above those who remain (at home)…" (verse: 95)

قال الإمام البخاري رحمه الله (2831): حدثنا أبو الوليد حدثنا شعبة عن أبي إسحاق قال سمعت البراء رضي الله عنه يقول: لما نزلت: (لَّا يَسْتَوِى ٱلْقَٰعِدُونَ مِنَ ٱلْمُؤْمِنِينَ) دعا رسول الله ﷺ زيدا فجاءه بكتف فكتبها وشكا ابن أم مكتوم ضرارته فنزلت: (لَّا يَسْتَوِى ٱلْقَٰعِدُونَ مِنَ ٱلْمُؤْمِنِينَ غَيْرُ أُو۟لِى ٱلضَّرَرِ).

Al-Baraa said, "When this verse descended,

$$\text{لَّا يَسْتَوِى ٱلْقَٰعِدُونَ مِنَ ٱلْمُؤْمِنِينَ}$$

'Not equal are those of the believers who remain (at home)…'

The Messenger of Allaah ﷺ called for Zaid who came to him with a shoulder bone and wrote the verse on it. Ibn Ummi Maktoom then complained about his disability and thereafter the following descended:

$$ لَّا يَسْتَوِى ٱلْقَٰعِدُونَ مِنَ ٱلْمُؤْمِنِينَ غَيْرُ أُو۟لِى ٱلضَّرَرِ $$

"Not equal are those of the believers who remain (at home), except those who are disabled…"

In regards to this *hadeeth*, Al-Bukhaaree transmitted it in his *Saheeh* (2831) and Muslim in his *Saheeh* (1898).

قال الإمام البخاري رَحِمَهُ اللهُ (2832): حدثنا عبد العزيز بن عبد الله حدثنا إبراهيم بن سعد الزهري قال حدثني صالح بن كيسان عن ابن شهاب عن سهل بن سعد الساعدي ﷺ أنه قال: رأيت مروان بن الحكم جالسا في المسجد فأقبلت حتى جلست إلى جنبه فأخبرنا أن زيد بن ثابت أخبره أن رسول الله ﷺ أملى عليّ: لا يستوي القاعدون من المؤمنين والمجاهدون في سبيل الله قال: فجاءه ابن أم مكتوم وهو يملّها عليّ فقال: يا رسول الله لو أستطيع الجهاد لجاهدت وكان رجلا أعمى فأنزل الله تبارك وتعالى على رسوله ﷺ فخذه على فخذي فثقلت عليّ حتى خفت أن ترضّ فخذي ثم سرّي عنه فأنزل الله عز وجل: (غَيْرُ أُو۟لِى ٱلضَّرَرِ).

Sahl ibn Sa'd As-Saa'idee ﷺ said, "I saw Marwaan ibn Al-Hakam sitting in the *masjid* so I went to him and sat at his side. He then narrated to us that Zaid ibn Thaabit narrated to him (saying), "The Messenger of Allaah ﷺ dictated to me:

لا يستوي القاعدون من المؤمنين والمجاهدون في سبيل الله

'Not equal are those of the believers who remain (at home) and those who fight in the cause of Allaah…'

Ibn Ummi Maktoom, who was a blind man, came to him while he was dictating it to me and said, "O Messenger of Allaah, if I were able to fight I would have fought." Then Allaah ﷻ sent down revelation to His Messenger ﷺ while his thigh was resting on my thigh. It became extremely heavy on me to the point that I became scared that my thigh would be crushed. Then it passed and Allaah ﷻ sent down:

$$ غَيْرُ أُو۟لِى ٱلضَّرَرِ $$

"Except those who are disabled.""

This *hadeeth*, Al-Bukhaaree transmitted it in his *Saheeh* (2832).

قال الإمام ابن حبان ﵀ كما في الإحسان (ج 7 ص 105-106): أخبرنا أحمد بن علي بن المثنى حدثنا إبراهيم بن الحجاج السامي حدثنا عبد الواحد بن زياد حدثنا عاصم بن كليب حدثني أبي عن خالي الفَلَتَان بن عاصم ﵁ قال: كنا عند النبي ﷺ فأنزل عليه وكان إذا أنزل عليه رام ببصره وفرغ سمعه وقلبه مفتوحة عيناه لما يأتيه من الله فكنا نعرف ذلك فقال للكاتب: اكتب: لا يستوي القاعدون من المؤمنين والمجاهدون في سبيل الله قال: فقام الأعمى فقال: يا رسول الله ما ذنبنا فأنزل الله تعالى عليه فقلنا للأعمى: إنه ينزل على النبي ﷺ فبقي قائما ويقول: أعوذ بالله من غضب رسول الله ﷺ قال: فقال النبي ﷺ للكاتب: اكتب: (غَيْرُ أُولِي ٱلضَّرَرِ).

Al-Falataan ibn 'Aasim ؓ said, "We were with the Prophet ﷺ while revelation was sent down to him. When revelation was sent down to him he would lose his eyesight while his two eyes remained open, and his hearing and his heart would be occupied with what has come from Allaah. This would be something recognizable. Then he said to the scribe, 'Write:

لا يستوي القاعدون من المؤمنين والمجاهدون في سبيل الله

"Not equal are those of the believers who remain (at home) and those who fight in the cause of Allaah…"'

The blind man then stood up and said, "O Messenger of Allaah, what is our sin?" Then Allaah ﷻ sent down revelation to him and we said to the blind man, 'Verily revelation is being sent down to the Prophet ﷺ.' So he remained standing while saying, "I seek refuge in Allaah from the anger of the Messenger of Allaah ﷺ!" Then the Prophet ﷺ said to the scribe, 'Write:

غَيْرُ أُولِي ٱلضَّرَرِ

"Except those who are disabled."'

This *hadeeth* has been transmitted by Ibn Hibbaan as mentioned in *Al-Ihsaan*, volume 7, pages 105-106. Ash-Sheikh Muqbil ﵀ said, "This is a *hasan hadeeth*…".

قال الإمام الترمذي ﵀ (3032): حدثنا الحسن بن محمد الزعفراني نا الحجاج بن محمد عن ابن جريج قال أخبرني عبد الكريم سمع مقسما مولى عبد الله بن الحارث يحدث عن ابن عباس ﵄ أنه قال: (لَّا يَسْتَوِى ٱلْقَٰعِدُونَ مِنَ ٱلْمُؤْمِنِينَ غَيْرُ أُولِى ٱلضَّرَرِ) عن بدر والخارجون إلى بدر لما نزلت غزوة بدر قال عبد الله بن جحش وابن أم مكتوم: إنا أعميان يا رسول الله فهل لنا رخصة فنزلت:

(لَّا يَسْتَوِى ٱلْقَٰعِدُونَ مِنَ ٱلْمُؤْمِنِينَ غَيْرُ أُولِى ٱلضَّرَرِ وَٱلْمُجَٰهِدُونَ فِى سَبِيلِ ٱللَّهِ بِأَمْوَٰلِهِمْ

وَأَنفُسِهِمْ ۚ فَضَّلَ ٱللَّهُ ٱلْمُجَٰهِدِينَ بِأَمْوَٰلِهِمْ وَأَنفُسِهِمْ عَلَى ٱلْقَٰعِدِينَ دَرَجَةً) فهؤلاء القاعدون غير أولي الضرر (وَفَضَّلَ ٱللَّهُ ٱلْمُجَٰهِدِينَ عَلَى ٱلْقَٰعِدِينَ أَجْرًا عَظِيمًا) درجات منه على القاعدين من المؤمنين غير أولي الضرر.

Ibn 'Abbaas said:

لَّا يَسْتَوِى ٱلْقَٰعِدُونَ مِنَ ٱلْمُؤْمِنِينَ غَيْرُ أُو۟لِى ٱلضَّرَرِ

"Not equal are those of the believers who remain (at home), except those who are disabled…" '(Meaning) those who stayed behind from the battle of Badr and those who went out to Badr. When the battle of Badr occurred, 'Abdullaah ibn Jahsh[61] and Ibn Ummi Maktoom said, "Verily we are blind, O Messenger of Allaah. So are we excused?" Then it descended:

لَّا يَسْتَوِى ٱلْقَٰعِدُونَ مِنَ ٱلْمُؤْمِنِينَ غَيْرُ أُو۟لِى ٱلضَّرَرِ وَٱلْمُجَٰهِدُونَ فِى سَبِيلِ ٱللَّهِ بِأَمْوَٰلِهِمْ وَأَنفُسِهِمْ ۚ فَضَّلَ ٱللَّهُ ٱلْمُجَٰهِدِينَ بِأَمْوَٰلِهِمْ وَأَنفُسِهِمْ عَلَى ٱلْقَٰعِدِينَ دَرَجَةً

"Not equal are those of the believers who remain (at home), except those who are disabled, and those who fight in the cause of Allaah with their wealth and their lives. Allaah has preferred in grades those who fight with their wealth and their lives above those who remain (at home)…"[62]

These are those who stay behind while they are not disabled.

وَفَضَّلَ ٱللَّهُ ٱلْمُجَٰهِدِينَ عَلَى ٱلْقَٰعِدِينَ أَجْرًا عَظِيمًا

"And Allaah has preferred those who fight above those who remain (at home) with a great reward." [Meaning] Grades above those who stay behind while they are not disabled."'

At-Tirmidhee transmitted this *hadeeth* in his *Jaami'* (3032) and classified it to be *hasan ghareeb*.

---

[61] In a different narration of this *hadeeth* he was named: Abu Ahmad ibn Jahsh, and this is what is correct. As for 'Abdullaah, he was not blind as Ibn Hajar explained in *Fathul-Baaree* in the explanation of *hadeeth* (4595).

[62] From this point to the end of the *hadeeth* is not from Ibn 'Abbaas, rather it is from Ibn Juraij, one of the narrators in the chain, as Ibn Hajar mentioned in *Fathul-Baaree* in the explanation of *hadeeth* (4595).

His, the Exalted One's statement:

$$\text{إِنَّ الَّذِينَ تَوَفَّاهُمُ الْمَلَائِكَةُ ظَالِمِي أَنفُسِهِمْ قَالُوا فِيمَ كُنتُمْ ۖ قَالُوا كُنَّا مُسْتَضْعَفِينَ فِي الْأَرْضِ}$$

"Verily those whom the angels take at death while they are wronging themselves, they (the angels) say, "In what condition were you?" They reply, "We were weak and oppressed on the earth…" (verse: 97)

قال الإمام البخاري رحمه الله (4596): حدثنا عبد الله بن يزيد المقرئ حدثنا حيوة وغيره قالا حدثنا محمد بن عبد الرحمن أبو الأسود قال: قطع على أهل المدينة بعث فاكتتبت فيه فلقيت عكرمة مولى ابن عباس فأخبرته فنهاني عن ذلك أشد النهي ثم قال: أخبرني ابن عباس رضي الله عنهما أن ناسا من المسلمين كانوا مع المشركين يكثرون سواد المشركين على رسول الله ﷺ يأتي السهم يرمى به فيصيب أحدهم فيقتله أو يضرب فيقتل فأنزل الله: (إِنَّ الَّذِينَ تَوَفَّاهُمُ الْمَلَائِكَةُ ظَالِمِي أَنفُسِهِمْ) الآية. رواه الليث عن أبي الأسود.

Muhammad ibn 'Abdir-Rahmaan Abu Al-Aswad said, "The people of Madeenah were forced to form an army[63] and I was registered to be in it. I then met 'Ikrimah Mawlaa Ibn 'Abbaas and told him about that. He strictly forbade me from doing that and said, 'Ibn 'Abbaas narrated to me that some Muslims used to be with the polytheists (on the battleground) increasing the numbers of the polytheists against the Messenger of Allaah ﷺ. An arrow would be shot hitting and killing one of them or one of them would be struck (by a sword) and killed. Then Allaah sent down:

$$\text{إِنَّ الَّذِينَ تَوَفَّاهُمُ الْمَلَائِكَةُ ظَالِمِي أَنفُسِهِمْ}$$

"Verily those whom the angels take at death while they are wronging themselves…'" (verse 97).

Regarding this *hadeeth*, Al-Bukhaaree transmitted it in his *Saheeh* (4596).

---

[63] Ibn Hajar said in *Fathul-Baaree* in the explanation of this *hadeeth*, "The meaning of this is that they were forced to form an army to go fight the people of Shaam (Syria) at the time when 'Abdullaah ibn Az-Zubair was the leader in Makkah…and in this story is a proof that 'Ikrimah is free from what has been attributed to him that he had the ideology of the *Khawaarij*, for verily he went to the extreme in the prohibition against fighting the Muslims and of increasing the numbers of those who fight them."

His, the Exalted One's statement:

$$\text{وَمَن يَخْرُجْ مِنْ بَيْتِهِ مُهَاجِرًا إِلَى ٱللَّهِ وَرَسُولِهِ ثُمَّ يُدْرِكْهُ ٱلْمَوْتُ فَقَدْ وَقَعَ أَجْرُهُ عَلَى ٱللَّهِ}$$

"And whoever leaves his home migrating to Allaah and His Messenger and then death overtakes him, his reward has become incumbent upon Allaah…" (verse: 100)

قال الإمام ابن جرير ﷺ (ج 9 ص 118): حدثنا أحمد بن منصور الرمادي قال حدثنا أبو أحمد الزبيدي قال حدثنا شريك عن عمرو بن دينار عن عكرمة عن ابن عباس ﷺ قال: نزلت هذه الآية: (إِنَّ ٱلَّذِينَ تَوَفَّىٰهُمُ ٱلْمَلَٰٓئِكَةُ ظَالِمِىٓ أَنفُسِهِمْ) وكان بمكة رجل يقال له ضمرة من بني بكر وكان مريضا فقال لأهله: أخرجوني من مكة فإني أجد الحر فقالوا: أين نخرجك فأشار بيده نحو المدينة فنزلت هذه الآية: (وَمَن يَخْرُجْ مِنْ بَيْتِهِ مُهَاجِرًا إِلَى ٱللَّهِ وَرَسُولِهِ) إلى آخر الآية.

Ibn 'Abbaas ﷺ said, "The following verse descended:

$$\text{إِنَّ ٱلَّذِينَ تَوَفَّىٰهُمُ ٱلْمَلَٰٓئِكَةُ ظَالِمِىٓ أَنفُسِهِمْ}$$

"Verily those whom the angels take at death while they are wronging themselves…" while there was a man in Makkah called Damrah, from the tribe Banee Bakr. He was sick so he said to his family, 'Get me out of Makkah, for verily I feel the fever.' They said, "Where should we move you to?" He then pointed with his hand towards Madeenah. Then this verse descended:

$$\text{وَمَن يَخْرُجْ مِنْ بَيْتِهِ مُهَاجِرًا إِلَى ٱللَّهِ وَرَسُولِهِ}$$

"And whoever leaves his home migrating to Allaah and His Messenger…" up to the end of the verse."

This *hadeeth* has been transmitted by Ibn Jareer in his *Tafseer*, volume 9, page 118. Ash-Sheikh Muqbil ﷺ discerned that the correct position regarding this *hadeeth* is that it is *mursal*. However, he then mentioned that the *hadeeth* has other chains. Refer to the *Musnad* of Abu Ya'laa, *hadeeth* (2679), and the *Tafseer* of Ibn Katheer, volume 1, page 543, and the book *Al-Isaabah* by Ibn Hajar in the biography of Janda' ibn Damrah.

His, the Exalted One's statement:

$$\text{وَلَا جُنَاحَ عَلَيْكُمْ إِن كَانَ بِكُمْ أَذًى مِّن مَّطَرٍ أَوْ كُنتُم مَّرْضَىٰٓ أَن تَضَعُوٓا۟ أَسْلِحَتَكُمْ}$$

"And there is no sin on you for putting down your arms if you are inconvenienced by rain or if you are ill…" (verse: 102)

قال الإمام البخاري ﷺ (4599): حدثنا محمد بن مقاتل أبو الحسن أخبرنا حجاج عن ابن جريج قال أخبرني يعلى عن سعيد بن جبير عن ابن عباس ﷺ: (إِن كَانَ بِكُم أَذًى مِّن مَّطَرٍ أَوْ كُنتُم مَّرْضَىٰٓ) قال: عبد الرحمن بن عوف وكان جريحا.

On Ibn 'Abbaas ﷺ:

إِن كَانَ بِكُم أَذًى مِّن مَّطَرٍ أَوْ كُنتُم مَّرْضَىٰٓ

"If you are inconvenienced by rain or if you are ill."

He said, "That is referring to 'Abdur-Rahmaan ibn 'Awf. He was wounded."

Regarding this *hadeeth*, Al-Bukhaaree transmitted it in his *Saheeh* (4599) and Al-Haakim in *Al-Mustadrak*, volume 2, page 308. In *Al-Mustadrak* it was clearly stated that the verse descended because of 'Abdur-Rahmaan ibn 'Awf when he was wounded.

His, the Exalted One's statement:

وَلَآمُرَنَّهُمْ فَلَيُغَيِّرُنَّ خَلْقَ ٱللَّهِ

"And I will order them so they will change what Allaah has created…" (verse: 119)

قال الإمام ابن جرير ﷺ (ج 9 ص 215): حدثنا محمد بن بشار قال حدثنا عبد الرحمن قال حدثنا حماد بن سلمة عن عمار بن أبي عمار عن ابن عباس ﷺ أنه كره الإخصاء وقال: فيه نزلت: (وَلَآمُرَنَّهُمْ فَلَيُغَيِّرُنَّ خَلْقَ ٱللَّهِ).

Ibn 'Abbaas ﷺ used to dislike the practice of castrating animals and he said, "Because of that [practice] the verse descended,

وَلَآمُرَنَّهُمْ فَلَيُغَيِّرُنَّ خَلْقَ ٱللَّهِ

"And I will order them so they will change what Allaah has created…"

In regards to this *hadeeth*, Ibn Jareer transmitted it in his *Tafseer*, volume 9, page 215. Ash-Sheikh Muqbil ﷺ commented, "This hadeeth is *saheeh*, according to the standards of Muslim."

His, the Exalted One's statement:

$$وَيَسْتَفْتُونَكَ فِي ٱلنِّسَآءِ ۖ قُلِ ٱللَّهُ يُفْتِيكُمْ فِيهِنَّ$$

"They ask for your legal ruling concerning women. Say, Allaah gives you the ruling about them…" (verse: 127)

قال الإمام البخاري رَحِمَهُ اللهُ (2494): حدثنا الأويسي حدثنا إبراهيم بن سعد عن صالح عن ابن شهاب قال أخبرني عروة أنه سأل عائشة رَضِيَ اللهُ عَنْهَا وقال الليث حدثني يونس عن ابن شهاب قال أخبرني عروة بن الزبير أنه سأل عائشة رَضِيَ اللهُ عَنْهَا عن قول الله تعالى: (وَإِنْ خِفْتُمْ أَلَّا تُقْسِطُوا فِي ٱلْيَتَـٰمَىٰ) ، فذكرت له نحو ما تقدم في أول السورة ، قال عروة: قالت عائشة: ثم إن الناس استفتوا رسول الله ﷺ بعد هذه الآية فأنزل الله: (وَيَسْتَفْتُونَكَ فِي ٱلنِّسَآءِ) إلى قوله تعالى: (وَتَرْغَبُونَ أَن تَنكِحُوهُنَّ) الحديث.

'Urwah ibn Az-Zubair asked 'Aishah ؓ about the statement of Allaah ﷻ:

$$وَإِنْ خِفْتُمْ أَلَّا تُقْسِطُوا۟ فِى ٱلْيَتَـٰمَىٰ$$

"And if you fear that you will not be able to deal justly with the orphan girls…" (*An-Nisaa*: 3). (She then mentioned to him a *hadeeth* similar to what was earlier mentioned in the beginning of this *Soorah*) 'Urwah said, "'Aishah stated, 'Then the people asked the Messenger of Allaah ﷺ for the legal ruling after this verse had already been revealed. Then Allaah sent down:

$$وَيَسْتَفْتُونَكَ فِى ٱلنِّسَآءِ$$

"They ask for your legal ruling concerning women…"

up to His ﷻ statement:

$$وَتَرْغَبُونَ أَن تَنكِحُوهُنَّ$$

"And yet you desire to marry them."

As for this *hadeeth*, Al-Bukhaaree transmitted it in his *Saheeh* (2494) and Muslim in his *Saheeh* (3018). The *hadeeth* has been abbreviated with only its highlighting point mentioned.

His, the Exalted One's statement:

$$وَإِنِ ٱمْرَأَةٌ خَافَتْ مِنْ بَعْلِهَا نُشُوزًا أَوْ إِعْرَاضًا فَلَا جُنَاحَ عَلَيْهِمَا أَن يُصْلِحَا بَيْنَهُمَا صُلْحًا$$

"And if a woman fears from her husband mistreatment or desertion, there is no sin on them if they make a settlement between themselves…"
(verse: 128)

قال الإمام البخاري ﵀ (4601): حدثنا محمد بن مقاتل أخبرنا عبد الله أخبرنا هشام بن عروة عن أبيه عن عائشة ﵂: (وَإِنِ ٱمْرَأَةٌ خَافَتْ مِنْ بَعْلِهَا نُشُوزًا أَوْ إِعْرَاضًا) قالت: الرجل تكون عنده المرأة ليس بمستكثر منها يريد أن يفارقها فتقول: أجعلك من شأني في حل فنزلت هذه الآية في ذلك.

On 'Aishah ﵂:

وَإِنِ ٱمْرَأَةٌ خَافَتْ مِنْ بَعْلِهَا نُشُوزًا أَوْ إِعْرَاضًا

[Regarding the verse] "And if a woman fears from her husband mistreatment or desertion…"
She said, "A man has a wife whom he does not love a lot nor does he associate closely with her. He wants to divorce her so she says, 'I give you the advantage to deal freely concerning me.'[64] So this verse descended pertaining to that."

Al-Bukhaaree transmitted this *hadeeth* in his *Saheeh* (4601) and Muslim in his *Saheeh* (3021).

قال الإمام أبو داود ﵀ (2135): حدثنا أحمد بن يونس ثنا عبد الرحمن يعني ابن أبي الزناد عن هشام بن عروة عن أبيه قال قالت عائشة ﵂: يابن أختي كان رسول الله ﷺ لا يفضل بعضنا على بعض في القسم من مكثه عندنا وكان قل يوم إلا وهو يطوف علينا جميعا فيدنو من كل امرأة من غير مسيس حتى يبلغ إلى التي هو يومها فيبيت عندها ولقد قالت سودة بنت زمعة حين أسنت وفرقت أن يفارقها رسول الله ﷺ: يا رسول الله يومي لعائشة فقبل ذلك رسول الله ﷺ منها قالت: نقول: في ذلك أنزل الله تعالى وفي أشباهها أراه قال: (وَإِنِ ٱمْرَأَةٌ خَافَتْ مِنْ بَعْلِهَا نُشُوزًا).

'Aishah ﵂ said to 'Urwah, "O son of my sister, the Messenger of Allaah ﷺ did not give preference to some of us (his wives) over the others in the division of time he would spend with us. There would not be a day except that he would make a round visiting all of us. He would spend time with each wife without having sexual relations until he reached the one whose day it was. Then he would spend the night with her. When Sawdah bint Zam'ah grew old and was scared that the Messenger of Allaah ﷺ might divorce her, she said, 'O Messenger of Allaah, I give my day to 'Aishah,' and the Messenger of Allaah ﷺ accepted that from her."

---

[64] Meaning do as you want with regards to being intimate towards me, but do not divorce me. Refer to the narration of this *hadeeth* in Muslim (3021).

She ('Aishah) went on saying, "We say, because of her and those like her, Allaah ﷻ sent down:

$$وَإِنِ ٱمْرَأَةٌ خَافَتْ مِنْ بَعْلِهَا نُشُوزًا$$

"And if a woman fears from her husband mistreatment…"

Regarding this *hadeeth*, Abu Daawud transmitted it in *As-Sunan* (2135). Ash-Sheikh Muqbil ﷺ said, "There is no contradiction between these narrations, for verily the first *hadeeth* of 'Aishah is vague and the second *hadeeth* of hers clarifies that vagueness…"

His, the Exalted One's statement:

$$يَسْتَفْتُونَكَ قُلِ ٱللَّهُ يُفْتِيكُمْ فِى ٱلْكَلَٰلَةِ$$

"They ask you for a legal ruling. Say, Allaah gives you the legal ruling about *Al-Kalaalah*[65]…" (verse: 176)

قال الإمام مسلم ﷺ (1616 / 5): حدثنا عمرو بن محمد بن بكير الناقد حدثنا سفيان بن عيينة عن محمد بن المنكدر سمع جابر بن عبد الله ﷺ قال: مرضت فأتاني رسول الله ﷺ وأبو بكر يعوداني ماشيان فأغمي عليّ فتوضأ ثم صب عليّ من وَضوئه فأفقت قلت:

يا رسول الله كيف أقضي في مالي فلم يرد عليّ شيئًا حتى نزلت آية الميراث: (يَسْتَفْتُونَكَ قُلِ ٱللَّهُ يُفْتِيكُمْ فِى ٱلْكَلَٰلَةِ).

Jaabir ibn 'Abdillaah ﷺ said, "I became ill so the Messenger of Allaah ﷺ and Abu Bakr walked over to visit me. I was unconscious so he ﷺ made ablution and poured the water from his ablution over me. I then regained consciousness and said, "O Messenger of Allaah, how should I distribute my wealth?" He did not respond until the verse of inheritance descended:

$$يَسْتَفْتُونَكَ قُلِ ٱللَّهُ يُفْتِيكُمْ فِى ٱلْكَلَٰلَةِ$$

"They ask you for a legal ruling. Say, Allaah gives you the legal ruling about *Al-Kalaalah*…"

Muslim transmitted This *hadeeth* in his *Saheeh* (1616/5). It has already preceded that in another narration of this *hadeeth* the following verse descended:

---

[65] *Al-Kalaalah*: The majority of the Scholars say *Al-Kalaalah* is the person who dies leaving neither children nor parents to inherit from him thus the inheritance is divided among the other relatives. Refer to *Fathul-Baaree* in the explanation of *hadeeth* (6744) and *Tafseer Ibn Katheer* in the explanation of *Soorah An-Nisaa*, verse 12.

$$\text{يُوصِيكُمُ ٱللَّهُ فِىٓ أَوْلَٰدِكُمْ}$$

"Allaah commands you concerning your children's (inheritance)…"

(*An-Nisaa*: 11) Ash-Sheikh Muqbil ﷺ said, "There is nothing which prevents the two verses from being revealed together at the same time because of the story of Jaabir…"

سورة المائدة

Sooratul-Maa'idah

<u>His, the Exalted One's statement:</u>

يَـٰٓأَيُّهَا ٱلَّذِينَ ءَامَنُوٓا۟ إِذَا قُمْتُمْ إِلَى ٱلصَّلَوٰةِ فَٱغْسِلُوا۟ وُجُوهَكُمْ

"O you who believe, when you intend to offer prayer wash your faces..." (verse: 6)

قال الإمام البخاري رحمه الله (334): حدثنا عبد الله بن يوسف قال أخبرنا مالك عن عبد الرحمن ابن القاسم عن أبيه عن عائشة رضي الله عنها زوج النبي ﷺ قالت: خرجنا مع رسول الله ﷺ في بعض أسفاره حتى إذا كنا بالبيداء أو بذات الجيش انقطع عقد لي فأقام رسول الله ﷺ على التماسه وأقام الناس معه وليسوا على ماء فأتى الناس إلى أبي بكر الصديق فقالوا: ألا ترى ما صنعت عائشة أقامت برسول الله ﷺ والناس وليسوا على ماء وليس معهم ماء فجاء أبو بكر ورسول الله ﷺ واضع رأسه على فخذي قد نام فقال: حبست رسول الله ﷺ والناس وليسوا على ماء وليس معهم ماء فقالت عائشة: فعاتبني أبو بكر وقال ما شاء الله أن يقول وجعل يطعنني بيده في خاصرتي فلا يمنعني من التحرك إلا مكان رسول الله ﷺ على فخذي فقام رسول الله ﷺ حين أصبح على غير ماء فأنزل الله آية التيمم فتيمموا فقال أسيد ابن الحضير: ما هي بأول بركتكم يا آل أبي بكر قالت: فبعثنا البعير الذي كنت عليه فأصبنا العقد تحته.

'Aishah ؓ said, "We went with the Messenger of Allaah ﷺ on one of his journeys. When we reached Al-Baidaa or Dhaat Al-Jaish[66] a necklace[67] of mine broke off. The Messenger of Allaah ﷺ stopped to look for it and the people stopped with him. They were at a place that had no water. So the people went to Abu Bakr As-Siddeeq and said, 'Do you not see what 'Aishah has done? She has halted the Messenger of Allaah ﷺ and the people at a place that has no water, nor do they have water with them!'

Abu Bakr then came to me while the Messenger of Allaah ﷺ was sleeping with his head resting on my thigh. He said, "You have held back the Messenger of Allaah ﷺ and the people while they are at a place that has no water, nor do they have any water with them!" Abu Bakr reprimanded me saying what Allaah willed for him to say and he started to poke me with his hand on my hip. The only thing which prevented me from moving was the

---

[66] Al-Baidaa and Dhaat Al-Jaish are two places outside Madeenah on the path to Makkah.
[67] It was clarified in another narration of this *hadeeth* that the necklace belonged to her sister Asmaa who loaned it to 'Aishah.

Messenger of Allaah ﷺ on my thigh. In the morning the Messenger of Allaah ﷺ woke up at that place that had no water. Then Allaah sent down the verse of *At-Tayammum*[68] and they made *Tayammum*. Usaid ibn Al-Hudair then said, 'This is not the first blessing that has come because of you, O family of Abu Bakr.' We then urged the camel I was riding to get up and we found the necklace under it."

Al-Bukhaaree has transmitted this *hadeeth* in his *Saheeh* (334) and Muslim in his *Saheeh* (367). The verse of *At-Tayammum* was specified in another narration of this *hadeeth* in Al-Bukhaaree (4608) which reads, "Then it descended:

$$\text{يَا أَيُّهَا ٱلَّذِينَ ءَامَنُوٓا۟ إِذَا قُمْتُمْ إِلَى ٱلصَّلَوٰةِ}$$

'O you who believe, when you intend to offer prayer…' (Verse: 6).

His, the Exalted One's statement:

$$\text{إِنَّمَا جَزَٰٓؤُا۟ ٱلَّذِينَ يُحَارِبُونَ ٱللَّهَ وَرَسُولَهُۥ وَيَسْعَوْنَ فِى ٱلْأَرْضِ فَسَادًا}$$

"The recompense of those who wage war against Allaah and His Messenger and do mischief in the land…" (verse: 33)

قال الإمام أبو داود رحمه الله (4366): حدثنا محمد بن الصباح بن سفيان قال أخبرنا ح وثنا عمرو بن عثمان ثنا الوليد عن الأوزاعي عن يحيى يعني بن أبي كثير عن أبي قلابة عن أنس ابن مالك رضي الله عنه بهذا الحديث قال فيه: فبعث رسول الله ﷺ في طلبهم قافة فأتى بهم قال: فأنزل الله تبارك وتعالى في ذلك: (إِنَّمَا جَزَٰٓؤُا۟ ٱلَّذِينَ يُحَارِبُونَ ٱللَّهَ وَرَسُولَهُۥ وَيَسْعَوْنَ فِى ٱلْأَرْضِ فَسَادًا) الآية.

Anas ibn Maalik ؓ mentioned this *hadeeth*[69] and he said about it, "So the Messenger of Allaah ﷺ dispatched a search party to capture them and they

---

[68] *At-Tayammum* is the ritual of wiping the hands and face with dirt instead of making ablution when one is excused from making ablution.

[69] Abu Daawud is referring to *hadeeth* (4364) which he mentioned before this *hadeeth*:

قال الإمام أبو داود رحمه الله (4364): حدثنا سليمان بن حرب ثنا حماد عن أيوب عن أبي قلابة عن أنس بن مالك رضي الله عنه أن قوما من عكل أو قال من عرينة قدموا على رسول الله ﷺ فاجتووا المدينة فأمر لهم رسول الله ﷺ بلقاح وأمرهم أن يشربوا من أبوالها وألبانها فانطلقوا فلما صحوا قتلوا راعي رسول الله ﷺ واستاقوا النعم فبلغ النبي ﷺ خبرهم من أول النهار فأرسل النبي ﷺ في آثارهم فما ارتفع النهار حتى جيء بهم فأمر بهم فقطعت أيديهم وأرجلهم وسمر أعينهم وألقوا في الحرة يستسقون فلا يسقون قال أبو قلابة: فهؤلاء قوم سرقوا وقتلوا وكفروا بعد إيمانهم وحاربوا الله ورسوله.

were captured and brought back. Then Allaah ﷻ sent down, because of that, the following:

$$ \text{إِنَّمَا جَزَٰٓؤُاْ ٱلَّذِينَ يُحَارِبُونَ ٱللَّهَ وَرَسُولَهُۥ وَيَسْعَوْنَ فِى ٱلْأَرْضِ فَسَادًا} $$

"The recompense of those who wage war against Allaah and His Messenger and do mischief in the land…" (verse: 33).

Regarding this *hadeeth*, Abu Daawud transmitted it in *As-Sunan* (4366). The chain of this *hadeeth* has some weakness in it, however, in the footnote of the latest edition of the Sheikh's book it was said, "…but there are many other chains related to the reason why the verse was revealed which can be used as a proof and Ibn Jareer has mentioned them." Refer to *Tafseer Ibn Jareer*, volume 10, pages 244-246.

His, the Exalted One's statement:

$$ \text{يَٰٓأَيُّهَا ٱلرَّسُولُ لَا يَحْزُنكَ ٱلَّذِينَ يُسَٰرِعُونَ فِى ٱلْكُفْرِ} $$

"O Messenger, let not those who rush into disbelief grieve you…" (verses: 41-45).

قال الإمام مسلم رحمه الله (1700): حدثنا يحيى بن يحيى وأبو بكر بن أبي شيبة كلاهما عن أبي معاوية قال يحيى أخبرنا أبو معاوية عن الأعمش عن عبد الله بن مرة عن البراء بن عازب رضي الله عنه قال: مر على النبي ﷺ بيهودي محمما مجلودا فدعاهم ﷺ فقال: هكذا تجدون حد الزاني في كتابكم قالوا: نعم فدعا رجلا من علمائهم فقال: أنشدك بالله الذي أنزل التوراة على موسى أهكذا تجدون حد الزاني في كتابكم قال: لا ولولا أنك نشدتني بهذا لم أخبرك نجده الرجم ولكنه كثر في أشرافنا فكنا إذا أخذنا الشريف تركناه وإذا أخذنا الضعيف أقمنا عليه الحد قلنا تعالوا فلنجتمع على شيء نقيمه على الشريف والوضيع فجعلنا التحميم والجلد مكان الرجم فقال رسول الله ﷺ: اللهم إني أول من أحيا أمرك إذ

Anas ibn Maalik ؓ narrated that a group of people from 'Ukl or 'Urainah came to the Messenger of Allaah ﷺ. They had a problem with the weather of Madeenah and became sick. So the Messenger of Allaah ﷺ ordered them to go to the herd of female camels and drink from their urine and milk. They went and did that. Then when they regained their health they killed the herdsman of the Messenger of Allaah ﷺ and drove off with the camels. News of what they did reached the Prophet ﷺ first thing in the morning. So the Prophet ﷺ sent a group to track them down. They were captured and brought back before midday. He summoned them. Then he had their legs and arms cut off and their eyes gouged out with hot nails. They were cast away to Al-Harrah (a place in Madeenah covered by black rocks). They asked for drink and were not given drink. Abu Qilaabah (a narrator in the chain) said, "These were a people who stole, and committed murder, and disbelieved after having faith, and waged war against Allaah and His Messenger." This *hadeeth* is authentic and has also been transmitted by Al-Bukhaaree (233) and Muslim (1671).

أماتوه فأمر به فرجم فأنزل الله عز وجل: (يَٰٓأَيُّهَا ٱلرَّسُولُ لَا يَحْزُنكَ ٱلَّذِينَ يُسَٰرِعُونَ فِى ٱلْكُفْرِ) إلى قوله: (إِنْ أُوتِيتُمْ هَٰذَا فَخُذُوهُ) يقول: ائتوا محمدا فإن أمركم بالتحميم والجلد فخذوه وإن أفتاكم بالرجم فاحذروا فأنزل الله تعالى: (وَمَن لَّمْ يَحْكُم بِمَآ أَنزَلَ ٱللَّهُ فَأُوْلَٰٓئِكَ هُمُ ٱلْكَٰفِرُونَ) (وَمَن لَّمْ يَحْكُم بِمَآ أَنزَلَ ٱللَّهُ فَأُوْلَٰٓئِكَ هُمُ ٱلظَّٰلِمُونَ) (وَمَن لَّمْ يَحْكُم بِمَآ أَنزَلَ ٱللَّهُ فَأُوْلَٰٓئِكَ هُمُ ٱلْفَٰسِقُونَ) في الكفار كلها.

Al-Baraa ibn 'Aazib said, "A Jew that had been flogged and had is face blackened with charcoal was carried pass the Prophet . He then called them and said, 'Is this the legal punishment for the adulterer in your book?' They said, "Yes." He then called one of their scholars and said, "I implore you by Allaah, the one who revealed the Tawraah to Moosaa, is that what you have found to be the legal punishment for the adulterer in your book?" He said, 'No, and if it had not been that you implored me with this I would not have told you. We find the legal punishment to be stoning, however, it (adultery) became widespread amongst our noble people so what we would do if we caught a noble person [committing adultery] is let him go, and if we caught a common person [doing the same] we would execute the legal punishment on him.

Then we said, "Let us come together and agree on a punishment that we can execute on the noble person and the common person." So we chose flogging and blackening the face instead of stoning.' The Messenger of Allaah then said, "O Allaah, verily I am the first one to revive your command that they have abandoned." He then summonsed him (the adulterer) and had him stoned to death. Then Allaah sent down:

$$\text{يَٰٓأَيُّهَا ٱلرَّسُولُ لَا يَحْزُنكَ ٱلَّذِينَ يُسَٰرِعُونَ فِى ٱلْكُفْرِ}$$

'O Messenger, let not those who rush into disbelief grieve you…'

up to His statement:

$$\text{إِنْ أُوتِيتُمْ هَٰذَا فَخُذُوهُ}$$

"If you are given this, take it."

[Meaning the Jews say] "Go to Muhammad. If he orders you with flogging and blackening the face then accept that; however, if he gives you the legal ruling of stoning then beware." Then Allaah sent down:

$$\text{وَمَن لَّمْ يَحْكُم بِمَا أَنزَلَ اللَّهُ فَأُوْلَٰئِكَ هُمُ الْكَافِرُونَ}$$

"And whoever does not judge by what Allaah has revealed, then such are the disbelievers." (verse: 44)

$$\text{وَمَن لَّمْ يَحْكُم بِمَا أَنزَلَ اللَّهُ فَأُوْلَٰئِكَ هُمُ الظَّالِمُونَ}$$

"And whoever does not judge by what Allaah has revealed, then such are the wrongdoers." (verse: 45)

$$\text{وَمَن لَّمْ يَحْكُم بِمَا أَنزَلَ اللَّهُ فَأُوْلَٰئِكَ هُمُ الْفَاسِقُونَ}$$

"And whoever does not judge by what Allaah has revealed, then such are the disobedient." (verse: 47)

All of these (verses) were revealed because of the disbelievers."

This *hadeeth* has been transmitted by Muslim in his *Saheeh* (1700).

His, the Exalted One's statement:

$$\text{يَٰأَيُّهَا الرَّسُولُ بَلِّغْ مَا أُنزِلَ إِلَيْكَ مِن رَّبِّكَ ۖ وَإِن لَّمْ تَفْعَلْ فَمَا بَلَّغْتَ رِسَالَتَهُ ۚ وَاللَّهُ يَعْصِمُكَ مِنَ النَّاسِ}$$

"O Messenger, convey what has been sent down to you from your Lord, and if you do not, then you have not conveyed His message; and Allaah will protect you from the people…" (verse: 67)

قال الإمام ابن حبان رحمه الله كما في موارد الظمآن ص (430): أخبرنا عبد الله بن محمد الأزدي حدثنا إسحاق بن إبراهيم الحنظلي أنبأنا مؤمل بن إسماعيل حدثنا حماد بن سلمة حدثنا محمد ابن عمرو عن أبي سلمة عن أبي هريرة رضي الله عنه قال: كان رسول الله ﷺ إذا نزل منزلا نظروا أعظم شجرة يرونها فجعلوها للنبي ﷺ فينزل تحتها وينزل أصحابه بعد ذلك في ظل الشجر فبينما هو نازل تحت شجرة وقد علق السيف عليها إذ جاء أعرابي فأخذ السيف من الشجرة ثم دنا من النبي ﷺ وهو نائم فأيقظه فقال: يا محمد من يمنعك مني الليلة فقال النبي ﷺ: الله فأنزل الله: (يَٰأَيُّهَا الرَّسُولُ بَلِّغْ مَا أُنزِلَ إِلَيْكَ مِن رَّبِّكَ وَإِن لَّمْ تَفْعَلْ فَمَا بَلَّغْتَ رِسَالَتَهُ وَاللَّهُ يَعْصِمُكَ مِنَ النَّاسِ) الآية.

Abu Hurairah said, "When the Messenger of Allaah used to stop at a resting place, they would look for the biggest tree they could find and reserve it for the Prophet. He would then rest under it and after that his

Companions would rest in the shade of the trees. Once while he was resting under a tree with his sword hanging from it a Bedouin Arab suddenly came and took the sword from the tree. He then approached the Prophet ﷺ while he was asleep and awakened him. Then he said, 'O Muhammad, who will protect you from me tonight?' The Prophet ﷺ said, "Allaah." Then Allaah sent down:

$$\text{يَٰٓأَيُّهَا ٱلرَّسُولُ بَلِّغْ مَآ أُنزِلَ إِلَيْكَ مِن رَّبِّكَ ۖ وَإِن لَّمْ تَفْعَلْ فَمَا بَلَّغْتَ رِسَالَتَهُۥ ۚ وَٱللَّهُ يَعْصِمُكَ مِنَ ٱلنَّاسِ}$$

"O Messenger, convey that which has been sent down to you from your Lord, and if you do not, then you have not conveyed His message. Allaah will protect you from the people…" (verse: 67).

As for this *hadeeth*, Ibn Hibbaan transmitted it as mentioned in *Mawaarid Adh-Dham'aan*, page 430. Ash-Sheikh Muqbil ﷺ said, "This is a *hasan hadeeth*, for verily Muhammad ibn 'Amr, Adh-Dhahabee has said about him in *Al-Meezaan* that he is *hasanul-hadeeth*. Likewise Mu'ammal ibn Ismaa'eel; they have spoken about his memory, however, he has been supported as can be found in *Tafseer Ibn Katheer*, volume 2, page 79. Aadam, being Ibn Abee Iyaas, has supported him as Ibn Katheer mentioned with the chain of Ibn Mardawaih."

His, the Exalted One's statement:

$$\text{وَإِذَا سَمِعُوا۟ مَآ أُنزِلَ إِلَى ٱلرَّسُولِ تَرَىٰٓ أَعْيُنَهُمْ تَفِيضُ مِنَ ٱلدَّمْعِ مِمَّا عَرَفُوا۟ مِنَ ٱلْحَقِّ ۖ يَقُولُونَ رَبَّنَآ ءَامَنَّا فَٱكْتُبْنَا مَعَ ٱلشَّٰهِدِينَ ۝}$$

"And when they listen to what has been sent down to the Messenger, you see their eyes overflowing with tears because of what they have recognized of the truth. They say, "Our Lord, we believe so write us down among those who bear witness." (verse: 83)

قال الإمام ابن أبي حاتم ﷺ في التفسير (ج 3 ص 23): حدثنا أبي حدثنا عمرو بن علي حدثنا عمر بن علي المقدمي قال سمعت هشام بن عروة يحدث عن أبيه عن عبد الله بن الزبير ﷺ قال: نزلت هذه الآية في النجاشي وأصحابه: (وَإِذَا سَمِعُوا۟ مَآ أُنزِلَ إِلَى ٱلرَّسُولِ تَرَىٰٓ أَعْيُنَهُمْ تَفِيضُ مِنَ ٱلدَّمْعِ) الآية.

'Abdullaah ibn Az-Zubair ﷺ said, "This verse descended because of An-Najaashee and his companions:

$$\text{وَإِذَا سَمِعُوا مَا أُنزِلَ إِلَى ٱلرَّسُولِ تَرَىٰ أَعْيُنَهُمْ تَفِيضُ مِنَ ٱلدَّمْعِ}$$

"And when they listen to what has been sent down to the Messenger, you see their eyes overflowing with tears…" (verse: 83).

This *hadeeth* has been transmitted by Ibn Abee Haatim in his *Tafseer*, volume 3, page 23. Ash-Sheikh Muqbil ﷺ said, "The *hadeeth*, the people of its chain are people of the *Saheeh* (Al-Bukhaaree and/or Muslim) except for Muhammad ibn Idrees, the father of Ibn Abee Haatim, however, he is a great *haafidh*…"

His, the Exalted One's statement:

$$\text{مِنْ أَوْسَطِ مَا تُطْعِمُونَ أَهْلِيكُمْ}$$

"From the average of what you feed your own families…" (verse: 89)

قال الإمام أبو عبد الله بن ماجه ﷺ (2113): حدثنا محمد بن يحيى ثنا عبد الرحمن بن مهدي ثنا سفيان بن عيينة عن سليمان بن أبي المغيرة عن سعيد بن جبير عن ابن عباس ﷺ قال: كان الرجل يقوت أهله قوتا فيه سعة وكان الرجل يقوت أهله قوتا فيه شدة فنزلت: (مِنْ أَوْسَطِ مَا تُطْعِمُونَ أَهْلِيكُمْ).

Ibn 'Abbaas ﷺ said, "A man would sustain his family an abundant sustenance while another man would sustain his family sustenance of hardship. Then the verse descended:

$$\text{مِنْ أَوْسَطِ مَا تُطْعِمُونَ أَهْلِيكُمْ}$$

"From the average of what you feed your own families…"

Ibn Maajah transmitted this *hadeeth* in *As-Sunan* (2113). Ash-Sheikh Muqbil ﷺ commented, "This *hadeeth*, the people of its chain are people of the *Saheeh* (Al-Bukhaaree and/or Muslim) except for Sulaimaan ibn Abee Al-Mugheerah Al-'Absee, and Yahyaa ibn Ma'een has declared him to be trustworthy. Al-Buseeree said in *Misbaah Az-Zujaajah*, 'This chain is *mawqoof*[70] with a *saheeh* chain.' I say, it is in the category of the reasons for revelation so it has the ruling of *raf'*…[71]"

---

[70] *Mawqoof* is a *hadeeth* that has been attributed to a *Sahaabee*.
[71] Meaning it takes the ruling of a *hadeeth* attributed to the Prophet ﷺ.

His, the Exalted One's statement:

$$\text{يَا أَيُّهَا الَّذِينَ آمَنُوا إِنَّمَا الْخَمْرُ وَالْمَيْسِرُ وَالْأَنْصَابُ وَالْأَزْلَامُ رِجْسٌ مِنْ عَمَلِ الشَّيْطَانِ}$$

"O you who believe, indeed intoxicants, gambling, *Al-Ansaab*[72] and divination arrows are an abomination of Shaytaan's work..."
(verses: 90-91)

قال الإمام ابن جرير رحمه الله (ج 10 ص 571): حدثنا الحسين بن علي الصدائي قال ثنا حجاج ابن المنهال قال ثنا ربيعة بن كلثوم عن جبير عن أبيه عن سعيد بن جبير عن ابن عباس رضي الله عنهما قال: نزل تحريم الخمر في قبيلتين من قبائل الأنصار شربوا حتى إذا ثملوا عبث بعضهم ببعض فلما أن صحوا جعل الرجل منهم يرى الأثر بوجهه ولحيته فيقول: فعل بي هذا أخي فلان وكانوا إخوة ليس في قلوبهم ضغائن والله لو كان بي رءوفا رحيما ما فعل بي هذا حتى وقعت في قلوبهم الضغائن فأنزل الله: (إِنَّمَا الْخَمْرُ وَالْمَيْسِرُ) إلى قوله: (فَهَلْ أَنْتُمْ مُنْتَهُونَ)

فقال ناس من المتكلفين: هي رجس وهي في بطن فلان قتل يوم بدر وقتل فلان يوم أحد فأنزل الله: (لَيْسَ عَلَى الَّذِينَ آمَنُوا وَعَمِلُوا الصَّالِحَاتِ جُنَاحٌ فِيمَا طَعِمُوا) الآية.

Ibn 'Abbaas said, "The prohibition of alcoholic drink descended because of two tribes from the tribes of the *Ansaar*. They used to drink to the point that when they became intoxicated they would play and joke around with one another. When they would become sober one of them would look at the marks on his face and beard and he would say, 'My brother so-and-so did this to me!', They used to be brothers with no hatred in their hearts, 'By Allaah, if he had been compassionate and merciful towards me he would not have done this to me!' Then hatred fell into their hearts so Allaah sent down:

$$\text{إِنَّمَا الْخَمْرُ وَالْمَيْسِرُ}$$

"Indeed intoxicants, gambling..."

up to His statement:

$$\text{فَهَلْ أَنْتُمْ مُنْتَهُونَ}$$

"So will you not cease!"

Then some people who used to meddle into affairs that do not concern them said, 'It is an abomination and it is present in the stomach of so-and-so who

---

[72] *Al-Ansaab* are stone alters where the polytheists used to slaughter their sacrificial animals for their idols.

was killed on the day of Badr and so-and-so who was killed on the day of Uhud!' Then Allaah revealed:

$$\text{لَيْسَ عَلَى ٱلَّذِينَ ءَامَنُوا۟ وَعَمِلُوا۟ ٱلصَّٰلِحَٰتِ جُنَاحٌ فِيمَا طَعِمُوا۟}$$

"Those who believe and do righteous deeds, there is no sin on them for what they tasted in the past…'" (verses: 90-91).

As for this *hadeeth*, Ibn Jareer transmitted it in his *Tafseer*, volume 10, page 571. Ash-Sheikh Muqbil ﷺ said, "As for the chain of Ibn Jareer, the people of the chain are people of the *Saheeh* (Al-Bukhaaree and/or Muslim) except for Al-Husain ibn 'Ali As-Sudaa'ee, however, he is trustworthy. Furthermore, the *hadeeth* of Sa'd will later be mentioned in *Sooratul-'Ankaboot*, if Allaah wills."

His, the Exalted One's statement:

$$\text{لَيْسَ عَلَى ٱلَّذِينَ ءَامَنُوا۟ وَعَمِلُوا۟ ٱلصَّٰلِحَٰتِ جُنَاحٌ فِيمَا طَعِمُوا۟}$$

"Those who believe and do righteous deeds, there is no sin on them for what they tasted in the past…" (verse: 93).

قال الإمام البخاري رحمه الله (2464): حدثنا محمد بن عبد الرحيم أبو يحيى أخبرنا عفان حدثنا حماد بن زيد حدثنا ثابت عن أنس ﷺ: كنت ساقي القوم في منزل أبي طلحة وكان خمرهم يومئذ الفضيخ فأمر رسول الله ﷺ مناديا ينادي: ألا إن الخمر قد حرمت قال: فقال لي أبو طلحة: اخرج فأهرقها فخرجت فهرقتها فجرت في سكك المدينة فقال بعض القوم: قد قتل قوم وهي في بطونهم فأنزل الله: (لَيْسَ عَلَى ٱلَّذِينَ ءَامَنُوا۟ وَعَمِلُوا۟ ٱلصَّٰلِحَٰتِ جُنَاحٌ فِيمَا طَعِمُوا۟) الآية.

Anas ﷺ said, "I was the one who poured drinks for the people in Abu Talhah's house. The alcoholic drink for that day was *fadeekh*.[73] The Messenger of Allaah ﷺ then ordered someone to call out loud, 'Verily alcoholic drink has been prohibited!' Abu Talhah then said to me, "Go and pour it out." So I went and poured it out and it flowed in the streets of Madeenah. Then some people said, 'Some people were killed and died while it was in their stomachs.' Then Allaah sent down:

$$\text{لَيْسَ عَلَى ٱلَّذِينَ ءَامَنُوا۟ وَعَمِلُوا۟ ٱلصَّٰلِحَٰتِ جُنَاحٌ فِيمَا طَعِمُوا۟}$$

"Those who believe and do righteous deeds, there is no sin on them for what they tasted in the past…'" (verse: 93).

---

[73] *Fadeekh* is an alcoholic drink made from different types of dates.

Al-Bukhaaree transmitted this *hadeeth* in his *Saheeh* (2464) as well as Muslim in his *Saheeh* (1980/3).

His, the Exalted One's statement:

$$\text{يَٰٓأَيُّهَا ٱلَّذِينَ ءَامَنُوا۟ لَا تَسْـَٔلُوا۟ عَنْ أَشْيَآءَ إِن تُبْدَ لَكُمْ تَسُؤْكُمْ}$$

"O you who believe, do not ask about things which if made plain to you will distress you…" (verse: 101)

قال الإمام البخاري (4621): حدثنا منذر بن الوليد بن عبد الرحمن الجارودي حدثنا أبي حدثنا شعبة عن موسى بن أنس عن أنس قال: خطب رسول الله ﷺ خطبة ما سمعت مثلها قط قال: لو تعلمون ما أعلم لضحكتم قليلا ولبكيتم كثيرا قال: فغطى أصحاب رسول الله ﷺ وجوههم لهم خنين فقال رجل: من أبي قال: فلان فنزلت هذه الآية: (لَا تَسْـَٔلُوا۟ عَنْ أَشْيَآءَ إِن تُبْدَ لَكُمْ تَسُؤْكُمْ). رواه النضر وروح بن عبادة عن شعبة.

Anas said, "The Messenger of Allaah ﷺ gave us a sermon we never heard the likes of. He said, 'If you knew what I know you would laugh little and cry much.' The Companions of the Messenger of Allaah ﷺ then covered their faces whining. A man then said, "Who is my father?" He said, 'Your father is so-and-so.' Thereafter, this verse descended,

$$\text{لَا تَسْـَٔلُوا۟ عَنْ أَشْيَآءَ إِن تُبْدَ لَكُمْ تَسُؤْكُمْ}$$

"Do not ask about things which if made plain to you will distress you."

As for this *hadeeth*, Al-Bukhaaree has transmitted it in his *Saheeh* (4621) and Muslim in his *Saheeh* (2359).

قال الإمام البخاري (4622): حدثنا الفضل بن سهل حدثنا أبو النضر حدثنا أبو خيثمة حدثنا أبو الجويرية عن ابن عباس قال: كان قوم يسألون رسول الله ﷺ استهزاء فيقول الرجل: من أبي ويقول الرجل تضل ناقته: أين ناقتي فأنزل الله فيهم هذه الآية: (يَٰٓأَيُّهَا ٱلَّذِينَ ءَامَنُوا۟ لَا تَسْـَٔلُوا۟ عَنْ أَشْيَآءَ إِن تُبْدَ لَكُمْ تَسُؤْكُمْ) حتى فرغ من الآية كلها.

Ibn 'Abbaas said, "A group of people used to ask the Messenger of Allaah ﷺ out of mockery. A man would say, 'Who is my father?' And another man whose camel went astray would say, "Where is my camel?" Consequently, Allaah sent down this verse in their regard,

$$\text{يَٰأَيُّهَا ٱلَّذِينَ ءَامَنُوا۟ لَا تَسْـَٔلُوا۟ عَنْ أَشْيَآءَ إِن تُبْدَ لَكُمْ تَسُؤْكُمْ}$$

"O you who believe, do not ask about things which if made plain to you will distress you…" (5:101).

Al-Bukhaaree transmitted this *hadeeth* in his *Saheeh* (4622).

قال الإمام ابن جرير ﵁ (ج 11 ص 105): حدثني محمد بن علي بن الحسن بن شقيق قال سمعت أبي قال أخبرنا الحسين بن واقد عن محمد بن زياد قال سمعت أبا هريرة ﷺ يقول: خطبنا رسول الله ﷺ فقال: يأيها الناس كتب الله عليكم الحج فقام محصن الأسدي فقال: أفي كل عام يا رسول الله فقال: أما إني لو قلت نعم لوجبت ولو وجبت ثم تركتم لضللتم اسكتوا عنى ما سكت عنكم فإنما هلك من كان قبلكم بسؤالهم واختلافهم على أنبيائهم فأنزل الله تعالى: (يَٰأَيُّهَا ٱلَّذِينَ ءَامَنُوا۟ لَا تَسْـَٔلُوا۟ عَنْ أَشْيَآءَ إِن تُبْدَ لَكُمْ تَسُؤْكُمْ) إلى آخر الآية.

Abu Hurairah ؓ said, "The Messenger of Allaah ﷺ gave us a sermon saying, "O people, Allaah has prescribed for you the *hajj* (pilgrimage)." Then Mihsan Al-Ansaaree stood up and said, 'Every year, O Messenger of Allaah?' He said, "Verily if I were to have said yes it would have become incumbent upon you, and if it was made incumbent upon you and then you abandoned it you would have gone astray. Do not ask me about what has been left open for you for verily those who came before you were destroyed only because of their probing and differing with their Prophets." Then Allaah ﷻ sent down,

$$\text{يَٰأَيُّهَا ٱلَّذِينَ ءَامَنُوا۟ لَا تَسْـَٔلُوا۟ عَنْ أَشْيَآءَ إِن تُبْدَ لَكُمْ تَسُؤْكُمْ}$$

"O you who believe, do not ask about things which if made plain to you will distress you…" (5: 101).

Ibn Jareer transmitted this *hadeeth* in his *Tafseer*, volume 11, page 105, and the basis of the *hadeeth* is in Muslim.

قال الإمام ابن جرير ﵁ (ج 11 ص 107): حدثنا زكريا بن يحيى بن أبان المصري قال ثنا أبو زيد عبد الرحمن بن أبي الغمر قال ثنا أبو مطيع معاوية بن يحيى عن صفوان بن عمرو قال ثني سليم بن عامر قال سمعت أبا أمامة الباهلي ﷺ يقول: قام رسول الله ﷺ في الناس فقال: كتب عليكم الحج فقام رجل من الأعراب فقال: أفي كل عام قال: فعلا كلام رسول الله ﷺ وأسكت واستغضب فمكث طويلا ثم تكلم فقال: من السائل فقال الأعرابي: أنا ذا فقال: ويحك ماذا يؤمنك أن أقول نعم ولو قلت نعم لوجبت ولو وجبت لكفرتم ألا إنه إنما أهلك الذين قبلكم أئمة الحرج والله لو أني أحللت لكم جميع ما

119

في الأرض وحرمت عليكم منها موضع خف لوقعتم فيه قال: فأنزل الله تعالى عند ذلك: (يَٰٓأَيُّهَا ٱلَّذِينَ ءَامَنُوا۟ لَا تَسْـَٔلُوا۟ عَنْ أَشْيَآءَ).

Abu Umaamah Al-Baahilee ﷺ said, "The Messenger of Allaah ﷺ stood among the people and said, 'Hajj has been prescribed for you.' A man from the Bedouins stood up and said, "Every year?," cutting off the Messenger of Allaah ﷺ, so he (the Prophet ﷺ) remained silent. He was angered and it showed. Then after a while he spoke saying, 'Who is the questioner?' The Bedouin man said, "Here I am." He said, 'Woe to you, what protects you from me saying yes. And if I were to say yes it would be incumbent; And if it were made incumbent you would have disbelieved. Verily those before you were destroyed only by their leaders who made things difficult. By Allaah, if I were to make everything on earth permissible for you except for a spot the size of a camel's hoof, you would have fallen into it.' At that point Allaah ﷻ sent down,

يَٰٓأَيُّهَا ٱلَّذِينَ ءَامَنُوا۟ لَا تَسْـَٔلُوا۟ عَنْ أَشْيَآءَ

"O you who believe, do not ask about things…"

As for this *hadeeth*, Ibn Jareer transmitted it in his *Tafseer*, volume 11, page 107. In the chain of the *hadeeth* is 'Abdur-Rahmaan ibn Abee Al-Ghamr. Ash-Sheikh Muqbil ﷺ said about him, "'[Regarding] Abdur-Rahmaan ibn Abee Al-Ghamr, a group has narrated on him although he has not be declared trustworthy by someone whose declaration is regarded, so he can be used in a supporting role. In addition, Abu Mutee' Mu'aawiyah ibn Yahyaa, is someone whom there is a difference of opinion about his status and it appears that he is *hasanul-hadeeth*; and the *hadeeth* is regarded as a supporting *hadeeth* for the *hadeeth* of Abu Hurairah as you can see.

These are three different reasons for this verse's decision because the first, 'Abdullaah ibn Hudhaafah, did not ask out of mockery; however, Al-Haafidh said in *Al-Fath*, volume 9, page 351, (*hadeeth* 4622), 'There is nothing which prevents all of them from being reasons why it was revealed, and Allaah knows best.' He added on page 352, "In short, it (the verse) was revealed because of asking too many questions, whether it be out of mockery, or to test (the Prophet ﷺ), or to make something difficult which would have remained permissible, if it had not been asked about."

His, the Exalted One's statement:

$$\text{يَٰٓأَيُّهَا ٱلَّذِينَ ءَامَنُوا۟ شَهَٰدَةُ بَيْنِكُمْ إِذَا حَضَرَ أَحَدَكُمُ ٱلْمَوْتُ حِينَ ٱلْوَصِيَّةِ ٱثْنَانِ ذَوَا عَدْلٍ مِّنكُمْ أَوْ ءَاخَرَانِ مِنْ غَيْرِكُمْ}$$

"O you who believe, when death approaches one of you and you make a bequest, take the testimony of two just men from amongst you or two others besides yourselves…" to His ﷻ statement,

$$\text{وَٱللَّهُ لَا يَهْدِى ٱلْقَوْمَ ٱلْفَٰسِقِينَ}$$

"And Allaah does not guide the people who are disobedient." (verses: 106-108)

قال الإمام البخاري رحمه الله (2780): وقال لي علي بن عبد الله حدثنا يحيى بن آدم حدثنا ابن أبي زائدة عن محمد بن أبي القاسم عن عبد الملك بن سعيد بن جبير عن أبيه عن ابن عباس رضي الله عنهما قال: خرج رجل من بني سهم مع تميم الداري وعدي بن بداء فمات السهمي بأرض ليس بها مسلم فلما قدما بتركته فقدوا جاما من فضة مُخَوَّصا من ذهب فأحلفهما رسول الله ﷺ ثم وجد الجام بمكة فقالوا ابتعناه من تميم وعدي فقام رجلان من أولياء السهمي فحلفا: لشهادتنا أحق من شهادتهما وإن الجام لصاحبهم قال: وفيهم نزلت هذه الآية: (يَٰٓأَيُّهَا ٱلَّذِينَ ءَامَنُوا۟ شَهَٰدَةُ بَيْنِكُمْ إِذَا حَضَرَ أَحَدَكُمُ ٱلْمَوْتُ).

Ibn 'Abbaas ﷺ said, "A man from the tribe Banee Sahm departed along with Tameem Ad-Daaree and 'Adee ibn Baddaa. The man from the tribe of Sahm then died while in a land free of Muslims. When the two returned with his inheritance, the family of the deceased found that a silver vessel engraved with gold was missing. The Messenger of Allaah ﷺ made the two men swear [about what happened to the vessel and its whereabouts] and the vessel was later found in Makkah. The people who had the vessel said, 'We purchased it from Tameem[74] and 'Adee.' Then, two men who were relatives of the man from the tribe Sahm stood up and swore saying, "Indeed our testimony is more binding than the testimony of those two, and verily the vessel belongs to our companion." Because of them this verse descended,

---

[74] Note: Tameem Ad-Daaree was one of the noble Companions of the Messenger of Allaah ﷺ. This story occurred before he embraced Islaam. In some of the narrations of this *hadeeth* it was mentioned that after he embraced Islaam he went to the family of the deceased and told them what happened and gave them the money he received from selling the vessel, and Allaah knows best. Refer to *Fathul-Baaree* in the explanation of this *hadeeth* for more.

$$\text{يَـٰٓأَيُّهَا ٱلَّذِينَ ءَامَنُوا۟ شَهَـٰدَةُ بَيْنِكُمْ إِذَا حَضَرَ أَحَدَكُمُ ٱلْمَوْتُ}$$

"O you who believe, when death approaches one of you and you make a bequest…"

Al-Bukhaaree transmitted this *hadeeth* it his *Saheeh* (2780).

سورة الأنعام

Sooratul-An'aam

His, the Exalted One's statement:

وَلَا تَطْرُدِ ٱلَّذِينَ يَدْعُونَ رَبَّهُم بِٱلْغَدَوٰةِ وَٱلْعَشِىِّ يُرِيدُونَ وَجْهَهُۥ

"And do not turn away those who invoke their Lord morning and afternoon seeking His face…" (verse: 52)

قال الإمام مسلم ﵀ (2413 / 45): حدثنا زهير بن حرب حدثنا عبد الرحمن عن سفيان عن المقدام بن شريح عن أبيه عن سعد ﵁: فيَّ نزلت: (وَلَا تَطْرُدِ ٱلَّذِينَ يَدْعُونَ رَبَّهُم بِٱلْغَدَوٰةِ وَٱلْعَشِىِّ) قال: نزلت في ستة أنا وابن مسعود منهم وكان المشركون قالوا له: تدني هؤلاء.

Sa'd ibn Abee Waqqaas ﵁ said, "I was a reason for this verse's decsension:

وَلَا تَطْرُدِ ٱلَّذِينَ يَدْعُونَ رَبَّهُم بِٱلْغَدَوٰةِ وَٱلْعَشِىِّ

'And do not turn away those who invoke their Lord morning and afternoon…'.

It was revealed because of six people and Ibn Mas'ood and I were amongst them. The polytheists had said to him (the Prophet ﷺ), "You let the likes of these people get too close you to you!"

As for this *hadeeth*, Muslim transmitted it in his *Saheeh* (2413/45).

قال الإمام مسلم ﵀ (2413 / 46): حدثنا أبو بكر بن أبي شيبة حدثنا محمد بن عبد الله الأسدي عن إسرائيل عن المقدام بن شريح عن أبيه عن سعد ﵁ قال: كنا مع النبي ﷺ ستة نفر فقال المشركون للنبي ﷺ: اطرد هؤلاء لا يجترؤن علينا قال: وكنت أنا وابن مسعود ورجل من هذيل وبلال ورجلان لست أسمّيهما فوقع في نفس رسول الله ﷺ ما شاء أن يقع فحدث نفسه فأنزل الله عز وجل: (وَلَا تَطْرُدِ ٱلَّذِينَ يَدْعُونَ رَبَّهُم بِٱلْغَدَوٰةِ وَٱلْعَشِىِّ يُرِيدُونَ وَجْهَهُۥ).

[In another narration] Sa'd ibn Abee Waqqaas ﵁ said, "Six of us were with the Prophet ﷺ when the polytheists said to the him, "Turn away these people so they will not have the audacity to be seen with us." (The six were) me, Ibn Mas'ood, a man from the tribe Hudhail, Bilaal and two men that I will not name. Then something occurred to the Messenger of Allaah ﷺ that Allaah willed and he contemplated for some time. Then Allaah ﷻ sent down:

$$\text{وَلَا تَطْرُدِ ٱلَّذِينَ يَدْعُونَ رَبَّهُم بِٱلْغَدَوٰةِ وَٱلْعَشِيِّ يُرِيدُونَ وَجْهَهُ}$$

"And do not turn away those who invoke their Lord morning and afternoon seeking His face…"

This *hadeeth* has been transmitted by Muslim in his *Saheeh* (2413/46).

His, the Exalted One's statement:

$$\text{وَلَا تَأْكُلُوا۟ مِمَّا لَمْ يُذْكَرِ ٱسْمُ ٱللَّهِ عَلَيْهِ}$$

"And do not eat of that (meat) on which Allaah's name has not been pronounced…" (verse: 121)

قال الإمام أبو داود ﷺ (2818): حدثنا محمد بن كثير قال أنا إسرائيل حدثنا سماك عن عكرمة عن ابن عباس ﷺ في قوله: (وَإِنَّ ٱلشَّيَـٰطِينَ لَيُوحُونَ إِلَىٰٓ أَوْلِيَآئِهِمْ) يقولون: ما ذبح الله فلا تأكلوه وما ذبحتم أنتم فكلوه فأنزل الله: (وَلَا تَأْكُلُوا۟ مِمَّا لَمْ يُذْكَرِ ٱسْمُ ٱللَّهِ عَلَيْهِ).

Ibn 'Abbaas ﷺ said about His statement:

$$\text{وَإِنَّ ٱلشَّيَـٰطِينَ لَيُوحُونَ إِلَىٰٓ أَوْلِيَآئِهِمْ}$$

"And certainly the devils inspire their allies…" (verse: 121)

"They (the disbelievers) say, 'what Allaah has killed, do not eat it, and that which you yourselves slaughter, eat it?' Then Allaah sent down:

$$\text{وَلَا تَأْكُلُوا۟ مِمَّا لَمْ يُذْكَرِ ٱسْمُ ٱللَّهِ عَلَيْهِ}$$

"And do not eat of that (meat) on which Allaah's name has not been pronounced…"[75]

Regarding this *hadeeth*, Abu Daawud transmitted it in *As-Sunan* (2818) and Ash-Sheikh Muqbil ﷺ commented about it saying, "I say, the *hadeeth* is from

---

[75] The meaning of this *hadeeth* is the devils inspired their allies from the polytheists to present a specious argument to the believers about the issue of eating the meat of dead animals telling them to say to the believers, "That which Allaah has killed, do not eat it, and that which you yourselves slaughtered, eat it?" Meaning, you claim that you worship Allaah alone then when it comes to the issue of the dead animal which Allaah caused to die, you do not eat from it but you do eat from the animal that you yourselves slaughter. Why is that? This is the meaning of their statement. Then Allaah ﷻ sent down this verse refuting this false analogy. Refer to the *Tafseer* of Ibn Jareer, volume 12, pages 81-82.

the narrations of Simaak on 'Ikrimah and they are inconsistent so therefore, the *hadeeth* is weak by this chain; however, it has supporting chains which raise it to the level of being authentic, amongst them is what An-Nasaa'ee transmitted in *At-Tafseer*, volume 1, page 479 (*hadeeth* 191) and Abu Daawud, volume 3, page 246 (*hadeeth* 2819)."

سورة الأعراف

Sooratul-A'raaf

His, the Exalted One's statement:

يَٰبَنِىٓ ءَادَمَ خُذُواْ زِينَتَكُمْ عِندَ كُلِّ مَسْجِدٍ

"O children of Aadam, wear your adornment at every *masjid*..." (verse: 31)

قال الإمام مسلم ﵀ (3028): حدثنا محمد بن بشار حدثنا محمد بن جعفر ح وحدثني أبو بكر بن نافع واللفظ له حدثنا غندر حدثنا شعبة عن سلمة بن كهيل عن مسلم البطين عن سعيد بن جبير عن ابن عباس ﵄ قال: كانت المرأة تطوف بالبيت وهي عريانة فتقول: من يعيرني تطوافا تجعله على فرجها وتقول:

اليوم يبدو بعضه أو كله   فما بدا منه فلا أحله

فنزلت هذه الآية: (خُذُواْ زِينَتَكُمْ عِندَ كُلِّ مَسْجِدٍ).

Ibn 'Abbaas ﵄ said, "A woman would make *tawaaf* of the Sacred House naked saying, 'Who will lend me a *titwaaf*?'[76] She would then place it over her groin and say:

ليوم يبدو بعضه أو كله   فما بدا منه فلا أحله

Today, some of it or all of it shows,
and what shows I do not make permissible,

then this verse descended:

خُذُواْ زِينَتَكُمْ عِندَ كُلِّ مَسْجِدٍ

"Wear your adornment at every *masjid*."

Muslim transmitted this *hadeeth* in his *Saheeh* (3028).

His, the Exalted One's statement:

وَٱتْلُ عَلَيْهِمْ نَبَأَ ٱلَّذِىٓ ءَاتَيْنَٰهُ ءَايَٰتِنَا فَٱنسَلَخَ مِنْهَا

---

[76] A *titwaaf* is a small piece of clothing they used for making *tawaaf*.

"And recite to them the story of the one to whom We gave (knowledge of) our signs but he detached himself from them…" (verse: 175)

قال الإمام النسائي ﵀ في التفسير (212): أخبرنا محمد بن عبد الأعلى حدثنا خالد بن الحارث ثنا شعبة أخبرني يعلى بن عطاء قال سمعت نافع بن عاصم يقول قال عبد الله ﵁ في قوله تعالى: (ءَاتَيْنَٰهُ ءَايَٰتِنَا فَٱنسَلَخَ مِنْهَا) الآية نزلت في أمية.

'Abdullaah ibn 'Amr ﵁ said about His ﷻ statement:

ءَاتَيْنَٰهُ ءَايَٰتِنَا فَٱنسَلَخَ مِنْهَا

"The one to whom We gave (knowledge of) our signs but he detached himself from them…", "It descended because of Umaiyah."[77]

This *hadeeth*, An-Nasaa'ee transmitted it in his *Tafseer* (212).

---

[77] He is Umaiyah ibn Abee As-Salt. Ibn Katheer said about him in his *Tafseer* of this verse, "He had a lot of knowledge of the past revelations. However he did not benefit by his knowledge, for verily he reached the era of the Messenger of Allaah ﷺ. His distinguishing characteristics, signs and miracles reached him. These signs were clear to every person of insight, and with all of this, he met him and did not follow him, rather, he befriended the polytheists and helped and praised them. He elegized the polytheists who died at Badr with an eloquent elegy. May Allaah disfigure him."

سورة الأنفال

Sooratul-Anfaal

His, the Exalted One's statement:

$$\text{يَسْـَٔلُونَكَ عَنِ ٱلْأَنفَالِ ۖ قُلِ ٱلْأَنفَالُ لِلَّهِ وَٱلرَّسُولِ}$$

"They ask you about the spoils of war. Say: The spoils are for Allaah and the Messenger…" (verse: 1)

قال الإمام الترمذي رحمه الله (3079): حدثنا أبو كريب حدثنا أبو بكر بن عياش عن عاصم بن بهدلة عن مصعب بن سعد عن أبيه رضي الله عنه قال: لما كان يوم بدر جئت بسيف فقلت: يا رسول الله إن الله قد شفى صدري من المشركين ، أو نحو هذا ، هب لي هذا السيف فقال: هذا ليس لي ولا لك فقلت: عسى أن يعطى هذا من لا يبلي بلائي فجاءني الرسول ﷺ فقال: إنك سألتني وليست لي وقد صارت لي وهو لك قال: فنزلت : (يَسْـَٔلُونَكَ عَنِ ٱلْأَنفَالِ) الآية.

قال أبو عيسى: هذا حديث حسن صحيح وقد رواه سماك بن حرب عن مصعب أيضا وفي الباب عن عبادة بن الصامت.

Sa'd ibn Abee Waqqaas ؓ said, "On the day of Badr I brought a (captured) sword and said, 'O Messenger of Allaah, indeed Allaah has healed my breast from the polytheists,' or he said something similar to this, "Let me have this sword." He ﷺ said, "This is not mine nor is it yours." I said, "Perhaps it will be given to someone who is not able to do what I do on the battlefield." The Messenger of Allaah ﷺ then came to me and said, "Verily you asked me when it was not mine. It has become mine and now it is yours." Then it descended:

$$\text{يَسْـَٔلُونَكَ عَنِ ٱلْأَنفَالِ}$$

"They ask you about the spoils of war…"

At-Tirmidhee transmitted This hadeeth in his *Jaami'* (3079) and Muslim in his *Saheeh* in the book of *Jihaad* (1748/34) with a longer wording.

قال الإمام أحمد رحمه الله (ج 5 ص 323): ثنا معاوية بن عمرو ثنا أبو إسحاق عن عبد الرحمن ابن عياش ابن أبي ربيعة عن سليمان بن موسى عن أبي سلام عن أبي أمامة عن عبادة بن الصامت ﷺ قال: خرجنا مع النبي ﷺ فشهدت معه بدرا فالتقى الناس فهزم الله تبارك وتعالى العدو فانطلقت طائفة في آثارهم يهزمون ويقتلون فأكبت طائفة على العسكر يحوونه ويجمعونه وأحدقت طائفة برسول

الله ﷺ لا يصيب العدو منه غرة حتى إذا كان الليل وفاء الناس بعضهم إلى بعض قال الذين جمعوا الغنائم: نحن حويناها وجمعناها فليس لأحد فيها نصيب وقال الذين خرجوا في طلب العدو: لستم بأحق بها منا نحن نفينا عنها العدو وهزمناهم وقال الذين أحدقوا برسول الله ﷺ: لستم بأحق بها منا نحن أحدقنا برسول الله ﷺ وخفنا أن يصيب العدو منه غرة واشتغلنا به فنزلت: (يَسْـَٔلُونَكَ عَنِ ٱلْأَنفَالِ ۖ قُلِ ٱلْأَنفَالُ لِلَّهِ وَٱلرَّسُولِ ۖ فَٱتَّقُوا۟ ٱللَّهَ وَأَصْلِحُوا۟ ذَاتَ بَيْنِكُمْ) فقسمها رسول الله ﷺ على وفاق بين المسلمين.

'Ubaadah ibn As-Saamit ؓ said, "We departed with the Prophet ﷺ and I participated along with him in the battle of Badr. The people met in battle and Allaah ﷻ defeated the enemy. A group chased them down, routing them and killing them. Another group focused on the camp collecting the spoils of war while Another group surrounded the Messenger of Allaah ﷺ guarding him so the enemy would not be able to attack him abruptly. That night, everyone returned and gathered. The people who collected the spoils of war said, 'We collected the spoils of war so no one else gets a share of it.' However, the people who went and tracked down the enemy said, "You do not have more right to it than we do. We removed the enemy from the spoils and defeated them." The people who surrounded the Messenger of Allaah then asserted ﷺ said, 'You do not have more right to it than we do. We surrounded the Messenger of Allaah ﷺ out of fear that the enemy might attack him suddenly so we concerned ourselves with him." Then the verse descended:

يَسْـَٔلُونَكَ عَنِ ٱلْأَنفَالِ ۖ قُلِ ٱلْأَنفَالُ لِلَّهِ وَٱلرَّسُولِ ۖ فَٱتَّقُوا۟ ٱللَّهَ وَأَصْلِحُوا۟ ذَاتَ بَيْنِكُمْ

"They ask you about the spoils of war. Say: The spoils are for Allaah and the Messenger, so fear Allaah and correct the matters of difference between you…". Thereafter the Messenger of Allaah ﷺ divided it evenly between the Muslims."

As for this *hadeeth*, Al-Imaam Ahmad transmitted it in his *Musnad*, volume 5, page 323. Ash-Sheikh Muqbil ؒ in the latest edition of his book mentioned a beneficial footnote on this *hadeeth* explaining that Abu Salaam, one of the narrators in the chain, has heard from Abu Umaamah, the noble Companion and narrator on 'Ubaadah in the chain, as found in Muslim (804). This is contrary to what Abu Haatim has said negating that Abu Salaam has heard from Abu Umaamah.

قال الإمام أبو داود ؒ (2737): حدثنا وهب بن بقية قال أخبرنا خالد عن داود عن عكرمة عن ابن عباس ؓ قال: قال رسول الله ﷺ يوم بدر: من فعل كذا وكذا فله من النفل كذا وكذا قال فتقدم الفتيان ولزم المشيخة الرايات فلم يبرحوها فلما فتح الله عليهم قال المشيخة: كنا ردءا لكم لو انهزمتم

لفئتم إلينا فلا تذهبوا بالمغنم ونبقى فأبى الفتيان وقالوا: جعله رسول الله ﷺ لنا فأنزل الله: (يَسْـَٔلُونَكَ عَنِ ٱلْأَنفَالِ ۖ قُلِ ٱلْأَنفَالُ لِلَّهِ وَٱلرَّسُولِ) إلى قوله: (كَمَآ أَخْرَجَكَ رَبُّكَ مِنۢ بَيْتِكَ بِٱلْحَقِّ وَإِنَّ فَرِيقًا مِّنَ ٱلْمُؤْمِنِينَ لَكَٰرِهُونَ) يقول: فكان ذلك خيرا لهم فكذلك أيضا فأطيعوني فإني أعلم بعاقبة هذا منكم.

Ibn 'Abbaas ؓ said, "The Messenger of Allaah ﷺ said on the day of Badr, 'Whoever does such-and-such gets such-and-such from the spoils.' The younger men then went to the front lines while the older men stayed by the flags not moving away from them. Then when Allaah gave them victory the older men said, "We were your support. If you were to have been defeated you would have come back to us for support, so do not take the spoils and leave us with nothing." The younger men refused and said, 'The Messenger of Allaah ﷺ granted it to us.' Then Allaah sent down:

$$\text{يَسْـَٔلُونَكَ عَنِ ٱلْأَنفَالِ ۖ قُلِ ٱلْأَنفَالُ لِلَّهِ وَٱلرَّسُولِ}$$

"They ask you about the spoils of war. Say: The spoils are for Allaah and the Messenger...", up to His statement:

$$\text{كَمَآ أَخْرَجَكَ رَبُّكَ مِنۢ بَيْتِكَ بِٱلْحَقِّ وَإِنَّ فَرِيقًا مِّنَ ٱلْمُؤْمِنِينَ لَكَٰرِهُونَ}$$

"As your Lord caused you to go out from your home in truth while, indeed, a group among the believers disliked it." (verse: 5)

He is saying: So that (going out to Badr) was better for them and likewise (the distribution of the spoils is better for them), so obey me (the Prophet) for verily I know better than you how the distribution should go."

Abu Daawud transmitted This *hadeeth* in *As-Sunan* (2737). Ash-Sheikh Muqbil ؒ commented, "There is no contradiction between these two reasons (the story of Sa'd and the story of the groups) since there is nothing which prevents the verse from being revealed because of both of them, and Allaah knows best."

His, the Exalted One's statement:

$$\text{إِذْ تَسْتَغِيثُونَ رَبَّكُمْ فَٱسْتَجَابَ لَكُمْ أَنِّى مُمِدُّكُم بِأَلْفٍ مِّنَ ٱلْمَلَٰٓئِكَةِ مُرْدِفِينَ}$$

"(Remember) when you sought help from your Lord so He answered you (saying): 'will help you with a thousand of the angels each behind the other in succession.'" (verse: 9)

قال الإمام أحمد ﷺ (ج 1 ص 30): حدثنا أبو نوح قراد أنبأنا عكرمة بن عمار حدثنا سماك الحنفي أبو زميل حدثني ابن عباس حدثني عمر بن الخطاب ﷺ قال: لما كان يوم بدر قال: نظر النبي ﷺ إلى أصحابه وهم ثلاثمائة ونيف ونظر إلى المشركين فإذا هم ألف وزيادة فاستقبل النبي ﷺ القبلة ثم مد يديه وعليه رداؤه وإزاره ثم قال: اللهم أين ما وعدتني اللهم أنجز لي ما وعدتني اللهم إنك إن تهلك هذه العصابة من أهل الإسلام فلا تعبد في الأرض أبدا قال فما زال يستغيث ربه عز وجل ويدعوه حتى سقط رداؤه فأتاه أبو بكر فأخذ رداءه فرداه ثم التزمه من ورائه ثم قال: يا نبي الله كفاك مناشدتك ربك فإنه سينجز لك ما وعدك وأنزل الله عز وجل: (إِذْ تَسْتَغِيثُونَ رَبَّكُمْ فَاسْتَجَابَ لَكُمْ أَنِّي مُمِدُّكُم بِأَلْفٍ مِّنَ ٱلْمَلَٰٓئِكَةِ مُرْدِفِينَ)... الحديث.

'Umar ibn Al-Khattaab ﷺ said, "On the day of Badr the Prophet ﷺ looked towards his Companions who numbered just over three hundred. Then he looked towards the polytheists and found them to be over a thousand. The Prophet ﷺ then faced the *qiblah* (the direction for prayer) and extended his arms while wearing his *izaar* (lower garment) and his *ridaa* (upper garment) and then said, "O Allaah, where is what you promised me! O Allaah, fulfill for me what you promised me! O Allaah, if you allow this small group of Muslims to be destroyed you will never be worshipped on earth!" He continued to seek the aid of his Lord ﷺ and supplicate Him to the point where his upper garment fell off. So Abu Bakr came to him and picked up his upper garment and put it back on him and stood behind him saying, "O Prophet of Allaah, you imploring your Lord is sufficient, for verily He will fulfill for you what He promised you." In this regard Allaah ﷺ sent down:

$$\text{إِذْ تَسْتَغِيثُونَ رَبَّكُمْ فَاسْتَجَابَ لَكُمْ أَنِّي مُمِدُّكُم بِأَلْفٍ مِّنَ ٱلْمَلَٰٓئِكَةِ مُرْدِفِينَ}$$

"(Remember) when you sought help from your Lord so He answered you (saying): 'I will help you with a thousand of the angels each behind the other in succession.'

Al-Imaam Ahmad transmitted this *hadeeth* in his *Musnad*, volume 1, page 30, and has already been mentioned in entirety in *Soorah Aali 'Imraan*, verse 165. Muslim has also transmitted it in his *Saheeh* (1763).

His, the Exalted One's statement:

$$\text{وَمَن يُوَلِّهِمْ يَوْمَئِذٍ دُبُرَهُۥٓ إِلَّا مُتَحَرِّفًا لِّقِتَالٍ أَوْ مُتَحَيِّزًا إِلَىٰ فِئَةٍ فَقَدْ بَآءَ بِغَضَبٍ مِّنَ ٱللَّهِ وَمَأْوَىٰهُ جَهَنَّمُ وَبِئْسَ ٱلْمَصِيرُ ﴿١٦﴾}$$

"And whoever turns his back to them on such a day, unless it is a stratagem of war or to retreat to a troop (of his own), he indeed has drawn upon himself wrath from Allaah and his abode is hell, and worst indeed is that destination." (verse: 16)

قال الإمام أبو داود رحمه الله (2648): حدثنا محمد بن هشام المصري حدثنا بشر بن المفضل حدثنا داود عن أبي النضرة عن أبي سعيد رضي الله عنه قال: نزلت في يوم بدر: (وَمَن يُوَلِّهِمْ يَوْمَئِذٍ دُبُرَهُ).

Abu Sa'eed said, "this verse descended because of the day of Badr:

وَمَن يُوَلِّهِمْ يَوْمَئِذٍ دُبُرَهُ

"And whoever turns his back to them on such a day..."

Abu Daawud transmitted this *hadeeth* in *As-Sunan* (2648) and Ibn Katheer said in his *Tafseer*, volume 2, page 295, "This does not negate that fleeing from the advance is also forbidden for others, not only the people of badr, even if the verse descended because of them, because the previously mentioned *hadeeth* of Abu Hurairah proves that fleeing from the advance is a major sin according to the position of the majority of Scholars, and Allaah knows best."

His, the Exalted One's statement:

وَمَا رَمَيْتَ إِذْ رَمَيْتَ وَلَٰكِنَّ ٱللَّهَ رَمَىٰ

"And you threw not when you threw, rather Allaah threw…" (verse: 17)

قال الإمام الطبراني رحمه الله في الكبير (3128): حدثنا أحمد بن مابهرام الأيذجي ثنا محمد بن يزيد الأسفاطي ثنا إبراهيم بن يحيى الشجري حدثني أبي ثنا موسى بن يعقوب الزمعي عن عبد الله بن يزيد مولى الأسود بن سفيان عن أبي بكر بن سليمان بن أبي حثمة عن حكيم بن حزام رضي الله عنه قال: لما كان يوم بدر أمر رسول الله صلى الله عليه وسلم فأخذ كفا من الحصباء فاستقبلنا به فرمانا بها وقال: شاهت الوجوه فانهزمنا فأنزل الله عز وجل: (وَمَا رَمَيْتَ إِذْ رَمَيْتَ وَلَٰكِنَّ ٱللَّهَ رَمَىٰ).

Hakeem ibn Hizaam said, "On the day of Badr the Messenger of Allaah called for and took a handful of pebbles. He then faced us and threw them at us[78] and said, 'May their faces be disfigured.' At that point we were defeated and Allaah sent down:

---

[78] Hakeem ibn Hizaam was one of the noble Companions of the Prophet. At the time of Badr he had not yet embraced Islaam, rather, he fought on the side of the

$$\text{وَمَا رَمَيْتَ إِذْ رَمَيْتَ وَلَٰكِنَّ ٱللَّهَ رَمَىٰ}$$

"And you threw not when you threw, rather Allaah threw…"

As for this *hadeeth*, At-Tabaraanee transmitted it in *Al-Mu'jam Al-Kabeer* (3128). Al-Haithamee said in *Majma' Az-Zawaa'id*, volume 2, page 84, "Its chain is *hasan*." Ash-Sheikh Muqbil ﷺ added, "Perhaps he means it is *hasan li ghairihi*…". The Sheikh later commented, "And we said that perhaps Al-Haithamee classified the *hadeeth* to be *hasan* because of the supporting *ahaadeeth* that play a buttressing role because after declaring his classification he added: "And it has been narrated on Ibn 'Abbaas that the Prophet ﷺ said to 'Ali, 'Give me a handful of pebbles.' So he gave it to him and then he threw them at the faces of the people. There was not a single person except that his eyes were filled with pebbles. Then the verse descended:

$$\text{وَمَا رَمَيْتَ إِذْ رَمَيْتَ وَلَٰكِنَّ ٱللَّهَ رَمَىٰ}$$

"And you threw not when you threw, rather Allaah threw…".

Then he (Al-Haithamee) stated, "At-Tabaraanee transmitted it and the people of the chain are people of the *Saheeh* (Al-Bukhaaree and/or Muslim)."

His, the Exalted One's statement:

$$\text{إِن تَسْتَفْتِحُوا۟ فَقَدْ جَآءَكُمُ ٱلْفَتْحُ}$$

"If you (O disbelievers) ask for victory, the victory has already come (as you have asked for it)…" (verse: 19)

قال الإمام ابن جرير ﷺ (ج 13 ص 454): حدثنا يحيى بن آدم عن إبراهيم بن سعيد عن صالح بن كيسان عن الزهري عن عبد الله بن ثعلبة بن صُعير ﷺ قال: كان المستفتح يوم بدر أبا جهل قال: اللهم أقطعنا للرحم وآتانا بما لم نعرف فأحنه الغداة فأنزل الله: (إِن تَسْتَفْتِحُوا۟ فَقَدْ جَآءَكُمُ ٱلْفَتْحُ).

'Abdullaah ibn Tha'labah ibn Su'air ﷺ said, "The one (from the polytheists) who implored Allaah for victory on the day of Badr was Abu Jahl. He said, 'O Allaah, whoever amongst us (Abu Jahl or Muhammad ﷺ) is the most severe in cutting family ties and in introducing novelties that we don not recognize to be right, destroy him on this morning." Then Allaah sent down:

---

polytheists. He embraced Islaam the year that Makkah was conquered and later participated in the battle of Hunain. Refer to the book *Al-Isaabah* for more.

$$\text{إِن تَسۡتَفۡتِحُواْ فَقَدۡ جَآءَكُمُ ٱلۡفَتۡحُۖ}$$

"If you (O disbelievers) ask for victory, the victory has already come (as you have asked for it)…"

Ibn Jareer transmitted this *hadeeth* it in his *Tafseer*, volume 13, page 454, and likewise Al-Haakim in *Al-Mustadrak*, volume 2, page 328 and he classified it to be authentic according to the standards of the two Sheikhs (Al-Bukhaaree and Muslim) although they did not transmit it. Ash-Sheikh Muqbil mentioned in this regard that "Muslim did not transmit on 'Abdullaah ibn Tha'labah so the *hadeeth* meets the standards of Al-Bukhaaree…".

His, the Exalted One's statement:

$$\text{وَمَا كَانَ ٱللَّهُ لِيُعَذِّبَهُمۡ وَأَنتَ فِيهِمۡۚ وَمَا كَانَ ٱللَّهُ مُعَذِّبَهُمۡ وَهُمۡ يَسۡتَغۡفِرُونَ ۝}$$

"Allaah would not punish them while you are amongst them, nor would Allaah not punish them while they seek forgiveness." (verse: 33)

قال الإمام البخاري (4648): حدثني أحمد حدثنا عبيد الله بن معاذ حدثنا أبي حدثنا شعبة عن عبد الحميد هو ابن كُردِيد صاحب الزيادي سمع أنس بن مالك ﷺ: قال أبو جهل: اللهم إن كان هذا هو الحق من عندك فأمطر علينا حجارة من السماء أو ائتنا بعذاب أليم فنزلت: (وَمَا كَانَ ٱللَّهُ لِيُعَذِّبَهُمۡ وَأَنتَ فِيهِمۡ وَمَا كَانَ ٱللَّهُ مُعَذِّبَهُمۡ وَهُمۡ يَسۡتَغۡفِرُونَ) (وَمَا لَهُمۡ أَلَّا يُعَذِّبَهُمُ ٱللَّهُ وَهُمۡ يَصُدُّونَ عَنِ ٱلۡمَسۡجِدِ ٱلۡحَرَامِ) الآية.

Anas ibn Maalik said, "Abu Jahl said, 'O Allaah, if this is the truth from you then rain down upon us stones from the heavens or inflict us with a painful punishment." Then the following verse(s) descended:

$$\text{وَمَا كَانَ ٱللَّهُ لِيُعَذِّبَهُمۡ وَأَنتَ فِيهِمۡۚ وَمَا كَانَ ٱللَّهُ مُعَذِّبَهُمۡ وَهُمۡ يَسۡتَغۡفِرُونَ}$$

"Allaah would not punish them while you are amongst them, nor would Allaah punish them while they seek forgiveness."

$$\text{وَمَا لَهُمۡ أَلَّا يُعَذِّبَهُمُ ٱللَّهُ وَهُمۡ يَصُدُّونَ عَنِ ٱلۡمَسۡجِدِ ٱلۡحَرَامِ}$$

"And why should Allaah not punish them while they prevent (people) from the Sacred *Masjid*…" the verse (verse: 34).

Al-Bukhaaree has transmitted this *hadeeth* in his *Saheeh* (4648) and Muslim in his *Saheeh* (2796).

قال الإمام ابن جرير ﵀ (ج 13 ص 511): حدثنا أحمد بن منصور الرمادي قال ثنا أبو حذيفة قال ثنا عكرمة عن أبي زميل عن ابن عباس ﵄: إن المشركين كانوا يطوفون بالبيت يقولون: لبيك لبيك لا شريك لك فيقول النبي ﷺ: قد قد فيقولون: إلا شريك هو لك تملكه وما ملك ويقولون: غفرانك غفرانك فأنزل الله: (وَمَا كَانَ ٱللَّهُ لِيُعَذِّبَهُمْ وَأَنتَ فِيهِمْ ۚ وَمَا كَانَ ٱللَّهُ مُعَذِّبَهُمْ وَهُمْ يَسْتَغْفِرُونَ) فقال ابن عباس: كان فيهم أمانان نبي الله والاستغفار قال: فذهب النبي وبقي الاستغفار (وَمَا لَهُمْ أَلَّا يُعَذِّبَهُمُ ٱللَّهُ وَهُمْ يَصُدُّونَ عَنِ ٱلْمَسْجِدِ ٱلْحَرَامِ وَمَا كَانُوٓا۟ أَوْلِيَآءَهُۥٓ ۚ إِنْ أَوْلِيَآؤُهُۥٓ إِلَّا ٱلْمُتَّقُونَ) قال: فهذا عذاب الآخرة قال: وذاك عذاب الدنيا.

Ibn 'Abbaas ؓ narrated that the polytheists used to make *tawaaf* of the Sacred House saying, "We obey your call! We obey your call! You have no partner!" The Prophet ﷺ would then say, "Enough! Enough!" Then they would say, "Except a partner that is yours, You own him and that which he possesses!" They would also say, "We seek your forgiveness! We seek your forgiveness!" Then Allaah sent down:

وَمَا كَانَ ٱللَّهُ لِيُعَذِّبَهُمْ وَأَنتَ فِيهِمْ ۚ وَمَا كَانَ ٱللَّهُ مُعَذِّبَهُمْ وَهُمْ يَسْتَغْفِرُونَ

"Allaah would not punish them while you are amongst them, nor would Allaah punish them while they seek forgiveness."
Ibn 'Abbaas said, "They had two safeguards: the Prophet of Allaah and seeking forgiveness."

وَمَا لَهُمْ أَلَّا يُعَذِّبَهُمُ ٱللَّهُ وَهُمْ يَصُدُّونَ عَنِ ٱلْمَسْجِدِ ٱلْحَرَامِ وَمَا كَانُوٓا۟ أَوْلِيَآءَهُۥٓ ۚ إِنْ أَوْلِيَآؤُهُۥٓ إِلَّا ٱلْمُتَّقُونَ

"And why should Allaah not punish them while they prevent (people) from the Sacred *Masjid* and they are not its guardians. None can be its guardians except those who fear Allaah…"; He (Ibn 'Abbaas) said, "So this (verse: 34) pertains to the punishment in the hereafter and that (verse: 33) pertains to the punishment of this life."

As for this *hadeeth*, Ibn Jareer transmitted it in his *Tafseer*, volume 13, page 511. Ash-Sheikh Muqbil ﵀ said, "This is a *hasan hadeeth*," and then added, "There is nothing which prevents the verse from being revealed because of this situation as well as the other, or even that both of them together were the reason why the verse was revealed, and Allaah knows best."

His, the Exalted One's statement:

$$\text{ٱلْـٰٔنَ خَفَّفَ ٱللَّهُ عَنكُمْ وَعَلِمَ أَنَّ فِيكُمْ ضَعْفًا ۚ فَإِن يَكُن مِّنكُم مِّائَةٌ صَابِرَةٌ يَغْلِبُوا۟ مِائَتَيْنِ}$$

"Now Allaah has lightened your task and He knows that there is weakness in you. So if there are from amongst you one hundred steadfast persons they shall overcome two hundred…" (verse: 66)

قال الإمام البخاري ﵁ (4653): حدثنا يحيى بن عبد الله السلمي أخبرنا عبد الله بن المبارك أخبرنا جرير بن حازم قال أخبرني الزبير بن الخِرِّيت عن عكرمة عن ابن عباس ﵄ قال: لما نزلت: (إن يَكُن مِّنكُمْ عِشْرُونَ صَابِرُونَ يَغْلِبُوا۟ مِائَتَيْنِ) شق ذلك على المسلمين حين فرض عليهم أن لا يفر واحد من عشرة فجاء التخفيف فقال: (ٱلْـٰٔنَ خَفَّفَ ٱللَّهُ عَنكُمْ وَعَلِمَ أَنَّ فِيكُمْ ضَعْفًا ۚ فَإِن يَكُن مِّنكُم مِّائَةٌ صَابِرَةٌ يَغْلِبُوا۟ مِائَتَيْنِ) قال: فلما خفف الله عنهم من العدة نقص من الصبر ما خفف عنهم.

Ibn 'Abbaas ﵄ said, "When the following verse descended:

$$\text{إِن يَكُن مِّنكُمْ عِشْرُونَ صَابِرُونَ يَغْلِبُوا۟ مِائَتَيْنِ}$$

"If there are twenty, steadfast amongst you, they shall overcome two hundred…" (verse: 65), it became a heavy burden on the Muslims when it was made incumbent that one person must stand and fight and not flee from ten. Then the lightening of that burden ensued,

$$\text{ٱلْـٰٔنَ خَفَّفَ ٱللَّهُ عَنكُمْ وَعَلِمَ أَنَّ فِيكُمْ ضَعْفًا ۚ فَإِن يَكُن مِّنكُم مِّائَةٌ صَابِرَةٌ يَغْلِبُوا۟ مِائَتَيْنِ}$$

"Now Allaah has lightened your task and He knows that there is weakness in you. So if there are from amongst you one hundred steadfast persons they shall overcome two hundred…"
So when Allaah lessened the number for them, the obligation to remain steadfast was lightened in accordance with the reduction of numbers."

Al-Bukhaaree transmitted this *hadeeth* in his *Saheeh* (4653).

His, the Exalted One's statement:

$$\text{مَا كَانَ لِنَبِيٍّ أَن يَكُونَ لَهُ أَسْرَىٰ حَتَّىٰ يُثْخِنَ فِي ٱلْأَرْضِ}$$

"It is not for a Prophet that he should have prisoners of war until he has made a great slaughter (amongst his enemies, gaining the upper-hand) in the land…" (verse: 67)

قال الحاكم رحمه الله (ج 2 ص 329): أخبرنا أبو العباس محمد بن أحمد المحبوبي حدثنا سعيد بن مسعود حدثنا عبيد الله بن موسى حدثنا إسرائيل عن إبراهيم بن مهاجر عن مجاهد عن ابن عمر رضي الله عنهما قال: استشار رسول الله ﷺ في الأسارى أبا بكر فقال: قومك وعشيرتك فخل سبيلهم فاستشار عمر فقال: اقتلهم قال: ففداهم رسول الله ﷺ فأنزل الله عز وجل: (مَا كَانَ لِنَبِيٍّ أَن يَكُونَ لَهُ أَسْرَىٰ حَتَّىٰ يُثْخِنَ فِي ٱلْأَرْضِ) إلى قوله : (فَكُلُوا مِمَّا غَنِمْتُمْ حَلَالًا طَيِّبًا) قال: فلقي النبي ﷺ عمر قال: كاد أن يصيبنا في خلافك بلاء.

هذا حديث صحيح الإسناد ولم يخرجاه.

Ibn 'Umar said, "The Messenger of Allaah ﷺ sought advice from Abu Bakr on what to do with the prisoners of war. So he (Abu Bakr) said, 'They are your people and relatives so let them go.' He then sought advice from 'Umar who said, "Kill them." The Messenger of Allaah ﷺ then ransomed them, [taking the advice of Abu Bakr]. In this regard Allaah sent down the following:

$$\text{مَا كَانَ لِنَبِيٍّ أَن يَكُونَ لَهُ أَسْرَىٰ حَتَّىٰ يُثْخِنَ فِي ٱلْأَرْضِ}$$

"It is not for a Prophet that he should have prisoners of war until he has made a great slaughter (amongst his enemies gaining the upper-hand) in the land," up to His statement,

$$\text{فَكُلُوا مِمَّا غَنِمْتُمْ حَلَالًا طَيِّبًا}$$

"So enjoy what you have captured of the booty of war, lawful and good." (verse: 69)

The Prophet ﷺ then met 'Umar and said, 'We were close to being afflicted with a tribulation for differing with your advice."

Al-Haakim transmitted this *hadeeth* in *Al-Mustadrak*, volume 2, page 329 and considered its chain to be authentic. Adh-Dhahabee asserted, "I say, it is up to the standards of Muslim." The *hadeeth* of 'Umar has already been mentioned in *Soorah Aal 'Imraan*.

His, the Exalted One's statement:

$$\text{لَوْلَا كِتَابٌ مِّنَ اللَّهِ سَبَقَ لَمَسَّكُمْ فِيمَا أَخَذْتُمْ عَذَابٌ عَظِيمٌ ۝ فَكُلُوا مِمَّا غَنِمْتُمْ حَلَالًا طَيِّبًا ۚ وَاتَّقُوا اللَّهَ ۚ إِنَّ اللَّهَ غَفُورٌ رَّحِيمٌ ۝}$$

"Were it not for a previous ordainment from Allaah, a severe torment would have touched you for what you took. So enjoy what you have captured of the booty of war, lawful and good, and fear Allaah. Verily Allaah is Oft-Forgiving Most-Merciful." (verse: 68-69)

قال الإمام أبو داود الطيالسي ﵀ (2429): حدثنا سلام عن الأعمش عن أبي صالح عن أبي هريرة ﵁ قال: لما كان يوم بدر تعجل الناس إلى الغنائم فأصابوها فقال رسول الله ﷺ: إن الغنيمة لا تحل لأحد سود الرؤوس غيركم وكان النبي وأصحابه إذا غنموا الغنيمة جمعوها ونزلت نار من السماء فأكلتها فأنزل الله هذه الآية: (لَوْلَا كِتَابٌ مِّنَ اللَّهِ سَبَقَ) إلى آخر الآيتين.

Abu Hurairah ﵁ said, "On the day of Badr the people rushed to the spoils of war and took them, so the Messenger of Allaah ﷺ said, 'Verily the spoils of war have not been made permissible for anyone of the children of Aadam other than you. The Prophet[79] and his companions, when they would win the spoils of war, they would gather it and then fire would descend from the sky destroying it.' Then Allaah sent down this verse:

$$\text{لَوْلَا كِتَابٌ مِّنَ اللَّهِ سَبَقَ}$$

"Were it not for a previous ordainment from Allaah...", to the end of the two verses."

Regarding this *hadeeth*, At-Tayaalisee transmitted it in his *Musnad* (2429) and At-Tirmidhee in his *Jaami'*, and he classified it to be *hasan saheeh*.

قال الحاكم ﵀ (ج 2 ص 329): حدثنا الشيخ أبو بكر بن إسحاق أنبأ محمد بن شاذان الجوهري حدثنا زكريا بن عدي حدثنا عبيد الله بن عمرو الرقي عن زيد بن أبي أنيسة عن عمرو بن مرة عن خيثمة قال: كان سعد بن أبي وقاص ﵁ في نفر فذكروا عليا فشتموه فقال سعد: مهلا عن أصحاب رسول الله ﷺ فإنا أصبنا دنيا مع رسول الله ﷺ فأنزل الله عز وجل: (لَوْلَا كِتَابٌ مِّنَ اللَّهِ سَبَقَ

---

[79] Meaning the Prophet from amongst the Prophets before Muhammad, may the peace and praise of Allaah be upon them, as is made clear in the narration of this *hadeeth* in the book *Mushkil Al-Aathaar hadeeth* (3310).

لَمَسَّكُمْ فِيمَآ أَخَذْتُمْ عَذَابٌ عَظِيمٌ) فأرجو أن تكون رحمة من عند الله سبقت لنا فقال بعضهم: فوالله إنه كان يبغضك ويسميك الأخنس فضحك سعد حتى استعلاه الضحك ثم قال: أليس قد يجد المرء على أخيه في الأمر يكون بينه وبينه ثم لا يبلغ ذلك أمانته وذكر كلمة أخرى.

هذا حديث صحيح على شرط الشيخين ولم يخرجاه.

Sa'd ibn Abee Waqqaas was with a group of people who mentioned 'Ali and began reviling him so Sa'd said, "Slow down and be easy on the Companions of the Messenger of Allaah, for verily we obtained some worldly goods with the Messenger of Allaah and then Allaah sent down:

لَوْلَا كِتَٰبٌ مِّنَ ٱللَّهِ سَبَقَ لَمَسَّكُمْ فِيمَآ أَخَذْتُمْ عَذَابٌ عَظِيمٌ

'Were it not for a previous ordainment from Allaah, a severe torment would have touched you for what you took."

So I hope that mercy from Allaah has preceded for us." Then one of them said, 'By Allaah, he used to despise you and call you the pug-nosed one.' Sa'd then laughed to the point where he was overtaken by laughter and then said, "Is it not possible that a person can have a problem with his brother because of a personal thing between them but it does not reach the point where his loyalty to him is broken?" And he mentioned another statement.

Al-Haakim transmitted this *hadeeth* in *Al-Mustadrak*, volume 2, page 329 and classified it to be authentic according to the standards of the two Sheikhs (Al-Bukhaaree and Muslim).

His, the Exalted One's statement:

وَأُوْلُوا۟ ٱلْأَرْحَامِ بَعْضُهُمْ أَوْلَىٰ بِبَعْضٍ فِى كِتَٰبِ ٱللَّهِ

"And blood relatives have more right to one another in the decree of Allaah…" (verse: 75)

قال الإمام أبو داود الطيالسي (2676): حدثنا سليمان عن سماك عن عكرمة عن ابن عباس قال: آخى رسول الله بين أصحابه وورث بعضهم من بعض حتى نزلت: (وَأُوْلُوا۟ ٱلْأَرْحَامِ بَعْضُهُمْ أَوْلَىٰ بِبَعْضٍ فِى كِتَٰبِ ٱللَّهِ) فتركوا ذلك وتوارثوا بالنسب.

Ibn 'Abbaas said, "The Messenger of Allaah made his Companions associate with one another as brothers (each Companion having his own brotherly companion) and they used to inherit from one another until the verse descended:

$$\text{وَأُو۟لُوا۟ ٱلْأَرْحَامِ بَعْضُهُمْ أَوْلَىٰ بِبَعْضٍ}$$

'And blood relatives have more right to one another...'

So they stopped doing that and inherited from one another through family ties."

At-Tayaalisee transmitted this *hadeeth* in his *Musnad* (2676). A similar *hadeeth* on Az-Zubair has been transmitted by Ibn Abee Haatim in his *Tafseer*, volume 4, page 24. Ash-Sheikh Muqbil ﷺ commented, pertaining to the chain of the *hadeeth* of Ibn 'Abbaas, "The narrations of Simaak on 'Ikrimah are inconsistent; however, this *hadeeth* is supported by the *hadeeth* of Az-Zubair and is therefore raised to the level of authenticity, and Allaah knows best.

سورة التوبة

Sooratut-Tawbah

His, the Exalted One's statement:

$$\text{أَجَعَلْتُمْ سِقَايَةَ ٱلْحَاجِّ وَعِمَارَةَ ٱلْمَسْجِدِ ٱلْحَرَامِ كَمَنْ ءَامَنَ بِٱللَّهِ وَٱلْيَوْمِ ٱلْأَخِرِ وَجَٰهَدَ فِى سَبِيلِ ٱللَّهِ ۚ لَا يَسْتَوُۥنَ عِندَ ٱللَّهِ}$$

"Do you consider the providing of drinking water to the pilgrims and the maintenance of the Sacred *Masjid* equal to those who believe in Allaah and the last day and fight in the cause of Allaah? They are not equal in the sight of Allaah…" (verse: 19)

قال الإمام مسلم ﷺ (1879): حدثني حسن بن علي الحلواني حدثنا أبو توبة حدثنا معاوية بن سلام عن زيد بن سلام أنه سمع أبا سلام قال حدثني النعمان بن بشير ﷺ قال: كنت عند منبر رسول الله ﷺ فقال رجل: ما أبالي أن لا أعمل عملا بعد الإسلام إلا أن أسقي الحاج وقال آخر: ما أبالي أن لا أعمل عملا بعد الإسلام إلا أن أعمر المسجد الحرام وقال آخر: الجهاد في سبيل الله أفضل مما قلتم فزجرهم عمر وقال: لا ترفعوا أصواتكم عند منبر رسول الله ﷺ وهو يوم الجمعة ولكن إذا صليت الجمعة دخلت فاستفتيته فيما اختلفتم فيه فأنزل الله عز وجل: (أَجَعَلْتُمْ سِقَايَةَ ٱلْحَاجِّ وَعِمَارَةَ ٱلْمَسْجِدِ ٱلْحَرَامِ كَمَنْ ءَامَنَ بِٱللَّهِ وَٱلْيَوْمِ ٱلْأَخِرِ) الآية إلى آخرها.

An-Nu'maan ibn Basheer said, "I was at the *minbar*[80] of the Messenger of Allaah when a man said, 'It does not matter to me if I were to do no other deed after Islaam other than providing drinking water for the pilgrims.' Another man said, "It does not matter to me if I were to do no other deed after Islaam other than maintaining the Sacred *Masjid*." Another man said, 'Fighting in the path of Allaah is better than what you mentioned.' 'Umar then scolded them and said, "Do not raise your voices at the *minbar* of the Messenger of Allaah on the day of *Jumu'ah*! Rather, after I pray the

---

[80] The *minbar* was a small wooden pulpit with three steps which the Prophet used to stand upon when giving his sermons, and he would sit down on the third step as is mentioned in the *hadeeth* of Anas transmitted by Ad-Daarimee, *hadeeth* (42). Ash-Sheikh Muqbil mentioned it in his book *Al-Jaami' As-Saheeh Mimmaa laisa fee As-Saheehain*, volume 2, page 186, and ruled it to be *hasan*. Ash-Sheikh Muhammad ibn 'Abdil-Wahhaab Al-Yemenee Al-Wusaabee has written a small treatise about the number of steps of the *minbar* called *Al-Jawhar fee 'Adad Darajaat Al-Minbar*, and he came to the conclusion that the Sunnah of the *minbar* is that it have three steps only, and that the *Khateeb* (lecturer) stands on the second step and sits on the third step.

Jumu'ah prayer, I will go to (the Messenger of Allaah ﷺ) and ask for his judgment regarding your differing." Then Allaah ﷻ sent down:

$$\text{أَجَعَلْتُمْ سِقَايَةَ ٱلْحَآجِّ وَعِمَارَةَ ٱلْمَسْجِدِ ٱلْحَرَامِ كَمَنْ ءَامَنَ بِٱللَّهِ وَٱلْيَوْمِ ٱلْءَاخِرِ}$$

"Do you consider the providing of drinking water to the pilgrims and the maintenance of the Sacred *Masjid* equal to those who believe in Allaah and the last day…".

Muslim transmitted this *hadeeth* in his *Saheeh* (1879).

<u>His, the Exalted One's statement:</u>

$$\text{وَٱلَّذِينَ يَكْنِزُونَ ٱلذَّهَبَ وَٱلْفِضَّةَ وَلَا يُنفِقُونَهَا فِى سَبِيلِ ٱللَّهِ فَبَشِّرْهُم بِعَذَابٍ أَلِيمٍ}$$

"And those who hoard gold and silver, and spend it not in the path of Allaah, announce unto them a painful torment." (verse: 34)

قال الإمام البخاري ﷺ (1406): حدثنا علي سمع هشيما أخبرنا حصين عن زيد بن وهب قال مررت بالربذة فإذا أنا بأبي ذر ﷺ فقلت له: ما أنزلك منزلك هذا قال: كنت بالشام فاختلفت أنا ومعاوية في: (وَٱلَّذِينَ يَكْنِزُونَ ٱلذَّهَبَ وَٱلْفِضَّةَ وَلَا يُنفِقُونَهَا فِى سَبِيلِ ٱللَّهِ) قال معاوية: نزلت في أهل الكتاب فقلت: نزلت فينا وفيهم فكان بيني وبينه في ذاك وكتب إلى عثمان ﷺ يشكوني فكتب إليَّ عثمان أن اقدم المدينة فقدمتها فكثر عليَّ الناس حتى كأنهم لم يروني قبل ذلك فذكرت ذاك لعثمان فقال لي: إن شئت تنحيت فكنت قريبا فذاك الذي أنزلني هذا المنزل ولو أمروا عليَّ حبشيا لسمعت وأطعت.

Zaid ibn Wahb said, "I passed by Ar-Rabdhah[81] and ran into Abu Dhar ﷺ so I said, 'What brings you here?' He said, "I was in Shaam and I differed with Mu'aawiyah about the verse,

$$\text{وَٱلَّذِينَ يَكْنِزُونَ ٱلذَّهَبَ وَٱلْفِضَّةَ وَلَا يُنفِقُونَهَا فِى سَبِيلِ ٱللَّهِ}$$

'And those who hoard gold and silver, and spend it not in the path of Allaah…'

Mu'aawiyah said, "It descended because of the people of the book." I said, 'It descended because of us as well as them (the people of the book).' So a disagreement occurred between the two of us because of this differing. He then wrote to 'Uthmaan ﷺ complaining about me. 'Uthmaan then wrote me a letter telling me to come to Madeenah, so I went there. On arrival, the people

---

[81] Ar-Rabdhah is a place between Makkah and Madeenah.

gathered around me as if they had never seen me before and I mentioned that to 'Uthmaan so he said to me, "If you wish, retire to a nearby place." So that is what brought me here and if they were to put a man from Habashah (Abyssinia) in authority over me, I would hear and obey."

Al-Bukhaaree transmitted this *hadeeth* in his *Saheeh* (1406).

His, the Exalted One's statement:

وَمِنْهُم مَّن يَلْمِزُكَ فِي ٱلصَّدَقَٰتِ فَإِنْ أُعْطُواْ مِنْهَا رَضُواْ وَإِن لَّمْ يُعْطَوْاْ مِنْهَآ إِذَا هُمْ يَسْخَطُونَ ۝

"And amongst them are those who accuse you in the matter of the distribution of the alms. If they are given a part thereof they are pleased, but if they are not given thereof, behold, they are angry." (verse: 58)

قال الإمام البخاري ﷺ (6933): حدثنا عبد الله بن محمد حدثنا هشام أخبرنا معمر عن الزهري عن أبي سلمة عن أبي سعيد ﷺ قال: بينا النبي ﷺ يقسم جاء عبد الله بن ذي الخويصرة التميمي فقال: اعدل يا رسول الله فقال: ويحك ومن يعدل إذا لم أعدل قال عمر بن الخطاب: ائذن لي فأضرب عنقه قال: دعه فإن له أصحابا يحقر أحدكم صلاته مع صلاته وصيامه مع صيامه يمرقون من الدين كما يمرق السهم من الرمية ينظر في قُذَذه فلا يوجد فيه شيء ثم ينظر إلى نصله فلا يوجد فيه شيء ثم ينظر إلى رصافه فلا يوجد فيه شيء ثم ينظر في نضيّه فلا يوجد فيه شيء قد سبق الفرث والدم آيتهم رجل إحدى يديه ، أو قال ، ثدييه مثل ثدي المرأة ، أو قال ، مثل البضعة تدردر يخرجون على حين فرقة من الناس قال أبو سعيد: أشهد سمعت من النبي ﷺ وأشهد أن عليا قتلهم وأنا معه جيء بالرجل على النعت الذي نعته النبي ﷺ قال فنزلت فيه: (وَمِنْهُم مَّن يَلْمِزُكَ فِي ٱلصَّدَقَٰتِ).

Abu Sa'eed ﷺ said, "While the Prophet ﷺ was distributing the alms, 'Abdullaah ibn Dhil-Khuwaisirah At-Tameemee came to him and said, 'Be just, O Messenger of Allaah!' He ﷺ said, "Woe unto you! Who will be just if I am not just?" 'Umar ibn Al-Khattaab said, 'Let me strike his neck (chopping off his head).' He ﷺ said, "Leave him, for verily he has companions whom one of you will regard his prayer to be insignificant in comparison to their prayer, and his fasting to be insignificant in comparison to their fasting. They will pass through the *deen* (religion) as an arrow passes through the game animal. The feathers of the arrow are looked at with no traces of the animal on them. The tip of the arrow is then looked at with no traces of the animal on it. The *risaaf* (tendons used as string and wound to tighten the tip of the arrow) are then looked at with no traces of the animal on them. The shaft of the arrow is then looked at with no traces of the animal on it. It passed by the blood and the *farth* (the excrements in the stomach)

without any of that clinging to it. Their sign is a man whom one of his arms, or he said breasts, is like the breast of a woman, or he said, like a piece of meat that shakes. They will emerge when the Muslims are divided."
Abu Sa'eed said, "I bear witness that I heard this from the Prophet ﷺ and I bear witness that 'Ali killed them while I was with him. The man was brought according to the description that the Prophet ﷺ had described." He (Abu Sa'eed) said, "It (the verse in question) descended because of him ('Abdullaah ibn Dhil-Khuwaisirah):

$$\text{وَمِنْهُم مَّن يَلْمِزُكَ فِي ٱلصَّدَقَٰتِ}$$

"And amongst them are those who accuse you in the matter of the distribution of the alms…"

Al-Bukhaaree transmitted this *hadeeth* in his *Saheeh* (6933).

<u>His, the Exalted One's statement:</u>

$$\text{وَلَئِن سَأَلْتَهُمْ لَيَقُولُنَّ إِنَّمَا كُنَّا نَخُوضُ وَنَلْعَبُ قُلْ أَبِٱللَّهِ وَءَايَٰتِهِۦ وَرَسُولِهِۦ كُنتُمْ تَسْتَهْزِءُونَ}$$

"And if you ask them they say, 'We were only talking idly and joking.' Say: Was it at Allaah and His signs and His Messenger that you were mocking!" (verse: 65)

قال الإمام ابن أبي حاتم ﵀ في التفسير (ج 4 ص 63): حدثنا يونس بن عبد الأعلى حدثنا عبد الله بن وهب أخبرني هشام بن سعد عن زيد بن أسلم عن عبد الله بن عمر ﵄ قال: قال رجل في غزوة تبوك في مجلس يوماً: ما رأيت مثل مثل قرائنا هؤلاء لا أرغب بطوناً ولا أكذب ألسنة ولا أجبن عند اللقاء فقال رجل في المجلس: كذبت ولكنك منافق لأخبرن رسول الله ﷺ فبلغ ذلك النبي ﷺ ونزل القرآن قال عبد الله: فأنا رأيته متعلقاً بحقب ناقة رسول الله ﷺ تنكبه الحجارة وهو يقول: يا رسول الله إنما كنا نخوض ونلعب ورسول الله ﷺ يقول: أبالله آياته ورسوله كنتم تستهزءون.

'Abdullaah ibn 'Umar ﵄ said, "One day a man said while in a gathering on the way to the battle of Tabook, 'I have not seen the likes of our reciters. I have not seen a people having stomachs with a greater appetite, tongues that lie with greater frequency, or people that are more cowardly when confronting the enemy than them.' A man in the gathering then said, "You lie! Rather, you are a hypocrite! I will indeed inform the Messenger of Allaah ﷺ." News of that incident reached the Prophet ﷺ and Qur'aan descended."
'Abdullaah (ibn 'Umar) said, "I saw him hanging onto the straps of the camel of the Messenger of Allaah ﷺ while being hurt by stones on the ground saying: 'O Messenger of Allaah, we were only talking idly and joking!' The

Messenger of Allaah ﷺ would respond saying, "Was it at Allaah and His signs and His Messenger that you were mocking!"

Regarding this *hadeeth*, Ibn Abee Haatim transmitted it in his *Tafseer*, volume 4, page 63. Ash-Sheikh Muqbil ﷺ commented saying, "[Concerning] The *hadeeth*, the people of its chain are people of the *Saheeh* (Al-Bukhaaree and/or Muslim) except for Hishaam ibn Sa'd. Muslim only mentioned him in a supporting role as mentioned in *Al-Meezaan*. At-Tabaree also transmitted it by way of his (Hishaam's) chain, volume 10, page 172, and it has a supporting *hadeeth* with a chain that is *hasan* mentioned by Ibn Abee Haatim, volume 4, page 64, from the *hadeeth* of Ka'b ibn Maalik."

<u>His, the Exalted One's statement:</u>

يَحْلِفُونَ بِٱللَّهِ مَا قَالُوا۟ وَلَقَدْ قَالُوا۟ كَلِمَةَ ٱلْكُفْرِ وَكَفَرُوا۟

"They swear by Allaah that they said nothing (bad), but really they said a word of disbelief and they disbelieved..." (verse: 74)

قال الإمام ابن جرير رحمه الله (ج 14 ص 363): حدثني أيوب بن إسحاق بن إبراهيم قال ثنا عبد الله بن رجاء قال ثنا إسرائيل عن سماك عن سعيد بن جبير عن ابن عباس رضي الله عنهما قال: كان رسول الله ﷺ جالسا في ظل شجرة فقال: إنه سيأتيكم إنسان فينظر إليكم بعيني شيطان فإذا جاء فلا تكلموه فلم يلبث أن طلع رجل أزرق فدعاه رسول الله ﷺ فقال: علام تشتمني أنت وأصحابك فانطلق الرجل فجاء بأصحابه فحلفوا بالله ما قالوا وما فعلوا حتى تجاوز عنهم فأنزل الله: (يَحْلِفُونَ بِٱللَّهِ مَا قَالُوا۟) ثم نعتهم جميعا إلى آخر الآية.

Ibn 'Abbaas ﷺ said, "The Messenger of Allaah ﷺ was sitting in the shade of a tree and he said, 'Indeed a person will soon come to you and he will look at you with the two eyes of a devil, so when he comes do not speak to him.' Then, after a short period of time, a blue-eyed man emerged and the Messenger of Allaah ﷺ called him over and said, "On what basis do you and your comrades revile me?" The man then left and came back with his comrades. They swore by Allaah that they did not say or do anything until he finally pardoned them. Then Allaah sent down the following,

يَحْلِفُونَ بِٱللَّهِ مَا قَالُوا۟

'They swear by Allaah that they said nothing...'

Then He (Allaah) described them all concluding the verse."

Ibn Jareer transmitted this *hadeeth* in his *Tafseer*, volume 14, page 363.

His, the Exalted One's statement:

$$\text{ٱلَّذِينَ يَلْمِزُونَ ٱلْمُطَّوِّعِينَ مِنَ ٱلْمُؤْمِنِينَ فِي ٱلصَّدَقَٰتِ}$$

"Those who blame the believers who give charity voluntarily…" (verse: 79)

قال الإمام البخاري رحمه الله (1415): حدثنا عبيد الله بن سعيد حدثنا أبو النعمان الحكم هو ابن عبد الله البصري حدثنا شعبة عن سليمان عن أبي وائل عن أبي مسعود رضي الله عنه قال: لما نزلت آية الصدقة كنا نحامل فجاء رجل فتصدق بشيء كثير فقالوا: مرائي وجاء رجل فتصدق بصاع فقالوا: إن الله لغني عن صاع هذا فنزلت: (ٱلَّذِينَ يَلْمِزُونَ ٱلْمُطَّوِّعِينَ مِنَ ٱلْمُؤْمِنِينَ فِي ٱلصَّدَقَٰتِ وَٱلَّذِينَ لَا يَجِدُونَ إِلَّا جُهْدَهُمْ) الآية.

Abu Mas'ood ؓ said, "During the time the verse regarding charity was revealed, we used to carry things on our backs for money. A man would come and give a lot of charity and they (the hypocrites) would say, 'Show off.' Another man would come and give one *Saa'* (four double handfuls) in charity and they (the hypocrites) would say, "Allaah is in no need of this man's *Saa'*." Then the verse descended,

$$\text{ٱلَّذِينَ يَلْمِزُونَ ٱلْمُطَّوِّعِينَ مِنَ ٱلْمُؤْمِنِينَ فِي ٱلصَّدَقَٰتِ وَٱلَّذِينَ لَا يَجِدُونَ إِلَّا جُهْدَهُمْ}$$

'Those who blame the believers who give charity voluntarily and those who can not find something to give except what is available to them…" (verse: 79)

Al-Bukhaaree transmitted this *hadeeth* in his *Saheeh* (1415) as well as Muslim in his *Saheeh* (1018).

His, the Exalted One's statement:

$$\text{وَلَا تُصَلِّ عَلَىٰ أَحَدٍ مِّنْهُم مَّاتَ أَبَدًا}$$

"And do not ever pray for any of them who has died…" (verse: 84)

قال الإمام البخاري رحمه الله (1269): حدثنا مسدد قال حدثنا يحيى بن سعيد عن عبيد الله قال حدثني نافع عن ابن عمر رضي الله عنهما أن عبد الله بن أبي لما توفي جاء ابنه إلى النبي ﷺ فقال: يا رسول الله أعطني قميصك أكفنه فيه وصلّ عليه واستغفر له فأعطاه النبي ﷺ قميصه فقال: آذني أصلي عليه فآذنه

146

فلما أراد أن يصلي عليه جذبه عمر ﷺ فقال: أليس الله نهاك أن تصلي على المنافقين فقال: أنا بين خيرتين قال: (اَسْتَغْفِرْ لَهُمْ أَوْ لَا تَسْتَغْفِرْ لَهُمْ إِن تَسْتَغْفِرْ لَهُمْ سَبْعِينَ مَرَّةً فَلَن يَغْفِرَ ٱللَّهُ لَهُمْ) فصلى عليه فنزلت: (وَلَا تُصَلِّ عَلَىٰ أَحَدٍ مِّنْهُم مَّاتَ أَبَدًا).

Ibn 'Umar ﷺ narrated that when 'Abdullaah ibn Ubay died his son went to the Prophet ﷺ and said, "O Messenger of Allaah, let me have your *qamees* (long outer garment) so I can shroud him in it, and pray for him and seek forgiveness for him." The Prophet ﷺ then gave him his *qamees* and said, 'Give me permission to pray (the funeral prayer) for him.' So he gave him permission. Then, when he was about to pray for him, 'Umar pulled him back and said, "Has not Allaah prohibited you from praying for the hypocrites?" He said, 'I am between two choices, He has said,

اَسْتَغْفِرْ لَهُمْ أَوْ لَا تَسْتَغْفِرْ لَهُمْ إِن تَسْتَغْفِرْ لَهُمْ سَبْعِينَ مَرَّةً فَلَن يَغْفِرَ ٱللَّهُ لَهُمْ

"Whether you ask forgiveness for them or you do not ask forgiveness for them, if you ask seventy times for their forgiveness, Allaah will not forgive them." So he prayed for him and thereafter this verse descended,

وَلَا تُصَلِّ عَلَىٰ أَحَدٍ مِّنْهُم مَّاتَ أَبَدًا

"And do not ever pray for any of them who has died…".

This *hadeeth* has been transmitted by Al-Bukhaaree in his *Saheeh* (1269) as well as Muslim in his *Saheeh* (2400).

His, the Exalted One's statement:

سَيَحْلِفُونَ بِٱللَّهِ لَكُمْ إِذَا ٱنقَلَبْتُمْ إِلَيْهِمْ لِتُعْرِضُوا۟ عَنْهُمْ ۖ فَأَعْرِضُوا۟ عَنْهُمْ ۖ إِنَّهُمْ رِجْسٌ ۖ وَمَأْوَىٰهُمْ جَهَنَّمُ جَزَآءً بِمَا كَانُوا۟ يَكْسِبُونَ ۝ يَحْلِفُونَ لَكُمْ لِتَرْضَوْا۟ عَنْهُمْ ۖ فَإِن تَرْضَوْا۟ عَنْهُمْ فَإِنَّ ٱللَّهَ لَا يَرْضَىٰ عَنِ ٱلْقَوْمِ ٱلْفَٰسِقِينَ ۝

"They will swear to you by Allaah when you return to them that you may turn away from them. So turn away from them. Surely they are impure and hell is their dwelling place, a recompense for that which they used to earn. They swear to you that you may be pleased with them, but if you are pleased with them, certainly Allaah is not pleased with the people who are disobedient." (verses: 95-96)

قال الإمام ابن جرير ﷺ (ج 14 ص 427): حدثني يونس قال أخبرنا ابن وهب قال أخبرني يونس عن ابن شهاب قال أخبرني عبد الرحمن بن عبد الله بن كعب بن مالك أن عبد الله بن كعب قال سمعت كعب بن مالك ﷺ يقول: لما قدم رسول الله ﷺ من تبوك جلس للناس فلما فعل ذلك جاءه المخلفون فطفقوا يعتذرون إليه ويحلفون له وكانوا بضعة وثمانين رجلا فقبل منهم رسول الله ﷺ علانيتهم وبايعهم واستغفر لهم ووكل سرائرهم إلى الله وصدقته حديثي فقال كعب: والله ما أنعم الله علي من نعمة قط بعد أن هداني للإسلام أعظم في نفسي من صدقي رسول الله ﷺ أن لا أكون كذبته فأهلك كما هلك الذين كذبوا إن الله قال للذين كذبوا حين أنزل الوحي شر ما قال لأحد: (سَيَحْلِفُونَ بِٱللَّهِ لَكُمْ إِذَا ٱنقَلَبْتُمْ إِلَيْهِمْ لِتُعْرِضُوا۟ عَنْهُمْ ۖ فَأَعْرِضُوا۟ عَنْهُمْ ۖ إِنَّهُمْ رِجْسٌ ۖ وَمَأْوَىٰهُمْ جَهَنَّمُ جَزَآءً بِمَا كَانُوا۟ يَكْسِبُونَ)

إلى قوله: (فَإِنَّ ٱللَّهَ لَا يَرْضَىٰ عَنِ ٱلْقَوْمِ ٱلْفَٰسِقِينَ).

Ka'b ibn Maalik ؓ said, "When the Messenger of Allaah ﷺ came back from Tabook he sat down in order for the people to come to him. When he did that the people who stayed behind went to him giving him their excuses and swearing to him. They numbered over eighty men. He accepted from them what they outwardly said, and accepted their pledge of allegiance, and asked forgiveness for them, and entrusted whatever they may have concealed to Allaah. I told him the truth in what I said." Ka'b then said, "By Allaah, Allaah has never granted me a favor, after guiding me to Islaam, greater to me than (the favor) of me telling the truth to the Messenger of Allaah ﷺ and that I did not lie to him which would have ruined me as the people who lied were ruined. For verily Allaah said to those who lied when He sent down the revelation the worst thing He said to anyone:

سَيَحْلِفُونَ بِٱللَّهِ لَكُمْ إِذَا ٱنقَلَبْتُمْ إِلَيْهِمْ لِتُعْرِضُوا۟ عَنْهُمْ ۖ فَأَعْرِضُوا۟ عَنْهُمْ ۖ إِنَّهُمْ رِجْسٌ وَمَأْوَىٰهُمْ جَهَنَّمُ جَزَآءً بِمَا كَانُوا۟ يَكْسِبُونَ

'They will swear to you by Allaah when you return to them that you may turn away from them. So turn away from them. Surely they are impure and hell is their dwelling place, a recompense for that which they used to earn,' up to His statement,

فَإِنَّ ٱللَّهَ لَا يَرْضَىٰ عَنِ ٱلْقَوْمِ ٱلْفَٰسِقِينَ

'Certainly Allaah is not pleased with the people who are disobedient.'

Ibn Jareer transmitted this *hadeeth* in his *Tafseer*, volume 14, page 427. Ash-Sheikh Muqbil ؓ said, "The *hadeeth*, the people of its chain are people of the

Saheeh (Al-Bukhaaree and/or Muslim)...and similar to this hadeeth is what has been recorded in *Saheeh Al-Bukhaaree* at the end of the *hadeeth* of Ka'b ibn Maalik in the book of military expeditions in the chapter, The battle of Tabook (4418)."

His, the Exalted One's statement:

$$\text{مَا كَانَ لِلنَّبِيِّ وَٱلَّذِينَ ءَامَنُوٓا۟ أَن يَسْتَغْفِرُوا۟ لِلْمُشْرِكِينَ وَلَوْ كَانُوٓا۟ أُو۟لِى قُرْبَىٰ مِنۢ بَعْدِ مَا تَبَيَّنَ لَهُمْ أَنَّهُمْ أَصْحَابُ ٱلْجَحِيمِ ۝}$$

"It is not (proper) for the Prophet and those who believe to ask forgiveness for the polytheists, even if they be of kin, after it has become clear to them that they are the dwellers of the fire." (verse: 113)

قال الإمام البخاري رَحِمَهُ اللهُ (1360): حدثنا إسحاق أخبرنا يعقوب بن إبراهيم قال حدثني أبي عن صالح عن ابن شهاب قال أخبرني سعيد بن المسيب عن أبيه رَضِيَ اللهُ عَنْهُ أنه أخبره أنه لما حضرت أبا طالب الوفاة جاءه رسول الله ﷺ فوجد عنده أبا جهل بن هشام وعبد الله بن أبي أمية بن المغيرة قال رسول الله ﷺ لأبي طالب: يا عم قل لا إله إلا الله كلمة أشهد لك بها عند الله فقال أبو جهل وعبد الله بن أبي أمية: يا أبا طالب أترغب عن ملة عبد المطلب فلم يزل رسول الله ﷺ يعرضها عليه ويعودان بتلك المقالة حتى قال أبو طالب آخر ما كلمهم: هو على ملة عبد المطلب وأبى أن يقول لا إله إلا الله فقال رسول الله ﷺ: أما والله لأستغفرن لك ما لم أنه عنك فأنزل الله تعالى فيه: (مَا كَانَ لِلنَّبِيِّ) الآية.

Al-Musayyab ؓ narrated that when death approached Abu Taalib, the Messenger of Allaah ﷺ went to him and found Abu Jahl ibn Hishaam and 'Abdullaah ibn Abee Umaiyah ibn Al-Mugheerah there with him. The Messenger of Allaah ﷺ said to Abu Taalib, "O my uncle, say: *Laa Ilaaha Illallaah* (there is no deity who deserves to be worshipped except Allaah), a word that I will use to testify on your behalf with Allaah." Abu Jahl and 'Abdullaah ibn Abee Umaiyah then said, 'Do you prefer other than the religion of 'Abdul-Muttalib?' The Messenger of Allaah ﷺ continued to encourage him and they would respond with the same statement until Abu Taalib uttered to them his final words saying that he is on the religion of 'Abdul-Muttalib he refused to say, *Laa Ilaaha Illallaah* (there is no deity who deserves to be worshipped except Allaah). The Messenger of Allaah ﷺ then said, "Verily, by Allaah, I will seek forgiveness for you as long as I am not prohibited from doing so for you." Because of this, Allaah ﷻ then sent down,

$$\text{مَا كَانَ لِلنَّبِيِّ}$$

"It is not (proper) for the Prophet…" (verse: 113) .

Al-Bukhaaree transmitted this *hadeeth* in his *Saheeh* (1360) as well as Muslim in his *Saheeh* (24).

His, the Exalted One's statement:

لَقَد تَّابَ ٱللَّهُ عَلَى ٱلنَّبِيِّ وَٱلْمُهَٰجِرِينَ وَٱلْأَنصَارِ ٱلَّذِينَ ٱتَّبَعُوهُ فِى سَاعَةِ ٱلْعُسْرَةِ

"Allaah has forgiven the Prophet and the emigrants and the *Ansaar* (the helpers), those who followed him in the time of difficulty…" up to His statement:

يَٰٓأَيُّهَا ٱلَّذِينَ ءَامَنُوا۟ ٱتَّقُوا۟ ٱللَّهَ وَكُونُوا۟ مَعَ ٱلصَّٰدِقِينَ

"O you who believe, fear Allaah and be with those who are truthful." (verses:117-119)

قال الإمام البخاري ﷺ (4418): حدثنا يحيى بن بكير حدثنا الليث عن عقيل عن ابن شهاب عن عبد الرحمن بن عبد الله بن كعب بن مالك أن عبد الله بن كعب بن مالك وكان قائد كعب من بنيه حين عمي قال سمعت كعب بن مالك ﷺ يحدث حين تخلف عن قصة تبوك قال كعب: لم أتخلف عن رسول الله ﷺ في غزوة غزاها إلا في غزوة تبوك غير أني كنت تخلفت في غزوة بدر ولم يعاتب أحدا تخلف عنها إنما خرج رسول الله ﷺ يريد عير قريش حتى جمع الله بينهم وبين عدوهم على غير ميعاد ولقد شهدت مع رسول الله ﷺ ليلة العقبة حين تواثقنا على الإسلام وما أحب أن لي بها مشهد بدر وإن كانت بدر أذكر في الناس منها من خبري أني لم أكن قط أقوى ولا أيسر حين تخلفت عنه في تلك الغزاة والله ما اجتمعت عندي قبله راحلتان قط حتى جمعتهما في تلك الغزوة ولم يكن رسول الله ﷺ يريد غزوة إلا ورّى بغيرها حتى كانت تلك الغزوة غزاها رسول الله ﷺ في حر شديد واستقبل سفرا بعيدا ومفازا وعدوا كثيرا فجلى للمسلمين أمرهم ليتأهبوا أهبة غزوهم فأخبرهم بوجهه الذي يريد والمسلمون مع رسول الله ﷺ كثير ولا يجمعهم كتاب حافظ ، يريد الديوان ، قال كعب: فما رجل يريد أن يتغيب إلا ظن أن سيخفى له ما لم ينزل فيه وحي الله وغزا رسول الله ﷺ تلك الغزوة حين طابت الثمار والظلال وتجهز رسول الله ﷺ والمسلمون معه فطفقت أغدو لكي أتجهز معهم فأرجع ولم أقض شيئا فأقول في نفسي أنا قادر عليه فلم يزل يتمادى بي حتى اشتد بالناس الجد فأصبح رسول الله ﷺ والمسلمون معه ولم أقض من جهازي شيئا فقلت أتجهز بعده بيوم أو يومين ثم ألحقهم فغدوت بعد أن فصلوا لأتجهز فرجعت ولم أقض شيئا ثم غدوت ثم رجعت ولم أقض شيئا فلم يزل بي حتى أسرعوا وتفارط الغزو وهممت أن أرتحل فأدركهم وليتني فعلت فلم يقدر لي ذلك فكنت إذا خرجت في الناس بعد خروج رسول الله ﷺ فطفت فيهم أحزنني أني لا أرى إلا رجلا مغموصا عليه النفاق أو رجلا ممن عذر الله من الضعفاء ولم يذكرني رسول الله ﷺ

150

حتى بلغ تبوك فقال وهو جالس في القوم بتبوك: ما فعل كعب فقال رجل من بني سلمة: يا رسول الله حبسه برداه ونظره في عطفيه فقال معاذ بن جبل: بئس ما قلت والله يا رسول الله ما علمنا عليه إلا خيرا فسكت رسول الله ﷺ قال كعب ابن مالك: فلما بلغني أنه توجه قافلا حضرني همي وطفقت أتذكر الكذب وأقول بماذا أخرج من سخطه غدا واستعنت على ذلك بكل ذي رأي من أهلي فلما قيل إن رسول الله ﷺ قد أظل قادما زاح عني الباطل وعرفت أني لن أخرج منه أبدا بشيء فيه كذب فأجمعت صدقه وأصبح رسول الله ﷺ قادما وكان إذا قدم من سفر بدأ بالمسجد فيركع فيه ركعتين ثم جلس للناس فلما فعل ذلك جاءه المخلفون فطفقوا يعتذرون إليه ويحلفون له وكانوا بضعة وثمانين رجلا فقبل منهم رسول الله ﷺ علانيتهم وبايعهم واستغفر لهم ووكل سرائرهم إلى الله فجئته فلما سلمت عليه تبسم تبسم المغضب ثم قال: تعال فجئت أمشي حتى جلست بين يديه فقال لي: ما خلفك ألم تكن قد ابتعت ظهرك فقلت: بلى إني والله يا رسول الله لو جلست عند غيرك من أهل الدنيا لرأيت أن أخرج من سخطه بعذر ولقد أعطيت جدلا ولكني والله لقد علمت لئن حدثتك اليوم حديث كذب ترضى به عني ليوشكن الله أن يسخطك علي ولئن حدثتك حديث صدق تجد علي فيه إني لأرجو فيه عفو الله لا والله ما كان لي من عذر والله ما كنت قط أقوى ولا أيسر مني حين تخلفت عنك فقال رسول الله ﷺ: أما هذا فقد صدق فقم حتى يقضي الله فيك فقمت وثار رجال من بني سلمة فاتبعوني فقالوا لي: والله ما علمناك كنت أذنبت ذنبا قبل هذا ولقد عجزت أن لا تكون اعتذرت إلى رسول الله ﷺ بما اعتذر إليه المتخلفون قد كان ذنبك استغفار رسول الله ﷺ لك فوالله ما زالوا يؤنبونني حتى أردت أن أرجع فأكذب نفسي ثم قلت لهم هل لقي هذا معي أحد قالوا: نعم رجلان قالا مثل ما قلت فقيل لهما مثل ما قيل لك فقلت: من هما قالوا: مرارة بن الربيع العمري وهلال بن أمية الواقفي فذكروا لي رجلين صالحين قد شهدا بدرا فيهما أسوة فمضيت حين ذكروهما لي ونهى رسول الله ﷺ المسلمين عن كلامنا أيها الثلاثة من بين من تخلف عنه فاجتنبنا الناس وتغيروا لنا حتى تنكرت في نفسي الأرض فما هي التي أعرف فلبثنا على ذلك خمسين ليلة فأما صاحباي فاستكانا وقعدا في بيوتهما يبكيان وأما أنا فكنت أشب القوم وأجلدهم فكنت أخرج فأشهد الصلاة مع المسلمين وأطوف في الأسواق ولا يكلمني أحد وآتي رسول الله ﷺ فأسلم عليه وهو في مجلسه بعد الصلاة فأقول في نفسي هل حرك شفتيه برد السلام علي أم لا ثم أصلي قريبا منه فأسارقه النظر فإذا أقبلت على صلاتي أقبل إلي وإذا التفت نحوه أعرض عني حتى إذا طال علي ذلك من جفوة الناس مشيت حتى تسورت جدار حائط أبي قتادة وهو ابن عمي وأحب الناس إلي فسلمت عليه فوالله ما رد علي السلام فقلت: يا أبا قتادة أنشدك بالله هل تعلمني أحب الله ورسوله فسكت فعدت له فنشدته فسكت فعدت له فنشدته فقال: الله ورسوله أعلم ففاضت عيناي وتوليت حتى تسورت الجدار قال: فبينا أنا أمشي بسوق المدينة إذا نبطي من أنباط أهل الشام ممن قدم بالطعام يبيعه بالمدينة يقول: من يدل على كعب ابن مالك فطفق الناس يشيرون له حتى إذا جاءني دفع إلي كتابا من ملك غسان فإذا فيه: أما بعد فإنه قد بلغني أن صاحبك قد جفاك ولم يجعلك الله بدار هوان ولا مضيعة فالحق بنا نواسك فقلت لما قرأتها: وهذا أيضا من البلاء فتيممت بها التنور فسجرته بها حتى إذا مضت أربعون ليلة من الخمسين إذا رسول رسول

الله ﷺ يأتيني فقال: إن رسول الله ﷺ يأمرك أن تعتزل امرأتك فقلت: أطلقها أم ماذا أفعل قال: لا بل اعتزلها ولا تقربها وأرسل إلى صاحبي مثل ذلك فقلت لامرأتي الحقي بأهلك فتكوني عندهم حتى يقضي الله في هذا الأمر قال كعب: فجاءت امرأة هلال بن أمية رسول الله ﷺ فقالت: يا رسول الله إن هلال بن أمية شيخ ضائع ليس له خادم فهل تكره أن أخدمه قال: لا ولكن لا يقربك قالت: إنه والله ما به حركة إلى شيء والله ما زال يبكي منذ كان من أمره ما كان إلى يومه هذا فقال لي بعض أهلي: لو استأذنت رسول الله ﷺ في امرأتك كما أذن لامرأة هلال ابن أمية أن تخدمه فقلت: والله لا أستأذن فيها رسول الله ﷺ وما يدريني ما يقول رسول الله ﷺ إذا استأذنته فيها وأنا رجل شاب فلبثت بعد ذلك عشر ليال حتى كملت لنا خمسون ليلة من حين نهى رسول الله ﷺ عن كلامنا فلما صليت صلاة الفجر صبح خمسين ليلة وأنا على ظهر بيت من بيوتنا فبينا أنا جالس على الحال التي ذكر الله قد ضاقت علي نفسي وضاقت علي الأرض بما رحبت سمعت صوت صارخ أوفى على جبل سلع بأعلى صوته: يا كعب بن مالك أبشر قال: فخررت ساجدا وعرفت أن قد جاء فرج وآذن رسول الله ﷺ بتوبة الله علينا حين صلى صلاة الفجر فذهب الناس يبشروننا وذهب قبل صاحبي مبشرون وركض إلي رجل فرسا وسعى ساع من أسلم فأوفى على الجبل وكان الصوت أسرع من الفرس فلما جاءني الذي سمعت صوته يبشرني نزعت له ثوبي فكسوته إياهما ببشراه والله ما أملك غيرهما يومئذ واستعرت ثوبين فلبستهما وانطلقت إلى رسول الله ﷺ فيتلقاني الناس فوجا فوجا يهنونني بالتوبة يقولون: لتهنك توبة الله عليك قال كعب: حتى دخلت المسجد فإذا رسول الله ﷺ جالس حوله الناس فقام إلي طلحة بن عبيد الله يهرول حتى صافحني وهناني والله ما قام إلي رجل من المهاجرين غيره ولا أنساها لطلحة قال كعب: فلما سلمت على رسول الله ﷺ قال رسول الله ﷺ وهو يبرق وجهه من السرور: أبشر بخير يوم مر عليك منذ ولدتك أمك قال قلت: أمن عندك يا رسول الله أم من عند الله قال: لا بل من عند الله وكان رسول الله ﷺ إذا سر استنار وجهه حتى كأنه قطعة قمر وكنا نعرف ذلك منه فلما جلست بين يديه قلت: يا رسول الله إن من توبتي أن أنخلع من مالي صدقة إلى الله وإلى رسول الله قال رسول الله ﷺ: أمسك عليك بعض مالك فهو خير لك قلت: فإني أمسك سهمي الذي بخيبر فقلت: يا رسول الله إن الله إنما نجاني بالصدق وإن من توبتي أن لا أحدث إلا صدقا ما بقيت فوالله ما أعلم أحدا من المسلمين أبلاه الله في صدق الحديث منذ ذكرت ذلك لرسول الله ﷺ أحسن مما أبلاني ما تعمدت منذ ذكرت ذلك لرسول الله ﷺ إلى يومي هذا كذبا وإني لأرجو أن يحفظني الله فيما بقيت وأنزل الله على رسوله ﷺ: (لَّقَد تَّابَ ٱللَّهُ عَلَى ٱلنَّبِىِّ وَٱلْمُهَٰجِرِينَ وَٱلْأَنصَارِ) إلى قوله: (وَكُونُوا۟ مَعَ ٱلصَّٰدِقِينَ) فوالله ما أنعم الله علي من نعمة قط بعد أن هداني للإسلام أعظم في نفسي من صدقي لرسول الله ﷺ أن لا أكون كذبته فأهلك كما هلك الذين كذبوا فإن الله قال للذين كذبوا حين أنزل الوحي شر ما قال لأحد فقال تبارك وتعالى: (سَيَحْلِفُونَ بِٱللَّهِ لَكُمْ إِذَا ٱنقَلَبْتُمْ) إلى قوله:

152

(فَإِنَّ ٱللَّهَ لَا يَرْضَىٰ عَنِ ٱلْقَوْمِ ٱلْفَٰسِقِينَ) قال كعب: وكنا تخلفنا أيها الثلاثة عن أمر أولئك الذين قبل منهم رسول الله ﷺ حين حلفوا له فبايعهم واستغفر لهم وأرجأ رسول الله ﷺ أمرنا حتى قضى الله فيه فبذلك قال الله: (وَعَلَى ٱلثَّلَٰثَةِ ٱلَّذِينَ خُلِّفُوا۟) وليس الذي ذكر الله مما خلفنا عن الغزو إنما هو تخليفه إيانا وإرجاؤه أمرنا عمن حلف له واعتذر إليه فقبل منه.

Ka'b ibn Maalik ؓ narrated about the story of Tabook when he stayed behind saying, "I never abstained from the Messenger of Allaah ﷺ not partaking in a battle that he fought except for the battle of Tabook; however, I was absent during the battle of Badr but he did not blame anyone who was absent from that battle for verily the Messenger of Allaah ﷺ only set out wanting to raid a caravan of Quraish. Allaah then caused them and their enemies to encounter without notice. However, I was present with the Messenger of Allaah ﷺ on the night of Al-'Aqabah when we took covenants from one another pledging our allegiance to Islaam, and I would not like to have the battle of Badr as a replacement for it,[82] even if Badr is more remembered by the people.

A part of my story (about Tabook) is that I had never been stronger or wealthier than when I was refrained from travelling with him not participating in that battle. By Allaah, I never had two riding animals at one time until the time of that battle. The Messenger of Allaah ﷺ would not got out for a battle except that he feigned that he was going out for a different one until the time for the intended battle came. The Messenger of Allaah ﷺ prepared for the battle of Tabook at a time when the weather was extremely hot. He faced a long journey through the desert as well as a large enemy so [on this occasion] he made clear to the Muslims their situation so they could prepare the equipment they would need for their battle, and he also told them the intended destination.

The Muslims with the Messenger of Allaah ﷺ at that time were many. In fact a register would not be able to fit all of their names. There was not a man who wanted to stay behind except that he thought his affair would remain hidden for him (the prophet) as long as no revelation from Allaah descending thereby exposing him. Furthermore, the Messenger of Allaah ﷺ prepared for that battle at a time when the fruits were ripe and there was good shade. The Messenger of Allaah ﷺ and the Muslims with him started to get ready [to depart]. I would go out as to get ready along with them, then I would come back without accomplishing anything. I would say to myself, 'I am able to get ready (later).'

---

[82] Ibn Hajar explained the wisdom behind this statement in *Fathul-Baaree* in the explanation of *hadeeth* (3889) saying, "Because whoever was present at Badr, even if he is distinguished because it was the first battle where Islaam was victorious, however, the pledge at Al-'Aqabah was the reason why Islaam spread and because of it the battle of Badr took place."

I kept delaying up to the time when the people began to diligently prepare for departure. By morning, the Messenger of Allaah ﷺ and the Muslims along with him were fully prepared and I had not gotten any of my preparations done. I said [to myself], 'I will get ready a day or two after them, then I will catch up with them.' I went out to get ready after they had already departed, then I returned, again not accomplishing anything. Then I went out once more, then I returned not accomplishing anything. I continued doing this until they were long gone and the battle had passed me by. I considered going out to try and catch them. If only I did that [things would have been different], but that was not destined for me. When I would walk among the people after the Messenger of Allaah ﷺ had left, it saddened me that I would only see a man accused of hypocrisy or a weak man that Allaah has excused.

The Messenger of Allaah ﷺ did not mention me until he reached Tabook. He said, "What did Ka'b do?" A man from the tribe Banee Salimah said, 'O Messenger of Allaah, his outer garment held him back, (he was) constantly looking at its sides (out of vainglory).' Mu'aadh ibn Jabal said, "What a terrible thing you said! O Messenger of Allaah, we know nothing but good about him." The Messenger of Allaah ﷺ was silent. When news reached me that he had started to head back my grief set in. I started to think of a lie to say, saying to myself, 'How will I remove myself from his displeasure tomorrow?' I sought help from everyone in my family who had an idea. Then when it was said, "Indeed the Messenger of Allaah ﷺ is about to arrive," all of those false ideas left me and I knew that I will never be able to remove myself from his displeasure by something rooted in lying, so I decided to tell him the truth.

The Messenger of Allaah ﷺ arrived in the morning. What he used to do when he returned from a journey is first go to the *masjid* and pray two rak'ahs, then he would sit down for the people. When he did that, the people who stayed behind went to him giving him their excuses and swearing to him. They numbered over eighty men. He accepted from them what they outwardly said and accepted their pledge of allegiance and asked forgiveness for them and entrusted what they may have concealed to Allaah. I then went to him. When I gave him the salaams he smiled the smile of someone angry and then he said, 'Come here.' I walked over and sat in front of him and then he said to me, "What made you stay behind? Did you not purchase a riding animal?" I said, 'Certainly. By Allaah, O Messenger of Allaah, if I were sitting with someone other than you from the people of this world you would have seen me escape his displeasure with an excuse. By Allaah, I have been given eloquent speech; however, by Allaah, I truly know that if I were to tell you a lie which makes you pleased with me, Allaah will soon make you displeased with me, and if I tell you the truth, which may anger you, I hope for Allaah's forgiveness. No, by Allaah, I have no excuse. No, by Allaah, I have never been stronger or wealthier than I was when I refrained from departing with you.'

The Messenger of Allaah ﷺ said, "As for this one, indeed, he has told the truth. Stand (and go about your business) until Allaah judges in your affair." So I stood. A group of men from the tribe Banee Salimah jumped up and followed me. They said to me, 'By Allaah, we have not known you to have committed a sin before this, yet you were unable to give the Messenger of Allaah ﷺ an excuse as the people who stayed behind gave him! The Messenger of Allaah ﷺ, asking forgiveness for you would have been sufficient to expiate your sin!" By Allaah, they continued blaming me to the point where I nearly went back and declared myself a liar. Then I said to them, 'Did anyone experience what happened to me?' They said, "Yes, two men said something similar to what you said, and something similar to what was said to you, was said to them." I said, "Who are they?" They said, "Muraarah ibn Ar-Rabee' Al-'Amree and Hilaal ibn Umaiyah Al-Waaqidee." They mentioned to me two righteous men who participated in the battle of Badr. [I thought to myself], I can find consolation with them. I then departed after they mentioned those two to me.

The Messenger of Allaah ﷺ prohibited the Muslims from talking to us three exclusively, not the rest of those who stayed behind, so we stayed away from the people. They seemed different [in their behavior] toward us. Even the earth seemed different to me, as if it was not the earth that I knew. We remained in that state fifty nights. As for my two companions, they kept low and sat in their houses crying. As for me, I was the youngest and strongest of the three so I would go and attend the prayer with the Muslims and walk around the markets, and no one would talk to me. I would go to the Messenger of Allaah ﷺ and give him salaams while he was in his place of sitting after the prayer and I would say to myself, 'Did he move his lips returning my salaams or not?' I would then pray close to him and glance at him. When I would focus on my prayer he would look at me and when I would turn towards him he would turn away.

When my alienation from the people became prolonged and extensive, I went and climbed over the wall of Abu Qataadah who was the son of my uncle and the most beloved person to me. I gave him salaams. By Allaah, he did not return the salaams so I said, 'O Abaa Qataadah, I implore you by Allaah. Do you know me to love Allaah and His Messenger?' He was silent so I repeated that to him imploring him. He was silent so I repeated that to him imploring him once more. He said, "Allaah and His Messenger know best." My eyes then overflowed with tears. I then turned back and climbed back over the wall. Later, while I was walking in the market of Madeenah, I came across a Nabatean[83] from the Nabateans of the people of Shaam, who was one those groups who arrived with food to sell in Madeenah. He was saying, 'Who will point out for me Ka'b ibn Maalik?' The people then started to point me out

---

[83] Ibn Hajar said in *Fathul-Baaree* in the explanation of this hadeeth, "This is an ascription to the discovery of water and the extraction of it. These people at that time were people of agriculture and this Nabatean from Shaam was a Christian…"

for him so he came to me and handed me a letter from the King of Ghassaan. I found in it: "To Proceed: Verily it has reached me that your companion has treated you harshly. Allaah has not placed you in an abode of degradation or in an abode where your rights are at loss, so join us. We will assist you and be charitable to you." When I read that I said, 'This is also from the trial.' I took it to the oven, igniting it with it.

In addition to this, when forty of the fifty nights passed, the messenger of the Messenger of Allaah ﷺ came to me and said, "Verily, the Messenger of Allaah ﷺ orders you to dissociate yourself from your wife." I said, 'Should I divorce her or what should I do?' He said, "No, instead dissociate yourself from her and do not go near her." He then conveyed the same message to my two companions. I then said to my wife, 'Go stay with your family until Allaah judges in this affair.' The wife of Hilaal ibn Umaiyah then went to the Messenger of Allaah ﷺ and said, "O Messenger of Allaah, verily Hilaal ibn Umaiyah is a poor old man and he does not have a servant. So do you find anything wrong with me serving him?" He said, 'No; however, he must not approach you.' She said, "By Allaah, he has not been doing anything. By Allaah, he has not stopped crying since the start of his current situation up to this day." One of my relatives then said to me, 'Why don't you seek permission from the Messenger of Allaah ﷺ for your wife [to serve you] as he gave permission to the wife of Hilaal ibn Umaiyah to serve him?' I said, "By Allaah, I will not seek permission from the Messenger of Allaah ﷺ for my wife [to serve me]. I do not even know what he would say if I were to ask permission from him for her [to serve me] considering I am a young man."

I endured ten more days after that, reaching totaling fifty days for us since the Messenger of Allaah ﷺ first prohibited (the people) from talking to us. Then, when I prayed the *Fajr* prayer on the morning of the fiftieth night on top of one of our houses, while I was sitting in the state that Allaah mentioned, my soul was anguished and the earth, vast as it is, seemed cramped to me, I heard the voice of someone shouting from the top of the mountain Sal'. He shouted with his loudest voice, 'O Ka'b ibn Maalik, Rejoice!' I then fell down in prostration knowing the relief had come. The Messenger of Allaah ﷺ announced after he prayed the *Fajr* prayer that Allaah had accepted our repentance. Then the people came to give us the good news. [Some] People went to my two companions giving them the good news. One man rode his horse to reach me while another man from the tribe Aslam ran and climbed the mountain and his voice preceded the horse. When the person whose voice I heard giving me the good news came to me I took off my two pieces of clothing and gave them to him to wear, in exchange for his good news. By Allaah, at that time I did not own other [clothing] besides them. I then borrowed two pieces of clothing, put them on, and headed for the Messenger of Allaah ﷺ. The people received me in groups congratulating me for the acceptance of my repentance saying, "Be delighted by Allaah's acceptance of your repentance!" I then entered the *masjid* and found the Messenger of Allaah ﷺ surrounded by the people. Talhah ibn 'Ubaidillah got up and rushed over to me shaking my hand and congratulating me. By Allaah, no one other than him from the *Muhaajireen* (emigrants) got up and came over to me. I will never forget that about Talhah.

Then when I gave the Messenger of Allaah ﷺ the salaams, the Messenger of Allaah ﷺ said with his face shining from happiness, 'Be delighted by the good news of the best day you ever had since your mother gave birth to you.' When the Messenger of Allaah ﷺ would get happy, his face would shine as if it were a piece of the moon and we could recognize that [shine emanating] from him. When I sat in front of him I said, "O Messenger of Allaah, verily a part of my repentance is that I want to give charity from my wealth to Allaah and His Messenger ﷺ." The Messenger of Allaah ﷺ said, 'Hold on to some of your wealth for that is better for you.' I said, "In that case, I will hold on to my portion of the war booty that I received from Khaibar." I then said, "O Messenger of Allaah, verily Allaah only saved me because of my truthfulness, so a part of my repentance is that I will only speak the truth as long as I live." By Allaah, I know of no one from the Muslims whom Allaah bestowed His favor upon for being truthful from the time I said that to the Messenger of Allaah ﷺ until today, a favor better than what He bestowed upon me as a favor. I have not intentionally lied from the time I mentioned that to the Messenger of Allaah ﷺ up to this day, and I hope that Allaah will protect me (from lying) in what remains of my life. Also, Allaah sent down to His Messenger:

$$\text{لَقَد تَّابَ ٱللَّهُ عَلَى ٱلنَّبِيِّ وَٱلْمُهَٰجِرِينَ وَٱلْأَنصَارِ}$$

'Allaah has forgiven the Prophet and the emigrants and the *Ansaar*…'
up to His statement:

$$\text{وَكُونُوا۟ مَعَ ٱلصَّٰدِقِينَ}$$

"And be with those who are truthful."

By Allaah, Allaah has never granted me a favor, after guiding me to Islaam, greater to me than the favor of me telling the truth to the Messenger of Allaah ﷺ and that I did not lie to him which would have ruined me as the people who lied were ruined, for verily Allaah said to those who lied, when he sent down the revelation, the worst thing He has said to anyone. He ﷻ said:

$$\text{سَيَحْلِفُونَ بِٱللَّهِ لَكُمْ إِذَا ٱنقَلَبْتُمْ}$$

"They will swear to you by Allaah when you return to them…"
up to His statement:

$$\text{فَإِنَّ ٱللَّهَ لَا يَرْضَىٰ عَنِ ٱلْقَوْمِ ٱلْفَٰسِقِينَ}$$

'Certainly Allaah is not pleased with the people who are disobedient.'

We three were left out of the judgment of those whom the Messenger of Allaah ﷺ accepted from them their excuses when they swore to him and he accepted their pledge of allegiance and asked forgiveness for them. The Messenger of Allaah ﷺ delayed our case until Allaah judged in its regard and pertaining to that Allaah said:

$$\text{وَعَلَى ٱلثَّلَٰثَةِ ٱلَّذِينَ خُلِّفُوا۟}$$

"And (He has also forgiven) the three whose case was deferred…"

What Allaah mentioned was not about when we stayed behind from the battle, rather, He only mentioned how He delayed our case and excluded us from those who swore to him (the Prophet ﷺ) and gave him an excuse, causing him to accept what they put forward."

Al-Bukhaaree transmitted this *hadeeth* in his *Saheeh* (4418) as well Muslim in his *Saheeh* (2769).

سورة هود

Sooratu Hud

His, the Exalted One's statement:

$$\text{أَلَا إِنَّهُمْ يَثْنُونَ صُدُورَهُمْ لِيَسْتَخْفُواْ مِنْهُ ۚ أَلَا حِينَ يَسْتَغْشُونَ ثِيَابَهُمْ يَعْلَمُ مَا يُسِرُّونَ وَمَا يُعْلِنُونَ ۚ إِنَّهُۥ عَلِيمٌۢ بِذَاتِ ٱلصُّدُورِ}$$

"Indeed they fold up their breasts that they may hide from Him. Surely, even when they cover themselves with their garments, He knows what they conceal and what they reveal. Verily He is All-Knower of the inner most secrets of the breasts." (verse: 5)

قال الإمام البخاري رحمه الله (4681): حدثنا الحسن بن محمد بن الصباح حدثنا حجاج قال قال ابن جريج أخبرني محمد بن عباد بن جعفر أنه سمع ابن عباس ﷺ يقرأ: (ألا إنهم تثنوني صدورهم) قال: سألته عنها فقال: أناس كانوا يستحيون أن يتخلوا فيفضوا إلى السماء وأن يجامعوا نساءهم فيفضوا إلى السماء فنزل ذلك فيهم.

Muhammad ibn 'Abbaad ibn Ja'far narrated that he heard Ibn 'Abbaas recite:

ألا إنهم تثنوني صدورهم[84]

"Indeed their breasts [are] folded up"

He (Muhammad ibn 'Abbaad) said, "I asked him about that so he said, 'A group of people used to be embarrassed to relieve themselves in the *khalaa*[85] exposing themselves to the sky, and they were embarrassed to have sexual intercourse with their wives (naked) exposing themselves to the sky. Then that [verse] descended because of them.'"

This *hadeeth* has been transmitted by Al-Bukhaaree in his *Saheeh* (4681).

His, the Exalted One's statement:

$$\text{وَأَقِمِ ٱلصَّلَوٰةَ طَرَفَىِ ٱلنَّهَارِ وَزُلَفًا مِّنَ ٱلَّيْلِ ۚ إِنَّ ٱلْحَسَنَٰتِ يُذْهِبْنَ ٱلسَّيِّـَٔاتِ ۚ ذَٰلِكَ ذِكْرَىٰ لِلذَّٰكِرِينَ}$$

---

[84] Ibn Hajar said about this recitation in *Fathul-Baaree* in the explanation of this *hadeeth*, "(تثنوني) on the pattern تَفَوْعَلَ."

[85] The *khalaa* is an empty remote area used as a place for relieving ones self.

"And perform the prayer at the two ends of the day and in some hours of the night. Verily the good deeds remove the evil deeds. That is a reminder for the mindful." (verse: 114)

قال الإمام البخاري ﵀ (526): حدثنا قتيبة قال حدثنا يزيد بن زريع عن سليمان التيمي عن أبي عثمان النهدي عن ابن مسعود ﵁ أن رجلا أصاب من امرأة قبلة فأتى النبي ﷺ فأخبره فأنزل الله: (وَأَقِمِ ٱلصَّلَوٰةَ طَرَفَيِ ٱلنَّهَارِ وَزُلَفًا مِّنَ ٱلَّيْلِ ۚ إِنَّ ٱلْحَسَنَاتِ يُذْهِبْنَ ٱلسَّيِّئَاتِ) فقال الرجل يا رسول الله ألي هذا قال: لجميع أمتي كلهم.

Ibn Mas'ood ﵁ narrated that a man kissed a woman, so he went to the Prophet ﷺ and told him about what happened. Then Allaah sent down:

$$\text{وَأَقِمِ ٱلصَّلَوٰةَ طَرَفَيِ ٱلنَّهَارِ وَزُلَفًا مِّنَ ٱلَّيْلِ ۚ إِنَّ ٱلْحَسَنَاتِ يُذْهِبْنَ ٱلسَّيِّئَاتِ}$$

"And perform the prayer at the two ends of the day and in some hours of the night. Verily the good deeds remove the evil deeds…"
The man said, "O Messenger of Allaah, is this for me (alone)?" He said, "For all of my nation."

This *hadeeth* has been transmitted by Al-Bukhaaree in his *Saheeh* (526) and by Muslim in his *Saheeh* (2763).

قال الإمام الترمذي ﵀ (3115): حدثنا عبد الله بن عبد الرحمن أخبرنا يزيد بن هارون أخبرنا قيس بن الربيع عن عثمان بن عبد الله بن موهب عن موسى بن طلحة عن أبي اليسر ﵁ قال: أتتني امرأة تبتاع تمرا فقلت إن في البيت تمرا أطيب منه فدخلت معي في البيت فأهويت إليها فقبلتها فأتيت أبا بكر فذكرت ذلك له قال: استر على نفسك وتب ولا تخبر أحدا فلم أصبر فأتيت عمر فذكرت ذلك له فقال: استر على نفسك وتب ولا تخبر أحدا فلم أصبر فأتيت النبي ﷺ فذكرت ذلك له فقال: أخلفت غازيا في سبيل الله في أهله بمثل هذا حتى تمنى أنه لم يكن أسلم إلا تلك الساعة حتى ظن أنه من أهل النار قال: وأطرق رسول الله ﷺ طويلا حتى أوحى الله إليه: (وَأَقِمِ ٱلصَّلَوٰةَ طَرَفَيِ ٱلنَّهَارِ وَزُلَفًا مِّنَ ٱلَّيْلِ) إلى قوله: (ذِكْرَىٰ لِلذَّاكِرِينَ) قال أبو اليسر: فأتيته فقرأها علي رسول الله ﷺ فقال أصحابه: يا رسول الله ألهذا خاصة أم للناس عامة قال: بل للناس عامة.

وهذا حديث حسن صحيح وقيس بن الربيع ضعفه وكيع وغيره وأبو اليسر هو كعب بن عمرو قال وروى شريك عن عثمان بن عبد الله هذا الحديث مثل رواية قيس بن الربيع قال وفي الباب عن أبي أمامة وواثلة بن الأسقع وأنس بن مالك.

160

Abu Al-Yasar ﷺ stated, "A woman came to me wanting to buy some dates so I said [to her], 'Verily inside the house are dates better than these.' So she entered the house with me and then I leaned over and kissed her. I went to Abu Bakr and told him about that. He said, "Conceal yourself, repent and do not tell anyone." I was not patient, so I went to 'Umar and told him about what happened. He said, "Conceal yourself, repent and do not tell anyone." Again I was not patient, so I went to the Prophet ﷺ and told him about what I did. He said, "You left the likes of this for a warrior in the path of Allaah who left behind his family (to come back to)!" (He scolded him) to the point that he wished that he had not embraced Islaam except at that moment, and to the point where he thought he was one of the people of the fire. He (Abu Al-Yasar) said, "The Messenger of Allaah ﷺ bowed his head for a long time until this verse was revealed to him:

$$\text{وَأَقِمِ ٱلصَّلَوٰةَ طَرَفِيِ ٱلنَّهَارِ وَزُلَفًا مِّنَ ٱلَّيْلِ}$$

"And perform the prayer at the two ends of the day and in some hours of the night…"
to His statement:

$$\text{ذِكْرَىٰ لِلذَّٰكِرِينَ}$$

'…a reminder for the mindful.'

Abu-Al-Yasar said, "I went to him and the Messenger of Allaah ﷺ recited it to me. His Companions then said, 'O Messenger of Allaah, is that for this person exclusively or for the people in general?' He said, "[No.] Rather, for the people in general."

This *hadeeth* has been transmitted by At-Tirmidhee in his *Jaami'* (3115), and An-Nasaa'ee in his *Tafseer* (268). Ash-Sheikh Muqbil ﷺ commented saying, "The *hadeeth* is *hasan li ghairihi* because Qais ibn Ar-Rabee' has been supported…".

سورة يوسف

Sooratu Yoosuf

His, the Exalted One's statement:

$$\text{نَحْنُ نَقُصُّ عَلَيْكَ أَحْسَنَ ٱلْقَصَصِ}$$

"We relate unto you the best of stories…" (verse: 3)

قال الإمام إسحاق بن راهويه ﵀ كما في المطالب العالية ص (440): حدثنا عمرو بن محمد حدثنا خلاد الصفار عن عمرو بن قيس الملائي عن عمرو بن مرة عن مصعب بن سعد عن سعد ﵁ في قول الله عز وجل: (نَحْنُ نَقُصُّ عَلَيْكَ أَحْسَنَ ٱلْقَصَصِ) الآية قال: أنزل الله القرآن على رسول الله ﷺ فتلاه عليهم زمانا فقالوا: يا رسول الله لو قصصت علينا فأنزل الله: (الٓرۚ تِلْكَ ءَايَٰتُ ٱلْكِتَٰبِ ٱلْمُبِينِ) إلى قوله: (نَحْنُ نَقُصُّ عَلَيْكَ أَحْسَنَ ٱلْقَصَصِ) الآية فتلاها رسول الله ﷺ زمانا فقالوا: يا رسول الله لو حدثتنا فأنزل الله تعالى: (ٱللَّهُ نَزَّلَ أَحْسَنَ ٱلْحَدِيثِ كِتَٰبًا مُّتَشَٰبِهًا) الآية.

Sa'd ibn Abee Waqqaas ﵁ said about the statement of Allaah ﷻ:

$$\text{نَحْنُ نَقُصُّ عَلَيْكَ أَحْسَنَ ٱلْقَصَصِ}$$

"We relate unto you the best of stories…" (verse:3),

He (Sa'd) said, "Allaah sent down [some] Qur'aan to the Messenger of Allaah ﷺ so he recited it to them (his Companions) for some time and then after some time they said, 'O Messenger of Allaah, if only you told us some stories.' In response Allaah sent down:

$$\text{الٓرۚ تِلْكَ ءَايَٰتُ ٱلْكِتَٰبِ ٱلْمُبِينِ}$$

"*Alif Laam Raa*, these are the verses of the clear book…" up to His statement:

$$\text{نَحْنُ نَقُصُّ عَلَيْكَ أَحْسَنَ ٱلْقَصَصِ}$$

'We relate unto you the best of stories…' (verse: 3).

The Messenger of Allaah ﷺ recited that [story] to them for some time and then they said, "O Messenger of Allaah, if only you were to give us a speech." Then Allaah ﷻ sent down:

$$ٱللَّهُ نَزَّلَ أَحْسَنَ ٱلْحَدِيثِ كِتَٰبًا مُّتَشَٰبِهًا$$

'Allaah has sent down the best speech, a book, its parts resembling each other..'' (*Az-Zumar*: 23).

Ishaaq ibn Raahawaih has transmitted this *hadeeth* as mentioned in *Al-Mataalib Al-'Aaliyah* page 440. Ash-Sheikh Muqbil ؓ stated, "As for this *hadeeth*, the people of its chain are people of the *Saheeh* (Al-Bukhaaree and/or Muslim) except for Khallaad As-Saffaar; however, he is trustworthy, and I have omitted the rest of the *hadeeth* because it is not *muttasil* (its chain is not connected)…"

سورة الرعد

Sooratul-Ra'd

His, the Exalted One's statement:

$$وَيُرْسِلُ ٱلصَّوَاعِقَ فَيُصِيبُ بِهَا مَن يَشَاءُ وَهُمْ يُجَٰدِلُونَ فِى ٱللَّهِ وَهُوَ شَدِيدُ ٱلْمِحَالِ$$

"And He sends the thunderbolts and therewith He strikes whomsoever He wills while they dispute about Allaah, and He is mighty in strength, severe in punishment." (verse: 13)

قال الإمام البزار رَحِمَهُ اللهُ كما في كشف الأستار (ج 3 ص 54): حدثنا عبدة بن عبد الله أنبأ يزيد ابن هارون أنبأ ديلم بن غزوان ثنا ثابت عن أنس رَضِيَ اللهُ عَنْهُ قال: بعث رسول الله ﷺ رجلاً من أصحابه إلى رجل من عظماء الجاهلية يدعوه إلى الله تبارك وتعالى فقال: أيش ربك الذي تدعوني إليه هو من حديد هو من نحاس هو من فضة هو من ذهب هو فأتى النبي ﷺ فأخبره فأعاده النبي ﷺ الثانية فقال مثل ذلك فأرسله إليه الثالثة فقال مثل ذلك فأتى النبي ﷺ فأخبره فأرسل الله تبارك وتعالى عليه صاعقة فأحرقته فقال رسول الله ﷺ: إن الله تبارك وتعالى قد أرسل على صاحبك صاعقة فأحرقته فنزلت هذه الآية: (وَيُرْسِلُ ٱلصَّوَاعِقَ فَيُصِيبُ بِهَا مَن يَشَاءُ وَهُمْ يُجَٰدِلُونَ فِى ٱللَّهِ وَهُوَ شَدِيدُ ٱلْمِحَالِ).

Anas ؓ said, "The Messenger of Allaah ﷺ sent one of his Companions to a man who was a leader in the days of *Jaahiliyah* to call him to Allaah ﷻ. So he said, 'What is your Lord which you call me to? Is he made of steel? Is he made of copper? Is he made of silver? Is he made of gold?' He returned to the Prophet ﷺ and informed him about that so the Prophet ﷺ sent him back a second time. He (the leader) then repeated the same thing. He then sent him back a third time whereupon he said the same thing. He returned to the Prophet ﷺ and informed him about that. Allaah ﷻ then sent down upon him a thunderbolt burning him. The Messenger of Allaah ﷺ then said, "Verily Allaah ﷻ has sent down a thunderbolt upon your associate burning him." Then this verse descended:

$$وَيُرْسِلُ ٱلصَّوَاعِقَ فَيُصِيبُ بِهَا مَن يَشَاءُ وَهُمْ يُجَٰدِلُونَ فِى ٱللَّهِ وَهُوَ شَدِيدُ ٱلْمِحَالِ$$

"And He sends the thunderbolts and therewith He strikes whom He wills while they dispute about Allaah, and He is mighty in strength, severe in punishment."

Al-Bazzaar transmitted this *hadeeth* as mentioned in *Kashf Al-Astaar* volume 3, page 54, and Abu Ya'laa in his *Musnad*, volume 6, page 87. Ash-Sheikh Muqbil ﷺ explained that in some of the chains of this *hadeeth*, 'Ali ibn Abee Saarah is present who is very weak and then he said, "So based on this, reliance is placed on the first chain (the above mentioned chain) and the hadeeth rises to the level of authentic, and Allaah knows best."

سورة إبراهيم

Sooratu Ibraaheem

His, the Exalted One's statement:

يُثَبِّتُ ٱللَّهُ ٱلَّذِينَ ءَامَنُوا۟ بِٱلْقَوْلِ ٱلثَّابِتِ فِى ٱلْحَيَوٰةِ ٱلدُّنْيَا وَفِى ٱلْءَاخِرَةِ

"Allaah will keep firm those who believe with the word that stands firm in this world and in the hereafter..." (verse: 27)

قال الإمام مسلم ﷺ (2871 / 74): حدثنا أبو بكر بن أبي شيبة ومحمد بن المثنى وأبو بكر ابن نافع قالوا حدثنا عبد الرحمن يعنون ابن مهدي عن سفيان عن أبيه عن خيثمة عن البراء ابن عازب ﷺ: (يُثَبِّتُ ٱللَّهُ ٱلَّذِينَ ءَامَنُوا۟ بِٱلْقَوْلِ ٱلثَّابِتِ فِى ٱلْحَيَوٰةِ ٱلدُّنْيَا وَفِى ٱلْءَاخِرَةِ) قال: نزلت في عذاب القبر.

On Al-Baraa ibn 'Aazib ﷺ:

يُثَبِّتُ ٱللَّهُ ٱلَّذِينَ ءَامَنُوا۟ بِٱلْقَوْلِ ٱلثَّابِتِ فِى ٱلْحَيَوٰةِ ٱلدُّنْيَا وَفِى ٱلْءَاخِرَةِ

"Allaah will keep firm those who believe with the word that stands firm, in this world and in the hereafter..."
He said, "It descended regarding the punishment of the grave."

This *hadeeth* has been transmitted by Muslim in his *Saheeh* (2871/74).

قال الإمام النسائي ﷺ في المجتبى (ج 4 ص 101-102): أخبرنا محمد بن بشار قال حدثنا محمد قال حدثنا شعبة عن علقمة بن مرثد عن سعد بن عبيدة عن البراء بن عازب ﷺ عن النبي ﷺ قال: (يُثَبِّتُ ٱللَّهُ ٱلَّذِينَ ءَامَنُوا۟ بِٱلْقَوْلِ ٱلثَّابِتِ فِى ٱلْحَيَوٰةِ ٱلدُّنْيَا وَفِى ٱلْءَاخِرَةِ) قال: نزلت في عذاب القبر يقال له: من ربك فيقول: ربي الله وديني دين محمد ﷺ فذلك قوله: (يُثَبِّتُ ٱللَّهُ ٱلَّذِينَ ءَامَنُوا۟ بِٱلْقَوْلِ ٱلثَّابِتِ فِى ٱلْحَيَوٰةِ ٱلدُّنْيَا وَفِى ٱلْءَاخِرَةِ).

Al-Baraa ibn 'Aazib ﷺ on the Prophet ﷺ:

$$يُثَبِّتُ ٱللَّهُ ٱلَّذِينَ ءَامَنُوا۟ بِٱلْقَوْلِ ٱلثَّابِتِ فِى ٱلْحَيَوٰةِ ٱلدُّنْيَا وَفِى ٱلْءَاخِرَةِ$$

"Allaah will keep firm those who believe with the word that stands firm, in this world and in the hereafter…"

He said, "It descended because of the punishment of the grave. It will be said to him (the believer in the grave), 'Who is your Lord?' He will then say, "Allaah is my Lord and my religion is the religion of Muhammad ﷺ." That is the meaning of His statement:

$$يُثَبِّتُ ٱللَّهُ ٱلَّذِينَ ءَامَنُوا۟ بِٱلْقَوْلِ ٱلثَّابِتِ فِى ٱلْحَيَوٰةِ ٱلدُّنْيَا وَفِى ٱلْءَاخِرَةِ$$

'Allaah will keep firm those who believe with the word that stands firm, in this world and in the hereafter…"

An-Nasaa'ee transmitted this *hadeeth* in *Al-Mujtabaa*, volume 4, pages 101-102. And the *hadeeth* is in Al-Bukhaaree (1369) and Muslim (2871/73) with a similar wording.

سورة النحل

Sooratun-Nahl

<u>His, the Exalted One's statement:</u>

ضَرَبَ ٱللَّهُ مَثَلًا عَبْدًا مَّمْلُوكًا لَّا يَقْدِرُ عَلَىٰ شَيْءٍ

"Allaah puts forward the example of a slave under the possession of another, he has no power of any sort…" (verses: 75-76)

قال الإمام ابن جرير ﵀ (ج 17 ص 263-264): حدثنا الحسن بن الصباح البزار قال ثنا يحيى بن إسحاق السيلحيني قال ثنا حماد عن عبد الله بن عثمان بن خثيم عن إبراهيم عن عكرمة عن يعلى بن أمية عن ابن عباس ﵄ في قوله: (ضَرَبَ ٱللَّهُ مَثَلًا عَبْدًا مَّمْلُوكًا) قال: نزلت في رجل من قريش وعبده وفي قوله: (وَضَرَبَ ٱللَّهُ مَثَلًا رَّجُلَيْنِ أَحَدُهُمَا أَبْكَمُ لَا يَقْدِرُ عَلَىٰ شَيْءٍ) إلى قوله: (وَهُوَ عَلَىٰ صِرَاطٍ مُّسْتَقِيمٍ) قال: هو عثمان بن عفان قال: والأبكم الذي أينما يوجه لا يأت بخير ذاك مولى عثمان بن عفان كان عثمان ينفق عليه ويكفله ويكفيه المئونة وكان الآخر يكره الإسلام ويأباه وينهاه عن الصدقة والمعروف فنزلت فيهما.

Ibn 'Abbaas ﵄ said about His statement:

ضَرَبَ ٱللَّهُ مَثَلًا عَبْدًا مَّمْلُوكًا

"Allaah puts forward the example of a slave under the possession of another…"
"It descended because of a man from Quraish and his slave." And he also said about His statement:

وَضَرَبَ ٱللَّهُ مَثَلًا رَّجُلَيْنِ أَحَدُهُمَا أَبْكَمُ لَا يَقْدِرُ عَلَىٰ شَيْءٍ

"And Allaah puts forward the example of two men, one of them dumb who has no power over anything…"
up to where He states:

وَهُوَ عَلَىٰ صِرَاطٍ مُّسْتَقِيمٍ

"…while he is on a straight path."

He said, "He is 'Uthmaan ibn 'Affaan, and the dumb man, the one who wherever he is directed brings no good is the slave of 'Uthmaan ibn 'Affaan. 'Uthmaan used to spend on him and support him giving him sufficient provisions while the other man ('Uthmaan's slave) used to detest Islaam and reject it and even tried to prevent him from giving charity and doing what is right. Then the verse descended because of those two."

This *hadeeth* has been transmitted by Ibn Jareer in his *Tafseer*, volume 17, page 263-264. Ash-Sheikh Muqbil ﷺ commented about it, "[As for] The *hadeeth*, the people of its chain are people of the *Saheeh* (Al-Bukhaaree and/or Muslim)."

His, the Exalted One's statement:

وَلَقَدْ نَعْلَمُ أَنَّهُمْ يَقُولُونَ إِنَّمَا يُعَلِّمُهُ بَشَرٌ لِّسَانُ الَّذِى يُلْحِدُونَ إِلَيْهِ أَعْجَمِىٌّ وَهَٰذَا لِسَانٌ عَرَبِىٌّ مُّبِينٌ ﴿١٠٣﴾

"And indeed We know that they say: "It is only a human being that teaches him." The tongue of the one they refer to is foreign while this is a clear Arabic tongue." (verse: 103)

قال الإمام ابن جرير ﷺ (ج 17 ص 300): حدثني المثنى قال ثنا عمرو بن عون قال أخبرنا هشيم عن حصين عن عبد الله بن مسلم الحضرمي ﷺ أنه كان لهم عبدان من أهل اليمن وكانا طفلين وكان يقال لأحدهما يسار والآخر جبر فكانا يقرآن التوراة وكان رسول الله ﷺ ربما جلس إليهما فقال كفار قريش: إنما يجلس إليهما يتعلم منهما فأنزل الله تعالى: (لِّسَانُ الَّذِى يُلْحِدُونَ إِلَيْهِ أَعْجَمِىٌّ وَهَٰذَا لِسَانٌ عَرَبِىٌّ مُّبِينٌ).

'Abdullaah ibn Muslim Al-Hadramee ﷺ narrated that they used to own two slaves who were captured from a group of people on a caravan from Yemen. They were two small boys, one was named Yasaar and the other was named Jabr. They used to recite the Tawraah and the Messenger of Allaah ﷺ would, at times, sit and listen to them. So the disbelievers of Quraish said, "He only sits and listens to them so he can learn from them." Then Allaah ﷻ sent down:

لِّسَانُ الَّذِى يُلْحِدُونَ إِلَيْهِ أَعْجَمِىٌّ وَهَٰذَا لِسَانٌ عَرَبِىٌّ مُّبِينٌ

"The tongue of the one they refer to is foreign while this is a clear Arabic tongue."

As for this *hadeeth*, Ibn Jareer transmitted it in his *Tafseer*, volume 17, page 300. Ash-Sheikh Muqbil ﷺ asserted, "[Regarding] The *hadeeth*, the people of its chain are people of the *Saheeh* (Al-Bukhaaree and/or Muslim) except for Al-Muthannaa and he is ibn Ibraaheem Al-Aamulee and I have not found a person who has mentioned a biography for him; however, he was supported by Sufyaan ibn Wakee' and there is some talk about him. As for Hushaim, he is ibn Basheer and he is a *mudallis* and he has not explicitly stated (that he heard the *hadeeth* from his Sheikh). However, he has been supported by Khaalid ibn 'Abdillaah, and he is At-Tahhaan, and by Muhammad ibn Fudail… and the *hadeeth* has a supporting *hadeeth* from the *hadeeth* of Ibn 'Abbaas…"

قال الحاكم ﷺ (ج 2 ص 357): أخبرني عبد الرحمن بن الحسن بن أحمد الأسدي بهمدان حدثنا إبراهيم بن الحسين ثنا آدم بن أبي إياس حدثنا ورقاء عن بن أبي نجيح عن مجاهد عن ابن عباس ﷺ في قوله عز وجل: (إِنَّمَا يُعَلِّمُهُۥ بَشَرٌ ۗ لِّسَانُ ٱلَّذِى يُلْحِدُونَ إِلَيْهِ أَعْجَمِىٌّ وَهَٰذَا لِسَانٌ عَرَبِىٌّ مُّبِينٌ) قالوا إنما يعلم محمدا عبد ابن الحضرمي وهو صاحب الكتب فقال الله: (لِّسَانُ ٱلَّذِى يُلْحِدُونَ إِلَيْهِ أَعْجَمِىٌّ وَهَٰذَا لِسَانٌ عَرَبِىٌّ مُّبِينٌ) (إِنَّمَا يَفْتَرِى ٱلْكَذِبَ ٱلَّذِينَ لَا يُؤْمِنُونَ بِـَٔايَٰتِ ٱللَّهِ).

هذا حديث صحيح الإسناد ولم يخرجاه.

Ibn 'Abbaas ﷺ said about His ﷻ statement:

إِنَّمَا يُعَلِّمُهُۥ بَشَرٌ ۗ لِّسَانُ ٱلَّذِى يُلْحِدُونَ إِلَيْهِ أَعْجَمِىٌّ وَهَٰذَا لِسَانٌ عَرَبِىٌّ مُّبِينٌ

"It is only a human being that teaches him." The tongue of the one they refer to is foreign while this is a clear Arabic tongue."

"They (the polytheists) said, "Verily it is only the slave of Ibn Al-Hadramee who teaches Muhammad;" He was a person versed in the scriptures. So Allaah said in response:

لِّسَانُ ٱلَّذِى يُلْحِدُونَ إِلَيْهِ أَعْجَمِىٌّ وَهَٰذَا لِسَانٌ عَرَبِىٌّ مُّبِينٌ

"The tongue of the one they refer to is foreign while this is a clear Arabic tongue."

إِنَّمَا يَفْتَرِى ٱلْكَذِبَ ٱلَّذِينَ لَا يُؤْمِنُونَ بِـَٔايَٰتِ ٱللَّهِ

"It is only those who believe not in the signs of Allaah who fabricate falsehood…" (verse: 105)

Al-Haakim transmitted this *hadeeth* in *Al-Mustadrak*, volume 2, page 357.

His, the Exalted One's statement:

$$\text{ثُمَّ إِنَّ رَبَّكَ لِلَّذِينَ هَاجَرُوا۟ مِنۢ بَعْدِ مَا فُتِنُوا۟ ثُمَّ جَٰهَدُوا۟ وَصَبَرُوٓا۟ إِنَّ رَبَّكَ مِنۢ بَعْدِهَا لَغَفُورٌۭ رَّحِيمٌۭ}$$

"Then verily your Lord, for those who emigrated after they had been put to trials and thereafter fought and were patient, verily your Lord after that is Oft-Forgiving Most Merciful." (verse: 110)

قال الإمام ابن جرير ﷺ (ج 17 ص 307): حدثنا أحمد بن منصور الرمادي قال ثنا أبو أحمد الزبيري قال ثنا محمد بن شريك عن عمرو بن دينار عن عكرمة عن ابن عباس ﷺ قال: كان قوم من أهل مكة أسلموا وكانوا يستخفون بالإسلام فأخرجهم المشركون يوم بدر معهم فأصيب بعضهم وقتل بعض فقال المسلمون: كان أصحابنا هؤلاء مسلمين وأكرهوا فاستغفروا لهم فنزلت: (إِنَّ ٱلَّذِينَ تَوَفَّىٰهُمُ ٱلْمَلَٰٓئِكَةُ ظَالِمِىٓ أَنفُسِهِمْ قَالُوا۟ فِيمَ كُنتُمْ) الآية قال: فكتب إلى من بقي بمكة من المسلمين بهذه الآية وأنه لا عذر لهم قال: فخرجوا فلحقهم المشركون فأعطوهم الفتنة فنزلت فيهم: (وَمِنَ ٱلنَّاسِ مَن يَقُولُ ءَامَنَّا بِٱللَّهِ فَإِذَآ أُوذِىَ فِى ٱللَّهِ) إلى آخر الآية فكتب المسلمون إليهم بذلك فحزنوا وأيسوا من كل خير ثم نزلت فيهم: (ثُمَّ إِنَّ رَبَّكَ لِلَّذِينَ هَاجَرُوا۟ مِنۢ بَعْدِ مَا فُتِنُوا۟ ثُمَّ جَٰهَدُوا۟ وَصَبَرُوٓا۟ إِنَّ رَبَّكَ مِنۢ بَعْدِهَا لَغَفُورٌۭ رَّحِيمٌۭ) فكتبوا إليهم بذلك إن الله قد جعل لكم مخرجا فخرجوا فأدركهم المشركون فقاتلوهم حتى نجا من نجا وقتل من قتل.

Ibn 'Abbaas ﷺ said, "A group from the people of Makkah had embraced Islaam and used to hide their Islaam. The polytheists forced them to go out with them on the day of Badr. In consequence, some of them were injured and others were killed so the Muslims said, 'These companions of ours were Muslims. They were forced to come out, so ask forgiveness for them.' Then it descended:

$$\text{إِنَّ ٱلَّذِينَ تَوَفَّىٰهُمُ ٱلْمَلَٰٓئِكَةُ ظَالِمِىٓ أَنفُسِهِمْ قَالُوا۟ فِيمَ كُنتُمْ}$$

"Verily those whom the angels take at death while they are wronging themselves, they (the angels) say, "In what condition were you?..." (*An-Nisaa*: 97)

This verse was written down and sent to the Muslims who remained in Makkah and they were informed that they had no excuse (for remaining in Makkah). They then went to leave and the polytheists caught up with them and gave them a trying punishment. Then the following verse descended because of them:

$$\text{وَمِنَ ٱلنَّاسِ مَن يَقُولُ ءَامَنَّا بِٱللَّهِ فَإِذَآ أُوذِىَ فِى ٱللَّهِ}$$

'And from mankind are those who say: "We believe in Allaah," but when he is harmed for the sake of Allaah…' (*Al-'Ankaboot*:10).

The Muslims wrote down that verse and sent it to them. They were saddened and gave up hope of any good. Then the following verse descended because of them:

$$\text{ثُمَّ إِنَّ رَبَّكَ لِلَّذِينَ هَاجَرُواْ مِنۢ بَعْدِ مَا فُتِنُواْ ثُمَّ جَهَدُواْ وَصَبَرُواْ إِنَّ رَبَّكَ مِنۢ بَعْدِهَا لَغَفُورٌ رَّحِيمٌ}$$

"Then verily your Lord, for those who emigrated after they had been put to trials and thereafter fought and were patient, verily your Lord after that is Oft-Forgiving Most Merciful."

They wrote that to them letting them know that Allaah has made a way out for them. So they set out to leave and the polytheists caught up with them; so they fought them until some of them escaped and some of them were killed."

Ibn Jareer transmitted this hadeeth in his *Tafseer*, volume 17, page 307. Al-Haithamee said about it in *Majma' Az-Zawaa'id*, volume 7, page 10: "The people of its chain are people of the *Saheeh* (Al-Bukhaaree and/or Muslim) except for Muhammad ibn Shareek, although he is trustworthy."

His, the Exalted One's statement:

$$\text{وَإِنْ عَاقَبْتُمْ فَعَاقِبُواْ بِمِثْلِ مَا عُوقِبْتُم بِهِۦ وَلَئِن صَبَرْتُمْ لَهُوَ خَيْرٌ لِّلصَّـٰبِرِينَ}$$

"And if you punish, then punish with the like of that which you were afflicted, and if you endure patiently, verily it is better for the patient." (verse: 126)

قال الإمام الترمذي ﵀ (3129): حدثنا أبو عمار حدثنا الفضل بن موسى عن عيسى بن عبيد عن الربيع بن أنس عن أبي العالية قال حدثني أبي بن كعب ﵁ قال: لما كان يوم أحد أصيب من الأنصار أربعة وستون رجلا ومن المهاجرين ستة فيهم حمزة فمثلوا بهم فقالت الأنصار: لئن أصبنا منهم يوما مثل هذا لنربين عليهم قال: فلما كان يوم فتح مكة أنزل الله: (وَإِنْ عَاقَبْتُمْ فَعَاقِبُواْ بِمِثْلِ مَا عُوقِبْتُم بِهِۦ وَلَئِن صَبَرْتُمْ لَهُوَ خَيْرٌ لِّلصَّـٰبِرِينَ) فقال رجل: لا قريش بعد اليوم فقال رسول الله ﷺ: كفوا عن القوم إلا أربعة.

قال: هذا حديث حسن غريب من حديث أبي بن كعب.

Ubay ibn Ka'b said, "On the day of Uhud sixty four men from the *Ansaar* were killed and six men from the *Muhaajireen* (emigrants) were killed; one of them was Hamzah. They (the polytheists) had mutilated them so the *Ansaar* said, 'If we encounter them on a day similar to this, we will mutilate them worse than this.' Then on the day of the conquest of Makkah, Allaah sent down:

$$وَإِنْ عَاقَبْتُمْ فَعَاقِبُوا بِمِثْلِ مَا عُوقِبْتُم بِهِ ۖ وَلَئِن صَبَرْتُمْ لَهُوَ خَيْرٌ لِّلصَّابِرِينَ$$

"And if you punish, then punish with the like of that which you were afflicted, and if you endure patiently, verily it is better for the patient."
A man said, "There will be no Quraish after today." So the Messenger of Allaah said, "Restrain yourselves from (killing) the people except for four people."[86]

---

[86] The four were named in the *hadeeth* of Sa'd ibn Abee Waqqaas transmitted by An-Nasaa'ee in *Al-Mujtabaa*, volume 7, pages 105-106, and Abu Daawud (2683) and (4359) and by others: "'Ikrimah ibn Abee Jahl, and 'Abdullaah ibn Khatal, and Miqyas ibn Subaabah, and 'Abdullaah ibn Sa'd ibn Abee Sarh." However, in the chain of this *hadeeth* is Asbaat ibn Nasr whom the Scholars have differed on his status. Our Sheikh Muqbil said about him in his footnotes on *Tafseer Ibn Katheer* in the explanation of *Soortul-Baqarah*: 267, "Asbaat ibn Nasr is closer to being weak." However, portions of this *hadeeth* are supported by other *ahaadeeth*. Ibn Khatal being one of them is supported by the *hadeeth* of Anas transmitted by Al-Bukhaaree (1846), (3044), (4286), (5808) and Muslim (1357). The historians say he committed murder and then left Islaam. He used to ridicule the Prophet with poetry and he had two slave girls who used to sing poetry ridiculing the Prophet . He was killed on the day of the conquest of Makkah while hanging on to the drapes of the Ka'bah. 'Abdullaah ibn Sa'd ibn Abee Sarh being one of them is supported by the *hadeeth* of Ibn 'Abbaas transmitted by Abu Daawud (4358) and An-Nasaa'ee in *Al-Mujtabaa*, volume 7, page 107, and others. Ash-Sheikh Al-Albaanee ruled the chain of Abu Daawud to be *hasan*. 'Abdullaah used to be amongst those who write the revelation for the Prophet and then he left Islaam. On the day of the conquest, 'Uthmaan ibn 'Affaan, his brother by way of wet nurse, sought protection for him. The Prophet granted him protection. 'Abdullaah re-embraced Islaam and later participated with 'Amr ibn Al-'Aas in the conquest of Misr (Egypt). Miqyas ibn Subaabah being one of them is supported by the *hadeeth* of Sa'eed ibn Yarboo' transmitted by Abu Daawud (2684) and Ad-Daaraqutnee, volume 4, page 168, and by others. In the wording of Ad-Daaraqutnee the four were named as previously mentioned except that Al-Huwairith ibn Nuqaid was mentioned in place of 'Ikrimah ibn Abee Jahl. In the chain of this *hadeeth* is 'Umar ibn 'Uthmaan who is *majhool* (his status is not known) so the *hadeeth* is weak, however, it, along with other narrations that the historians mention, supports Miqyas ibn Subaabah being one of them. Miqyas's brother was accidentally killed. Miqyas was given the blood money. He then killed the one who accidentally killed his brother and left Islaam and abided in Makkah. He was killed on the day of the conquest of Makkah. As for the story of 'Ikrimah ibn Abee Jahl, he was the son the famous polytheist Abu Jahl. He was similar to his father in his enmity towards Islaam. In the *hadeeth* of Sa'd ibn Abee Waqqaas it was mentioned that he fled and boarded a ship. The ship ran into a storm so the people on the ship said, "Be sincere (supplicate Allaah alone), for verily your gods are of no avail to you here!" 'Ikrimah then said, "By Allaah, if nothing other than

At-Tirmidhee transmitted this hadeeth in his *Jaami'* (3129) and classified it to be *hasan ghareeb*.

---

sincerity (in worshipping Allaah alone) can save me in the ocean then nothing other than it can save me on land..." He then went to the Prophet ﷺ and embraced Islaam. This story is supported by narrations the historians mention like the narration of Ibn Abee Mulaikah transmitted by Ibn Sa'd in *At-Tabaqaat* and At-Tabaraanee in *Al-Mu'jam Al-Kabeer*, volume 17, page 372 and by others, and like the narration of 'Urwah transmitted by Al-Haakim, volume 3, page 241 and by others. As for Al-Huwairith ibn Nuqaid who was mentioned in the *hadeeth* of Sa'eed ibn Yarboo', the historians say he used to annoy the Prophet ﷺ in Makkah and was killed on the day of the conquest. The historians have also mentioned other people whom the Prophet ﷺ ordered to be killed on the day of the conquest. This does not contradict the *hadeeth* in which he said to restrain except from four people. Sheikhul-Islaam Ibn Taymiyah explained that in his book *As-Saarim Al-Maslool 'alaa Shaatim Ar-Rasool*, page 143, saying, "...and that is, it is possible that the Prophet ﷺ prohibited his Companions from fighting except those who fought them and except for the four people and then afterwards he ordered that they kill this one and others..."

سورة الإسراء

Sooratul-Israa

His, the Exalted One's statement:

قُلِ ٱدْعُوا۟ ٱلَّذِينَ زَعَمْتُم مِّن دُونِهِۦ فَلَا يَمْلِكُونَ كَشْفَ ٱلضُّرِّ عَنكُمْ وَلَا تَحْوِيلًا ۝

أُو۟لَـٰٓئِكَ ٱلَّذِينَ يَدْعُونَ يَبْتَغُونَ إِلَىٰ رَبِّهِمُ ٱلْوَسِيلَةَ

"Say: Call upon those besides Him whom you claim (to be gods). They do not have the power to remove the adversity from you or to even shift it from you to someone else. Those whom they call upon desire for themselves means of access to their Lord…" (verses: 56-57)

قال الإمام مسلم رحمه الله (3030): حدثني أبو بكر بن نافع العبدي حدثنا عبد الرحمن حدثنا سفيان عن الأعمش عن إبراهيم عن أبي معمر عن عبد الله ﷺ: (أُو۟لَـٰٓئِكَ ٱلَّذِينَ يَدْعُونَ يَبْتَغُونَ إِلَىٰ رَبِّهِمُ ٱلْوَسِيلَةَ) قال: كان نفر من الإنس يعبدون نفرا من الجن فأسلم النفر من الجن واستمسك الإنس بعبادتهم فنزلت: (أُو۟لَـٰٓئِكَ ٱلَّذِينَ يَدْعُونَ يَبْتَغُونَ إِلَىٰ رَبِّهِمُ ٱلْوَسِيلَةَ).

On 'Abdullaah ibn Mas'ood:

أُو۟لَـٰٓئِكَ ٱلَّذِينَ يَدْعُونَ يَبْتَغُونَ إِلَىٰ رَبِّهِمُ ٱلْوَسِيلَةَ

"Those whom they call upon desire for themselves means of access to their Lord…"

He said, "A group from mankind used to worship a group of *Jinn*. The group of *Jinn* later embraced Islaam and the group from mankind continued worshipping them. Then it descended:

أُو۟لَـٰٓئِكَ ٱلَّذِينَ يَدْعُونَ يَبْتَغُونَ إِلَىٰ رَبِّهِمُ ٱلْوَسِيلَةَ

"Those whom they call upon desire for themselves means of access to their Lord…"

As for this *hadeeth*, Muslim has transmitted it in his *Saheeh* (3030); and in another narration of this *hadeeth* in Muslim it was stated: "…The *Jinn* then embraced Islaam while the group from mankind who used to worship them were unaware. Then the verse descended…" Al-Bukhaaree also transmitted the *hadeeth* in his *Saheeh* (4714), however, the verse being revealed was not mentioned.

His, the Exalted One's statement:

$$\text{وَمَا مَنَعَنَا أَن نُّرْسِلَ بِٱلْآيَاتِ إِلَّا أَن كَذَّبَ بِهَا ٱلْأَوَّلُونَ}$$

"And nothing prevents us from sending the signs except that the people of old denied them…" (verse: 59)

قال الإمام أحمد ﷺ (ج 1 ص 258): ثنا عثمان بن محمد وسمعته أنا منه ثنا جرير عن الأعمش عن جعفر بن إياس عن سعيد بن جبير عن ابن عباس ﷺ قال: سأل أهل مكة النبي ﷺ أن يجعل لهم الصفا ذهبا وأن ينحى الجبال عنهم فيزدرعوا فقيل له: إن شئت أن تستأني بهم وإن شئت أن تؤتيهم الذي سألوا فإن كفروا أهلكوا كما أهلكت من قبلهم قال: لا بل أستأني بهم فأنزل الله عز وجل هذه الآية: (مَنَعَنَا أَن نُّرْسِلَ بِٱلْآيَاتِ إِلَّا أَن كَذَّبَ بِهَا ٱلْأَوَّلُونَ وَءَاتَيْنَا ثَمُودَ ٱلنَّاقَةَ مُبْصِرَةً).

Ibn 'Abbaas ﷺ said, "The people of Makkah asked the Prophet ﷺ to turn the mountain of As-Safaa into gold for them and that he move the mountains away from them so they could use that area for agriculture. It was then said to him, 'If you wish, wait and be patient with them, or if you wish, We will give them what they asked for. Then if they disbelieve they will be destroyed as I destroyed those before them.' He said, "No, rather I will wait and be patient with them." Then Allaah ﷺ sent down this verse:

$$\text{وَمَا مَنَعَنَا أَن نُّرْسِلَ بِٱلْآيَاتِ إِلَّا أَن كَذَّبَ بِهَا ٱلْأَوَّلُونَ وَءَاتَيْنَا ثَمُودَ ٱلنَّاقَةَ مُبْصِرَةً}$$

"And nothing prevents us from sending the signs except that the people of old denied them. And We sent the she-camel to Thamood as a clear sign…"

Al-Imaam Ahmad transmitted this hadeeth in his *Musnad*, volume 1, page 258. Ibn Katheer, in *Al-Bidaayah wa An-Nihaayah*, volume 3, page 52, said, "Its chain is *jayyid*." Al-Haithamee said in *Majma' Az-Zawaa'id*, volume 7, page 50, "Its people are people of the *Saheeh* (Al-Bukhaaree and/or Muslim)."

His, the Exalted One's statement:

$$\text{وَيَسْأَلُونَكَ عَنِ ٱلرُّوحِ ۖ قُلِ ٱلرُّوحُ مِنْ أَمْرِ رَبِّي وَمَا أُوتِيتُم مِّنَ ٱلْعِلْمِ إِلَّا قَلِيلًا}$$

"And they ask you about the spirit. Say: The spirit is from the matters of my Lord. And of knowledge you have only been given a little." (verse: 85)

قال الإمام البخاري رحمه الله (125): حدثنا قيس بن حفص قال حدثنا عبد الواحد قال حدثنا الأعمش سليمان عن إبراهيم عن علقمة عن عبد الله ﷺ قال: بينا أنا أمشي مع النبي ﷺ في خَرِب المدينة وهو يتوكأ على عسيب فمر بنفر من اليهود فقال بعضهم لبعض: سلوه عن الروح وقال بعضهم: لا تسألوه لا يجيء فيه بشيء تكرهونه فقال بعضهم: لنسألنه فقام رجل منهم فقال: يا أبا القاسم ما الروح فسكت فقلت: إنه يوحى إليه فقمت فلما انجلى عنه فقال: (ويسألونك عن الروح قل الروح من أمر ربي وما أوتوا من العلم إلا قليلا). قال الأعمش: هكذا في قراءتنا.

'Abdullaah ibn Mas'ood ؓ said, "As I was walking with the Prophet ﷺ in the area of the ruins of Madeenah, while he was supporting himself with an *'aseeb* (a cane made from a date palm branch), he passed by a group of Jews. So they said to one another, 'Ask him about the spirit.' One of them said, "Do not ask him. That way he does not mention something about it which you dislike." Then one of them said, 'We will indeed ask him.' A man from them then stood up and said, "O Abaal-Qaasim, what is the spirit?" He was silent. Then I said, 'Verily revelation is being revealed to him.' Then I stood. It then passed from him so he said:

ويسألونك عن الروح قل الروح من أمر ربي وما أوتوا من العلم إلا قليلا

"And they ask you about the spirit. Say: The spirit is from the matters of my Lord. And of knowledge they have only been given a little."
Al-A'mash (a narrator in the chain) said, "That is how it is in our recitation."[87]

Al-Bukhaaree transmitted this hadeeth in his *Saheeh* (125) and Muslim in his *Saheeh* (2794).

قال الإمام الترمذي رحمه الله (3140): حدثنا قتيبة حدثنا يحيى بن زكريا بن أبي زائدة عن داود بن أبي هند عن عكرمة عن ابن عباس ؓ قال: قالت قريش لليهود: أعطونا شيئا نسأل هذا الرجل فقال: سلوه عن الروح فسألوه عن الروح فأنزل الله: (وَيَسْـَٔلُونَكَ عَنِ ٱلرُّوحِ ۖ قُلِ ٱلرُّوحُ مِنْ أَمْرِ رَبِّى وَمَآ أُوتِيتُم مِّنَ ٱلْعِلْمِ إِلَّا قَلِيلًا) قالوا: أوتينا علما كثيرا أوتينا التوراة ومن أوتي التوراة فقد أوتي خيرا كثيرا فأنزلت: (قُل لَّوْ كَانَ ٱلْبَحْرُ مِدَادًا لِّكَلِمَـٰتِ رَبِّى لَنَفِدَ ٱلْبَحْرُ) إلى آخر الآية.
قال: هذا حديث حسن صحيح غريب من هذا الوجه.

Ibn 'Abbaas ؓ said, "Quraish said to the Jews, 'Give us something to ask this man.' They said, "Ask him about the spirit." Then Allaah sent down:

---

[87] Meaning the recitation of Al-A'mash is (أوتوا) instead of (أوتيتم).

176

$$وَيَسْـَٔلُونَكَ عَنِ ٱلرُّوحِ ۖ قُلِ ٱلرُّوحُ مِنْ أَمْرِ رَبِّى وَمَآ أُوتِيتُم مِّنَ ٱلْعِلْمِ إِلَّا قَلِيلًا$$

'And they ask you about the spirit. Say: The spirit is from the matters of my Lord. And of knowledge you have only been given a little.'

They (the Jews) said, "We have been given vast knowledge. We have been given the Tawraah, and whoever has been given the Tawraah, he has been given vast knowledge." Then this verse descended,

$$قُل لَّوْ كَانَ ٱلْبَحْرُ مِدَادًا لِّكَلِمَٰتِ رَبِّى لَنَفِدَ ٱلْبَحْرُ$$

"Say: If the ocean were ink for writing the words of my Lord, surely the ocean would be exhausted…" (*Al-Kahf*: 109).

This *hadeeth* has been transmitted by At-Tirmidhee transmitted in his *Jaami'* (3140). Al-Haafidh Ibn Katheer commented on the first *hadeeth*, the *hadeeth* of Ibn Mas'ood in his *Tafseer*, volume 3, page 60, saying, "And this wording demands, at first thought, that this verse is *Madaniyah* (a verse that descended after the *hijrah*) and that it was revealed when the Jews asked him about that [issue] in Madeenah despite the fact that the entire *Soorah* is *Makkiyah* (that which descended before the *hijrah*). This can be answered by saying the verse was revealed to him a second time in Madeenah, as it was revealed to him beforehand in Makkah. Or it could be said that revelation was sent down to him telling him to answer them with the verse that had already been revealed to him aforetime."

His, the Exalted One's statement:

$$وَلَا تَجْهَرْ بِصَلَاتِكَ وَلَا تُخَافِتْ بِهَا وَٱبْتَغِ بَيْنَ ذَٰلِكَ سَبِيلًا$$

"And offer your prayer neither aloud nor in a low voice, but follow a way between." (verse: 110)

قال الإمام البخاري رَحِمَهُ اللهُ (4722): حدثنا يعقوب بن إبراهيم حدثنا هشيم حدثنا أبو بشر عن سعيد بن جبير عن ابن عباس رَضِيَ اللهُ عَنْهُ في قوله تعالى ﷺ: (وَلَا تَجْهَرْ بِصَلَاتِكَ وَلَا تُخَافِتْ بِهَا) قال: نزلت ورسول الله ﷺ مختف بمكة كان إذا صلى بأصحابه رفع صوته بالقرآن فإذا سمع المشركون سبوا القرآن ومن أنزله ومن جاء به فقال الله تعالى لنبيه ﷺ: (وَلَا تَجْهَرْ بِصَلَاتِكَ) أي بقراءتك فيسمع المشركون فيسبوا القرآن (وَلَا تُخَافِتْ بِهَا) عن أصحابك فلا تسمعهم (وَٱبْتَغِ بَيْنَ ذَٰلِكَ سَبِيلًا).

Ibn 'Abbaas said about His statement:

$$\text{وَلَا تَجْهَرْ بِصَلَاتِكَ وَلَا تُخَافِتْ بِهَا}$$

"And offer your prayer neither aloud nor in a low voice…"

He (Ibn 'Abbaas) said, "It descended when the Messenger of Allaah ﷺ was in hiding in Makkah. When he used to pray with his Companions he would raise his voice with the Qur'aan. When the polytheists heard that they would revile the Qur'aan and the one who revealed it and the one who brought it [to them]. So Allaah ﷻ said to His Prophet ﷺ:

$$\text{وَلَا تَجْهَرْ بِصَلَاتِكَ}$$

"And offer your prayer neither aloud"

Meaning your recitation which leads the polytheists to hear it and revile the Qur'aan.

$$\text{وَلَا تُخَافِتْ بِهَا}$$

"nor in a low voice"

Making it low on your Companions which leads them not to hear you.

$$\text{وَابْتَغِ بَيْنَ ذَٰلِكَ سَبِيلًا}$$

"but follow a way between."

Al-Bukhaaree transmitted this hadeeth in his *Saheeh* (4722) and Muslim in his *Saheeh* (446).

قال الإمام البخاري رحمه الله (6327): حدثنا علي حدثنا مالك بن سُعير حدثنا هشام بن عروة عن أبيه عن عائشة رضي الله عنها: (وَلَا تَجْهَرْ بِصَلَاتِكَ وَلَا تُخَافِتْ بِهَا) أنزلت في الدعاء.

On 'Aishah:

$$\text{وَلَا تَجْهَرْ بِصَلَاتِكَ وَلَا تُخَافِتْ بِهَا}$$

"And offer your prayer neither aloud nor in a low voice…"

"It was sent down in regards to supplication."

Al-Bukhaaree transmitted this *hadeeth* in his *Saheeh* (6327) as well as Muslim in his *Saheeh* (447).

قال الإمام ابن جرير ﷺ (ج 17 ص 585): حدثنا أبو كريب قال ثنا يونس ثنا محمد بن إسحاق قال ثني داود بن الحصين عن عكرمة عن ابن عباس ﷺ قال: كان رسول الله ﷺ إذا جهر بالقرآن وهو يصلي تفرقوا وأبوا أن يستمعوا منه فكان الرجل إذا أراد أن يستمع من رسول الله ﷺ بعض ما يتلو وهو يصلي استرق السمع دونهم فرقا منهم فإن رأى أنهم قد عرفوا أنه يستمع ذهب خشية أذاهم فلم يستمع فإن خفض رسول الله ﷺ صوته لم يستمع الذين يستمعون من قراءته شيئا فأنزل الله عليه: (وَلَا تَجْهَرْ بِصَلَاتِكَ وَلَا تُخَافِتْ بِهَا) فيتفرقوا عنك فلا تسمع من أراد أن يسمعها ممن يسترق ذلك دونهم لعله يرعوي إلى بعض ما يسمع فينتفع به (وَابْتَغِ بَيْنَ ذَلِكَ سَبِيلًا).

Ibn 'Abbaas ﷺ said, "When the Messenger of Allaah ﷺ used to raise his voice with the Qur'aan while praying they (the polytheists) would disperse and refuse to listen to him. If a man wanted to listen to some of what the Messenger of Allaah ﷺ was reciting while praying, he would have to eavesdrop alongside of them out of fear of . If he thought they knew he was listening he would leave out of fear of their harm and not listen. If the Messenger of Allaah ﷺ were to lower his voice the people who wanted to listen would not hear any of his recitation. Then Allaah sent down to him:

$$\text{وَلَا تَجْهَرْ بِصَلَاتِكَ}$$

"And offer your prayer neither aloud"

because this would cause them to disperse from you.

$$\text{وَلَا تُخَافِتْ بِهَا}$$

"nor in a low voice"

This would cause the person who wanted to hear by eavesdropping alongside of them not to hear. Perhaps he will take heed to something that he hears and benefit thereby.

$$\text{وَابْتَغِ بَيْنَ ذَلِكَ سَبِيلًا}$$

"but follow a way between."

Ibn Jareer transmitted this hadeeth in his *Tafseer*, volume 17, page 585. Ash-Sheikh Muqbil ﷺ commented, "There is no contradiction between these different reasons because it is possible that the polytheists used to revile the Qur'aan and the one who brought it [to them], and that they used to harm whoever they saw listening to the Qur'aan, as it is also possible that what is meant by:

$$\text{وَلَا تَجْهَرْ بِصَلَاتِكَ}$$

"And offer your prayer neither aloud"

is your supplication in the prayer, and the narration which mentions that to be in *tashahhud* as mentioned in Ibn Jareer, volume 15, page 187,[88] is an explanation for the place of the supplication, and Allaah knows best."

---

[88] The Sheikh uses the older printed version of *Tafseer Ibn Jareer* for reference which is different from the version checked by Mahmood Shaakir which I used for quoting the *ahaadeeth*.

سورة مريم

Sooratu Maryam

His, the Exalted One's statement:

$$وَمَا نَتَنَزَّلُ إِلَّا بِأَمْرِ رَبِّكَ ۖ لَهُ مَا بَيْنَ أَيْدِينَا وَمَا خَلْفَنَا$$

"And we (the angels) descend not except by the command of your Lord. To him belongs what is before us and what is behind us…" (verse: 64)

قال الإمام البخاري رَحِمَهُ اللهُ (4731): حدثنا أبو نعيم حدثنا عمر بن ذر قال سمعت أبي عن سعيد ابن جبير عن ابن عباس رَضِيَ اللهُ عَنْهُ قال: قال رسول الله ﷺ لجبريل: ما يمنعك أن تزورنا أكثر مما تزورنا فنزلت: (وَمَا نَتَنَزَّلُ إِلَّا بِأَمْرِ رَبِّكَ ۖ لَهُ مَا بَيْنَ أَيْدِينَا وَمَا خَلْفَنَا).

Ibn 'Abbaas said, "The Messenger of Allaah said to Jibreel, 'What prevents you from visiting us more often?' Then this verse descended,

$$وَمَا نَتَنَزَّلُ إِلَّا بِأَمْرِ رَبِّكَ ۖ لَهُ مَا بَيْنَ أَيْدِينَا وَمَا خَلْفَنَا$$

"And we (the angels) descend not except by the command of your Lord. To him belongs what is before us and what is behind us…"

Al-Bukhaaree transmitted this hadeeth in his *Saheeh* (4731).

His, the Exalted One's statement:

$$أَفَرَأَيْتَ الَّذِي كَفَرَ بِآيَاتِنَا وَقَالَ لَأُوتَيَنَّ مَالًا وَوَلَدًا ۝ أَطَّلَعَ الْغَيْبَ أَمِ اتَّخَذَ عِندَ الرَّحْمَٰنِ عَهْدًا ۝ كَلَّا ۚ سَنَكْتُبُ مَا يَقُولُ وَنَمُدُّ لَهُ مِنَ الْعَذَابِ مَدًّا ۝ وَنَرِثُهُ مَا يَقُولُ وَيَأْتِينَا فَرْدًا ۝$$

"Have you seen the one who disbelieved in our signs and said, 'I shall certainly be given wealth and children.' Does he know the unseen or has he taken a covenant from the Most-Beneficent? Nay, We shall record what he says and We shall increase his torment. And We shall inherit from him all that he speaks of and he shall come to Us alone." (verses: 77-80)

قال الإمام البخاري رَحِمَهُ اللهُ (2091): حدثني محمد بن بشار حدثنا ابن أبي عدي عن شعبة عن سليمان عن أبي الضحى عن مسروق عن خباب رَضِيَ اللهُ عَنْهُ قال: كنت قينا في الجاهلية وكان لي على العاصي بن

وائل دين فأتيته أتقاضاه قال: لا أعطيك حتى تكفر بمحمد فقلت: لا أكفر حتى يميتك الله ثم تبعث قال: دعني حتى أموت وأبعث فسأوتى مالا وولدا فأقضيك فنزلت: (أَفَرَءَيْتَ ٱلَّذِى كَفَرَ بِـَٔايَـٰتِنَا وَقَالَ لَأُوتَيَنَّ مَالًا وَوَلَدًا) (أَطَّلَعَ ٱلْغَيْبَ أَمِ ٱتَّخَذَ عِندَ ٱلرَّحْمَـٰنِ عَهْدًا).

Khabbaab ﷺ said, "I was a blacksmith in *Jaahiliyah*. Al-'Aasee ibn Waa'il was indebted to me so I went to him demanding payment from him. He said, 'No, I will not give you until you disbelieve in Muhammad.' I said, "I will not disbelieve until Allaah causes you to die and you are resurrected."[89] He said, 'Leave me until I die and am resurrected, for I will be given wealth and children and then I will pay you back.' Then it descended:

أَفَرَءَيْتَ ٱلَّذِى كَفَرَ بِـَٔايَـٰتِنَا وَقَالَ لَأُوتَيَنَّ مَالًا وَوَلَدًا

"Have you seen the one who disbelieved in our signs and said, 'I shall certainly be given wealth and children."

أَطَّلَعَ ٱلْغَيْبَ أَمِ ٱتَّخَذَ عِندَ ٱلرَّحْمَـٰنِ عَهْدًا

"Does he know the unseen or has he taken a covenant from the Most-Beneficent?"

This *hadeeth* has been transmitted by Al-Bukhaaree in his *Saheeh* (2091) and by Muslim in his *Saheeh* (2795).

---

[89] Ibn Hajar said in *Fathul-Baaree* in the explanation of *hadeeth* (4732), "It could be understood from this that he will then disbelieve, however, he did not mean that because disbelief at that time is unthinkable so it is as if he said I will never disbelieve."

سورة الأنبياء

Sooratul-Anbiyaa

His, the Exalted One's statement:

$$\text{إِنَّ ٱلَّذِينَ سَبَقَتْ لَهُم مِّنَّا ٱلْحُسْنَىٰ أُو۟لَـٰٓئِكَ عَنْهَا مُبْعَدُونَ}$$

"Verily those for whom the good has preceded from Us, they will be placed far away from it (hell)." (verse: 101)

قال الإمام الطحاوي رحمه الله في مشكل الآثار (986): حدثنا عبيد بن رجال حدثنا الحسن بن علي حدثنا يحيى بن آدم حدثنا أبو بكر بن عياش ثنا عاصم عن أبي رزين عن أبي يحيى عن ابن عباس رضي الله عنهما قال: آية في كتاب الله عز وجل لا يسألني الناس عنها ولا أدري أعرفوها فلا يسألوني عنها أم جهلوها فلا يسألوني عنها قيل: ما هي قال: آية لما نزلت: (إِنَّكُمْ وَمَا تَعْبُدُونَ مِن دُونِ ٱللَّهِ حَصَبُ جَهَنَّمَ أَنتُمْ لَهَا وَٰرِدُونَ) شق ذلك على أهل مكة وقالوا: شتم محمد آلهتنا فقام ابن الزبعرى فقال: ما شأنكم قالوا: شتم محمد آلهتنا قال: وما قال قالوا: قال (إِنَّكُمْ وَمَا تَعْبُدُونَ مِن دُونِ ٱللَّهِ حَصَبُ جَهَنَّمَ أَنتُمْ لَهَا وَٰرِدُونَ) قال: ادعوه لي فدعي محمد ﷺ فقال ابن الزبعرى: يا محمد هذا شيء لآلهتنا خاصة أم لكل ما عبد من دون الله قال: بل لكل ما عبد من دون الله عز وجل قال فقال: خصمناه ورب البنية يا محمد ألست تزعم أن عيسى عبد صالح وعزيرا عبد صالح والملائكة عباد صالحون قال: بلى قال: فهذه النصارى تعبد عيسى وهذه اليهود تعبد عزيرا وهذه بنو مليح تعبد الملائكة قال فضج أهل مكة فنزلت: (إِنَّ ٱلَّذِينَ سَبَقَتْ لَهُم مِّنَّا ٱلْحُسْنَىٰ أُو۟لَـٰٓئِكَ عَنْهَا مُبْعَدُونَ) قال ونزلت: (وَلَمَّا ضُرِبَ ٱبْنُ مَرْيَمَ مَثَلًا إِذَا قَوْمُكَ مِنْهُ يَصِدُّونَ) وهو الضجيج.

Ibn 'Abbaas said, "[There is] A verse in the book of Allaah which the people do not ask me about it and I do not know [if it is because] they do not understand it so they do not ask me about it or, if it is that they are ignorant of it so they do not ask me about it?" It was said, "What is it?" He said, "When the verse descended:

$$\text{إِنَّكُمْ وَمَا تَعْبُدُونَ مِن دُونِ ٱللَّهِ حَصَبُ جَهَنَّمَ أَنتُمْ لَهَا وَٰرِدُونَ}$$

'Certainly you (disbelievers) and what you worship besides Allaah are fuel for hell. You will enter it.' (*Al-Anbiyaa*: 98)

It was hard on the people of Makkah and they said, "Muhammad has reviled our gods." Ibn Az-Ziba'raa stood up and said, 'What is with you?' They said, "Muhammad has reviled our gods." He responded, "And what did he say?" They said, 'He said:

$$\text{إِنَّكُمْ وَمَا تَعْبُدُونَ مِن دُونِ ٱللَّهِ حَصَبُ جَهَنَّمَ أَنتُمْ لَهَا وَارِدُونَ}$$

"Certainly you (disbelievers) and what you worship besides Allaah are fuel for hell. You will enter it."

He said, "Call him over for me." Muhammad ﷺ was then called so Ibn Az-Ziba'raa said, 'O Muhammad, is this something for our gods in particular or for everything that is worshipped besides Allaah?' He said, "[No] Rather [it is] for everything that is worshipped besides Allaah ﷻ." So he said, 'We have beaten him in the argument, by the Lord of this structure (the *Ka'bah*). O Muhammad, do you not claim that 'Eesaa is a righteous servant and that 'Uzair is a righteous servant and that the angels are righteous servants?' He said, "Certainly." He said, 'These are the Christians, they worship 'Eesaa, and these are the Jews, they worship 'Uzair, and these are the tribe Banu Maleeh, they worship the angels.' The people of Makkah then went into an uproar. Then this verse descended:

$$\text{إِنَّ ٱلَّذِينَ سَبَقَتْ لَهُم مِّنَّا ٱلْحُسْنَىٰ أُوْلَـٰٓئِكَ عَنْهَا مُبْعَدُونَ}$$

"Verily those for whom the good has preceded from Us, they will be placed far away from it (hell)."

And this verse descended:

$$\text{وَلَمَّا ضُرِبَ ٱبْنُ مَرْيَمَ مَثَلًا إِذَا قَوْمُكَ مِنْهُ يَصِدُّونَ}$$

"And when the son of Maryam is quoted as an example, behold, your people cry aloud." (*Az-Zukhruf*: 57)
That was the uproar."

This *hadeeth* has been transmitted by At-Tahaawee in *Mushkil Al-Aathaar* (986). Ash-Sheikh Muqbil ؓ pointed out the weakness in the chain and then mentioned supporting chains transmitted by At-Tahaawee in *Mushkil Al-Aathaar* (985) and (988), and by At-Tabaraanee in *Al-Mu'jam Al-Kabeer*, volume 12, page 153, and by Al-Haakim in *Al-Mustadrak*, volume 2, page 384, and by Al-Khateeb in *Al-Faqeeh wa Al-Mutafaqqih* page 70. Ash-Sheikh Muqbil ؓ said, "The *hadeeth,* along with the previous chains is *saheeh li ghairihi*, and Allaah knows best."

سورة الحج

Sooratul-Hajj

His, the Exalted One's statement:

هَـٰذَانِ خَصْمَانِ ٱخْتَصَمُواْ فِى رَبِّهِمْ

"These two opponents dispute with each other about their Lord…" (verse: 19)

قال الإمام البخاري ﷺ (3969): حدثنا يعقوب بن إبراهيم حدثنا هشيم أخبرنا أبو هاشم عن أبي مجلز عن قيس بن عباد قال سمعت أبا ذر ﷺ يقسم قسما أن هذه الآية: (هَـٰذَانِ خَصْمَانِ ٱخْتَصَمُواْ فِى رَبِّهِمْ) نزلت في الذين برزوا يوم بدر حمزة وعلي وعبيدة بن الحارث وعتبة وشيبة ابني ربيعة والوليد بن عتبة.

Qais ibn 'Ubaad said, "I heard Abu Dhar ﷺ swear that this verse:

هَـٰذَانِ خَصْمَانِ ٱخْتَصَمُواْ فِى رَبِّهِمْ

"These two opponents dispute with each other about their Lord…"

descended because of those who came forward to duel (with one another) on the day of Badr: Hamzah, and 'Ali, and 'Ubaidah bin Al-Haarith, and 'Utbah and Shaibah, the two sons of Rabee'ah, and Al-Waleed ibn 'Utbah."[90]

Al-Bukhaaree transmitted this *hadeeth* it in his *Saheeh* (3969) and Muslim in his *Saheeh* (3033).

---

[90] 'Ali, Hamzah, and 'Ubaidah represented the Muslims while 'Utbah, Shaibah, and Al-Waleed represented the polytheists. 'Ali and Hamzah both killed their opponents while 'Ubaidah and his opponent exchanged blows. 'Ubaidah was struck and then 'Ali and Hamzah came over and helped him kill his opponent. The narrations differ as to who faced off with who.

سورة المـؤمـنون

Sooratul-Mu'minoon

His, the Exalted One's statement:

$$\text{وَلَقَدْ أَخَذْنَٰهُم بِٱلْعَذَابِ فَمَا ٱسْتَكَانُوا۟ لِرَبِّهِمْ وَمَا يَتَضَرَّعُونَ ۝}$$

"And indeed We inflicted them with suffering but they did not submit to their Lord nor did they humble themselves." (verse: 76)

قال الإمام ابن جرير ﵀ (ج 19 ص 60): حدثنا ابن حميد قال ثنا أبو تميلة عن الحسين عن يزيد عن عكرمة عن ابن عباس ﵄ قال: جاء أبو سفيان إلى النبي ﷺ فقال: يا محمد أنشدك الله والرحم فقد أكلنا العلهز يعني الوبر والدم فأنزل الله: (وَلَقَدْ أَخَذْنَٰهُم بِٱلْعَذَابِ فَمَا ٱسْتَكَانُوا۟ لِرَبِّهِمْ وَمَا يَتَضَرَّعُونَ).

Ibn 'Abbaas said, "Abu Sufyaan went to the Prophet and said, 'O Muhammad, I implore you by Allaah and by the ties of the womb, for verily we have eaten *al-ilhiz*!' Meaning camels' fur and blood. Then Allaah sent down:

$$\text{وَلَقَدْ أَخَذْنَٰهُم بِٱلْعَذَابِ فَمَا ٱسْتَكَانُوا۟ لِرَبِّهِمْ وَمَا يَتَضَرَّعُونَ ۝}$$

"And indeed We inflicted them with suffering but they did not submit to their Lord nor did they humble themselves."

Ibn Jareer transmitted this *hadeeth* in his *Tafseer*, volume 19, page 60, and An-Nasaa'ee in his *Tafseer* (372), and Al-Haakim in *Al-Mustadrak*, volume 2, page 394, and Al-Baihaqee in *Dalaa'il An-Nubuwah*, volume 2, page 328. Ash-Sheikh Muqbil classified it to be *saheeh li ghairihi*.

سورة النور

Sooratun-Noor

<u>His, the Exalted One's statement:</u>

ٱلزَّانِى لَا يَنكِحُ إِلَّا زَانِيَةً أَوْ مُشْرِكَةً وَٱلزَّانِيَةُ لَا يَنكِحُهَآ إِلَّا زَانٍ أَوْ مُشْرِكٌ ۚ وَحُرِّمَ ذَٰلِكَ عَلَى ٱلْمُؤْمِنِينَ ۞

"The fornicator marries not but a fornicatress or a polytheist woman, and the fornicatress, none marries her except a fornicator or a polytheist, and such a thing is forbidden to the believers." (verse: 3)

قال الإمام الترمذي ﵀ (3177): حدثنا عبد بن حميد حدثنا روح بن عبادة عن عبيد الله بن الأخنس أخبرني عمرو بن شعيب عن أبيه عن جده ﵁ قال: كان رجل يقال له مرثد بن أبي مرثد وكان رجلا يحمل الأسرى من مكة حتى يأتي بهم المدينة قال: وكانت امرأة بغي بمكة يقال لها عناق وكانت صديقة له وإنه كان وعد رجلا من أسارى مكة يحمله قال: فجئت حتى انتهيت إلى ظل حائط من حوائط مكة في ليلة مقمرة قال: فجاءت عناق فأبصرت سواد ظلي بجنب الحائط فلما انتهت إلي عرفته فقالت: مرثد فقلت: مرثد فقالت: مرحبا وأهلا هلم فبت عندنا الليلة قال قلت: يا عناق حرم الله الزنى قالت: يا أهل الخيام هذا الرجل يحمل أسراكم قال: فتبعني ثمانية وسلكت الخندمة فانتهيت إلى كهف أو غار فدخلت فجاءوا حتى قاموا على رأسي فبالوا فطل بولهم على رأسي وأعماهم الله عني قال: ثم رجعوا ورجعت إلى صاحبي فحملته وكان رجلا ثقيلا حتى انتهيت إلى الإذخر ففككت عنه كبله فجعلت أحمله ويعينني حتى قدمت المدينة فأتيت رسول الله ﷺ فقلت: يا رسول الله أنكح عناقا فأمسك رسول الله ﷺ فلم يرد علي شيئا حتى نزلت: (ٱلزَّانِى لَا يَنكِحُ إِلَّا زَانِيَةً أَوْ مُشْرِكَةً وَٱلزَّانِيَةُ لَا يَنكِحُهَآ إِلَّا زَانٍ أَوْ مُشْرِكٌ ۚ وَحُرِّمَ ذَٰلِكَ عَلَى ٱلْمُؤْمِنِينَ) فقال رسول الله ﷺ: يا مرثد الزاني لا ينكح إلا زانية أو مشركة والزانية لا ينكحها إلا زان أو مشرك فلا تنكحها.
قال أبو عيسى: هذا حديث حسن غريب لا نعرفه إلا من هذا الوجه.

'Abdullaah ibn 'Amr ﵁ said, "There was a man called Marthad ibn Abee Marthad who used to transport the prisoners (freeing them) from Makkah bringing them to Madeenah, and there was a whore in Makkah called 'Anaaq who used to be his girlfriend. He had promised to transport a man who was a prisoner in Makkah. He (told his story) saying, 'I arrived and then wound up stopping at one of the walls of Makkah on a moonlit night. 'Anaaq then approached and saw my shadow on the side of the wall. When she came closer she recognized me and said, "Marthad?" I said, 'Marthad.' She said, "Welcome! Come spend the night with us tonight." I said, 'O 'Anaaq, Allaah has made fornication forbidden.' She said, "O residents of the tents, this man is transporting your prisoners!" Eight men started to chase me. I headed for Al-Khandamah (the name of a mountain) and wound up at a cave and entered. They then came and stood over my head and they urinated. Their urine sprinkled on to my head; however, Allaah had blinded them from seeing me. They turned [away] going back so I went back to my comrade and carried him and he was a heavy man. When I reached Al-Idhkhir (a place outside of Makkah) I broke open his shackles and transported him with his help until we finally arrived at Madeenah. I went to the Messenger of Allaah ﷺ and said, 'O Messenger of Allaah, can I marry 'Anaaq?' The Messenger of Allaah ﷺ was silent. He did not respond to me until this verse descended:

$$\text{ٱلزَّانِى لَا يَنكِحُ إِلَّا زَانِيَةً أَوْ مُشْرِكَةً وَٱلزَّانِيَةُ لَا يَنكِحُهَآ إِلَّا زَانٍ أَوْ مُشْرِكٌ ۚ وَحُرِّمَ ذَٰلِكَ عَلَى ٱلْمُؤْمِنِينَ}$$

"The fornicator marries not but a fornicatress or a polytheist woman, and the fornicatress, none marries her except a fornicator or a polytheist, and such a thing is forbidden to the believers."

Then the Messenger of Allaah ﷺ said, "O Marthad, the fornicator marries not but a fornicatress or a polytheist woman, and the fornicatress, none marries her except a fornicator or a polytheist, so do not marry her."

This *hadeeth* has been transmitted by At-Tirmidhee transmitted in his *Jaami'* (3177), and Al-Haakim in *Al-Mustadrak*, volume 2, page 166, and he classified its chain to be authentic.

His, the Exalted One's statement:

$$\text{وَٱلَّذِينَ يَرْمُونَ أَزْوَٰجَهُمْ وَلَمْ يَكُن لَّهُمْ شُهَدَآءُ إِلَّآ أَنفُسُهُمْ فَشَهَٰدَةُ أَحَدِهِمْ أَرْبَعُ شَهَٰدَٰتٍۭ بِٱللَّهِ ۙ إِنَّهُۥ لَمِنَ ٱلصَّٰدِقِينَ}$$

"And for those who accuse their wives but have no witnesses except themselves, let the testimony of one of them be four testimonies by Allaah that he is one of those who speak the truth..." (verses: 6-9)

قال الإمام البخاري رَحِمَهُ اللهُ (4745): حدثنا إسحاق حدثنا محمد بن يوسف حدثنا الأوزاعي قال حدثني الزهري عن سهل بن سعد رَضِيَ اللهُ عَنْهُ أن عويمرا أتى عاصم بن عدي وكان سيد بني عجلان فقال: كيف تقولون في رجل وجد مع امرأته رجلا أيقتله فتقتلونه أم كيف يصنع سل لي رسول الله ﷺ عن ذلك فأتى عاصم النبي ﷺ فقال: يا رسول الله فكره رسول الله ﷺ المسائل فسأله عويمر فقال: إن رسول الله ﷺ كره المسائل وعابها قال عويمر: والله لا أنتهي حتى أسأل رسول الله ﷺ عن ذلك فجاء عويمر فقال: يا رسول الله رجل وجد مع امرأته رجلا أيقتله فتقتلونه أم كيف يصنع فقال رسول الله

ﷺ قد أنزل الله القرآن فيك وفي صاحبتك فأمرهما رسول الله ﷺ بالملاعنة بما سمى الله في كتابه فلاعنها ثم قال:

يا رسول الله إن حبستها فقد ظلمتها فطلقها فكانت سنة لمن كان بعدهما في المتلاعنين ثم قال رسول الله ﷺ: انظروا فإن جاءت به أسحم أدعج العينين عظيم الأليتين خدلج الساقين فلا أحسب عويمرا إلا قد صدق عليها وإن جاءت به أحيمر كأنه وحرة فلا أحسب عويمرا إلا قد كذب عليها فجاءت به على النعت الذي نعت به رسول الله ﷺ من تصديق عويمر فكان بعد ينسب إلى أمه.

Sahl ibn Sa'd ؓ narrated that 'Uwaimir went to 'Aasim ibn 'Adee who was the leader of the tribe Banee 'Ajlaan and said, "What do you say about a man who finds his wife with another man? Should he kill him, which will cause you to kill him or, what should be done? Ask the Messenger of Allaah ﷺ about that for me." So 'Aasim went to the Prophet ﷺ and said, "O Messenger of Allaah…(asking the question)". The Messenger of Allaah ﷺ showed [his] dislike for the questions and disapproved of them. 'Uwaimir then asked him ('Aasim [about the answer to his questions]) so he said, "Verily the Messenger of Allaah ﷺ showed dislike for the questions and disapproved of them." 'Uwaimir said, "By Allaah, I will not give up until I ask the Messenger of Allaah ﷺ about that [myself]."

So 'Uwaimir went and said, "O Messenger of Allaah, [suppose] a man finds his wife with another man, should he kill him which will cause you to kill him or, what should be done?" The Messenger of Allaah ﷺ said, "Allaah has sent down Qur'aan in regards to you and your wife." The Messenger of Allaah ﷺ then ordered the two of them to take the oath of condemnation as Allaah stated in His book. So he made his sworn allegation against her and then he said, "O Messenger of Allaah, if I keep her I will have oppressed her." So he divorced her and that became the normal procedure for those who came after them in dealing with the two who take the oath of condemnation. The Messenger of Allaah ﷺ then said, "Look and see, if she has it (the baby) black with black eyes and a large backside and large shins then I think not except that 'Uwaimir was truthful in his accusation against her, and if she has it small and red like a *waharah*[91] then I think not except that 'Uwaimir has lied against her." She then had it on the description that the Messenger of Allaah ﷺ described confirming the truthfulness of 'Uwaimir so it afterwards was attributed to its mother.

This *hadeeth* has been transmitted by Al-Bukhaaree in his *Saheeh* (4745) and Muslim in his *Saheeh* (1492).

قال الإمام البخاري ؓ (4747): حدثني محمد بن بشار حدثنا ابن أبي عدي عن هشام بن حسان حدثنا عكرمة عن ابن عباس ؓ أن هلال بن أمية قذف امرأته عند النبي ﷺ بشريك بن سحماء

---

[91] A *waharah* is a small animal which looks like a lizard. It is white with red spots.

فقال النبي ﷺ: البينة أو حد في ظهرك فقال: يا رسول الله إذا رأى أحدنا على امرأته رجلا ينطلق يلتمس البينة فجعل النبي ﷺ يقول: البينة وإلا حد في ظهرك فقال هلال: والذي بعثك بالحق إني لصادق فلينزلن الله ما يبرئ ظهري من الحد فنزل جبريل وأنزل عليه: (وَٱلَّذِينَ يَرْمُونَ أَزْوَٰجَهُمْ) فقرأ حتى بلغ: (إِن كَانَ مِنَ ٱلصَّٰدِقِينَ) فانصرف النبي ﷺ فأرسل إليها فجاء هلال فشهد والنبي ﷺ يقول: إن الله يعلم أن أحدكما كاذب فهل منكما تائب ثم قامت فشهدت فلما كانت عند الخامسة وقفوها وقالوا: إنها موجبة قال ابن عباس: فتلكأت ونكصت حتى ظننا أنها ترجع ثم قالت: لا أفضح قومي سائر اليوم فمضت فقال النبي ﷺ: أبصروها فإن جاءت به أكحل العينين سابغ الأليتين خدلج الساقين فهو لشريك ابن سحماء فجاءت به كذلك فقال النبي ﷺ: لولا ما مضى من كتاب الله لكان لي ولها شأن.

Ibn 'Abbaas ؓ narrated that Hilaal bin Umaiyah accused his wife of committing adultery with Shareek ibn Sahmaa so the Prophet ﷺ said, "[Provide] the proof, or the legal punishment will be inflicted on your back (flogging)." He said, "O Messenger of Allaah, when one of us sees a man on top of his wife, does he go searching for proof?" The Prophet ﷺ said again, "The proof or the legal punishment will be inflicted on your back." Hilaal then said, "By the one who sent you with the truth, I am being truthful and indeed Allaah will send down what will free my back from the legal punishment." Jibreel then descended and sent down to him:

$$\text{وَٱلَّذِينَ يَرْمُونَ أَزْوَٰجَهُمْ}$$

"And for those who accuse their wives…"

He recited it until he reached:

$$\text{إِن كَانَ مِنَ ٱلصَّٰدِقِينَ}$$

"…if he speaks the truth."

The Prophet ﷺ then left and sent for her. Hilaal came and gave his testimony while the Prophet ﷺ was saying, "Indeed Allaah knows that one of you are lying so is there not among you two one who will repent!" She then stood up and gave her testimony. When she was about to make the fifth testimony they stopped her and said, "It will make it binding!" She hesitated and shrunk back to the point where we thought she would repeal and then she said, "I will not have my people be in disgrace for the rest of the day." So she went ahead (with the fifth testimony). The Prophet ﷺ then said, "Look at her, if she has it (the baby) with black eyes and a large backside and large shins then it was by Shareek ibn Sahmaa." She later gave birth to a baby with that description, so the Prophet ﷺ said, "If it were not for what has preceded from the book of Allaah, there would have been a matter to resolve between myself and her."

This *hadeeth* has been transmitted by Al-Bukhaaree in his *Saheeh* (4747).

قال الإمام مسلم ﵀ (1493): حدثنا محمد بن عبد الله بن نمير حدثنا أبي ح وحدثنا أبو بكر ابن أبي شيبة واللفظ له حدثنا عبد الله بن نمير حدثنا عبد الملك بن أبي سليمان عن سعيد بن جبير قال: سئلت عن المتلاعنين في إمرة مصعب أيفرق بينهما قال فما دريت ما أقول فمضيت إلى منزل ابن عمر بمكة فقلت للغلام: استأذن لي قال: إنه قائل فسمع صوتي قال: ابن جبير قلت: نعم قال: ادخل فوالله ما جاء بك هذه الساعة إلا حاجة فدخلت فإذا هو مفترش برذعة متوسد وسادة حشوها ليف قلت: أبا عبد الرحمن المتلاعنان أيفرق بينهما قال: سبحان الله نعم إن أول من سأل عن ذلك فلان بن فلان قال: يا رسول الله أرأيت أن لو وجد أحدنا امرأته على فاحشة كيف يصنع إن تكلم تكلم بأمر عظيم وإن سكت سكت على مثل ذلك قال: فسكت النبي ﷺ فلم يجبه فلما كان بعد ذلك أتاه فقال: إن الذي سألتك عنه قد ابتليت به فأنزل الله عز وجل هؤلاء الآيات في سورة النور: (وَٱلَّذِينَ يَرْمُونَ أَزْوَٰجَهُمْ) فتلاهن عليه ووعظه وذكره وأخبره أن عذاب الدنيا أهون من عذاب الآخرة قال: لا والذي بعثك بالحق ما كذبت عليها ثم دعاها فوعظها وذكرها وأخبرها أن عذاب الدنيا أهون من عذاب الآخرة قالت: لا والذي بعثك بالحق إنه لكاذب فبدأ بالرجل فشهد أربع شهادات بالله إنه لمن الصادقين والخامسة أن لعنة الله عليه إن كان من الكاذبين ثم ثنى بالمرأة فشهدت أربع شهادات بالله إنه لمن الكاذبين والخامسة أن غضب الله عليها إن كان من الصادقين ثم فرق بينهما.

Sa'eed ibn Jubair stated, "I was asked in the era when Mus'ab was in leadership about the two spouses who take the oath of condemnation; 'Are they to be separated?' I did not know what to say so I went to Ibn 'Umar's house in Makkah and said to the boy servant, "Ask permission for me [to enter]." He said, 'Verily he is resting.' He heard my voice and said, "Ibn Jubair?" I said, 'Yes.' He said, "Enter, for, by Allaah, nothing brings you here at this hour except an urgent need." So I entered and found him lying down on a donkey's saddle blanket with a pillow stuffed with palm fibers. I said, 'O Abaa 'Abdir-Rahmaan, the two spouses who take the oath of condemnation are they to be separated?' He said, "*Subhaanallaah* (Glorified be Allaah)! Yes. Verily the first person who asked about that was so-and-so." He said, "O Messenger of Allaah, tell me, if one of us were to find his wife committing adultery what should be done? If he speaks he has spoken about a serious matter, and if he is quiet he has been silent about something like that!" The Prophet ﷺ was silent and did not answer him. Thereafter he went to him and said, 'Verily that which I asked you about I have been tried with.' Then Allaah ﷻ sent down these verses from *Sooratun-Noor*:

وَٱلَّذِينَ يَرْمُونَ أَزْوَٰجَهُمْ

"And for those who accuse their wives…"

So he recited it to him, and warned him, and reminded him, and told him that the punishment of this world is easier than the punishment of the hereafter. He said, "No, by the one who sent you with the truth, I did not lie against her." He then summonsed her and warned her, and reminded her, and told her that the punishment of this world is easier than the punishment of the hereafter. She said, 'No, by the one who sent you with the truth, verily he is lying.' He then started with the man. He made four testimonies swearing by Allaah that he is truthful and the fifth testimony that the curse of Allaah be upon him if he is a liar. He then repeated that [process] with the woman so she made four testimonies swearing by Allaah that he is a liar and the fifth testimony [asking] that the anger of Allaah be upon her if he is being truthful. He then separated them."

As for this *hadeeth*, Muslim transmitted it in his *Saheeh* (1493). In some narrations of this *hadeeth* it was mentioned that the man who asked and later took the oath of condemnation was the man from the tribe Banee 'Ajlaan (Meaning 'Uwaimir).

قال الإمام مسلم ﵀ (1495): حدثنا زهير بن حرب وعثمان بن أبي شيبة وإسحاق بن إبراهيم واللفظ لزهير قال إسحاق أخبرنا وقال الآخران حدثنا جرير عن الأعمش عن إبراهيم عن علقمة عن عبد الله ﵁ قال: إنا ليلة الجمعة في المسجد إذ جاء رجل من الأنصار فقال: لو أن رجلا وجد مع امرأته رجلا فتكلم جلدتموه أو قتل قتلتموه وإن سكت سكت على غيظ والله لأسألن عنه رسول الله ﷺ فلما كان من الغد أتى رسول الله ﷺ فسأله فقال: لو أن رجلا وجد مع امرأته رجلا فتكلم جلدتموه أو قتل قتلتموه أو سكت سكت على غيظ فقال: اللهم افتح وجعل يدعو فنزلت آية اللعان: (وَٱلَّذِينَ يَرۡمُونَ أَزۡوَٰجَهُمۡ وَلَمۡ يَكُن لَّهُمۡ شُهَدَآءُ إِلَّآ أَنفُسُهُمۡ) هذه الآيات فابتلى به ذلك الرجل من بين الناس فجاء هو وامرأته إلى رسول الله ﷺ فتلاعنا فشهد الرجل أربع شهادات بالله إنه لمن الصادقين ثم لعن الخامسة أن لعنة الله عليه إن كان من الكاذبين فذهبت لتلعن فقال لها رسول الله ﷺ: مه، فأبت فلعنت فلما أدبرا قال لعلها أن تجيء به أسود جعدا فجاءت به أسود جعدا.

'Abdullaah ibn Mas'ood ﵁ said, "We were in the *masjid* on the night of *Jumu'ah* when a man from the *Ansaar* came and said, 'If a man were to find a man with his wife and then he spoke (exposing her) you would flog him, or if he killed him you would kill him, and if he kept quiet he would be keeping quiet about something that enrages him. By Allaah, I will indeed ask the Messenger of Allaah ﷺ about that.' When the next day came he went to the Messenger of Allaah ﷺ and asked him saying, 'If a man were to find a man with his wife and then he spoke (exposing her) you would flog him, or if he killed him you would kill him, and if he kept quiet he would be keeping quiet about something that enrages him.' He (the *Ansaaree* man) then said, "O

Allaah, make it clear!" And he began to supplicate. Then the verse of *Al-li'aan* (the oath of condemnation) descended:

$$\text{وَٱلَّذِينَ يَرْمُونَ أَزْوَٰجَهُمْ وَلَمْ يَكُن لَّهُمْ شُهَدَآءُ إِلَّآ أَنفُسُهُمْ}$$

"And for those who accuse their wives but have no witnesses except themselves…" these verses.

Out of all the people, that man was tried with that [situation] happening to him. He and his wife then went to the Messenger of Allaah ﷺ and took the oath of condemnation. The man made four testimonies swearing by Allaah that he is of the truthful, and then he made the fifth testimony that the curse of Allaah be upon him if he is of the liars. She then started to take the oath of condemnation. The Messenger of Allaah ﷺ said to her, 'Refrain!' She refused and took the oath of condemnation. When they departed he said, "Perhaps she will give birth to a (baby that is) black with curly hair." Consequently, she gave birth to a baby that was black with curly hair."

Muslim transmitted this *hadeeth* in his *Saheeh* (1495).

قال الإمام مسلم ﵀ (1496): وحدثنا محمد بن المثنى حدثنا عبد الأعلى حدثنا هشام عن محمد قال سألت أنس بن مالك ﵁ وأنا أرى أن عنده منه علما فقال: إن هلال بن أمية قذف امرأته بشريك بن سحماء وكان أخا البراء بن مالك لأمه وكان أول رجل لاعن في الإسلام قال: فلاعنها فقال رسول الله ﷺ: أبصروها فإن جاءت به أبيض سبطا قضيئ العينين فهو لهلال بن أمية وإن جاءت به أكحل جعدا حمش الساقين فهو لشريك بن سحماء قال: فأنبئت أنها جاءت به أكحل جعدا حمش الساقين.

Muhammad Ibn Seereen said, "I asked Anas ibn Maalik ﵁ assuming that he had knowledge about [situation] and so he said, 'Verily Hilaal ibn Umaiyah accused his wife of committing adultery with Shareek ibn Sahmaa. He was the brother of Al-Baraa ibn Maalik by his mother and he was the first man to take the oath of condemnation in Islaam. He took the oath of condemnation accusing her, which caused the Messenger of Allaah ﷺ to say, "Look at her, if she has (the baby) of white [complexion] with flat hair and bad eyes (because of excessive tearing or redness) then it is by Hilaal ibn Umaiyah; and if she has it of black [complexion] with curly hair and skinny shins, then it is by Shareek ibn Sahmaa." He (Anas) said, 'I was informed that she gave birth to a black baby with curly hair and skinny shins."

Muslim transmitted this *hadeeth* in his *Saheeh* (1496). Ash-Sheikh Muqbil ﵀ harmonized between these different *ahaadeeth* saying, "The strongest opinion to me is that Hilaal ibn Umaiyah asked, and his asking coincided with the man from the tribe Banee 'Ajlaan coming forward, and then the verse descended because of both of them, and Allaah knows best."

His, the Exalted One's statement:

$$﴿إِنَّ ٱلَّذِينَ جَآءُو بِٱلْإِفْكِ عُصْبَةٌ مِّنكُمْ ۚ لَا تَحْسَبُوهُ شَرًّا لَّكُم ۖ بَلْ هُوَ خَيْرٌ لَّكُمْ ۚ لِكُلِّ ٱمْرِئٍ مِّنْهُم مَّا ٱكْتَسَبَ مِنَ ٱلْإِثْمِ ۚ وَٱلَّذِى تَوَلَّىٰ كِبْرَهُۥ مِنْهُمْ لَهُۥ عَذَابٌ عَظِيمٌ﴾$$

"Verily those who brought forth the slander are a group among you. Consider it not a bad thing for you, rather, it is good for you. For each person among them is what he has earned of the sin, and as for the one amongst them who had the greater share therein, for him is a great punishment..." (verses: 11-22)

قال الإمام البخاري ﵀ (2661): حدثنا أبو الربيع سليمان بن داود وأفهمني بعضه أحمد بن يونس حدثنا فليح بن سليمان عن ابن شهاب الزهري عن عروة بن الزبير وسعيد بن المسيب وعلقمة بن وقاص الليثي وعبيد الله بن عبد الله بن عتبة عن عائشة ﵂ زوج النبي ﷺ حين قال لها أهل الإفك ما قالوا فبرأها الله منه قال الزهري وكلهم حدثني طائفة من حديثها وبعضهم أوعى من بعض وأثبت له اقتصاصا وقد وعيت عن كل واحد منهم الحديث الذي حدثني عن عائشة وبعض حديثهم يصدق بعضا زعموا أن عائشة قالت: كان رسول الله ﷺ إذا أراد أن يخرج سفرا أقرع بين أزواجه فأيتهن خرج سهمها خرج بها معه فأقرع بيننا في غزاة غزاها فخرج سهمي فخرجت معه بعد ما أنزل الحجاب فأنا أحمل في هودج وأنزل فيه فسرنا حتى إذا فرغ رسول الله ﷺ من غزوته تلك وقفل ودنونا من المدينة آذن ليلة بالرحيل فقمت حين آذنوا بالرحيل فمشيت حتى جاوزت الجيش فلما قضيت شأني أقبلت إلى الرحل فلمست صدري فإذا عقد لي من جزع أظفار قد انقطع فرجعت فالتمست عقدي فحبسني ابتغاؤه فأقبل الذين يرحلون لي فاحتملوا هودجي فرحلوه على بعيري الذي كنت أركب وهم يحسبون أني فيه وكان النساء إذ ذاك خفافا لم يثقلن ولم يغشهن اللحم وإنما يأكلن العلقة من الطعام فلم يستنكر القوم حين رفعوه ثقل الهودج فاحتملوه وكنت جارية حديثة السن فبعثوا الجمل وساروا فوجدت عقدي بعد ما استمر الجيش فجئت منزلهم وليس فيه أحد فأممت منزلي الذي كنت به فظننت أنهم سيفقدونني فيرجعون إلي فبينا أنا جالسة غلبتني عيناي فنمت وكان صفوان بن المعطل السلمي ثم الذكواني من وراء الجيش فأصبح عند منزلي فرأى سواد إنسان نائم فأتاني وكان يراني قبل الحجاب فاستيقظت باسترجاعه حتى أناخ راحلته فوطئ يدها فركبتها فانطلق يقود بي الراحلة حتى أتينا الجيش بعد ما نزلوا معرسين في نحر الظهيرة فهلك من هلك وكان الذي تولى الإفك عبد الله بن أبي ابن سلول فقدمنا المدينة فاشتكيت بها شهرا يفيضون من قول أصحاب الإفك ويريبني في وجعي أني لا أرى من النبي ﷺ اللطف الذي كنت أرى منه حين أمرض إنما يدخل فيسلم ثم يقول: كيف تيكم لا أشعر بشيء من ذلك حتى نقهت فخرجت أنا وأم مسطح قبل المناصع متبرزنا لا نخرج إلا ليلا إلى ليل وذلك قبل أن نتخذ الكنف قريبا من بيوتنا وأمرنا أمر العرب الأول في البرية أو في التنزه فأقبلت أنا وأم مسطح بنت أبي رهم نمشي فعثرت في مرطها فقالت: تعس مسطح فقلت لها: بئس ما قلت أتسبين رجلا شهد بدرا فقالت يا هنتاه ألم تسمعي ما قالوا فأخبرتني بقول أهل الإفك فازددت مرضا إلى مرضي فلما

194

رجعت إلى بيتي دخل علي رسول الله ﷺ فسلم فقال: كيف تيكم قالت: ائذن لي إلى أبوي قلت: وأنا حينئذ أريد أن أستيقن الخبر من قبلهما فأذن لي رسول الله ﷺ فأتيت أبوي فقلت لأمي: ما يتحدث به الناس فقالت: يا بنية هوني على نفسك الشأن فوالله لقلما كانت امرأة قط وضيئة عند رجل يحبها ولها ضرائر إلا أكثرن عليها فقلت: سبحان الله ولقد يتحدث الناس بهذا قالت فبت الليلة حتى أصبحت لا يرقأ لي دمع ولا أكتحل بنوم ثم أصبحت فدعا رسول الله ﷺ علي بن أبي طالب وأسامة ابن زيد حين استبطث الوحي يستشيرهما في فراق أهله فأما أسامة فأشار عليه بالذي يعلم في نفسه من الود لهم فقال أسامة: أهلك يا رسول الله ولا نعلم والله إلا خيرا وأما علي بن أبي طالب فقال: يا رسول الله لم يضيق الله عليك والنساء سواها كثير وسل الجارية تصدقك فدعا رسول الله ﷺ بريرة فقال: يا بريرة هل رأيت فيها شيئا يريبك فقالت بريرة: لا والذي بعثك بالحق إن رأيت منها أمرا أغمصه عليها أكثر من أنها جارية حديثة السن تنام عن العجين فتأتي الداجن فتأكله فقام رسول الله ﷺ من يومه فاستعذر من عبد الله بن أبي ابن سلول فقال رسول الله ﷺ: من يعذرني من رجل بلغني أذاه في أهلي فوالله ما علمت على أهلي إلا خيرا وقد ذكروا رجلا ما علمت عليه إلا خيرا وما كان يدخل على أهلي إلا معي فقام سعد بن معاذ فقال: يا رسول الله أنا والله أعذرك منه إن كان من الأوس ضربنا عنقه وإن كان من إخواننا من الخزرج أمرتنا ففعلنا في أمرك فقام سعد بن عبادة وهو سيد الخزرج وكان قبل ذلك رجلا صالحا ولكن احتملته الحمية فقال: كذبت لعمر الله لا تقتله ولا تقدر على ذلك فقام أسيد بن الحضير فقال: كذبت لعمر الله ولنقتلنه فإنك منافق تجادل عن المنافقين فثار الحيان الأوس والخزرج حتى هموا ورسول الله ﷺ على المنبر فنزل فخفضهم حتى سكتوا وسكت وبكيت يومي لا يرقأ لي دمع ولا أكتحل بنوم فأصبح عندي أبواي قد بكيت ليلتين ويوما حتى أظن أن البكاء فالق كبدي قالت: فبينا هما جالسان عندي وأنا أبكي إذ استأذنت امرأة من الأنصار فأذنت لها فجلست تبكي معي فبينا نحن كذلك إذ دخل رسول الله ﷺ فجلس ولم يجلس عندي من يوم قيل في ما قيل قبلها وقد مكث شهرا لا يوحى إليه في شأني شيء قالت: فتشهد ثم قال: يا عائشة فإنه بلغني عنك كذا وكذا فإن كنت بريئة فسيبرئك الله وإن كنت ألممت بشيء فاستغفري الله وتوبي إليه فإن العبد إذا اعترف بذنبه ثم تاب تاب الله عليه فلما قضى

رسول الله ﷺ مقالته قلص دمعي حتى ما أحس منه قطرة وقلت لأبي: أجب عني رسول الله ﷺ قال: والله ما أدري ما أقول لرسول الله ﷺ فقلت لأمي: أجيبي عني رسول الله ﷺ فيما قال قالت: والله ما أدري ما أقول لرسول الله ﷺ قالت: وأنا جارية حديثة السن لا أقرأ كثيرا من القرآن فقلت: إني والله لقد علمت أنكم سمعتم ما يتحدث به الناس ووقر في أنفسكم وصدقتم به ولئن قلت لكم إني بريئة والله يعلم إني لبريئة لا تصدقوني بذلك ولئن اعترفت لكم بأمر والله يعلم أني بريئة لتصدقني والله ما أجد لي ولكم مثلا إلا أبا يوسف إذ قال: (فَصَبْرٌ جَمِيلٌ وَاللَّهُ الْمُسْتَعَانُ عَلَىٰ مَا تَصِفُونَ) ثم تحولت على فراشي وأنا أرجو أن يبرئني الله ولكن والله ما ظننت أن ينزل في شأني وحيا ولأنا أحقر في نفسي من أن يتكلم بالقرآن في أمري ولكني كنت أرجو أن يرى

رسول الله ﷺ في النوم رؤيا يبرئني الله فوالله ما رام مجلسه ولا خرج أحد من أهل البيت حتى أنزل عليه الوحي فأخذه ما كان يأخذه من البرحاء حتى إنه ليتحدر منه مثل الجمان من العرق في يوم شات فلما سري عن رسول الله ﷺ وهو يضحك فكان أول كلمة تكلم بها أن قال لي: يا عائشة احمدي الله فقد برأك الله فقالت لي أمي: قومي إلى رسول الله ﷺ فقلت: لا والله لا أقوم إليه ولا أحمد إلا الله فأنزل الله تعالى: (إِنَّ ٱلَّذِينَ جَآءُو بِٱلۡإِفۡكِ عُصۡبَةٌ مِّنكُمۡ) الآيات فلما أنزل الله هذا في براءتي قال أبو بكر الصديق ﷺ وكان ينفق على مسطح بن أثاثة لقرابته منه: والله لا أنفق على مسطح شيئًا أبدًا بعد ما قال لعائشة فأنزل الله تعالى: (وَلَا يَأۡتَلِ أُوْلُواْ ٱلۡفَضۡلِ مِنكُمۡ وَٱلسَّعَةِ) إلى قوله: (أَلَا تُحِبُّونَ أَن يَغۡفِرَ ٱللَّهُ لَكُمۡۚ وَٱللَّهُ غَفُورٌ رَّحِيمٌ) فقال أبو بكر: بلى والله إني لأحب أن يغفر الله لي فرجع إلى مسطح الذي كان يجري عليه وكان رسول الله ﷺ يسأل زينب بنت جحش عن أمري فقال: يا زينب ما علمت ما رأيت فقالت: يا رسول الله أحمي سمعي وبصري والله ما علمت عليها إلا خيرًا قالت وهي التي كانت تساميني فعصمها الله بالورع.

قال وحدثنا فليح عن هشام بن عروة عن عروة عن عائشة وعبد الله بن الزبير مثله قال وحدثنا فليح عن ربيعة بن أبي عبد الرحمن ويحيى بن سعيد عن القاسم بن محمد بن أبي بكر مثله.

'Aishah ؓ said, "When the Messenger of Allaah ﷺ wanted to go out on a journey, he would draw lots between his wives and whichever wife's lot was drawn he would bring her out with him. [On one occasion], He drew lots between us due to a military expedition that he was to take part in and my lot was drawn so I set out with him. This took place after the verses of the veil had already been revealed. I was carried in a *hawdaj* (which is something that is mounted onto the camel for a woman to ride in, thus veiling her from the people) and I was lowered (from the camel) into it and thus we travelled.

When the Messenger of Allaah ﷺ was finished with his battle and began heading home approaching Madeenah, he announced during the night that we were soon to start moving again. I got up when they announced the departure and walked [away] leaving the army behind me. Then when I finished my business (in the bathroom) and headed back to the place where we stopped to rest, I felt my chest and found, to my surprise, that a necklace that I had made of incense rocks resembling pearls[92] had broken off. I went back to search for my necklace and the search preoccupied me. The people who prepared my camel for me picked up my *hawdaj* and strapped it onto my camel that I was riding. They did so thinking I was in it. The women at that time were light;

---

[92] It came in other narrations of this *hadeeth*: "made of pearls from Dhafaari (a city in Yemen)." Ibn Hajar said in *Fathul-Baaree* in the explanation of *hadeeth* (4750), "…and Ibn At-teen mentioned that it was worth twelve dirhams and this supports the position that it was not made of pearls from Dhafaari because if it were the price would have been more than that."

they were not heavy nor did they have a lot of meat on their bones. The women would only eat a small portion of food so the men did not find anything strange about the weight of the *hawdaj* when they lifted it, so they carried it [and proceeded normally]. [In addition to customoary eating habits of women at that time] I was also a girl of young age. Eventually they got the camels up and ready and started to travel. I found my necklace after the army had already left. I went to the place where they were but no one was there. I headed for my resting area that I was staying in, thinking that they would realize that I was missing and then come back for me. Then while sitting there my eyes overcame me and I fell asleep.

Safwaan ibn Al-Mu'attal As-Sulamee, then Adh-Dhakwaanee, was trailing the army. In the morning he reached my resting place and saw the silhouette of a sleeping person and came over to me. He used to see me before the obligation of the veil was revealed. I was awakened by his statement, '*Innaa lillah wa innaa ilaihi raaji'oon* (Verily we belong to Allaah and verily to Him we return).' He then made his camel kneel down and placed his foot on its front leg[93] and I mounted. He then started to lead the camel with me on it (by walking in front of the camel holding its reins while she rode the camel) until we reached the army after they had stopped to rest at the peak of the midday heat. Then the time came for those who were ruined to be ruined. The one who started the slander was 'Abdullaah ibn Ubay ibn Salool. Eventually we arrived at Madeenah. I was sick for one month while the people were engrossed in the statement of those who initiated the slander (and did not know anything about that).[94]

It made me suspicious during my illness that I was not seeing the affection from the Prophet ﷺ that I used to see when I was sick. He would just enter and give the salaams then say, "How is this one doing?" I did not know anything about what was happening until I began to recover. Umm Mistah and I went out to the open plateau on the outskirts of Madeenah, the place where we would go to relieve ourselves. We would not go except at nighttime. That was before we had lavatories close to our houses. Our condition was the condition of the Arabs of old in going far away from the houses. So Umm Mistah bint Abee Ruhm and I headed out walking. She then stumbled on her clothes and said, 'May Mistah fall on his face!' I said to her, "What a terrible thing you said! Do you revile a man who participated in Badr?" She said, 'O this one, have you not heard what they have said?' She then informed me about the statement of the people of the slander, and my illness increased. When I returned to my house, the Messenger of Allaah ﷺ entered upon me, gave me the salaams and said, "How is this one doing?" I said, 'Give me permission to go to my parents.' At that moment I wanted confirmation of the news from them.

---

[93] Ibn Hajar said in *Fathul-Baaree* in the explanation of *hadeeth* (4750), "So it would be easier to mount and so he would not have to touch her as she mounted."
[94] What is between parentheses was taken from the narration of this *hadeeth* in Muslim.

The Messenger of Allaah ﷺ granted me permission, so I went to my parents and said to my mother, "What are the people talking about?" She said, 'O beloved daughter, do not let the matter get to you, for, by Allaah, there was never a beautiful woman that had a man who loves her and she has co-wives except that they would speak bad about her.'[95] I said, "*Subhaanallaah* (Glorified be Allaah)! The people are talking about this!" I spent that night in constant tears with my eyes finding no sleep. I then encountered morning. When the revelation was delayed, the Messenger of Allaah ﷺ called for 'Ali ibn Abee Taalib and Usaamah ibn Zaid seeking their counsel on whether or not he should separate from his family. As for Usaamah, he advised him according to what he knew of the love he ﷺ had in his soul for them (his family) so Usaamah said, '(They) are your family, O Messenger of Allaah. We only know good about them.' As for 'Ali ibn Abee Taalib, he said, "O Messenger of Allaah, Allaah has not restricted you in as far as other women are concerned, there are many. Ask the female servant. She will tell you the truth." The Messenger of Allaah ﷺ then called for Bareerah and said, 'O Bareerah, have you seen anything in her which makes you suspicious?' Bareerah said, "No, by the one who sent you with the truth, I have never seen anything from her that I can find fault with, more than her being a girl of young age; she sleeps while waiting for the dough to rise and then the sheep comes and eats it."

The Messenger of Allaah ﷺ got up at that point and went to seek one who would see to it that justice is done to 'Abdullaah ibn Ubay ibn Salool. The Messenger of Allaah ﷺ said, 'Who will help me deal with a man whose harm has reached me by accusing my family? For, by Allaah, I only know good of my family. Furthermore, they [negatively] mentioned a man that I only know good about as well (Safwaan). He would only come around my family If I was present.' Sa'd ibn Mu'aadh stood and said, "O Messenger of

---

[95] Ibn Hajar said in *Fathul-Baaree* in the explanation of *hadeeth* (4750), "This speech contains cleverness on her mother's part along with superb gentleness in going about instructing her that can not be outdone, for verily she knew that (the slander) would be hard for her to handle so she made the matter easier on her by informing her that she is not alone in that, because a person finds comfort with others like him in dealing with that which has occurred to him, and she incorporated into that something that would please her, that she was superior in beauty and standing as that is something which delights a woman to be described with, along with what it (the speech) contained alluding to what occurred from Hamnah bint Jahsh (she was among those who spread the slander) and that the main factor which prompted her to do that was the fact that 'Aishah was the co-wife of her sister Zainab bint Jahsh. From this it is known that the exception in her statement, "except that they would talk a lot against her," is connected (to the co-wives) because she did not intend her situation specifically, rather, she mentioned the way co-wives are in general. As for her true co-wives, even though they did not do anything violating her rights that usually occurs from co-wives, however, that did not cease to occur from the one who is a means of access to them as occurred from Hamnah, for indeed the piety of her sister (Zainab) prevented her from slandering 'Aishah as it prevented the rest of the Mothers of the Believers."

Allaah, by Allaah, I will help you deal with him. If he is from the tribe Al-Aws, we will strike his neck (chopping off his head), and if he is from our brothers from the tribe Al-Khazraj, order us and we will do to him what you order." Sa'd ibn 'Ubaadah then stood, he was the chief of the tribe Al-Khazraj and prior to this he was a righteous man but pride overtook him so he said, 'You lie! The everlasting existence of Allaah as my oath, by Allaah, you will not kill him nor do you even have the power to do that!' Usaid ibn Hudair then stood and said, "You lie! The everlasting existence of Allaah as my oath, by Allaah, we will indeed kill him for verily you are a hypocrite, you argue in defense of the hypocrites!" The two tribes, Al-Aws and Al-Khazraj, then became infuriated to the point where they were about to fight one another while the Messenger of Allaah ﷺ was on the *minbar*. He then descended and calmed them down until they were silent and he too was silent. I cried the rest of my day. The tears did not cease nor did my eyes find any sleep.

My parents came to me in the morning. I had cried [profusely] for two nights and one day to the point that I thought the crying would cause my liver to tear. Then while they were sitting with me as I cried, a woman from the *Ansaar* asked permission to enter so I gave her permission. She then sat and cried with me. Then while we were in that state, the Messenger of Allaah ﷺ entered and sat down. He had not sat down with me before this since the day that what was said about me was said. [At this point] He had gone one month without any revelation being revealed to him about my situation. He pronounced the *shahaadah* (I bear witness that there is no deity who deserves to be worshipped except Allaah and that Muhammad is His Slave and Messenger) and then he said, 'O 'Aishah, verily such-and-such news has reached me about you. If you are innocent, Allaah will clear you, and if you fell into a sin, seek Allaah's forgiveness and repent to Him, for verily the servant, when he admits his sin and then repents, Allaah accepts his repentance.'

When the Messenger of Allaah ﷺ finished his speech my tears stopped flowing to the point that I did not find a single teardrop. I said to my father, "Respond to the Messenger of Allaah ﷺ on my behalf." He said, 'By Allaah, I do not know what to say to the Messenger of Allaah ﷺ.' Then I said to my mother, "Respond on my behalf to the Messenger of Allaah ﷺ concerning what he said." She said, 'By Allaah, I do not know what to say to the Messenger of Allaah ﷺ.' I was a girl of young age not having read a lot of the Qur'aan,[96] so I said, "Verily, by Allaah, I know you have heard what the people have said and that it has settled in your souls and you have believed it; and if I say to you, 'I am innocent,' and Allaah knows I am innocent, you will not believe me, and if I admit to you a matter, and Allaah knows I am innocent, you will believe me. By Allaah, the only example I can find for you and I is the example of the father of Yoosuf when he said:

---

[96] She mentioned this to excuse herself for not recalling the name of Yoosuf's father, Ya'qoob, as Ibn Hajar mentioned in *Fathul-Baaree* in the explanation of *hadeeth* (4750).

$$\text{فَصَبْرٌ جَمِيلٌ ۖ وَاللَّهُ الْمُسْتَعَانُ عَلَىٰ مَا تَصِفُونَ}$$

"So pleasant patience[97] is most fitting, and Allaah is the one whose help is sought against that which you describe." (*Yoosuf*: 18).

I then turned facing the opposite direction on my bed hoping that Allaah will clear me; however, by Allaah, I did not think He would send down revelation because of my situation. In my eyes, I was too low for Qur'aan to be spoken because of my situation; rather, I hoped that the Messenger of Allaah ﷺ would see in his sleep, a dream that would clear me. Then, by Allaah, he did not part from the place he was sitting nor did anyone in the house leave until revelation was sent down to him. The pain and heat that used to overtake him (when revelation was revealed) overtook him. Drops of sweat that resembled pearls flowed down from him on a winter day. When that passed from the Messenger of Allaah ﷺ, the first thing he said, while laughing, was what he said to me, 'O 'Aishah, praise Allaah, for indeed Allaah has cleared you.' My mother said to me, "Get up and go to the Messenger of Allaah ﷺ." I said, 'No, by Allaah, I will not go over to him and I will not praise anyone except Allaah.' Allaah ﷻ had sent down:

$$\text{إِنَّ الَّذِينَ جَاءُوا بِالْإِفْكِ عُصْبَةٌ مِّنكُمْ}$$

"Verily those who brought forth the slander are a group among you..."

and the rest of the verses in this regard.
When Allaah sent that down clearing me, Abu Bakr As-Siddeeq ﷺ, who used to provide for Mistah ibn Uthaathah because of the family ties between them, said, 'By Allaah, I will never provide anything for Mistah after what he said about 'Aishah.' Then Allaah ﷻ sent down:

$$\text{وَلَا يَأْتَلِ أُولُو الْفَضْلِ مِنكُمْ وَالسَّعَةِ}$$

"And let not those among you who are blessed with graces and wealth swear not..."

up to His statement:

$$\text{أَلَا تُحِبُّونَ أَن يَغْفِرَ اللَّهُ لَكُمْ ۗ وَاللَّهُ غَفُورٌ رَّحِيمٌ}$$

'Do you not love that Allaah forgive you? And Allaah is Oft-Forgiving Most Merciful.' (verse: 22)

Abu Bakr then said, "Certainly, by Allaah, I love that Allaah forgive me." So he resumed giving Mistah what he used to give him. The Messenger of

---

[97] Pleasant or beautiful patience is patience in which there is no discontent or complaining to the creation as As-Sa'dee mentioned in his *Tafseer*.

Allaah ﷺ before this, had asked Zainab bint Jahsh about my situation saying, 'O Zainab, what do you know? What did you see?' She said, "O Messenger of Allaah ﷺ I guard my hearing and my sight (from ascribing to my hearing and sight something that I did not hear or see). By Allaah, I only know good of her." She was the one who use to vie with me for a superior standing (with the Prophet ﷺ), however, Allaah protected her through (her) piety."

Al-Bukhaaree transmitted this hadeeth in his *Saheeh* (2661) and Muslim in his *Saheeh* (2770).

His, the Exalted One's statement:

وَلَا تُكْرِهُوا فَتَيَاتِكُمْ عَلَى ٱلْبِغَاءِ إِنْ أَرَدْنَ تَحَصُّنًا لِّتَبْتَغُوا عَرَضَ ٱلْحَيَوٰةِ ٱلدُّنْيَا

"And force not your female servants to prostitution if they desire chastity in order that you make a gain in the goods of this worldly life…"
(verse: 33)

قال الإمام مسلم رحمه الله (3029): حدثنا أبو بكر بن أبي شيبة وأبو كريب جميعا عن أبي معاوية واللفظ لأبي كريب حدثنا أبو معاوية حدثنا الأعمش عن أبي سفيان عن جابر رضي الله عنه قال: كان عبد الله بن أبي ابن سلول يقول لجارية له: اذهبي فابتغينا شيئا فأنزل الله عز وجل: (وَلَا تُكْرِهُوا فَتَيَاتِكُمْ عَلَى ٱلْبِغَاءِ إِنْ أَرَدْنَ تَحَصُّنًا لِّتَبْتَغُوا عَرَضَ ٱلْحَيَوٰةِ ٱلدُّنْيَا وَمَن يُكْرِههُّنَّ فَإِنَّ ٱللَّهَ مِنْ بَعْدِ إِكْرَاهِهِنَّ) لهن (غَفُورٌ رَّحِيمٌ).

Jaabir ؓ said, "'Abdullaah ibn Ubay ibn Salool used to say to a female servant of his, 'Go out and do some prostitution for us.' Allaah ﷻ then revealed:

وَلَا تُكْرِهُوا فَتَيَاتِكُمْ عَلَى ٱلْبِغَاءِ إِنْ أَرَدْنَ تَحَصُّنًا لِّتَبْتَغُوا عَرَضَ ٱلْحَيَوٰةِ ٱلدُّنْيَا وَمَن يُكْرِههُّنَّ فَإِنَّ ٱللَّهَ مِنْ بَعْدِ إِكْرَاهِهِنَّ -لهن-[98] غَفُورٌ رَّحِيمٌ.

"And force not your female servants to prostitution if they desire chastity in order that you make a gain in the goods of this worldly life, and whoever compels them, then after such compulsion Allaah is Oft-Forgiving Most Merciful (towards them, the female servants)."

---

[98] (لهن) "Towards them, the female servants," is not part of the verse, rather, it is an explanation of the verse as An-Nawawee explained in his explanation of *Saheeh Muslim*.

Muslim transmitted this *hadeeth* in his *Saheeh* (3029).

His, the Exalted One's statement:

وَعَدَ ٱللَّهُ ٱلَّذِينَ ءَامَنُوا۟ مِنكُمْ وَعَمِلُوا۟ ٱلصَّٰلِحَٰتِ لَيَسْتَخْلِفَنَّهُمْ فِى ٱلْأَرْضِ كَمَا ٱسْتَخْلَفَ ٱلَّذِينَ مِن قَبْلِهِمْ وَلَيُمَكِّنَنَّ لَهُمْ دِينَهُمُ ٱلَّذِى ٱرْتَضَىٰ لَهُمْ وَلَيُبَدِّلَنَّهُم مِّنۢ بَعْدِ خَوْفِهِمْ أَمْنًا

"Allaah has promised those among you who believe and do righteous deeds that He will certainly grant them succession to (the present rulers) in the land as He granted to those before them, and that He will grant them the authority to perform their religion which He has chosen for them, and He will surely give them in exchange a safe security after their fear…" (verse: 55)

قال الحاكم ﷺ (ج 2 ص 401): حدثني محمد بن صالح بن هانئ حدثنا أبو سعيد محمد بن شاذان حدثنا أحمد بن سعيد الدارمي حدثنا علي بن الحسين بن واقد حدثني أبي عن الربيع ابن أنس عن أبي العالية عن أبي بن كعب ﷺ قال: لما قدم رسول الله ﷺ وأصحابه المدينة وآوتهم الأنصار رمتهم العرب عن قوس واحدة كانوا لا يبيتون إلا بالسلاح ولا يصبحون إلا فيه فقالوا: ترون أنا نعيش حتى نبيت آمنين مطمئنين لا نخاف إلا الله فنزلت: (وَعَدَ ٱللَّهُ ٱلَّذِينَ ءَامَنُوا۟ مِنكُمْ وَعَمِلُوا۟ ٱلصَّٰلِحَٰتِ لَيَسْتَخْلِفَنَّهُمْ فِى ٱلْأَرْضِ كَمَا ٱسْتَخْلَفَ ٱلَّذِينَ مِن قَبْلِهِمْ وَلَيُمَكِّنَنَّ لَهُمْ دِينَهُمُ ٱلَّذِى ٱرْتَضَىٰ لَهُمْ وَلَيُبَدِّلَنَّهُم مِّنۢ بَعْدِ خَوْفِهِمْ أَمْنًا) إلى: (وَمَن كَفَرَ بَعْدَ ذَٰلِكَ) يعني بالنعمة (فَأُو۟لَٰٓئِكَ هُمُ ٱلْفَٰسِقُونَ).

هذا حديث صحيح الإسناد ولم يخرجاه.

Ubay ibn Ka'b ﷺ said, "When the Messenger of Allaah ﷺ and his Companions arrived at Madeenah and the *Ansaar* gave them refuge, the Arabs took a unified stance in attacking them. They would not spend their nights except armed with weapons and they would not enter the morning except in that state, so they said, 'Do you think we will live to see the time when we spend the night in peace and security fearing none but Allaah?' Then the verse descended:

$$\text{وَعَدَ ٱللَّهُ ٱلَّذِينَ ءَامَنُوا۟ مِنكُمْ وَعَمِلُوا۟ ٱلصَّـٰلِحَـٰتِ لَيَسْتَخْلِفَنَّهُمْ فِى ٱلْأَرْضِ كَمَا ٱسْتَخْلَفَ ٱلَّذِينَ مِن قَبْلِهِمْ وَلَيُمَكِّنَنَّ لَهُمْ دِينَهُمُ ٱلَّذِى ٱرْتَضَىٰ لَهُمْ وَلَيُبَدِّلَنَّهُم مِّنۢ بَعْدِ خَوْفِهِمْ أَمْنًا}$$

"Allaah has promised those among you who believe and do righteous deeds that He will certainly grant them succession to (the present rulers) in the land as He granted to those before them, and that He will grant them the authority to perform their religion which He has chosen for them, and He will surely give them in exchange a safe security after their fear…"
up to,

$$\text{وَمَن كَفَرَ بَعْدَ ذَٰلِكَ}$$

"But whoever disbelieves after this…"

Meaning whoever denies the favor bestowed upon them.

$$\text{فَأُو۟لَـٰٓئِكَ هُمُ ٱلْفَـٰسِقُونَ}$$

"Those are the disobedient."

Al-Haakim transmitted this *hadeeth* in *Al-Mustadrak*, volume 2, page 401, and he classified its chain to be authentic and they (Al-Bukhaaree and Muslim) did not transmit it and Adh-Dhahabee was quiet about that (meaning he did not oppose that ruling). Ash-Sheikh Muqbil ﷺ mentioned that in the chain of the *hadeeth* is 'Ali ibn Husain ibn Waaqid whom the Scholars have differed about his status and then he said, "However, Al-Haithamee said in *Majma' Az-Zawaa'id*, volume 7, page 83, 'At-Tabaraanee transmitted it in *Al-Awsat* and its people (the people of the chain) are trustworthy.' And At-Tabaree mentioned it *mursal* on Abee 'Aaliyah, volume 18, page 159."[99]

His, the Exalted One's statement:

$$\text{لَّيْسَ عَلَى ٱلْأَعْمَىٰ حَرَجٌ وَلَا عَلَى ٱلْأَعْرَجِ حَرَجٌ وَلَا عَلَى ٱلْمَرِيضِ حَرَجٌ وَلَا عَلَىٰٓ أَنفُسِكُمْ أَن تَأْكُلُوا۟ مِنۢ بُيُوتِكُمْ}$$

---

[99] NOTE: The chain of At-Tabaraanee in *Al-Awsat* is also by way of 'Ali ibn Husain ibn Waaqid so the hadeeth's ruling depends on his status.

"There is no restriction on the blind, and there is no restriction on the lame, and there is no restriction on the sick, and there is no restriction on yourselves against eating from your houses…" (verse: 61)

قال الإمام أحمد بن عمرو بن عبد الخالق الشهير بالبزار ﷺ كما في كشف الأستار (ج 3 ص 61): حدثنا زيد بن أخزم أبو طالب الطائي ثنا بشر بن عمر ثنا إبراهيم بن سعد عن صالح ابن كيسان عن الزهري عن عروة عن عائشة ﷺ قالت: كان المسلمون يرغبون في النفير مع رسول الله ﷺ فيدفعون مفاتيحهم إلى ضمناهم ﷺ ويقولون لهم: قد أحللنا لكم أن تأكلوا ما أحببتم فكانوا يقولون: إنه لا يحل لنا إنهم أذنوا من غير طيب نفس فأنزل الله عز وجل: (لَّيْسَ عَلَى ٱلْأَعْمَىٰ حَرَجٌ وَلَا عَلَى ٱلْأَعْرَجِ حَرَجٌ وَلَا عَلَى ٱلْمَرِيضِ حَرَجٌ وَلَا عَلَىٰ أَنفُسِكُمْ أَن تَأْكُلُوا۟ مِنۢ بُيُوتِكُمْ أَوْ بُيُوتِ ءَابَآئِكُمْ أَوْ بُيُوتِ أُمَّهَٰتِكُمْ أَوْ بُيُوتِ إِخْوَٰنِكُمْ أَوْ بُيُوتِ أَخَوَٰتِكُمْ أَوْ بُيُوتِ أَعْمَٰمِكُمْ أَوْ بُيُوتِ عَمَّٰتِكُمْ) إلى قوله: (أَوْ مَا مَلَكْتُم مَّفَاتِحَهُ).

قال البزار: لا نعلمه رواه عن الزهري إلا صالح.

'Aishah ﷺ said, "The Muslims used to be eager to go out with the Messenger of Allaah ﷺ in battle and they would leave their keys (to their storage houses and belongings) with the chronically ill and they would say to them, 'We give you permission to eat what you wish.' They would say, "It is not permissible for us because they gave us permission unwillingly." Then Allaah ﷻ sent down:

لَّيْسَ عَلَى ٱلْأَعْمَىٰ حَرَجٌ وَلَا عَلَى ٱلْأَعْرَجِ حَرَجٌ وَلَا عَلَى ٱلْمَرِيضِ حَرَجٌ وَلَا عَلَىٰ أَنفُسِكُمْ أَن تَأْكُلُوا۟ مِنۢ بُيُوتِكُمْ أَوْ بُيُوتِ ءَابَآئِكُمْ أَوْ بُيُوتِ أُمَّهَٰتِكُمْ أَوْ بُيُوتِ إِخْوَٰنِكُمْ أَوْ بُيُوتِ أَخَوَٰتِكُمْ أَوْ بُيُوتِ أَعْمَٰمِكُمْ أَوْ بُيُوتِ عَمَّٰتِكُمْ

"There is no restriction on the blind, and there is no restriction on the lame, and there is no restriction on the sick, and there is no restriction on yourselves against eating from your houses, or the houses of your fathers, or the houses of your mothers, or the houses of your brothers, or the houses of your sisters, or the houses of your paternal uncles, or the houses of your paternal aunts…" up to His statement:

أَوْ مَا مَلَكْتُم مَّفَاتِحَهُ

"…or from those places whereof you hold keys."

---

[100] في النهاية: الضمنى: الزمنى جمع ضَمِن.

Al-Bazzaar transmitted this *hadeeth* as mentioned in *Kashf Al-Astaar*, volume 3, page 61. Al-Haithamee said in *Majma' Az-Zawaa'id*, volume 7, page 84, "The people of its chain are people of the *Saheeh* (Al-Bukhaaree and/or Muslim)." And As-Suyootee said in *Lubaab An-Nuqool*, "Its chain is *saheeh*."

سورة الفرقان

Sooratul-Furqaan

His, the Exalted One's statement:

$$\text{وَٱلَّذِينَ لَا يَدْعُونَ مَعَ ٱللَّهِ إِلَٰهًا ءَاخَرَ وَلَا يَقْتُلُونَ ٱلنَّفْسَ ٱلَّتِي حَرَّمَ ٱللَّهُ إِلَّا بِٱلْحَقِّ وَلَا يَزْنُونَ}$$

"And those who do not invoke any other deity along with Allaah, nor kill such person that Allaah has forbidden except for just cause, nor commit illegal sexual intercourse…" (verse: 68)

قال الإمام البخاري ﷺ (4761): حدثنا مسدد حدثنا يحيى عن سفيان قال حدثني منصور وسليمان عن أبي وائل عن أبي ميسرة عن عبد الله قال وحدثني واصل عن أبي وائل عن عبد الله ﷺ قال: سألت أو سئل رسول الله ﷺ أي الذنب عند الله أكبر قال: أن تجعل لله ندا وهو خلقك قلت: ثم أي قال: ثم أن تقتل ولدك خشية أن يطعم معك قلت: ثم أي قال: أن تزاني بحليلة جارك قال: ونزلت هذه الآية تصديقا لقول رسول الله ﷺ: (وَٱلَّذِينَ لَا يَدْعُونَ مَعَ ٱللَّهِ إِلَٰهًا ءَاخَرَ وَلَا يَقْتُلُونَ ٱلنَّفْسَ ٱلَّتِي حَرَّمَ ٱللَّهُ إِلَّا بِٱلْحَقِّ وَلَا يَزْنُونَ).

'Abdullaah ibn Mas'ood ﷺ said, "I asked, or the Messenger of Allaah ﷺ was asked, 'Which sin is the greatest with Allaah?' He said, "That you set up a partner with Allaah while He has created you." I said, 'Then what?' He said, "That you kill your child out of fear that he will eat with you." I said, 'Then what?' He said, "That you fornicate with your neighbor's wife." He ('Abdullaah ibn Mas'ood) said, 'This verse descended confirming what the Messenger of Allaah ﷺ said,'

$$\text{وَٱلَّذِينَ لَا يَدْعُونَ مَعَ ٱللَّهِ إِلَٰهًا ءَاخَرَ وَلَا يَقْتُلُونَ ٱلنَّفْسَ ٱلَّتِي حَرَّمَ ٱللَّهُ إِلَّا بِٱلْحَقِّ وَلَا يَزْنُونَ}$$

"And those who do not invoke any other deity along with Allaah, nor kill such person that Allaah has forbidden except for just cause, nor commit illegal sexual intercourse…"

This *hadeeth* has been transmitted by Al-Bukharee in his *Saheeh* (4761) and Muslim in his *Saheeh* (86).

قال الإمام البخاري ﷺ (4810): حدثني إبراهيم بن موسى أخبرنا هشام بن يوسف أن ابن جريج أخبرهم قال ابن يعلى إن سعيد بن جبير أخبره عن ابن عباس ﷺ أن ناسا من أهل الشرك كانوا قد قتلوا وأكثروا وزنوا وأكثروا فأتوا محمدا ﷺ فقالوا: إن الذي تقول وتدعوا إليه لحسن لو تخبرنا أن لما عملنا كفارة فنزل: (وَٱلَّذِينَ لَا يَدْعُونَ مَعَ ٱللَّهِ إِلَٰهًا ءَاخَرَ وَلَا يَقْتُلُونَ ٱلنَّفْسَ ٱلَّتِى حَرَّمَ ٱللَّهُ إِلَّا بِٱلْحَقِّ وَلَا يَزْنُونَ) ونزل: (قُلْ يَٰعِبَادِىَ ٱلَّذِينَ أَسْرَفُوا عَلَىٰ أَنفُسِهِمْ لَا تَقْنَطُوا مِن رَّحْمَةِ ٱللَّهِ).

Ibn 'Abbaas ﷺ narrated that a group of polytheists who had committed a lot of murder and fornication went to Muhammad ﷺ and said, 'Indeed what you say and call to is good, but if only you would inform us that there is an atonement for what we have done.' Then the verse descended:

وَٱلَّذِينَ لَا يَدْعُونَ مَعَ ٱللَّهِ إِلَٰهًا ءَاخَرَ وَلَا يَقْتُلُونَ ٱلنَّفْسَ ٱلَّتِى حَرَّمَ ٱللَّهُ إِلَّا بِٱلْحَقِّ وَلَا يَزْنُونَ

"And those who do not invoke any other deity along with Allaah, nor kill such person that Allaah has forbidden except for just cause, nor commit illegal sexual intercourse…"
Also, the following verse descended:

قُلْ يَٰعِبَادِىَ ٱلَّذِينَ أَسْرَفُوا عَلَىٰ أَنفُسِهِمْ لَا تَقْنَطُوا مِن رَّحْمَةِ ٱللَّهِ

'Say: O my slaves who have transgressed against themselves, despair not of the mercy of Allaah…' (*Az-Zumar*: 53)

Al-Bukhaaree transmitted this *hadeeth* in his *Saheeh* (4810) and Muslim in his *Saheeh* (122). Ash-Sheikh Muqbil ﷺ said, "There is nothing which prevents the verse from being revealed because of the two reasons simultaneously, and Allaah knows best."

His, the Exalted One's statement:

$$\text{إِلَّا مَن تَابَ وَءَامَنَ وَعَمِلَ عَمَلًا صَٰلِحًا فَأُو۟لَٰٓئِكَ يُبَدِّلُ ٱللَّهُ سَيِّـَٔاتِهِمْ حَسَنَٰتٍ ۗ وَكَانَ ٱللَّهُ غَفُورًا رَّحِيمًا}$$

"Except those who repent and believe and do righteous deeds, for those Allaah will change their sins into good deeds, and Allaah is Oft-Forgiving Most Merciful." (verse: 70)

قال الإمام البخاري رحمه الله (3855): حدثنا عثمان بن أبي شيبة حدثنا جرير عن منصور حدثني سعيد بن جبير أو قال حدثني الحكم عن سعيد بن جبير قال أمرني عبد الرحمن بن أبزى قال: سل ابن عباس عن هاتين الآيتين ما أمرهما: (وَلَا تَقْتُلُوا۟ ٱلنَّفْسَ ٱلَّتِى حَرَّمَ ٱللَّهُ إِلَّا بِٱلْحَقِّ) (وَمَن يَقْتُلْ مُؤْمِنًا مُّتَعَمِّدًا) فسألت ابن عباس ﷺ فقال: لما أنزلت التي في الفرقان قال مشركو أهل مكة: فقد قتلنا النفس التي حرم الله ودعونا مع الله إلها آخر وقد أتينا الفواحش فأنزل الله: (إِلَّا مَن تَابَ وَءَامَنَ) الآية فهذه لأولئك وأما التي في النساء الرجل إذا عرف الإسلام وشرائعه ثم قتل فجزاؤه جهنم.

فذكرته لمجاهد فقال: إلا من ندم.

Sa'eed ibn Jubair said, "'Abdur-Rahmaan ibn Abzaa commanded me saying, 'Ask Ibn 'Abbaas about these two verses; What are they regarding?"

$$\text{وَلَا تَقْتُلُوا۟ ٱلنَّفْسَ ٱلَّتِى حَرَّمَ ٱللَّهُ إِلَّا بِٱلْحَقِّ}$$

"And kill not such person that Allaah has forbidden except for just cause..." (*Al-An'aam*: 151 and *Al-Israa*: 33)[101]

$$\text{وَمَن يَقْتُلْ مُؤْمِنًا مُّتَعَمِّدًا}$$

"And whoever kills a believer intentionally..." (*An-Nisaa*: 93)

So I asked Ibn 'Abbaas and he said, 'When the verse in *Sooratul-Furqaan* descended, the polytheists from the people of Makkah said, "We have killed such a person that Allaah has forbidden and we have invoked another deity

---

[101] In other narrations of this *hadeeth* verse 68 of *Sooratul-Furqaan* was mentioned which is correct because it agrees with the text of the *hadeeth*.

along with Allaah and we have committed fornication." Then Allaah sent down:

$$\text{إِلَّا مَن تَابَ وَءَامَنَ}$$

'Except those who repent and believe…'.

As for the verse in *Sooratun-Nisaa*, if a man knows Islaam and its rulings and thereafter commits murder, his reward will be hell abiding therein.' I then mentioned that to Mujaahid so he added, "Except he who regrets."

This *hadeeth* has been transmitted by Al-Bukhaaree in his *Saheeh* (3855) and by Muslim in his *Saheeh* (3023).

سورة القصص

Sooratul-Qasas

His, the Exalted One's statement:

$$\text{وَلَقَدْ وَصَّلْنَا لَهُمُ ٱلْقَوْلَ لَعَلَّهُمْ يَتَذَكَّرُونَ}$$

"And indeed We have conveyed the word to them[102] in order that they may remember." (verse: 51)

قال الإمام ابن جرير ﷺ (ج 19 ص 594): حدثني بشر بن آدم قال حدثنا عفان بن مسلم قال حدثنا حماد بن سلمة قال حدثنا عمرو بن دينار عن يحيى بن جعدة عن رفاعة القرظي ﷺ قال: نزلت هذه الآية في عشرة أنا منهم: (وَلَقَدْ وَصَّلْنَا لَهُمُ ٱلْقَوْلَ لَعَلَّهُمْ يَتَذَكَّرُونَ).

Rifaa'ah Al-Quradhee ﷺ said, "The following verse descended because of ten people and I am one of them,

$$\text{وَلَقَدْ وَصَّلْنَا لَهُمُ ٱلْقَوْلَ لَعَلَّهُمْ يَتَذَكَّرُونَ}$$

"And indeed We have conveyed the word to them in order that they may remember."

Ibn Jareer transmitted this *hadeeth* in his *Tafseer*, volume 19, page 594, and At-Tabaraanee with two chains in *Al-Mu'jam Al-Kabeer*, volume 5, page 53. Al-Haithamee said in *Majma' Az-Zawaa'id*, volume 7, page 88, "At-Tabaraanee transmitted it with two chains, one of them is fully connected and the people of its chain are trustworthy…"

His, the Exalted One's statement:

$$\text{إِنَّكَ لَا تَهْدِى مَنْ أَحْبَبْتَ وَلَٰكِنَّ ٱللَّهَ يَهْدِى مَن يَشَآءُ}$$

"Verily you guide not whom you love[103] but Allaah guides whom He wills…" (verse: 56)

---

[102] There is a difference of opinion amongst the Scholars about who this verse is referring to. Some say it refers to Quraish while others say it refers to the Jews. Ibn Jareer mentioned this *hadeeth* under the position of those who say it refers to the Jews because Rifaa'ah was a Jew who embraced Islaam and became a Noble Companion of the Prophet ﷺ.

[103] There are two positions concerning the word love in this verse. One position is it means you guide not whom you love him for his family ties with you. The other position is it means you guide not whom you love him to be guided. Ibn Jareer

قال الإمام مسلم رَحِمَهُ اللهُ (25): حدثنا محمد بن عباد وابن أبي عمر قالا حدثنا مروان عن يزيد و هو ابن كيسان عن أبي حازم عن أبي هريرة رَضِيَ اللهُ عَنْهُ قال: قال رسول الله ﷺ لعمه عند الموت: قل لا إله إلا الله أشهد لك بها يوم القيامة فأبى فأنزل الله: (إِنَّكَ لَا تَهْدِي مَنْ أَحْبَبْتَ) الآية.

Abu Hurairah said, "The Messenger of Allaah said to his uncle at the time of his death, 'Say: *Laa Ilaaha Illallaah* (there is no deity who deserves to be worshipped except Allaah), I will testify to it on your behalf on the day of resurrection.' He refused. Then Allaah sent down:

$$\text{إِنَّكَ لَا تَهْدِي مَنْ أَحْبَبْتَ}$$

"Verily you guide not whom you love…" (verse: 56).

Muslim transmitted this *hadeeth* in his *Saheeh* (25). In another narration of this *hadeeth* in Muslim it was mentioned that Abu Taalib said, "If it were not that Quraish would have condemned me by saying, 'He only did that out of pity,' I would have delighted you with it."

---

mentioned these two positions in his *Tafseer*, volume 19, page 598 and Ibn Al-Jawzee in *Zaad Al-Maseer*, volume 6, page 232.

سورة العنكبوت

Sooratul-Ankaboot

His, the Exalted One's statement:

وَوَصَّيْنَا ٱلْإِنسَٰنَ بِوَٰلِدَيْهِ حُسْنًا ۖ وَإِن جَٰهَدَاكَ لِتُشْرِكَ بِى مَا لَيْسَ لَكَ بِهِۦ عِلْمٌ فَلَا تُطِعْهُمَآ

"And We have enjoined on man to be good and dutiful to his parents, but if they strive to make you join with Me, anything of which you have no knowledge, then obey them not…" (verse: 8)

قال الإمام مسلم ﷺ (43 / 1748): حدثنا أبو بكر بن أبي شيبة وزهير بن حرب قالا حدثنا الحسن بن موسى حدثنا زهير حدثنا سماك بن حرب حدثني مصعب بن سعد عن أبيه ﷺ أنه نزلت فيه آيات من القرآن قال: حلفت أم سعد أن لا تكلمه أبدا حتى يكفر بدينه ولا تأكل ولا تشرب قالت: زعمت أن الله وصاك بوالديك وأنا أمك وأنا آمرك بهذا قال: مكثت ثلاثا حتى غشي عليها من الجهد فقام ابن لها يقال له عمارة فسقاها فجعلت تدعو على سعد فأنزل الله عز وجل في القرآن هذه الآية: (وَوَصَّيْنَا ٱلْإِنسَٰنَ بِوَٰلِدَيْهِ حُسْنًا وَإِن جَٰهَدَاكَ لِتُشْرِكَ بِى) وفيها: (فَلَا تُطِعْهُمَا وَصَاحِبْهُمَا فِى ٱلدُّنْيَا مَعْرُوفًا) قال: وأصاب رسول الله ﷺ غنيمة عظيمة فإذا فيها سيف فأخذته فأتيت به الرسول ﷺ فقلت: نفلني هذا السيف فأنا من قد علمت حاله فقال: رده من حيث أخذته فانطلقت حتى إذا أردت أن ألقيه في القبض لامتني نفسي فرجعت إليه فقلت أعطنيه قال فشد لي صوته: رده من حيث أخذته قال: فأنزل الله عز وجل: (يَسْـَٔلُونَكَ عَنِ ٱلْأَنفَالِ) قال: ومرضت فأرسلت إلى النبي ﷺ فأتاني فقلت: دعني أقسم مالي حيث شئت قال فأبى قلت: فالنصف قال فأبى قلت: فالثلث قال فسكت فكان بعد الثلث جائزا قال وأتيت على نفر من الأنصار والمهاجرين فقالوا: تعال نطعمك ونسقيك خمرا وذلك قبل أن تحرم الخمر قال فأتيتهم في حش والحش البستان فإذا رأس جزور مشوي عندهم وزق من خمر قال فأكلت وشربت معهم قال فذكرت الأنصار والمهاجرون عندهم فقلت: المهاجرون خير من الأنصار قال فأخذ رجل أحد لحيي الرأس فضربني به فجرح بأنفي فأتيت رسول الله ﷺ فأخبرته فأنزل الله عز وجل فيَّ ، يعني نفسه ، شأن الخمر: (إِنَّمَا ٱلْخَمْرُ وَٱلْمَيْسِرُ وَٱلْأَنصَابُ وَٱلْأَزْلَٰمُ رِجْسٌ مِّنْ عَمَلِ ٱلشَّيْطَٰنِ).

Sa'd ibn Abee Waqqaas ؓ narrated that verses from the Qur'aan descended because of him. The mother of Sa'd took an oath that she will never speak to him again until he disbelieves in his religion and that she will neither eat nor drink until he does so. She said, "You claim that Allaah enjoins you to be dutiful to your parents. I am your mother and I order you to do this." She spent three days like that to the point where she passed out because of the strain. A son of hers called 'Umaarah then went over to her, giving her water to drink. (She regained consciousness) and started supplicating against Sa'd. Then Allaah ﷻ sent down this verse of the Qur'aan:

$$\text{وَوَصَّيْنَا ٱلْإِنسَٰنَ بِوَٰلِدَيْهِ حُسْنًا ۖ وَإِن جَٰهَدَاكَ لِتُشْرِكَ بِى}$$

"And We have enjoined on man to be good and dutiful to his parents but if they strive to make you join with Me…"

Included in this verse is the following:

$$\text{فَلَا تُطِعْهُمَا ۖ وَصَاحِبْهُمَا فِى ٱلدُّنْيَا مَعْرُوفًا}$$

"…then obey them not, but behave with them in the world kindly…"[104]

He (Sa'd) said, "Also, the Messenger of Allaah ﷺ had captured a large war booty and I found in it a sword. I took it and went with it to the Messenger of Allaah ﷺ and said, 'Let me have this sword from the war booty, since I am the one whose status is well known to (on the battle field)." He said, "Return it to the place you have taken it from." I went to put it back; however, when I was about to throw it into the pile of war booty my soul rebuked me, so I went back to him and said, 'Give it to me.' He said raising his voice at me, "Return it to the place you have taken it from!" Then Allaah ﷻ sent down:

$$\text{يَسْـَٔلُونَكَ عَنِ ٱلْأَنفَالِ}$$

"They ask you about the spoils of war…" (Al-Anfaal: 1)

Furthermore, I became ill so I sent for the Messenger of Allaah ﷺ. He came to me so I said, 'Let me distribute my wealth however I wish.' He refused. I said, 'Half?' He refused. I said, 'One third?' He was silent, so after that one third was permissible. In addition, I went to a group of people from the *Ansaar* and the *Muhaajireen* (emigrants). They then said, "Come with us. We will feed you and give you alcoholic drink." That was before alcoholic

---

[104] In this narration verse 8 of *Sooratul-'Ankaboot* was mixed with verse 15 of *Sooratu Luqmaan* while in other narrations verses 14 and 15 of *Sooratu Luqmaan* were only mentioned. Ash-Sheikh Muqbil ؒ said, "Either both verses were revealed or Simaak ibn Harb was inconsistent in his narration for verily he is inconsistent in many *ahaadeeth*."

drink was prohibited. I met them in a garden and found to my surprise the roasted head of a slaughtered camel and a wine sack. I then ate and drank with them and mentioned the *Ansaar* and the *Muhaajireen* in a conversation with them. I said, 'The *Muhaajiroon* are better than the *Ansaar*.' A man then took one of the jaw bones of the camel's head and hit me with it injuring my nose. I went to the Messenger of Allaah ﷺ and informed him about that. Then Allaah ﷻ sent down, because of me, the ruling on alcoholic drink:

$$\text{إِنَّمَا ٱلْخَمْرُ وَٱلْمَيْسِرُ وَٱلْأَنصَابُ وَٱلْأَزْلَـٰمُ رِجْسٌ مِّنْ عَمَلِ ٱلشَّيْطَـٰنِ}$$

"Indeed intoxicants, gambling, stone alters and divination arrows are an abomination of Shaytaan's work…" (*Al-Maa'idah*: 90-91).

Muslim transmitted this *hadeeth* in his *Saheeh* (1748/43).

His, the Exalted One's statement:

$$\text{وَمِنَ ٱلنَّاسِ مَن يَقُولُ ءَامَنَّا بِٱللَّهِ فَإِذَآ أُوذِىَ فِى ٱللَّهِ جَعَلَ فِتْنَةَ ٱلنَّاسِ كَعَذَابِ ٱللَّهِ}$$

"And from mankind are those who say: "We believe in Allaah," but when he is harmed for the sake of Allaah, he considers the trial of the people to be as if it were Allaah's punishment…" (verse: 10)

The reason for the revelation of this verse has already been mentioned in *Sooratun-Nahl*, verse: 110.

سورة لقمان

Sooratu Luqmaan

His, the Exalted One's statement:

$$إِنَّ ٱلشِّرْكَ لَظُلْمٌ عَظِيمٌ$$

"Verily joining others in worship with Allaah is a tremendous wrong." (verse: 13)

قال الإمام البخاري ﷺ (32): حدثنا أبو الوليد قال حدثنا شعبة ح قال وحدثني بشر قال حدثنا محمد عن شعبة عن سليمان عن إبراهيم عن علقمة عن عبد الله ﷺ قال: لما نزلت: (ٱلَّذِينَ ءَامَنُوا۟ وَلَمْ يَلْبِسُوٓا۟ إِيمَـٰنَهُم بِظُلْمٍ أُو۟لَـٰٓئِكَ لَهُمُ ٱلْأَمْنُ وَهُم مُّهْتَدُونَ) قال أصحاب النبي ﷺ: أينا لم يظلم فأنزل الله عز وجل: (إِنَّ ٱلشِّرْكَ لَظُلْمٌ عَظِيمٌ).

'Abdullaah ibn Mas'ood said, "When the following verse descended:

$$ٱلَّذِينَ ءَامَنُوا۟ وَلَمْ يَلْبِسُوٓا۟ إِيمَـٰنَهُم بِظُلْمٍ أُو۟لَـٰٓئِكَ لَهُمُ ٱلْأَمْنُ وَهُم مُّهْتَدُونَ$$

'Those who believe and mix not their faith with wrongdoing, those people, for them there is security, and they are guided.' (*Al-An'aam*: 82)
The Companions of the Prophet ﷺ said, "Which one of us has done no wrongdoing?" Then Allaah ﷻ sent down:

$$إِنَّ ٱلشِّرْكَ لَظُلْمٌ عَظِيمٌ$$

'Verily joining others in worship with Allaah is a tremendous wrong.'

This *hadeeth* has been transmitted by Al-Bukhaaree in his *Saheeh* (32).

NOTE: Al-Haafidh Ibn Hajar said in *Fathul-Baaree* in the explanation of *hadeeth* (32), "This narration of Shu'bah necessitates that this question was the reason why the other verse in *Sooratu Luqmaan* descended. However, Al-Bukhaaree and Muslim mentioned it with other chains leading to Al-A'mash[105] who is Sulaimaan, the aforementioned narrator in the chain of this *hadeeth*. In the narration of Jareer on him (Al-A'mash) it reads, "They said, 'Which one of us has not mixed his faith with wrongdoing?' So he said, "It is not like that.

---

[105] Al-A'mash is the Sheikh of Shu'bah in this *hadeeth*. Shu'bah narrated the *hadeeth* with the wording: "Then Allaah ﷻ sent down," while the other students of Al-A'mash did not.

Have you not heard the statement of Luqmaan?" And in the narration of Wakee' on him (Al-A'mash) it reads, "He said, 'It is not like you thought...' And in the narration of 'Eesaa on Yoonus it states, "Verily what is only meant is joining others in worship with Allaah. Have you not heard what Luqmaan said?" It appears from this that the verse in *Sooratu Luqmaan* was already known to them and that is why he pointed that out to them, or it is possible that it descended at that time, so he recited it to them and then he pointed that out to them, so the two different narrations are in harmony with each other."

سورة السجدة

Sooratus-Sajdah

His, the Exalted One's statement:

تَتَجَافَىٰ جُنُوبُهُمْ عَنِ ٱلْمَضَاجِعِ

"Their sides forsake their beds…" (verse: 16)

قال الإمام الترمذي رحمه الله (3196): حدثنا عبد الله بن أبي زياد حدثنا عبد العزيز بن عبد الله الأويسي عن سليمان بن بلال عن يحيى بن سعيد عن أنس بن مالك ﷺ أن هذه الآية: (تَتَجَافَىٰ جُنُوبُهُمْ عَنِ ٱلْمَضَاجِعِ) نزلت في انتظار هذه الصلاة التي تدعى العتمة.

قال أبو عيسى: هذا حديث حسن صحيح غريب لا نعرفه إلا من هذا الوجه.

Anas ibn Maalik narrated that this verse,

تَتَجَافَىٰ جُنُوبُهُمْ عَنِ ٱلْمَضَاجِعِ

"Their sides forsake their beds…"

descended because of waiting for this prayer known as *Al-'Atamah* (the *'Ishaa* prayer).[106]

At-Tirmidhee transmitted this *hadeeth* in his *Jaami'* (3196) and classified it to be *hasan saheeh ghareeb*. And Al-Haafidh Ibn Katheer said in his *Tafseer*, "Its chain is *jayyid*."

---

[106] *Al-'Atamah* is the *'Ishaa* prayer as is mentioned in numerous *ahaadeeth*. However, it is better to call this prayer *Al-'Ishaa* not *Al-'Atamah* because of the *hadeeth* of Ibn 'Umar in Muslim (644): "I heard the Messenger of Allaah say, "Do not let the Bedouins prevail over you in naming your prayer. Verily it is *Al-'Ishaa* while they milk the camels at *Al-'Atamah* (the time for *Al-'Ishaa* which the Bedouins used to call *Al-'Atamah*)."

سورة الأحزاب

Sooratul-Ahzaab

His, the Exalted One's statement:

$$\text{ٱدْعُوهُمْ لِآبَآئِهِمْ هُوَ أَقْسَطُ عِندَ ٱللَّهِ}$$

"Call them by the names of their fathers, that is more just with Allaah…" (verse: 5)

قال الإمام البخاري (4782): حدثنا معلى بن أسد حدثنا عبد العزيز بن المختار حدثنا موسى بن عقبة قال حدثني سالم عن عبد الله بن عمر إن زيد بن حارثة مولى رسول الله ﷺ ما كنا ندعوه إلا زيد بن محمد حتى نزل القرآن: (ٱدْعُوهُمْ لِآبَآئِهِمْ هُوَ أَقْسَطُ عِندَ ٱللَّهِ).

'Abdullaah ibn 'Umar said, "Verily Zaid ibn Haarithah, the *Mawlaa* (freed slave) of the Messenger of Allaah ﷺ, would only referred to by us as Zaid ibn Muhammad until Qur'aan descended,

$$\text{ٱدْعُوهُمْ لِآبَآئِهِمْ هُوَ أَقْسَطُ عِندَ ٱللَّهِ}$$

"Call them by the names of their fathers, that is more just with Allaah…" Al-Bukhaaree transmitted this *hadeeth* in his *Saheeh* (4782) as well as Muslim in his *Saheeh* (2425).

قال الإمام البخاري (5088): حدثنا أبو اليمان أخبرنا شعيب عن الزهري قال أخبرني عروة بن الزبير عن عائشة أن أبا حذيفة بن عتبة بن ربيعة بن عبد شمس وكان ممن شهد بدرا مع النبي ﷺ تبنى سالما وأنكحه بنت أخيه هند بنت الوليد بن عتبة بن ربيعة وهو مولى لامرأة من الأنصار كما تبنى النبي ﷺ زيدا وكان من تبنى رجلا في الجاهلية دعاه الناس إليه وورث من ميراثه حتى أنزل الله: (ٱدْعُوهُمْ لِآبَآئِهِمْ) إلى قوله:(وَمَوَٰلِيكُمْ) فردوا إلى آبائهم فمن لم يعلم له أب كان مولى وأخا في الدين فجاءت سهلة بنت سهيل بن عمرو القرشي ثم العامري وهي امرأة أبي حذيفة النبي ﷺ فقالت: يا رسول الله إنا كنا نرى سالما ولدا وقد أنزل الله فيه ما قد علمت ، فذكر الحديث.

'Aishah narrated that Abu Hudhaifah ibn 'Utbah ibn Rabee'ah ibn 'Abdi Shams, who was among those who participated in Badr with the Messenger of Allaah ﷺ, adopted Saalim as a son and married him to the daughter of his brother Hind bint Al-Waleed ibn 'Utbah ibn Rabee'ah. He (Saalim) was the freed slave of a woman from the *Ansaar* (then was adopted by Abu Hudhaifah) just as the Prophet ﷺ adopted Zaid. In the days of *Jaahiliyah* whoever adopted a son, the people would call him by his name and he would inherit from his inheritance until Allaah sent down [the following]:

$$\text{ٱدْعُوهُمْ لِآبَآئِهِمْ}$$

"Call them by the names of their fathers…"

up to His statement:

$$\text{وَمَوَٰلِيكُمْ}$$

"…and your freed slaves."

They were then returned to [being called by] their father's [names], and whoever was not known to have a father he was a *mawlaa* and a brother in the religion. Sahlah the daughter of Suhail ibn 'Amr Al-Qurashee, then Al-'Aamiree, the wife of Abu Hudhaifah ibn 'Utbah, then went to the Prophet ﷺ and said, "O Messenger of Allaah, verily we used to consider Saalim to be a child of ours but Allaah has sent down, because of him, what you know well…" then he mentioned the (rest of) the *hadeeth*.

This *hadeeth* has been transmitted by Al-Bukhaaree it in his *Saheeh* (5088). In some narrations of this *hadeeth,* it was worded: "Then Allaah sent down…" as mentioned in Ibn Al-Jaarood, page 231. Ash-Sheikh Muqbil ﷺ commented saying, "Perhaps the verse was revealed because of both of them (Zaid and Saalim), and Allaah knows best."

His, the Exalted One's statement:

$$\text{مِّنَ ٱلْمُؤْمِنِينَ رِجَالٌ صَدَقُوا۟ مَا عَـٰهَدُوا۟ ٱللَّهَ عَلَيْهِ ۖ فَمِنْهُم مَّن قَضَىٰ نَحْبَهُۥ وَمِنْهُم مَّن يَنتَظِرُ}$$

"Among the believers are men who have been true to their covenant with Allaah. Some of them have fulfilled their obligations (by being martyred) and some of them are still waiting…" (verse: 23)

قال الإمام البخاري ﷺ (2805): حدثنا محمد بن سعيد الخزاعي حدثنا عبد الأعلى عن حميد قال سألت أنسا حدثنا عمرو بن زرارة حدثنا زياد قال حدثني حميد الطويل عن أنس ﷺ قال: غاب عمي أنس بن النضر عن قتال بدر فقال: يا رسول الله غبت عن أول قتال قاتلت المشركين لئن الله أشهدني قتال المشركين ليرين الله ما أصنع فلما كان يوم أحد وانكشف المسلمون قال: اللهم إني أعتذر إليك مما صنع هؤلاء يعني أصحابه وأبرأ إليك مما صنع هؤلاء يعني المشركين ثم تقدم فاستقبله سعد بن معاذ فقال: يا سعد بن معاذ ورب النضر إني أجد ريحها من دون أحد قال سعد: فما استطعت يا رسول الله ما صنع قال أنس: فوجدنا به بضعا وثمانين ضربة بالسيف أو طعنه برمح أو رمية بسهم

ووجدناه قد قتل وقد مثل به المشركون فما عرفة أحد إلا أخته ببنانه قال أنس: كنا نرى أو نظن أن هذه الآية نزلت فيه وفي أشباهه: (مِّنَ ٱلْمُؤْمِنِينَ رِجَالٌ صَدَقُوا۟ مَا عَـٰهَدُوا۟ ٱللَّهَ عَلَيْهِ) إلى آخر الآية.

Anas ibn Maalik said, "My uncle Anas ibn An-Nadr was not present at the battle of Badr so he said, 'O Messenger of Allaah, I was not present at the first battle you fought against the polytheists. If Allaah allows me to be present at a battle against the polytheists, then indeed Allaah will see what I do.' Then on the day of the battle of Uhud when the Muslims suffered a blow, he (Anas ibn An-Nadr) said, "O Allaah, I seek your pardon for what these people have done," meaning his companions, "and I seek from you that I be cleared from what these people have done," meaning the polytheists. He then advanced forward. Sa'd ibn Mu'aadh then faced him so he said, 'O Sa'd ibn Mu'aadh, (I want) paradise, by the Lord of An-Nadr. Verily I find its fragrance just below Uhud.' Sa'd (later) said, "I was not able to do, O Messenger of Allaah, what he did." Anas (ibn Maalik) said, 'We later found with him over eighty wounds from strikes of the sword and stabs from the spear and shots from the arrow. We found him dead; the polytheists had mutilated him. No one could recognize him except his sister by the tips of his fingers. We used to think that this verse descended because of him and those like him:

مِّنَ ٱلْمُؤْمِنِينَ رِجَالٌ صَدَقُوا۟ مَا عَـٰهَدُوا۟ ٱللَّهَ عَلَيْهِ

"Among the believers are men who have been true to their covenant with Allaah..." (verse:23).

Al-Bukhaaree transmitted this *hadeeth* in his *Saheeh* (2805) and Muslim in his *Saheeh* (1903).

His, the Exalted One's statement:

وَكَفَى ٱللَّهُ ٱلْمُؤْمِنِينَ ٱلْقِتَالَ

"And Allaah spared the believers from fighting..." (verse: 25)

قال الإمام النسائي رحمه الله في المجتبى (ج 2 ص 17): أخبرنا عمرو بن علي قال حدثنا يحيى قال حدثنا ابن أبي ذئب قال حدثنا سعيد بن أبي عروبة عن عبد الرحمن بن أبي سعيد عن أبيه رضي الله عنه: شغلنا المشركون يوم الخندق عن صلاة الظهر حتى غربت الشمس وذلك قبل أن ينزل في القتال ما نزل فأنزل الله عز وجل: (وَكَفَى ٱللَّهُ ٱلْمُؤْمِنِينَ ٱلْقِتَالَ) فأمر رسول الله ﷺ بلالا فأقام لصلاة الظهر فصلاها كما كان يصليها لوقتها ثم أقام للعصر فصلاها كما كان يصليها في وقتها ثم أذن المغرب فصلاها كما كان يصليها في وقتها.

Abu Sa'eed Al-Khudree ﷺ said, "The polytheists had distracted us on the day of *Al-Khandaq* (the ditch) from performing the *Dhuhr* prayer until the sun had set. That was before the revelation about fighting had descended.[107] Then Allaah ﷻ sent down:

$$\text{وَكَفَى ٱللَّهُ ٱلْمُؤْمِنِينَ ٱلْقِتَالَ}$$

'And Allaah spared the believers from fighting…'.

The Messenger of Allaah ﷺ ordered Bilaal [to call the *iqaamah*], so he made the *Iqaamah* (the second call to prayer) for the *Dhuhr* prayer. He then prayed it as he would usually pray it in its proper time. Then he (Bilaal) made the *Iqaamah* for the *'Asr* Prayer and he prayed it as he would usually pray it in its proper time. Then he (Bilaal) called the *Adhaan* (the first call to prayer) for the *Maghrib* prayer and he prayed it as he would usually pray it in its proper time."

This *hadeeth* has been transmitted by An-Nasaa'ee in *Al-Mujtabaa*, volume 2, page 17. Ash-Sheikh Muqbil ﷺ said, "Regarding the *hadeeth*, the people of its chain are people of the *Saheeh* (Al-Bukhaaree and/or Muslim)."

<u>His, the Exalted One's statement:</u>

$$\text{يَٰٓأَيُّهَا ٱلنَّبِىُّ قُل لِّأَزْوَٰجِكَ إِن كُنتُنَّ تُرِدْنَ ٱلْحَيَوٰةَ ٱلدُّنْيَا وَزِينَتَهَا فَتَعَالَيْنَ أُمَتِّعْكُنَّ وَأُسَرِّحْكُنَّ سَرَاحًا جَمِيلًا}$$

"O Prophet, say to your wives: If you desire the life of this world and its glitter then come, I will make a provision for you and set you free in a handsome manner…" (verses: 28-29)

قال الإمام البخاري رحمه الله (2468): حدثنا يحيى بن بكير حدثنا الليث عن عقيل عن ابن شهاب قال أخبرني عبيد الله بن عبد الله بن أبي ثور عن عبد الله بن عباس رضي الله عنهما قال: لم أزل حريصا على أن أسأل عمر رضي الله عنه عن المرأتين من أزواج النبي ﷺ اللتين قال الله لهما: (إِن تَتُوبَا إِلَى ٱللَّهِ فَقَدْ صَغَتْ قُلُوبُكُمَا) فحججت معه فعدل معه بالإداوة فتبرز حتى جاء فسكبت على يديه من الإداوة فتوضأ فقلت: يا أمير المؤمنين من المرأتان من أزواج النبي ﷺ اللتان قال الله عز وجل لهما: (إِن تَتُوبَا إِلَى ٱللَّهِ فَقَدْ صَغَتْ قُلُوبُكُمَا) فقال: واعجبا لك يابن عباس عائشة وحفصة ثم استقبل عمر الحديث يسوقه فقال: إني كنت وجار لي من الأنصار في بني أمية بن زيد وهي من

---

[107] Meaning before the description of how to make the prayer in a state of fear was revealed.

عوالي المدينة وكنا نتناوب النزول على النبي ﷺ فينزل يوما وأنزل يوما فإذا نزلت جئته من خبر ذلك اليوم من الأمر وغيره وإذا نزل فعل مثله وكنا معشر قريش نغلب النساء فلما قدمنا على الأنصار إذا هم قوم تغلبهم نساؤهم فطفق نساؤنا يأخذن من أدب نساء الأنصار فصحت على امرأتي فراجعتني فأنكرت أن تراجعني فقالت: ولم تنكر أن أراجعك فوالله إن أزواج النبي ﷺ ليراجعنه وإن إحداهن لتهجره اليوم حتى الليل فأفزعتني فقلت: خابت من فعل منهن بعظيم ثم جمعت علي ثيابي فدخلت على حفصة فقلت: أي حفصة أتغاضب إحداكن رسول الله ﷺ اليوم حتى الليل فقالت: نعم فقلت: خابت وخسرت أفتأمن أن يغضب الله لغضب رسوله ﷺ فتهلكين لا تستكثري على رسول الله ﷺ ولا تراجعيه في شيء ولا تهجريه واسأليني ما بدا لك ولا يغرنك أن كانت جارتك هي أوضأ منك وأحب إلى رسول الله ﷺ يريد عائشة وكنا تحدثنا أن غسان تنعل النعال لغزونا فنزل صاحبي يوم نوبته فرجع عشاء فضرب بابي ضربا شديدا وقال: أنائم هو ففزعت فخرجت إليه وقال: حدث أمر عظيم قلت: ما هو أجاءت غسان قال: لا بل أعظم منه وأطول طلق رسول الله ﷺ نساءه قال: قد خابت حفصة وخسرت كنت أظن أن هذا يوشك أن يكون فجمعت علي ثيابي فصليت صلاة الفجر مع النبي ﷺ فدخل مشربة له فاعتزل فيها فدخلت على حفصة فإذا هي تبكي فقلت: ما يبكيك أو لم أكن حذرتك أطلقكن رسول الله ﷺ قالت: لا أدري هو ذا في المشربة فخرجت فجئت المنبر فإذا حوله رهط يبكي بعضهم فجلست معهم قليلا ثم غلبني ما أجد فجئت المشربة التي هو فيها فقلت لغلام له أسود: استأذن لعمر فدخل فكلم النبي ﷺ ثم خرج فقال: ذكرتك له فصمت فانصرفت حتى جلست مع الرهط الذين عند المنبر ثم جئت فذكر مثله فجلست مع الرهط الذين عند المنبر ثم غلبني ما أجد فجئت الغلام فقلت: استأذن لعمر فذكر مثله فلما وليت منصرفا فإذا الغلام يدعوني قال: أذن لك رسول الله ﷺ فدخلت عليه فإذا هو مضطجع على رمال حصير ليس بينه وبينه فراش قد أثر الرمال بجنبه متكئ على وسادة من أدم حشوها ليف فسلمت عليه ثم قلت: وأنا قائم: طلقت نساءك فرفع بصره إلي فقال: لا ثم قلت وأنا قائم أستأنس: يا رسول الله لو رأيتني وكنا معشر قريش نغلب النساء فلما قدمنا على قوم تغلبهم نساؤهم فذكره فتبسم النبي ﷺ ثم قلت: لو رأيتني ودخلت على حفصة فقلت: لا يغرنك أن كانت جارتك هي أوضأ منك وأحب إلى النبي ﷺ يريد عائشة فتبسم أخرى فجلست حين رأيته تبسم ثم رفعت بصري في بيته فوالله ما رأيت فيه شيئا يرد البصر غير أهبة ثلاثة فقلت: ادع الله فليوسع على أمتك فإن فارس والروم وسع عليهم وأعطوا الدنيا وهم لا يعبدون الله فقال: أو في شك أنت يا ابن الخطاب أولئك قوم عجلت لهم طيباتهم في الحياة الدنيا فقلت:

يا رسول الله استغفر لي فاعتزل النبي ﷺ من أجل ذلك الحديث حين أفشته حفصة إلى عائشة وكان قد قال ما أنا بداخل عليهن شهرا من شدة موجدته عليهن حين عاتبه الله فلما مضت تسع وعشرون دخل على عائشة فبدأ بها فقالت له عائشة: إنك أقسمت أن لا تدخل علينا شهرا وإنا أصبحنا لتسع وعشرين ليلة أعدها عدا فقال النبي ﷺ: الشهر تسع وعشرون وكان ذلك الشهر تسعا وعشرين قالت عائشة: فأنزلت آية التخيير فبدأ بي أول امرأة فقال: إني ذاكر لك أمرا ولا عليك أن لا تعجلي حتى

221

تستأمري أبويك قالت: قد أعلم أن أبوي لم يكونا يأمراني بفراقك ثم قال: إن الله قال: (يَٰٓأَيُّهَا ٱلنَّبِىُّ قُل لِّأَزْوَٰجِكَ) إلى قوله: (عَظِيمًا) قلت: أفي هذا أستأمر أبوي فإني أريد الله ورسوله والدار الآخرة ثم خير نساءه فقلن مثل ما قالت عائشة.

'Abdullaah ibn 'Abbaas ﷺ said, "I was always eager to ask 'Umar ﷺ about the two women from the wives of the Prophet ﷺ whom Allaah said to them:

$$إِن تَتُوبَآ إِلَى ٱللَّهِ فَقَدْ صَغَتْ قُلُوبُكُمَا$$

'If you two turn in repentance to Allaah, for your hearts are indeed so inclined (to oppose what the Prophet ﷺ likes)…' (*At-Tahreem*: 4)

So I made *hajj* with him. He turned off the road and I turned off with him carrying a small water sack. He relieved himself then came over, so I poured water from the sack onto his hands and he made *wudoo* (ablution). I said, "O Leader of the Believers, who are the two women from the wives of the Prophet ﷺ whom Allaah ﷻ said to them,

$$إِن تَتُوبَآ إِلَى ٱللَّهِ فَقَدْ صَغَتْ قُلُوبُكُمَا$$

'If you two turn in repentance to Allaah, for your hearts are indeed so inclined (to oppose what the Prophet ﷺ likes)…'

He said, "O how surprised I am at you, O Ibn 'Abbaas! 'Aishah and Hafsah." Then 'Umar began to tell the story saying, 'Verily, a neighbor of mine from the *Ansaar* and I used to reside in the village of the tribe Banee Umaiyah ibn Zaid which was one the villages of Madeenah. We used to take turns in going to sit with the Prophet ﷺ. He would go one day and I would go another day. When I would go I would return to him with the news of that day, news about commandments and other things, and when he would go he would do the same.

We, the community of Quraish in particular, used to dominate the women. Then when we came to the *Ansaar* we found them to be men whose women dominated them and our women started following the ways of the women of the *Ansaar*. [Once] I had shouted at my wife and then she talked back to me and I found it strange that she talked back to me. Then she said, "And why do you find it strange that I talk back to you? For, by Allaah, indeed the wives of the Prophet ﷺ talk back to him and at times one of them will avoid him from daytime to nightfall." She startled me so I said, 'Whoever does that from amongst them has done a tremendous thing.' I then put my clothes on and went to Hafsah and said, "O Hafsah, does is it true that one of you may be on bad terms with the Messenger of Allaah ﷺ from daytime to nightfall?" She said, 'Yes.' I said, "May she suffer ruin and loss. Is she safe from the anger of

Allaah due to the anger of His Messenger ﷺ? You will be destroyed!" Do not ask a lot from the Messenger of Allaah ﷺ and do not speak back to him whatever the case may be; and do not avoid him, and ask me about what comes to your mind and do not be deceived by your neighbor (co-wife) being more beautiful than you and more beloved to the Messenger of Allaah ﷺ," meaning 'Aishah.

It had reached us that Ghassaan was preparing horse shoes for our next military expedition. My companion went over on the day of his turn. He came back at night and knocked hard on my door and said, 'Is he there?' I was startled so I went out to him. He said, "A serious matter has occurred." I said, 'What is it? Did Ghassaan come?' He said, "No, rather, something greater than that and more alarming. The Messenger of Allaah ﷺ has divorced his wives." He ('Umar) said, 'Hafsah has suffered ruin and loss. I thought this was about to happen.' I then put on my clothes and prayed the *Fajr* prayer with the Prophet ﷺ. Afterwards, he went into an attic room of his, secluding himself in it. I entered where Hafsah was and found her crying. I said, "What makes you cry? Did I not warn you! Did the Messenger of Allaah ﷺ divorce you all?" She said, 'I don't know. There he is in the attic room.' I left and went to the *minbar* and found a group of people gathered around it, some of them crying. I sat with them for a little while until what I found in my heart overtook me, so I headed for the attic room that he was in. I said to a black servant boy of his, "Ask permission for 'Umar [to enter]." He entered and told the Prophet ﷺ [that I was seeking permission to enter] and then he came out and said, 'I mentioned you to him but he remained silent.' I then went away and sat with the group of people who were at the *minbar*. Then what I found in my heart overtook me so I went back. He (the servant boy) mentioned the same thing so I went and sat with the group of people who were at the *minbar* until what I found in my heart overtook me so I went to the servant boy and said, "Ask permission for 'Umar." He mentioned the same thing. Then when I turned back to leave the servant boy suddenly called me saying, 'The Messenger of Allaah ﷺ has given you permission.'

I entered and found him lying down on a woven mat with no bedding between him and it. The woven mat had left marks in his side. He was leaning on a leather pillow stuffed with palm fibers. I gave him the salaams and then I said while standing, "You divorced your wives?" He looked at me and said, 'No.' Then I said while standing trying to be social and break the atmosphere, "O Messenger of Allaah, if only you had seen me. We the community of Quraish used to dominate the women, then we came to a group of men that are dominated by their women." He then mentioned it (the story with his wife), so the Prophet ﷺ smiled. Then I said, 'If only you had seen me when I entered upon Hafsah and said, "Do not be deceived by your neighbor being more beautiful than you and more beloved to the Prophet ﷺ," meaning 'Aishah. So he smiled again.

I sat down when I saw him smiling and looked around his house. By Allaah, I did not see anything that would catch the eye other than three hides so I said, "Invoke Allaah that He enriches your nation for verily the Persians and the Romans have been enriched. They have been given the goods of this world yet they do not worship Allaah." He said while leaning, 'Are you in doubt, O son of Al-Khattaab? Those are a people who have been given, in advance, their delights in this world.' I said, "O Messenger of Allaah, ask forgiveness for me." The Prophet ﷺ had secluded himself because of that talk after Hafsah had passed it on to 'Aishah and he had said, 'I will not enter upon them for one month.' That was due to the extreme anger he held against them when Allaah censured him.[108] Then when twenty nine days had passed he entered upon 'Aishah starting his daily rounds with her. 'Aishah said to him, "Verily you swore not to enter upon us for one month and we have entered the morning of the twenty ninth night. I can count them off." The Prophet ﷺ said, 'A month is twenty nine days.' That month was twenty nine days. 'Aishah said, "Then the verse of the choice was revealed so the first woman he started with was me. He said, 'Verily I am about to mention to you a matter, and it is not upon you to rush and answer until you seek advice from your parents.' She said, "I know my parents will not order me to separate from you." Then he said, "Verily Allaah says:

$$\text{يَٰٓأَيُّهَا ٱلنَّبِىُّ قُل لِّأَزْوَٰجِكَ}$$

'O Prophet, say to your wives...'

up to His statement:

$$\text{عَظِيمًا}$$

"...an enormous reward."

I said, 'Do I need to seek advice from my parents for something like this? Indeed I choose Allaah and His Messenger and the abode of the hereafter.' He then made the rest of his wives choose, so they said the same thing that 'Aishah said."

Al-Bukhaaree transmitted this *hadeeth* in his *Saheeh* (2468) as well as Muslim in his *Saheeh* (1479/34).

قال الإمام مسلم ﵀ (1478): وحدثنا زهير بن حرب حدثنا روح بن عبادة حدثنا زكريا بن إسحاق حدثنا أبو الزبير عن جابر بن عبد الله ﵁ قال: دخل أبو بكر يستأذن على رسول الله ﷺ فوجد

---

[108] What is meant by the censure is the statement of Allaah ﷻ:

$$\text{(يَٰٓأَيُّهَا ٱلنَّبِىُّ لِمَ تُحَرِّمُ مَآ أَحَلَّ ٱللَّهُ لَكَ)}$$

"O Prophet, why do you forbid that which Allaah has made permissible for you..." (*At-Tahreem*: 1) Refer to *Fathul-Baaree* in the explanation of *hadeeth* (5191).

الناس جلوسا ببابه لم يؤذن لأحد منهم قال فأذن لأبي بكر فدخل ثم أقبل عمر فاستأذن فأذن له فوجد النبي ﷺ جالسا حوله نساؤه واجما ساكتا قال فقال: لأقولن شيئا أضحك النبي ﷺ فقال: يا رسول الله لو رأيت بنت خارجة سألتني النفقة فقمت إليها فوجأت عنقها فضحك رسول الله ﷺ وقال: هن حولي كما ترى يسألنني النفقة فقام أبو بكر إلى عائشة يجأ عنقها فقام عمر إلى حفصة يجأ عنقها كلاهما يقول: تسألن رسول الله ﷺ ما ليس عنده فقلن: والله لا نسأل رسول الله ﷺ شيئا أبدا ليس عنده ثم اعتزلهن شهرا أو تسعا وعشرين يوما ثم نزلت عليه هذه الآية: (يَـٰٓأَيُّهَا ٱلنَّبِىُّ قُل لِّأَزْوَٰجِكَ)

حتى بلغ: (لِلْمُحْسِنَـٰتِ مِنكُنَّ أَجْرًا عَظِيمًا) قال فبدأ بعائشة فقال: يا عائشة إني أريد أن أعرض عليك أمرا أحب أن لا تعجلي فيه حتى تستشيري أبويك قالت: وما هو يا رسول الله فتلا عليها الآية قالت: أفيك يا رسول الله أستشير أبوي بل أختار الله ورسوله والدار الآخرة وأسألك أن لا تخبر امرأة من نسائك بالذي قلت قال: لا تسألني امرأة منهن إلا أخبرتها إن الله لم يبعثني معنتا ولا متعنتا ولكن بعثني معلما ميسرا.

Jaabir ibn 'Abdillaah ؓ said, "Abu Bakr came asking permission to enter upon the Messenger of Allaah ﷺ. He found a group of people sitting at his door and none of them were given permission to enter. However, Abu Bakr was granted permission, so he entered. Then 'Umar came and asked permission [to enter] and was also granted permission. He (Abu Bakr) found the Prophet ﷺ sitting down depressed in silence with his wives around him, so he said, 'I will indeed say something that will make the Prophet ﷺ laugh.' He then said, "O Messenger of Allaah, if only you had seen when the daughter of Khaarijah asked me for provision and I got up and poked her in the neck." The Messenger of Allaah ﷺ laughed and said, 'They are around me, as you see, asking me for provision.' Abu Bakr then got up and poked 'Aishah in her neck and 'Umar got up and poked Hafsah in her neck both of them saying, "Do you ask the Messenger of Allaah ﷺ for what he does not have!" They said, 'By Allaah, we will never ask the Messenger of Allaah ﷺ for anything he does not have.' He then dissociated himself from them for one month or twenty nine days and then this verse was revealed to him,

$$\text{يَـٰٓأَيُّهَا ٱلنَّبِىُّ قُل لِّأَزْوَٰجِكَ}$$

"O Prophet, say to your wives…"

up to where Allah mentions,

$$\text{لِلْمُحْسِنَـٰتِ مِنكُنَّ أَجْرًا عَظِيمًا}$$

'…for the good doers amongst you an enormous reward.'

He then started with 'Aishah saying, "O 'Aishah, verily I am about to present to you a matter and I hope you will not rush to answer until you seek the advice of your parents." She said, 'And what is that, O Messenger of Allaah?' He then recited to her the verse. She said, 'About you, O Messenger of Allaah, do I seek advice from my parents? Rather, I choose Allaah and His Messenger and the abode of the hereafter, and I ask that you not tell any of your wives what I said.' He said, "None of them will ask me except that I will tell her; Indeed Allaah has not sent me to be harsh or to cause distress, rather, He has sent me to instruct and make things easy."

Muslim transmitted this *hadeeth* in his *Saheeh* (1478).

His, the Exalted One's statement:

$$إِنَّمَا يُرِيدُ ٱللَّهُ لِيُذْهِبَ عَنكُمُ ٱلرِّجْسَ أَهْلَ ٱلْبَيْتِ وَيُطَهِّرَكُمْ تَطْهِيرًا$$

"Allaah wants only to remove evil deeds from you, O members of the family, and to purify you." (verse: 33)

قال الإمام ابن أبي حاتم ﷺ كما في تفسير ابن كثير (ج 3 ص 484): حدثنا علي بن حرب الموصلي حدثنا زيد بن الحباب حدثنا الحسين بن واقد عن يزيد النحوي عن عكرمة عن ابن عباس ﷺ في قوله تعالى: (إِنَّمَا يُرِيدُ ٱللَّهُ لِيُذْهِبَ عَنكُمُ ٱلرِّجْسَ أَهْلَ ٱلْبَيْتِ) قال: نزلت في نساء النبي ﷺ خاصة.

Ibn 'Abbaas ﷺ said about His ﷻ statement,

$$إِنَّمَا يُرِيدُ ٱللَّهُ لِيُذْهِبَ عَنكُمُ ٱلرِّجْسَ أَهْلَ ٱلْبَيْتِ$$

"Allaah wants only to remove evil deeds from you, O members of the family…"
that " it descended because of the wives of the Prophet ﷺ in particular."

Ibn Abee Haatim transmitted this *hadeeth* as mentioned in *Tafseer Ibn Katheer*, volume 3, page 484.

His, the Exalted One's statement:

$$إِنَّ ٱلْمُسْلِمِينَ وَٱلْمُسْلِمَٰتِ$$

"Verily the Muslim men and the Muslim women…" (verse: 35)

قال الإمام الترمذي رَحِمَهُ اللهُ (3211): حدثنا عبد بن حميد حدثنا محمد بن كثير حدثنا سليمان بن كثير عن حسين عن عكرمة عن أم عمارة الأنصارية رَضِيَ اللهُ عَنْها أنها أتت النبي ﷺ فقالت: ما أرى كل شيء إلا للرجال وما أرى النساء يذكرن بشيء فنزلت هذه الآية:

(إِنَّ ٱلْمُسْلِمِينَ وَٱلْمُسْلِمَٰتِ وَٱلْمُؤْمِنِينَ وَٱلْمُؤْمِنَٰتِ) الآية.

قال أبو عيسى: هذا حديث حسن غريب وإنما يعرف هذا الحديث من هذا الوجه.

Umm 'Umaarah Al-Ansaariyah ؓ narrated that she went to the Prophet ﷺ and said, "I only see everything to be for the men and I do not see the women mentioned in anything." Then the following verse descended,

$$\text{إِنَّ ٱلْمُسْلِمِينَ وَٱلْمُسْلِمَٰتِ وَٱلْمُؤْمِنِينَ وَٱلْمُؤْمِنَٰتِ}$$

"Verily the Muslim men and the Muslim women and the believing men and the believing women…" (verse: 35).

This *hadeeth* has been transmitted by At-Tirmidhee in his *Jaami'* (3211) and classified it to be *hasan ghareeb*. A similar *hadeeth* has also been narrated on Umm Salamah which has been transmitted by Al-Haakim in *Al-Mustadrak*, volume 2, page 416, and An-Nasaa'ee in his *Tafseer* (425), and Ibn Katheer in his *Tafseer*, volume 3, page 47.

<u>His, the Exalted One's statement:</u>

$$\text{وَتُخْفِى فِى نَفْسِكَ مَا ٱللَّهُ مُبْدِيهِ}$$

"But you hide in yourself what Allaah is to disclose…" (verse: 37)

قال الإمام البخاري رَحِمَهُ اللهُ (4787): حدثنا محمد بن عبد الرحيم حدثنا معلى بن منصور عن حماد بن زيد حدثنا ثابت عن أنس بن مالك ﷺ أن هذه الآية: (وَتُخْفِى فِى نَفْسِكَ مَا ٱللَّهُ مُبْدِيهِ) نزلت في شأن زينب بنت جحش وزيد بن حارثة.

Anas ibn Maalik ؓ narrated that this verse,

$$\text{وَتُخْفِى فِى نَفْسِكَ مَا ٱللَّهُ مُبْدِيهِ}$$

"But you hide in yourself what Allaah is to disclose…"

descended because of Zainab bint Jahsh and Zaid ibn Haarithah.[109]

Al-Bukhaaree transmitted this *hadeeth* in his *Saheeh* (4787).

<u>His, the Exalted One's statement:</u>

فَلَمَّا قَضَىٰ زَيْدٌ مِّنْهَا وَطَرًا زَوَّجْنَٰكَهَا

"So when Zaid fulfilled his need for her, We gave her to you in marriage…" (verse: 37)

قال الإمام ابن سعد ﷺ في الطبقات (ج 8 ص 103): أخبرنا عارم بن الفضل حدثنا حماد بن زيد عن ثابت عن أنس ﷺ قال: نزلت في زينب بنت جحش: (فَلَمَّا قَضَىٰ زَيْدٌ مِّنْهَا وَطَرًا زَوَّجْنَٰكَهَا)

قال: فكانت تفخر على نساء النبي ﷺ تقول: زوجكن أهلكن وزوجني الله من فوق سبع سموات.

Anas ﷺ said, "This verse descended because of Zainab bint Jahsh:

فَلَمَّا قَضَىٰ زَيْدٌ مِّنْهَا وَطَرًا زَوَّجْنَٰكَهَا

'So when Zaid fulfilled his need for her, We gave her to you in marriage…'
She used to boast [about this occurrence in relation to] the wives of the Prophet ﷺ saying, "Your families married you off while Allaah, from above the seven heavens, married me off."

This *hadeeth* has been transmitted by Ibn Sa'd it in *At-Tabaqaat Al-Kubraa*, volume 8, page 103. Ash-Sheikh Muqbil ﷺ said, "The people of its chain are people of the *Saheeh* (Al-Bukhaaree and/or Muslim)." The latter portion of the *hadeeth* is in Al-Bukhaaree (7420).

قال الإمام ابن سعد ﷺ في الطبقات (ج8 ص 104): أخبرنا عفان بن مسلم و عمرو بن عاصم الكلابي قالا حدثنا سليمان بن المغيرة عن ثابت عن أنس بن مالك ﷺ قال: لما انقضت عدة زينب بنت جحش قال رسول الله ﷺ لزيد بن حارثة: ما أجد أحدا آمن عندي وأوثق في نفسي منك ائت إلى زينب فاخطبها علي قال: فانطلق زيد فأتاها وهي تخمر عجينها فلما رأيتها عظمت في صدري فلم أستطع أن أنظر إليها حين عرفت أن رسول الله ﷺ قد ذكرها فوليتها ظهري ونكصت على عقبي

---

[109] Ibn Hajar said in *Fathul-Baaree* in the explanation of this *hadeeth*, "In short, that which the Prophet ﷺ was hiding was that which Allaah had informed him that she will become his wife, and that which prompted him to hide that was his fear that the people would say he married the wife of his son, but Allaah wanted to nullify that which the people of *Jaahiliyah* were upon from the rules of adoption with a command that nothing could be more effective than it, that being the marriage of the wife of he who was called a son and having that happen from the leader of the Muslims…"

وقلت: يا زينب أبشري إن رسول الله ﷺ يذكرك قالت: ما أنا بصانعة شيئا حتى أوامر ربي فقامت إلى مسجدها ونزل القرآن: (فَلَمَّا قَضَىٰ زَيْدٌ مِنْهَا وَطَرًا زَوَّجْنَاكَهَا).

Anas ibn Maalik ؓ said, "When Zainab's waiting period was complete, the Messenger of Allaah ﷺ said to Zaid ibn Haarithah, 'I do not find anyone more reliable and trustworthy to me than you. Go to Zainab and propose to her on my behalf.' Zaid then went and entered upon her while she was preparing her dough. (Zaid said), "When I saw her,[110] inside my chest she became grand, so I was not able to look at her after knowing the Messenger of Allaah ﷺ was interested in her so I turned my back to her and turned back on my heels and said, 'O Zainab be delighted, for verily the Messenger of Allaah ﷺ mentions you in interest.' She said, "I will not do anything until I consult my Lord." She then went to her prayer area and Qur'aan descended:

فَلَمَّا قَضَىٰ زَيْدٌ مِنْهَا وَطَرًا زَوَّجْنَاكَهَا

'So when Zaid fulfilled his need for her We gave her to you in marriage…'

Ibn Sa'd transmitted this *hadeeth* in *At-Tabaqaat Al-Kubraa*, volume 8, page 104, as well as Muslim in his *Saheeh* (1428/89).

His, the Exalted One's statement:

تُرْجِى مَن تَشَآءُ مِنْهُنَّ وَتُـْٔوِى إِلَيْكَ مَن تَشَآءُ

"You can postpone[111] [your time with] whomsoever you will of them and you may receive whom you will…" (verse: 51)

قال الإمام البخاري ؒ (4788): حدثنا زكريا بن يحيى حدثنا أبو أسامة قال هشام حدثنا عن أبيه عن عائشة ؓ قالت: كنت أغار على اللاتي وهبن أنفسهن لرسول الله ﷺ وأقول: أتهب المرأة نفسها

---

[110] An-Nawawee said in his explanation of *Saheeh Muslim*, "This was before the veil had been revealed."

[111] There is a difference of opinion about what is meant by postpone and receive. The majority of Scholars take the position that it is dealing with the division of time spent with his wives. The Prophet ﷺ was given the free hand to postpone anyone of his wives' days giving it to another wife. From their proof is *hadeeth* (4789) in Al-Bukhaaree. The second position is that he may divorce or keep whoever he wills. The third position is that he may accept the proposal of those women who grant themselves to him or he can deny their proposal. Ibn Hajar mentioned these positions in *Fathul-Baaree* in the explanation of *hadeeth* (4788).

فلما أنزل الله تعالى: (تُرْجِي مَن تَشَاءُ مِنْهُنَّ وَتُؤْوِي إِلَيْكَ مَن تَشَاءُ ۖ وَمَنِ ٱبْتَغَيْتَ مِمَّنْ عَزَلْتَ فَلَا جُنَاحَ عَلَيْكَ) قلت: ما أرى ربك إلا يسارع في هواك.

'Aishah ؓ said, "I used to be jealous of those women who granted themselves (for marriage without dowry) to the Messenger of Allaah ﷺ, and I would say, 'Does a woman grant herself?'[112] Then when Allaah ﷻ sent down the following,

تُرْجِي مَن تَشَاءُ مِنْهُنَّ وَتُؤْوِي إِلَيْكَ مَن تَشَاءُ ۖ وَمَنِ ٱبْتَغَيْتَ مِمَّنْ عَزَلْتَ فَلَا جُنَاحَ عَلَيْكَ

"You can postpone [your time with] whomsoever you will of them and you may receive whom you will. And whomever you desire of those whom you have set aside there is no sin on you (to receive her again)"
I said, 'I do not find your Lord except in a rush to please you.'

Al-Bukhaaree transmitted this *hadeeth* in his *Saheeh* (4788) and Muslim in his *Saheeh* (1464/49). Al-Haakim also transmitted it in *Al-Mustadrak*, volume 2, page 436, with the following wording: "Then Allaah sent down this verse in relation to the wives of the Prophet ﷺ…"

His, the Exalted One's statement:

يَـٰٓأَيُّهَا ٱلَّذِينَ ءَامَنُوا۟ لَا تَدْخُلُوا۟ بُيُوتَ ٱلنَّبِىِّ إِلَّآ أَن يُؤْذَنَ لَكُمْ

"O you who believe, enter not the Prophet's houses unless permission is given to you…" (verse: 53)

قال الإمام البخاري ؒ (4794): حدثنا إسحاق بن منصور أخبرنا عبد الله بن بكر السهمي حدثنا حميد عن أنس ؓ قال: أولم رسول الله ﷺ حين بنى بزينب بنت جحش فأشبع الناس خبزا ولحما ثم خرج إلى حجر أمهات المؤمنين كما كان يصنع صبيحة بنائه فيسلم عليهن ويسلمن عليه ويدعو لهن ويدعون له فلما رجع إلى بيته رأى رجلين جرى بهما الحديث فلما رآهما رجع عن بيته فلما رأى

---

[112] This is something which was exclusive for the Prophet ﷺ, that if a believing woman said to him, "I grant myself to you," he could marry her by that statement without dowry. However, it has been narrated that the Prophet ﷺ did not marry any of the women who granted themselves to him as Ibn Hajar mentioned in *Fathul-Baaree* in the explanation of *hadeeth* (4788). The proof that this was exclusive for him is the statement of Allaah ﷻ:

وَٱمْرَأَةً مُّؤْمِنَةً إِن وَهَبَتْ نَفْسَهَا لِلنَّبِىِّ إِنْ أَرَادَ ٱلنَّبِىُّ أَن يَسْتَنكِحَهَا خَالِصَةً لَّكَ مِن دُونِ ٱلْمُؤْمِنِينَ

"And a believing woman if she grants herself to the Prophet and the Prophet wishes to marry her, a privilege for you only not for the rest of the believers…" (*Al-Ahzaab*: 50)

الرجلان نبي الله ﷺ رجع عن بيته وثبا مسرعين فما أدري أنا أخبرته بخروجهما أم أخبر فرجع حتى دخل البيت وأرخى الستر بيني وبينه وأنزلت آية الحجاب.

وقال ابن أبي مريم أخبرنا يحيى حدثني حميد سمع أنسا عن النبي ﷺ.

Anas ؓ said, "The Messenger of Allaah ﷺ held a wedding feast after he consummated the marriage of Zainab bint Jahsh. The people filled their appetites with bread and meat. He then went to the living quarters of the Mothers of the Believers as he usually does on the morning of his consummation night giving them salaams and supplicating for them, and they would return the salaams and supplicate for him. Then when he started to return to his house he saw two men having a conversation. When he saw them he turned back from going to his house. The two men, when they saw the Prophet of Allaah ﷺ turn back from going to his house, jumped up and left in a hurry. I do not recall whether I told him they had left or if someone else told him, causing he returned. Then when he entered the house he set the curtain, hanging it down between myself and him, and the verse of the veil was then sent down."

This *hadeeth* has been transmitted by Al-Bukhaaree in his *Saheeh* (4794) as well as Muslim in his *Saheeh* (1428/92). In another narration of this *hadeeth* in Al-Bukhaaree (4799), it reads, "Then Allaah sent down:

$$\text{يَٰٓأَيُّهَا ٱلَّذِينَ ءَامَنُوا۟ لَا تَدْخُلُوا۟ بُيُوتَ ٱلنَّبِىِّ}$$

"O you who believe, enter not the Prophet's houses…"

قال الإمام البخاري ؒ (146): حدثنا يحيى بن بكير قال حدثنا الليث قال حدثني عقيل عن ابن شهاب عن عروة عن عائشة ؓ أن أزواج النبي ﷺ كن يخرجن بالليل إذا تبرزن إلى المناصع وهو صعيد أفيح فكان عمر يقول للنبي ﷺ: احجب نساءك فلم يكن رسول الله ﷺ يفعل فخرجت سودة بنت زمعة زوج النبي ﷺ ليلة من الليالي عشاء وكانت امرأة طويلة فناداها عمر: ألا قد عرفناك يا سودة حرصا على أن ينزل الحجاب فأنزل الله آية الحجاب.

'Aishah ؓ narrated that the wives of the Prophet ﷺ used to go out at night, when they needed to relieve themselves, to Al-Manaasi' which was an open plateau. 'Umar used to say to the Prophet ﷺ, "Veil your wives." But the Messenger of Allaah would not do that. One night, Sawdah bint Zam'ah, the wife of the Prophet ﷺ went out. She was a tall woman so 'Umar called out to her, "Indeed we have recognized you, O Sawdah!" He did that hoping that the veil would be revealed. Then Allaah sent down the verse of the veil.

Al-Bukhaaree transmitted this *hadeeth* in his *Saheeh* (146) and likewise Muslim in his *Saheeh* (2170/18).

قال الإمام الطبراني ﵀ في المعجم الصغير ص (83-84): حدثنا إبراهيم بن بندار الأصبهاني حدثنا محمد بن أبي عمر العدني حدثنا سفيان بن عيينة عن مسعر عن موسى بن أبي كثير عن مجاهد عن عائشة ﵂ قالت: كنت آكل مع النبي ﷺ حيسا في قعب فمر عمر ﵁ فدعاه فأكل فأصابت أصبعه أصبعي فقال: حسِّ أوّه أوّه لو أُطاع فيكن ما رأتكن عين فنزلت آية الحجاب.

'Aishah ﵂ said, "I was eating with the Prophet ﷺ some *hais*[113] in a large bowl. 'Umar ﵁ then passed by, so he (the prophet) called him over. He ate (with us) then his finger touched my finger and he said, '*Hassi*[114] Owe, Owe. If my opinion concerning you (the wives of the Prophet ﷺ) were to be approved of, not a single eye would see you.' Then the verse of the veil descended."

This *hadeeth* has been transmitted by At-Tabaraanee in *Al-Mu'jam As-Sagheer*, pages 83-84, and An-Nasaa'ee in his *Tafseer* (439).

قال الإمام النسائي ﵀ في التفسير (441): أخبرنا عمرو بن علي حدثنا أبو قتيبة حدثنا عيسى ابن طهمان قال سمعت أنس بن مالك ﵁ يقول: (وَإِذَا سَأَلْتُمُوهُنَّ مَتَاعًا فَاسْأَلُوهُنَّ مِن وَرَاءِ حِجَابٍ) الآية نزلت في زينب بنت جحش.

Anas ibn Maalik ﵁ said:

وَإِذَا سَأَلْتُمُوهُنَّ مَتَاعًا فَاسْأَلُوهُنَّ مِن وَرَاءِ حِجَابٍ

"[The verse] 'And when you ask them for something, ask them from behind a veil,'
descended because of Zainab bint Jahsh."

An-Nasaa'ee transmitted this *hadeeth* in his *Tafseer* (441).

The way to harmonize these different narrations: Al-Haafidh Ibn Hajar said in *Fathul-Baaree* in the explanation of *hadeeth* (146), "The way to harmonize between them is to say that the reasons for the revelation of the veil were numerous and the story of Zainab was the last of them because her story was explicitly mentioned in the verse, and what is meant by the verse of the veil in some of the narrations is His ﷻ statement:

---

[113] *Hais* is a meal prepared from dates, cottage cheese, and butter. Flour or bread crumbs is sometimes used in place of the cottage cheese. Refer to *An-Nihaayah* by Ibn Al-Atheer, volume 1, page 467.
[114] *Hassi* is a word said when someone accidentally touches something that hurts or burns him. Refer to *An-Nihaayah* by Ibn Al-Atheer, volume 1, page 385.

$$\text{يُدْنِينَ عَلَيْهِنَّ مِن جَلَٰبِيبِهِنَّ}$$

'...draw their cloaks over their bodies." (*Al-Ahzaab*: 59)

Ash-Sheikh Muqbil ﷺ said, "I say, to say what is meant by the verse of the veil is His statement:

$$\text{يُدْنِينَ عَلَيْهِنَّ مِن جَلَٰبِيبِهِنَّ}$$

'...draw their cloaks over their bodies,'

is something which needs to be reconsidered because the narrations explicitly stated in the story of Zainab that His statement descended,

$$\text{يَٰٓأَيُّهَا ٱلَّذِينَ ءَامَنُوا۟ لَا تَدْخُلُوا۟ بُيُوتَ ٱلنَّبِيِّ}$$

"O you who believe, enter not the Prophet's houses…".

Also, it was explicitly stated in the story of 'Umar (with Sawdah) as mentioned in *At-Tabaree*, volume 20, page 315, 'Then Allaah sent down the verse of the veil. Allaah says:

$$\text{يَٰٓأَيُّهَا ٱلَّذِينَ ءَامَنُوا۟ لَا تَدْخُلُوا۟}$$

"O you who believe, enter not…" (verse: 53).

So the opinion that there was more than one reason is more befitting."

IMPORTANT NOTE: It could be understood from this *hadeeth* (the story of 'Umar and Sawdah) that the statement of 'Umar: "We have recognized you, O Sawdah," was before the veil; however, in some of the narrations it was stated that it was after the veil. The correct understanding of that is what Al-Haafidh said in *Fathul-Baaree*, volume 10, page 150 (explanation of *hadeeth* 4794), "Al-Karmaanee said, 'If you were to say, here it has occurred after the veil while it has preceded in the chapter of *Wudoo* that it was before the veil? The answer to that is perhaps it occurred twice.'

Al-Haafidh Ibn Hajar then said, "I say, nay. Rather what was meant by the first veil is something other than the second veil. In short, 'Umar had a dislike in his heart to strangers looking at the Prophet's wives to the point that he clearly stated to him ﷺ, 'Veil your wives,' and he emphasized that up until the verse of the veil descended. Then he aimed to have them not even show their figures even if they were completely veiled. He was excessive in that [request] and was not granted that. Therefore, it was permissible for them to go out for their needs while being free from unnecessary hardship and relieved of an unnecessary restriction."

سورة يس

Sooratu Yaa Seen

<u>His, the Exalted One's statement:</u>

وَنَكْتُبُ مَا قَدَّمُوا وَءَاثَرَهُمْ

"And We record what they have put forth and their traces…"(verse: 12)

قال الإمام أبو بكر البزار ﷺ كما في تفسير ابن كثير (ج 3 ص 566): حدثنا عباد بن زياد الساجي حدثنا عثمان بن عمر حدثنا شعبة عن الجريري عن أبي نضرة عن أبي سعيد الخدري ﷺ قال: إن بني سلمة شكوا إلى رسول الله ﷺ بعد منازلهم من المسجد فنزلت: (وَنَكْتُبُ مَا قَدَّمُوا وَءَاثَرَهُمْ) فأقاموا في مكانهم.

وحدثنا محمد بن المثنى حدثنا عبد الأعلى حدثنا الجريري سعيد بن إياس عن أبي نضرة عن أبي سعيد ﷺ عن النبي ﷺ بنحوه.

Abu Sa'eed Al-Khudree ؓ said, "The tribe Banee Salimah complained to the Messenger of Allaah ﷺ that their houses were far away from the *masjid*. Then this verse descended:

وَنَكْتُبُ مَا قَدَّمُوا وَءَاثَرَهُمْ

'And We record what they have put forth and their traces…', so they remained in their area."

Al-Bazzaar transmitted this *hadeeth* as mentioned in *Tafseer Ibn Katheer*, volume 3, page 566. Ibn Katheer commented, "It has some peculiarly about it due to the mention of the revelation of the verse, as the *Soorah* in its entirety is *Makkiyah* (verses that descended before the *hijrah*)." Ash-Sheikh Muqbil ؓ said, "[As for] The *hadeeth*, the people of its chain are people of the *Saheeh* (Al-Bukhaaree and/or Muslim) except for 'Abbaad ibn Ziyaad and there is some talk about his status, as mentioned in *Tahdheeb At-Tahdheeb*; however, he has been supported as you see…". "…The *hadeeth* also has a supporting *hadeeth* in (*Tafseer*) Ibn Jareer (volume 20, page 497) on Ibn 'Abbaas ؓ he said, 'The houses of the *Ansaar* were far away from the *masjid* so they wanted to move closer to the *masjid*. Then the following descended,

$$\text{وَنَكْتُبُ مَا قَدَّمُوا۟ وَءَاثَـٰرَهُمْ}$$

"And We record what they have put forth and their traces…"

So they said, "We will remain in our area."
Its chain is by way of Simaak on 'Ikrimah and the narrations of Simaak on 'Ikrimah are inconsistent; nonetheless, it is in a supporting role as you see. As for the statement of Al-Haafidh Ibn Katheer, "It has some peculiarity about it because the *Soorah* in its entirety is *Makkiyah*," the point from this is not clear to me because if it stands true that this verse was revealed in Makkah, there is nothing which prevents it from being revealed twice, and if it being revealed in Makkah does not stand true then a *Soorah* can be *Makkiyah* except for one verse as is well known, and Allaah knows best."

His, the Exalted One's statement:

$$\text{أَوَلَمْ يَرَ ٱلْإِنسَـٰنُ أَنَّا خَلَقْنَـٰهُ مِن نُّطْفَةٍ}$$

"Does man not see that We have created him from a semen drop…" (verses: 77-83)

قال الإمام ابن أبي حاتم ﷺ كما في تفسير ابن كثير (ج 3 ص 581): حدثنا علي بن الحسين ابن الجنيد حدثنا محمد بن العلاء حدثنا عثمان بن سعيد الزيات عن هشيم عن أبي بشر عن سعيد بن جبير عن ابن عباس ﷺ قال: إن العاص بن وائل أخذ عظما من البطحاء ففتّه بيده ثم قال لرسول الله ﷺ: أيحيي الله هذا بعدما أرم فقال رسول الله ﷺ: نعم يميتك الله ثم يحييك ثم يدخلك جهنم قال: نزلت الآيات من آخر يس.

Ibn 'Abbaas ﷺ said, "Al-'Aas ibn Waa'il took an old bone from the flatland and crumbled it up in his hand and said to the Messenger of Allaah ﷺ, 'Will Allaah bring this back to life after being rotted to dust!' The Messenger of Allaah ﷺ said, "Yes. Allaah causes you to die, then He brings you back to life, then He will put you in hell." He (Ibn 'Abbaas) said, '[Thereafter] The last verses of *Sooratu Yaa Seen* descended."

Ibn Abee Haatim transmitted this *hadeeth* as mentioned in *Tafseer Ibn Katheer*, volume 3, page 581, and Al-Haakim in *Al-Mustadrak*, volume 2, page 429, and he ruled it to be authentic according to the standards of the two Sheikhs (Al-Bukhaaree and/or Muslim) although they did not transmit it.

سورة الزمر

Sooratuz-Zumar

His, the Exalted One's statement:

ٱللَّهُ نَزَّلَ أَحْسَنَ ٱلْحَدِيثِ

"Allaah has sent down the best speech…" (verses: 23-25)

The reason for this verse's revelation has been mentioned in *Sooratu Yoosuf*, verse 3.

His, the Exalted One's statement:

قُلْ يَـٰعِبَادِىَ ٱلَّذِينَ أَسْرَفُوا۟ عَلَىٰٓ أَنفُسِهِمْ لَا تَقْنَطُوا۟ مِن رَّحْمَةِ ٱللَّهِ

"Say: O My servants who have transgressed against themselves, despair not of the mercy of Allaah…" (verse: 53)

قال الإمام البخاري رَحِمَهُ اللهُ (4810): حدثني إبراهيم بن موسى أخبرنا هشام بن يوسف أن ابن جريج أخبرهم قال إن يعلى قال أخبره سعيد بن جبير عن ابن عباس رَضِيَ اللهُ عَنْهُمَا أن ناسا من أهل الشرك كانوا قد قتلوا وأكثروا وزنوا وأكثروا فأتوا محمدا ﷺ فقالوا: إن الذي تقول وتدعوا إليه لحسن لو تخبرنا أن لما عملنا كفارة فنزل: (وَٱلَّذِينَ لَا يَدْعُونَ مَعَ ٱللَّهِ إِلَـٰهًا ءَاخَرَ وَلَا يَقْتُلُونَ ٱلنَّفْسَ ٱلَّتِى حَرَّمَ ٱللَّهُ إِلَّا بِٱلْحَقِّ وَلَا يَزْنُونَ) ونزل: (قُلْ يَـٰعِبَادِىَ ٱلَّذِينَ أَسْرَفُوا۟ عَلَىٰٓ أَنفُسِهِمْ لَا تَقْنَطُوا۟ مِن رَّحْمَةِ ٱللَّهِ).

Ibn 'Abbaas ؓ narrated that a group of polytheists who had committed a lot of murder and fornication went to Muhammad ﷺ and said, "Indeed what you say and call to is good, but if only you would inform us that there is an atonement for what we have done." Then this verse descended,

وَٱلَّذِينَ لَا يَدْعُونَ مَعَ ٱللَّهِ إِلَـٰهًا ءَاخَرَ وَلَا يَقْتُلُونَ ٱلنَّفْسَ ٱلَّتِى حَرَّمَ ٱللَّهُ إِلَّا بِٱلْحَقِّ وَلَا يَزْنُونَ

"And those who do not invoke any other deity along with Allaah, nor kill such a person that Allaah has forbidden except for just cause, nor commit illegal sexual intercourse…" (*Al-Furqaan*: 68)

As well as this verse,

$$\text{قُلْ يَٰعِبَادِىَ ٱلَّذِينَ أَسْرَفُوا۟ عَلَىٰٓ أَنفُسِهِمْ لَا تَقْنَطُوا۟ مِن رَّحْمَةِ ٱللَّهِ}$$

"Say: O my slaves who have transgressed against themselves, despair not of the mercy of Allaah…"

Al-Bukhaaree transmitted this *hadeeth* in his *Saheeh* (4810) and Muslim in his *Saheeh* (122).

قال الحاكم ﷺ في المستدرك (ج 2 ص 435): حدثني أبو إسحاق إبراهيم بن إسماعيل القارئ حدثنا عثمان بن سعيد الدارمي حدثنا الحسن بن الربيع حدثنا عبد الله بن إدريس حدثني محمد بن إسحاق قال وأخبرني نافع عن عبد الله بن عمر عن عمر ﷺ قال: كنا نقول ما لمفتتن توبة وما الله بقابل منه شيئا فلما قدم رسول الله ﷺ المدينة أنزل فيهم: (قُلْ يَٰعِبَادِىَ ٱلَّذِينَ أَسْرَفُوا۟ عَلَىٰٓ أَنفُسِهِمْ لَا تَقْنَطُوا۟ مِن رَّحْمَةِ ٱللَّهِ إِنَّ ٱللَّهَ يَغْفِرُ ٱلذُّنُوبَ جَمِيعًا إِنَّهُ هُوَ ٱلْغَفُورُ ٱلرَّحِيمُ) والآيات التي بعدها قال عمر: فكتبتها ﷺ بيدي في صحيفة وبعث بها إلى هشام بن العاص قال هشام ابن العاص: فلما أتتني جعلت أقرؤها بذي طوى أصعد بها فيه وأصوب ولا أفهمها حتى قلت: اللهم فهمنيها قال فألقى الله تعالى في قلبي أنها إنما أنزلت فينا وفيما كنا نقول في أنفسنا ويقال فينا قال: فرجعت إلى بعيري فجلست عليه فلحقت برسول الله ﷺ وهو بالمدينة.

هذا حديث صحيح على شرط مسلم ولم يخرجاه.

'Umar ﷺ said, "We used to say there is no repentance for a *muftatin*[116] and Allaah would not accept any deed from him. Then when the Messenger of Allaah ﷺ came to Madeenah, the following descended because of them:

$$\text{قُلْ يَٰعِبَادِىَ ٱلَّذِينَ أَسْرَفُوا۟ عَلَىٰٓ أَنفُسِهِمْ لَا تَقْنَطُوا۟ مِن رَّحْمَةِ ٱللَّهِ إِنَّ ٱللَّهَ يَغْفِرُ ٱلذُّنُوبَ جَمِيعًا إِنَّهُ هُوَ ٱلْغَفُورُ ٱلرَّحِيمُ}$$

'Say: O My servants who have transgressed against themselves, despair not of the mercy of Allaah, verily Allaah forgives all sins. Truly He is Oft-Forgiving Most Merciful,' along with the verses after it.

'Umar added, "I then wrote it down on a scroll with my own hand and sent it to Hishaam ibn Al-'Aas."

---

[115] قال الشيخ مقبل ﷺ: من هنا من السيرة بهذا السند في السياق في المستدرك غير مفهوم وقع فيه سقط وهو في مجمع الزوائد كما في السيرة.

[116] *Muftatin* here means a person who embraced Islaam in Makkah and then was tried and tortured because of his Islaam and then gave in and returned back to disbelief.

Hishaam ibn Al-'Aas said, "When it reached me I went to Dhee Tuwaa (a place at the entrance to Makkah). I climbed [to a spot] there with [the scroll in my hand] and tried to read it while glancing at it but I could not understand it until I said, 'O Allaah, make me understand it. Then Allaah ﷻ cast into my heart that it was sent down because of us and because of that which we used to say within ourselves and what was said about us. So I returned to my riding camel and mounted it, then I joined up with the Messenger of Allaah ﷺ in Madeenah."

This *hadeeth* has been transmitted by Al-Haakim in *Al-Mustadrak*, volume 2, page 435, and he classified it to be authentic commensurate with the standards of Muslim although they (Al-Bukhaaree and Muslim) did not transmit it. Al-Bazzaar also transmitted it as mentioned in *Kashf Al-Astaar*, volume 2, page 302, as well as Ibn Ishaaq as mentioned in *Seerah Ibn Hishaam*, volume 1, page 475. Most of the wording was taken from *Seerah Ibn Hishaam* because the wording of Al-Haakim was unclear.

<u>His, the Exalted One's statement:</u>

$$\text{وَمَا قَدَرُواْ ٱللَّهَ حَقَّ قَدْرِهِ}$$

"And they made not a just estimate of Allaah such that is due to Him..." (verse: 67)

قال الإمام أحمد رَحِمَهُ (ج 1 ص 378): حدثنا أبو معاوية حدثنا الأعمش عن إبراهيم عن علقمة عن عبد الله رَضِيَ قال: جاء رجل إلى النبي ﷺ من أهل الكتاب فقال يا أبا القاسم أبلغك أن الله عز وجل يحمل الخلائق على أصبع والسموات على أصبع والأرضين على أصبع والشجر على أصبع والثرى على أصبع فضحك النبي ﷺ حتى بدت نواجذه فأنزل الله عز وجل: (وَمَا قَدَرُواْ ٱللَّهَ حَقَّ قَدْرِهِ) الآية.

'Abdullaah ibn Mas'ood ﴿ said, "A man from the people of the book came to the Prophet ﷺ and said, 'O Abaa Al-Qaasim, has it reached you that Allaah ﷻ will hold the creatures on a finger, and the heavens on a finger, and the earths on a finger, and the trees on a finger, and the soil on a finger?' The Prophet ﷺ then laughed to the point where his back molar teeth appeared. Then Allaah ﷻ sent down:

$$\text{وَمَا قَدَرُواْ ٱللَّهَ حَقَّ قَدْرِهِ}$$

"And they made not a just estimate of Allaah such that is due to Him..." (verse:67).

This *hadeeth* has been transmitted by Al-Imaam Ahmad in his *Musnad*, volume 1, page 378. Ash-Sheikh Muqbil ﷺ said, ", the people of the *hadeeth*'s chain are people of the *Saheeh* (Al-Bukhaaree and/or Muslim)."

NOTE: Al-Haafidh As-Suyootee said in *Al-Itqaan*, volume 1, page 34, "The *hadeeth* is in the *Saheeh* (Al-Bukhaaree and Muslim) with the wording: "Then the Messenger of Allaah ﷺ recited…," and this is more befitting because the verse is *Makkiyah*." Ash-Sheikh Muqbil ﷺ said, "I say, the wording, 'he recited,' which is in the *Saheeh* does not contradict that it descended and thereafter the Messenger of Allaah ﷺ recited it. As for it being *Makkiyah*, if it stands true that this was revealed in Makkah, then there is nothing which prevents it from being revealed twice; and if it does not stand true through an authentic chain that it was revealed in Makkah, then a *Soorah* can be *Makkiyah* except for one verse, and Allaah knows best."

سورة فصلت

Sooratu Fussilat

His, the Exalted One's statement:

وَمَا كُنتُمْ تَسْتَتِرُونَ أَن يَشْهَدَ عَلَيْكُمْ سَمْعُكُمْ وَلَا أَبْصَارُكُمْ وَلَا جُلُودُكُمْ وَلَٰكِن ظَنَنتُمْ أَنَّ ٱللَّهَ لَا يَعْلَمُ كَثِيرًا مِّمَّا تَعْمَلُونَ ۝

"And you were not hiding yourselves out of fear that your ears and your eyes and your skins will testify against you, rather you thought that Allaah knew not much of what you were doing." (verse: 22)

قال الإمام البخاري ﵀ (4816): حدثنا الصلت بن محمد حدثنا يزيد بن زريع عن روح بن القاسم عن منصور عن مجاهد عن أبي معمر عن ابن مسعود ﵁: (وَمَا كُنتُمْ تَسْتَتِرُونَ أَن يَشْهَدَ عَلَيْكُمْ سَمْعُكُمْ) الآية كان رجلان من قريش وختن لهما من ثقيف أو رجلان من ثقيف وختن لهما من قريش في بيت فقال بعضهم لبعض: أترون أن الله يسمع حديثنا قال بعضهم: يسمع بعضه وقال بعضهم: لئن كان يسمع بعضه لقد يسمع كله فأنزلت: (وَمَا كُنتُمْ تَسْتَتِرُونَ أَن يَشْهَدَ عَلَيْكُمْ سَمْعُكُمْ وَلَا أَبْصَارُكُمْ) الآية.

'Abdullaah Ibn Mas'ood ﵁ narrated [about the verse],

وَمَا كُنتُمْ تَسْتَتِرُونَ أَن يَشْهَدَ عَلَيْكُمْ سَمْعُكُمْ

"And you were not hiding yourselves out of fear that your ears…will testify against you…" (verse: 22),

That there were two men from Quraish and a relative of theirs through marriage from Thaqeef, or two men from Thaqeef and a relative of theirs through marriage from Quraish in a house. They said to one another, "Do you think Allaah hears our conversation?" One of them said, "He hears some of it." Another one said, "If He is able to hear some of it He hears all of it." Then the verse descended,

وَمَا كُنتُمْ تَسْتَتِرُونَ أَن يَشْهَدَ عَلَيْكُمْ سَمْعُكُمْ وَلَا أَبْصَارُكُمْ

"And you were not hiding yourselves out of fear that your ears and your eyes…will testify against you…" (verse: 22).

Al-Bukhaaree transmitted this *hadeeth* in his *Saheeh* (4816) and Muslim in his *Saheeh* (2775).

سورة الـشورى

Sooratush-Shooraa

His, the Exalted One's statement:

$$\text{قُل لَّآ أَسْـَٔلُكُمْ عَلَيْهِ أَجْرًا إِلَّا ٱلْمَوَدَّةَ فِى ٱلْقُرْبَىٰ}$$

"Say: No reward do I ask of you for this except love for kinship…" (verse: 23)

قال الإمام أحمد ﷺ (ج 1 ص 229): حدثنا يحيى عن شعبة حدثني عبد الملك بن ميسرة عن طاووس قال أتى ابن عباس رجل فسأله ، وسليمان بن داود قال أخبرنا شعبة أنبأني عبد الملك قال سمعت طاووسا يقول: سأل رجل ابن عباس المعنى عن قول الله عز وجل: (قُل لَّآ أَسْـَٔلُكُمْ عَلَيْهِ أَجْرًا إِلَّا ٱلْمَوَدَّةَ فِى ٱلْقُرْبَىٰ) فقال سعيد بن جبير: قربى محمد ﷺ قال ابن عباس ﷺ: عجلت إن رسول الله ﷺ لم يكن بطن من قريش إلا لرسول الله ﷺ فيهم قرابة فنزلت: (قُل لَّآ أَسْـَٔلُكُمْ عَلَيْهِ أَجْرًا إِلَّا ٱلْمَوَدَّةَ فِى ٱلْقُرْبَىٰ) إلا أن تصلوا قرابة ما بيني وبينكم.

Taawoos said, "A man asked Ibn 'Abbaas ﷺ about the meaning of His ﷻ statement,

$$\text{قُل لَّآ أَسْـَٔلُكُمْ عَلَيْهِ أَجْرًا إِلَّا ٱلْمَوَدَّةَ فِى ٱلْقُرْبَىٰ}$$

'Say: No reward do I ask of you for this except love for kinship…',

So Sa'eed ibn Jubair said, "[What is meant is] the relatives of Muhammad ﷺ." Ibn 'Abbaas said, 'You were hasty! [As for]The Messenger of Allaah ﷺ, there was not a tribe of Quraish except that the Messenger of Allaah ﷺ had family ties with them, so the verse descended,

$$\text{قُل لَّآ أَسْـَٔلُكُمْ عَلَيْهِ أَجْرًا إِلَّا ٱلْمَوَدَّةَ فِى ٱلْقُرْبَىٰ}$$

"Say: No reward do I ask of you for this except love for kinship…"

(Meaning) Except that you keep the family ties between me and you."[117]

Al-Imaam Ahmad transmitted this *hadeeth* in his *Musnad*, volume 1, page 229, and it is in Al-Bukhaaree (3497) and (4818) without the wording: "so it descended."

His, the Exalted One's statement:

$$وَلَوْ بَسَطَ ٱللَّهُ ٱلرِّزْقَ لِعِبَادِهِۦ لَبَغَوْا۟ فِى ٱلْأَرْضِ وَلَـٰكِن يُنَزِّلُ بِقَدَرٍ مَّا يَشَآءُ$$

"And if Allaah were to extend the provision profusely to His slaves they would transgress in the land, but He sends down by measure what He wills…" (verse: 27)

قال الإمام ابن جرير ﷺ (ج 21 ص 535-536): حدثني يونس قال أخبرنا ابن وهب قال قال أبو هانئ سمعت عمرو بن حريث وغيره يقولون: إنما أنزلت هذه الآية في أصحاب الصفة: (وَلَوْ بَسَطَ ٱللَّهُ ٱلرِّزْقَ لِعِبَادِهِۦ لَبَغَوْا۟ فِى ٱلْأَرْضِ وَلَـٰكِن يُنَزِّلُ بِقَدَرٍ مَّا يَشَآءُ) ذلك بأنهم قالوا: لو أن لنا فتمنوا.

حدثنا محمد بن سنان القزاز قال حدثنا أبو عبد الرحمن المقرئ قال حدثنا حيوة قال أخبرني أبو هانئ أنه سمع عمرو بن حريث يقول: إنما أنزلت هذه الآية وذكره مثله.

Abu Haani' said, "I hear 'Amr ibn Huraith and others say, 'This verse was sent down only because of the people of *As-Suffah* (the area of the Prophet's *masjid* where the poor would sleep),

$$وَلَوْ بَسَطَ ٱللَّهُ ٱلرِّزْقَ لِعِبَادِهِۦ لَبَغَوْا۟ فِى ٱلْأَرْضِ وَلَـٰكِن يُنَزِّلُ بِقَدَرٍ مَّا يَشَآءُ$$

"And if Allaah were to extend the provision profusely to His slaves they would transgress in the land, but He sends down by measure what He wills…". That was because they had said, "If we only had it…" so they wished [for extended provision]."

---

[117] Ibn Hajar said in *Fathul-Baaree* in the explanation of *hadeeth* (4818), "In short, Sa'eed ibn Jubair and those who agreed with him like 'Ali ibn Al-Husain and As-Suddee and 'Amr ibn Shu'aib as At-Tabaree transmitted on them took the verse to mean that the people being addressed were ordered to love the relatives of the Prophet ﷺ while Ibn 'Abbaas took it to mean that they were ordered to love the Prophet ﷺ because of the family ties between him and them. On the first opinion the address is general for all people held accountable for their actions while on the second opinion the address is specifically for Quraish. This opinion is supported by the fact that the *Soorah* is *Makkiyah* (that which descended before the *hijrah*)."

This *hadeeth* has been transmitted by Ibn Jareer transmitted in his *Tafseer*, volume 21, pages 535-536. And Al-Haakim transmitted a similar *hadeeth* on 'Ali ibn Abee Taalib in *Al-Mustadrak*, volume 2, page 445, and classified its chain to be authentic; and Adh-Dhahabee pointed out that it is on par with the standards of the two Sheikhs (Al-Bukhaaree and Muslim).

NOTE: There is a difference of opinion about whether or not 'Amr ibn Huraith is a *Sahaabee* as mentioned in *Al-Isaabah*.[118]

---

[118] Abu Khaithamah and after him Abu Ya'laa took the position that he is a *Sahaabee*. Al-Bukhaaree, Abu Haatim, Yahyaa ibn Ma'een, Ya'qoob Al-Fasawee and others took the position that he is not a *Sahaabee*. NOTE: There is another 'Amr ibn Huraith who is a *Sahaabee* known as 'Amr ibn Huraith Al-Makhzoomee who is different from 'Amr ibn Huraith the narrator of this *hadeeth*.

سورة الزخرف

Sooratuz-Zukhruf

His, the Exalted One's statement:

$$\text{وَلَمَّا ضُرِبَ ابْنُ مَرْيَمَ مَثَلاً إِذَا قَوْمُكَ مِنْهُ يَصِدُّونَ}$$

"And when the son of Maryam is quoted as an example, behold, your people cry aloud." (verse: 57)

قال الإمام أحمد ﷺ (ج 1 ص 317): ثنا هاشم بن القاسم ثنا شيبان عن عاصم عن أبي رزين عن أبي يحيى مولى ابن عقيل الأنصاري قال: قال ابن عباس ﷺ: لقد علمت آية من القرآن ما سألني عنها رجل قط فما أدري أعلمها الناس فلم يسألوا عنها أم لم يفطنوا لها فيسألوا عنها ثم طفق يحدثنا فلما قام تلاومنا أن لا نكون سألناه عنها فقلت: أنا له إذا راح غدا فلما راح الغد قلت: يابن عباس ذكرت أمس أن آية من القرآن لم يسألك عنها رجل قط فلا تدري أعلمها الناس فلم يسألوا عنها أم لم يفطنوا لها فقلت: أخبرني عنها وعن اللاتي قرأت قبلها قال: نعم إن رسول الله ﷺ قال لقريش: يا معشر قريش إنه ليس أحد يعبد من دون الله فيه خير وقد علمت قريش أن النصارى تعبد عيسى بن مريم وما تقول في محمد ﷺ فقالوا: يا محمد ألست تزعم أن عيسى كان نبيا وعبدا من عباد الله صالحا فلئن كنت صادقا فإن آلهتهم كما تقول قال: فأنزل الله عز وجل: (وَلَمَّا ضُرِبَ ابْنُ مَرْيَمَ مَثَلاً إِذَا قَوْمُكَ مِنْهُ يَصِدُّونَ) قال قلت: ما يصدون قال: يضجون (وَإِنَّهُ لَعِلْمٌ لِلسَّاعَةِ) قال: هو خروج عيسى بن مريم عليه السلام قبل يوم القيامة.

Abu Yahyaa Mawlaa ibn 'Aqeel Al-Ansaaree said, "Ibn 'Abbaas ﷺ stated, 'Indeed I know of a verse in the Qur'aan that no man has ever asked me about, and I do not know whether that was because people understand it or if they failed to take notice to ask about it." He then began to narrate to us. When he got up and left we blamed ourselves for not asking him about that so I said, 'I will do that [ask him] when he comes tomorrow.' When he came the next day I said, "O Ibn 'Abbaas, you mentioned yesterday that there is a verse in the Qur'aan that no man has ever asked you about and you do not know whether that is because the people understand it or if they fail to take notice of it. Inform me about it and those verses that you read before it." He said, 'Yes, the Messenger of Allaah ﷺ said to Quraish, "O Community of Quraish, verily there is no one worshipped besides Allaah who has good in him." Quraish knew that the Christians worship 'Eesaa the son of Mary and they knew what Muhammad was saying so they said, 'O Muhammad, do you not

---

[119] في مجمع الزوائد: (وما يقول محمد).

claim that 'Eesaa was a Prophet and a righteous servant from the servants of Allaah? If you are truthful in what you say then their deities are as you say.' Then Allaah ﷻ sent down this verse,

$$\text{وَلَمَّا ضُرِبَ ٱبْنُ مَرْيَمَ مَثَلًا إِذَا قَوْمُكَ مِنْهُ يَصِدُّونَ}$$

"And when the son of Maryam is quoted as an example, behold, your people cry aloud."

I said, 'What does يصدون mean?' He said, "They went into an uproar."

$$\text{وَإِنَّهُ لَعِلْمٌ لِّلسَّاعَةِ}$$

'And verily he is a sign of the hour…?'

He said, "This is dealing with the coming of 'Eesaa the son of Mary, peace be upon him, before the day of resurrection."

This *hadeeth* has been transmitted by Al-Imaam Ahmad in his *Musnad*, volume 1, page 317, and it has already been mentioned in *Sooratul-Anbiyaa* that it has other chains that strengthen it.

سورة الدخان

Sooratud-Dukhaan

His, the Exalted One's statement:

$$\text{فَٱرْتَقِبْ يَوْمَ تَأْتِى ٱلسَّمَآءُ بِدُخَانٍ مُّبِينٍ}$$

"Then wait for the day when the sky will bring forth a visible smoke."

Up to His statement:

$$\text{إِنَّا كَاشِفُوا ٱلْعَذَابِ قَلِيلاً إِنَّكُمْ عَآئِدُونَ}$$

"Verily We shall remove the torment for a while. Indeed you will revert." (verses:10-15)

قال الإمام البخاري رحمه الله (4821): حدثنا يحيى حدثنا أبو معاوية عن الأعمش عن مسلم عن مسروق قال قال عبد الله ﷺ: إنما كان هذا لأن قريشا لما استعصوا على النبي ﷺ دعا عليهم بسنين كسني يوسف فأصابهم قحط وجهد حتى أكلوا العظام فجعل الرجل ينظر إلى السماء فيرى ما بينه وبينها كهيئة الدخان من الجهد فأنزل الله تعالى: (فَٱرْتَقِبْ يَوْمَ تَأْتِى ٱلسَّمَآءُ بِدُخَانٍ مُّبِينٍ ۝ يَغْشَى ٱلنَّاسَ هَـٰذَا عَذَابٌ أَلِيمٌ ۝) قال: فأتى رسول الله ﷺ فقيل: يا رسول الله استسق لمضر فإنها قد هلكت قال: لمضر إنك لجريء فاستسقى فسقوا فنزلت: (إِنَّكُمْ عَآئِدُونَ) فلما أصابتهم الرفاهية عادوا إلى حالهم حين أصابتهم الرفاهية فأنزل الله عز وجل: (يَوْمَ نَبْطِشُ ٱلْبَطْشَةَ ٱلْكُبْرَىٰ إِنَّا مُنتَقِمُونَ) قال: يعني يوم بدر.

'Abdullaah ibn Mas'ood ﷺ said, "This only occurred because of Quraish; when they opposed the Prophet ﷺ he supplicated against them [asking] that years of drought, like the drought of Yoosuf befall them. They were then inflicted with drought and hard times to the point that they began eating bones. A man would look to the sky and see between him and it what appeared to be smoke from extreme exhaustion. Then Allaah ﷻ sent down the following:

$$\text{فَٱرْتَقِبْ يَوْمَ تَأْتِى ٱلسَّمَآءُ بِدُخَانٍ مُّبِينٍ ۝ يَغْشَى ٱلنَّاسَ هَـٰذَا عَذَابٌ أَلِيمٌ ۝}$$

'Then wait for the day when the sky will bring forth a visible smoke, covering the people; this is a painful torment.'

Someone then went to the Messenger of Allaah ﷺ saying to him, "O Messenger of Allaah, invoke Allaah for rain for the tribe Mudar for verily they have been ruined." He said, 'For Mudar? Indeed you are bold.' He then prayed for rain and rain fell upon them. Then the verse descended:

$$إِنَّكُمْ عَآئِدُونَ$$

"Indeed you will revert."

Then when easy times came to them they returned to their old ways. Then Allaah ﷻ sent down:

$$يَوْمَ نَبْطِشُ ٱلْبَطْشَةَ ٱلْكُبْرَىٰ إِنَّا مُنتَقِمُونَ$$

"On the day when We will seize with the greatest grasp, verily We will exact retribution."
Meaning the day of Badr."

Al-Bukhaaree transmitted this *hadeeth* in his *Saheeh* (4821) and Muslim in his *Saheeh* (2798).

سورة الجاثية

Sooratul-Jaathiyah

His, the Exalted One's statement:

وَقَالُوا۟ مَا هِىَ إِلَّا حَيَاتُنَا ٱلدُّنْيَا نَمُوتُ وَنَحْيَا وَمَا يُهْلِكُنَآ إِلَّا ٱلدَّهْرُ ۚ وَمَا لَهُم بِذَٰلِكَ مِنْ عِلْمٍ ۖ إِنْ هُمْ إِلَّا يَظُنُّونَ ۝

"And they say: "There is nothing but our life of this world, we die and we live and nothing destroys us except time." And they have no knowledge of that, they only conjecture." (verse: 24)

قال الإمام ابن جرير رحمه الله (ج 22 ص 79): حدثنا أبو كريب قال ثنا ابن عيينة عن الزهري عن سعيد بن المسيب عن أبي هريرة رضي الله عنه عن النبي ﷺ كان أهل الجاهلية يقولون: إنما يهلكنا الليل والنهار وهو الذي يهلكنا ويميتنا ويحيينا فقال الله في كتابه: (وَقَالُوا۟ مَا هِىَ إِلَّا حَيَاتُنَا ٱلدُّنْيَا نَمُوتُ وَنَحْيَا وَمَا يُهْلِكُنَآ إِلَّا ٱلدَّهْرُ) قال: فيسبون الدهر فقال الله تبارك وتعالى: يؤذيني ابن آدم يسب الدهر وأنا الدهر بيدي الأمر أقلب الليل والنهار.

حدثنا عمران بن بكار الكلاعي قال ثنا أبو روح قال ثنا سفيان بن عيينة عن الزهري عن سعيد بن المسيب عن أبي هريرة عن النبي ﷺ نحوه.

Abu Hurairah ؓ narrated on the Prophet ﷺ, "The people of *Jaahiliyah* used to say, 'We are only destroyed by the passing of the night and the day, that is what destroys us, causes us to die, and gives us life." So Allaah said in His book,

وَقَالُوا۟ مَا هِىَ إِلَّا حَيَاتُنَا ٱلدُّنْيَا نَمُوتُ وَنَحْيَا وَمَا يُهْلِكُنَآ إِلَّا ٱلدَّهْرُ

"And they say: "There is nothing but our life of this world, we die and we live and nothing destroys us except time."

So they revile the time, so Allaah ﷻ said (the English meaning is): 'The son of Aadam annoys Me,[120] for he reviles the time and I am the time.[121] In My hand is the command. I alternate the night and the day."

---

[120] Ash-Sheikh Ibnul-'Uthaimeen رحمه الله said as is mentioned in *Majmoo' Fataawaa wa Rasaa'il Ash-Sheikh Ibnil-'Uthaimeen*, volume 1, pages 163-164, "...meaning that He ﷻ gets annoyed at what was mentioned in the *hadeeth*, however, the annoyance that

249

Ibn Jareer transmitted this *hadeeth* in his *tafseer*, volume 22, page 79. Ash-Sheikh Muqbil ﷻ said after mentioning Ibn Katheer's statement that its wording is extremely odd, "And I do not know the basis for its wording being odd. As for the chain, its people are people of the *Saheeh* (Al-Bukhaaree and/or Muslim) and Al-Haafidh mentioned it in *Fathul-Baaree*, volume 10, page 195, and he was quiet about it."[122]

Allaah affirmed to Himself is not like the annoyance of the creation. The proof being His ﷻ statement:

$$\text{لَيْسَ كَمِثْلِهِ شَيْءٌ وَهُوَ ٱلسَّمِيعُ ٱلْبَصِيرُ}$$

"There is nothing like Him and He is the All-Hearer the All-Seer." (*Ash-Shooraa*: 11)
He mentioned the negation of similarity before affirmation in order for the affirmation (of attributes) to be received by a heart free from the delusion of similarity and therefore the affirmation will be in a manner befitting to Him ﷻ."

[121] Ash-Sheikh Ibnul-'Uthaimeen ﷻ said in *Al-Qawaa'id Al-Muthlaa*, pages 11-12, "THE SECOND PRINCIPLE: The names of Allaah are names and attributes. Names with regard to how they refer to the being and attributes with regard to how they have different meanings. They are similar in the first regard because they refer to one being, Allaah ﷻ. In the second regard they are different because each one refers to its specific meaning. For example: The Ever-Living, The All-Knowing, The All-Powerful, The All-Hearer, The All-Seer, The Most Beneficent, The Most Merciful, The All-Mighty, The All-Wise, they are all names for one being, Allaah ﷻ, however, the meaning of the Ever-Living is different from the meaning of the All-Knowing, and the meaning of the All-Knowing is different from the meaning of the All-Powerful and so on. We only said that they are names and attributes because the Qur'aan points to that as is in His ﷻ statement:

$$\text{وَهُوَ ٱلْغَفُورُ ٱلرَّحِيمُ}$$

"…and He is the Oft-Forgiving, the Most Merciful." (*Al-Ahqaaf*: 8)
And His statement:

$$\text{وَرَبُّكَ ٱلْغَفُورُ ذُو ٱلرَّحْمَةِ}$$

"…and your Lord is the Oft-Forgiving, the Possessor of Mercy." (*Al-Kahf*:58)
For verily the second verse demonstrates that the Most Merciful is the one who possesses the attribute of mercy… and from this it is also known that الدهر (the time) is not from the names of Allaah ﷻ because it is a *jaamid* noun (meaning it does not refer to an attribute and a being described with that attribute, rather it only refers to a name of something) it does not contain a meaning that enters it among the beautiful names (of Allaah) because it is just a name for time… so the meaning of His statement, "I am the time," is what He explained with His statement, "In My hand is the command. I alternate the night and the day." So He ﷻ is the Creator of the time and that which is in it. Also, He has made it clear that He alternates the night and the day, and they (the night and the day) are the time, and it is not possible that the one who alternates is that which is alternated. So with this it has become clear that it is not possible that what is meant by الدهر (the time) in this *hadeeth* is Allaah ﷻ."

[122] It seems that the oddity is in the first part of the *hadeeth* where it is as if the Prophet ﷺ said, "The people of *Jaahiliyah* used to say…" Allaah guided the *Sahaabah* from

سورة الفتح

Sooratul-Fath

قال الإمام البخاري رَحِمَهُ اللهُ (4844): حدثنا أحمد بن إسحاق السلمي يعلى حدثنا عبد العزيز ابن سياه عن حبيب بن أبي ثابت قال أتيت أبا وائل أسأله فقال: كنا بصفين فقال رجل: ألم تر إلى الذين يدعون إلى كتاب الله فقال علي: نعم فقال سهل بن حنيف ﷺ: اتهموا أنفسكم فلقد رأيتنا يوم الحديبية يعني الصلح الذي كان بين النبي ﷺ والمشركين ولو نرى قتالا لقاتلنا فجاء عمر فقال: ألسنا على الحق وهم على الباطل أليس قتلانا في الجنة وقتلاهم في النار قال: بلى قال: ففيم نعطي الدنية في ديننا ونرجع ولما يحكم الله بيننا فقال: يابن الخطاب إني رسول الله ولن يضيعني الله أبدا فرجع متغيظا فلم يصبر حتى جاء أبا بكر فقال: يا أبا بكر ألسنا على الحق وهم على الباطل قال: يابن الخطاب إنه رسول الله ﷺ ولن يضيعه الله أبدا فنزلت سورة الفتح.

Habeeb ibn Abee Thaabit said, "I went to Abu Waa'il to ask him [something] so he said, 'We were at Siffeen. A man (from Mu'aawiyah's side) said, "Have you not seen those who are being called to the book of Allaah?" So 'Ali said, 'Yes.' Sahl ibn Hunaif ﷺ then said, "Check yourselves (your opinions) for verily I saw us on the day of Al-Hudaibiyah," meaning the treaty that took place between the Prophet ﷺ and the polytheists, "if we would have had our opinion about fighting we would have fought. 'Umar came and said, 'Are we not on the truth and they are on falsehood? Are not our casualties in paradise and their casualties in the fire?' He (the Prophet ﷺ) said, "Certainly." He ('Umar) then said, 'For what reason do we offer weakness in our religion and we return while Allaah has yet judged between us?' He said, "O son of Al-Khattaab, verily I am the Messenger of Allaah and Allaah will never leave me to loss." He ('Umar) then turned back frustrated. His patience ran out so he went to Abu Bakr and said, 'O Abaa Bakr, are we not on the truth and they are on falsehood?' He said, "O son of Al-Khattaab, verily he is the Messenger of Allaah ﷺ and Allaah will never leave him to loss." Then *Sooratul-Fath* descended."

Al-Bukhaaree transmitted this *hadeeth* it in his *Saheeh* (4844) and Muslim in his *Saheeh* (1785/94).

---

the ignorance of *Jaahiliyah*. They used to live in *Jaahiliyah* so it seems odd that the Prophet ﷺ would speak to them as if they did not know what the people of *Jaahiliyah* used to say. In other narrations of this *hadeeth* it was clarified that the first portion of this *hadeeth* is not from the statement of the Prophet ﷺ, rather, it is the statement of Sufyaan ibn 'Uyainah, one of the narrators in the chain, and the *hadeeth* on the Prophet ﷺ starts with the statement: "Allaah ﷻ said (the English meaning is), "The son of Aadam annoys Me…" This clarification can be found in *Al-Ihsaan* (5715), and *Al-Mustadrak*, volume 2, page 453, and in *As-Sunan Al-Kubraa* by Al-Baihaqee, volume 3, page 365, and Allaah knows best.

قال الإمام ابن جرير رَحِمَهُ اللهُ (ج 22 ص 202): حدثني موسى بن سهل الرملي ثنا محمد بن عيسى قال ثنا مجمع بن يعقوب الأنصاري قال سمعت أبي يحدث عن عمه عبد الرحمن بن يزيد عن عمه مُجمِّع بن جارية الأنصاري رَضِيَ اللهُ عَنْهُ وكان أحد القراء الذين قرءوا القرآن قال: شهدنا الحديبية مع رسول الله ﷺ فلما انصرفنا عنها إذا الناس يهزون الأباعر فقال بعض الناس لبعض: ما للناس قالوا: أوحي إلى رسول الله ﷺ: (إِنَّا فَتَحْنَا لَكَ فَتْحًا مُبِينًا ۝ لِيَغْفِرَ لَكَ ٱللَّهُ) فقال رجل: أو فتح هو يا رسول الله قال: نعم والذي نفسي بيده إنه لفتح قال: فقسمت خيبر على أهل الحديبية لم يدخل معهم فيها أحد إلا من شهد الحديبية وكان الجيش ألفا وخمس مئة فيهم ثلاث مئة فارس فقسمها رسول الله ﷺ على ثمانية عشر سهما فأعطى الفارس سهمين وأعطى الراجل سهما.

Mujammi' ibn Jaariyah Al-Ansaaree ؓ said, "We were present with the Messenger of Allaah ﷺ at Al-Hudaibiyah. When we departed from there the people suddenly started to jolt their riding camels back and forth; so some of the people said to [the] others, 'What's up with the people?' They said, "[The following] has been revealed to the Messenger of Allaah ﷺ:

$$إِنَّا فَتَحْنَا لَكَ فَتْحًا مُبِينًا ۝ لِيَغْفِرَ لَكَ ٱللَّهُ$$

'Verily We have given you a manifest victory. That Allaah may forgive you your sins…'

A man then said, "Is it a victory, O Messenger of Allaah?" He said, 'Yes, by the one who my soul is in His hand, it is a victory.' The war booty from the battle of Khaibar was then distributed to the people who were at Al-Hudaibiyah. No one was given a share except those who participated in Al-Hudaibiyah. The army numbered one thousand five hundred [people] and amongst them were three hundred horsemen. The Messenger of Allaah ﷺ divided the war booty that was to be distributed into eighteen portions. The horseman was given two portions and the foot soldier was given one portion."

This *hadeeth* has been transmitted by Ibn Jareer in his *Tafseer*, volume 22, page 202.

His, the Exalted One's statement:

$$وَهُوَ ٱلَّذِى كَفَّ أَيْدِيَهُمْ عَنكُمْ وَأَيْدِيَكُمْ عَنْهُم بِبَطْنِ مَكَّةَ$$

"And He is the one who restrained their hands from you, and your hands from them in the midst of Makkah…" (verse: 24)

قال الإمام البخاري رَحِمَهُ اللهُ (2731) (2732): حدثني عبد الله بن محمد حدثنا عبد الرزاق أخبرنا معمر قال أخبرني الزهري قال أخبرني عروة بن الزبير عن المسور بن مخرمة ؓ ومروان يصدق كل واحد

منهما حديث صاحبه قالا: خرج رسول الله ﷺ زمن الحديبية حتى كانوا ببعض الطريق قال النبي ﷺ: إن خالد بن الوليد بالغميم في خيل لقريش طليعة فخذوا ذات اليمين فوالله ما شعر بهم خالد حتى إذا هم بقترة الجيش فانطلق يركض نذيرا لقريش وسار النبي ﷺ حتى إذا كان بالثنية التي يهبط عليهم منها بركت به راحلته فقال الناس: حل حل فألحت فقالوا: خلأت القصواء خلأت القصواء فقال النبي ﷺ: ما خلأت القصواء وما ذاك لها بخلق ولكن حبسها حابس الفيل ثم قال: والذي نفسي بيده لا يسألونني خطة يعظمون فيها حرمات الله إلا أعطيتهم إياها ثم زجرها فوثبت قال: فعدل عنهم حتى نزل بأقصى الحديبية على ثَمَد قليل الماء يتبرضه الناس تبرضا فلم يلبّثه الناس حتى نزحوه وشكي إلى رسول الله ﷺ العطش فانتزع سهما من كنانته ثم أمرهم أن يجعلوه فيه فوالله ما زال يجيش لهم بالري حتى صدروا عنه فبينما هم كذلك إذ جاء بديل بن ورقاء الخزاعي في نفر من قومه من خزاعة وكانوا عيبة نصح رسول الله ﷺ من أهل تهامة فقال: إني تركت كعب بن لؤي وعامر بن لؤي نزلوا أعداد مياه الحديبية ومعهم العوذ المطافيل وهم مقاتلوك وصادوك عن البيت فقال رسول الله ﷺ: إنا لم نجئ لقتال أحد ولكنا جئنا معتمرين وإن قريشا قد نهكتهم الحرب وأضرت بهم فإن شاءوا ماددتهم مدة ويخلوا بيني وبين الناس فإن أظهر فإن شاءوا أن يدخلوا فيما دخل فيه الناس فعلوا وإلا فقد جمّوا وإن هم أبوا فوالذي نفسي بيده لأقاتلنهم على أمري هذا حتى تتفرد سالفتي ولينفذن الله أمره فقال بديل: سأبلغهم ما تقول قال: فانطلق حتى أتى قريشا قال: إنا قد جئناكم من هذا الرجل وسمعناه يقول قولا فإن شئتم أن نعرضه عليكم فعلنا فقال سفهاؤهم: لا حاجة لنا أن تخبرنا عنه بشيء وقال ذوو الرأي منهم: هات ما سمعته يقول قال: سمعته يقول كذا وكذا فحدثهم بما قال النبي ﷺ فقام عروة بن مسعود فقال: أي قوم ألستم بالوالد قالوا: بلى قال: أو لست بالولد قالوا: بلى قال: فهل تتهمونني قالوا: لا قال: ألستم تعلمون أني استنفرت أهل عكاظ فلما بلحوا علي جئتكم بأهلي وولدي ومن أطاعني قالوا: بلى قال: فإن هذا قد عرض لكم خطة رشد اقبلوها ودعوني آتيه قالوا: ائته فأتاه فجعل يكلم النبي ﷺ فقال النبي ﷺ نحوا من قوله لبديل فقال عروة عند ذلك: أي محمد أرأيت إن استأصلت أمر قومك هل سمعت بأحد من العرب اجتاح أهله قبلك وإن تكن الأخرى فإني والله لأرى وجوها وإني لأرى أشوابا من الناس خليقا أن يفروا ويدعوك فقال له أبو بكر: امصص ببظر اللات أنحن نفر عنه وندعه فقال: من ذا قالوا: أبو بكر قال: أما والذي نفسي بيده لولا يد كانت لك عندي لم أجزك بها لأجبتك قال: وجعل يكلم النبي ﷺ فكلما تكلم أخذ بلحيته والمغيرة بن شعبة قائم على رأس النبي ﷺ ومعه السيف وعليه المغفر فكلما أهوى عروة بيده إلى لحية النبي ﷺ ضرب يده بنعل السيف وقال له: أخر يدك عن لحية

رسول الله ﷺ فرفع عروة رأسه فقال: من هذا قالوا: المغيرة بن شعبة فقال: أي غدر ألست أسعى في غدرتك وكان المغيرة صحب قوما في الجاهلية فقتلهم وأخذ أموالهم ثم جاء فأسلم فقال النبي ﷺ: أما الإسلام فأقبل وأما المال فلست منه في شيء ثم إن عروة جعل يرمق أصحاب النبي ﷺ بعينيه قال: فوالله ما تنخم رسول الله ﷺ نخامة إلا وقعت في كف رجل منهم فدلك بها وجهه وجلده وإذا أمرهم ابتدروا أمره وإذا توضأ كادوا يقتتلون على وضوئه وإذا تكلم خفضوا أصواتهم عنده وما يحدون إليه

النظر تعظيما له فرجع عروة إلى أصحابه فقال: أي قوم والله لقد وفدت على الملوك ووفدت على قيصر وكسرى والنجاشي والله إن رأيت ملكا قط يعظمه أصحابه ما يعظم أصحاب محمد ﷺ محمدا والله إن تتخم نخامة إلا وقعت في كف رجل منهم فدلك بها وجهه وجلده وإذا أمرهم ابتدروا أمره وإذا توضأ كادوا يقتتلون على وضوئه وإذا تكلم خفضوا أصواتهم عنده وما يحدون إليه النظر تعظيما له وإنه قد عرض عليكم خطة رشد فاقبلوها فقال رجل من بني كنانة: دعوني آتيه فقالوا: ائته فلما أشرف على النبي ﷺ وأصحابه قال رسول الله ﷺ: هذا فلان وهو من قوم يعظمون البدن فابعثوها له فبعثت له واستقبله الناس يلبون فلما رأى ذلك قال: سبحان الله ما ينبغي لهؤلاء أن يصدوا عن البيت فلما رجع إلى أصحابه قال: رأيت البدن قد قلدت وأشعرت فما أرى أن يصدوا عن البيت فقام رجل منهم يقال له مكرز بن حفص فقال: دعوني آتيه فقالوا: ائته فلما أشرف عليهم قال النبي ﷺ: هذا مكرز وهو رجل فاجر فجعل يكلم النبي ﷺ فبينما هو يكلمه إذ جاء سهيل بن عمرو قال معمر فأخبرني أيوب عن عكرمة أنه لما جاء سهيل بن عمرو قال النبي ﷺ: لقد سهل لكم من أمركم قال معمر قال الزهري في حديثه: فجاء سهيل ابن عمرو فقال: هات اكتب بيننا وبينكم كتابا فدعا النبي ﷺ الكاتب فقال النبي ﷺ: بسم الله الرحمن الرحيم قال سهيل: أما الرحمن فوالله ما أدري ما هو ولكن اكتب باسمك اللهم كما كنت تكتب فقال المسلمون: والله لا نكتبها إلا بسم الله الرحمن الرحيم فقال النبي ﷺ: اكتب باسمك اللهم ثم قال: هذا ما قاضى عليه محمد رسول الله فقال سهيل: والله لو كنا نعلم أنك رسول الله ما صددناك عن البيت ولا قاتلناك ولكن اكتب محمد بن عبد الله فقال النبي ﷺ: والله إني لرسول الله وإن كذبتموني اكتب محمد بن عبد الله قال الزهري: وذلك لقوله: لا يسألونني خطة يعظمون فيها حرمات الله إلا أعطيتهم إياها فقال له النبي ﷺ: على أن تخلوا بيننا وبين البيت فنطوف به فقال سهيل: والله لا تتحدث العرب أنا أخذنا ضغطة ولكن ذلك من العام المقبل فكتب فقال سهيل: وعلى أنه لا يأتيك منا رجل وإن كان على دينك إلا رددته إلينا قال المسلمون: سبحان الله كيف يرد إلى المشركين وقد جاء مسلما فبينما هم كذلك إذ دخل أبو جندل بن سهيل بن عمرو يرسف في قيوده وقد خرج من أسفل مكة حتى رمى بنفسه بين أظهر المسلمين فقال سهيل: هذا يا محمد أول ما أقاضيك عليه أن ترده إلي فقال النبي ﷺ: إنا لم ننقض الكتاب بعد قال: فوالله إذا لم أصالحك على شيء أبدا قال النبي ﷺ: فأجزه لي قال: ما أنا بمجيزه لك قال: بلى فافعل قال: ما أنا بفاعل قال مكرز: بل قد أجزناه لك قال أبو جندل: أي معشر المسلمين أرد إلى المشركين وقد جئت مسلما ألا ترون ما قد لقيت وكان قد عذب عذابا شديدا في الله قال فقال عمر بن الخطاب: فأتيت نبي الله ﷺ فقلت: ألست نبي الله حقا قال: بلى قلت: ألسنا على الحق وعدونا على الباطل قال: بلى فلم نعطي الدنية في ديننا إذا قال: إني رسول الله ولست أعصيه وهو ناصري قلت: أو ليس كنت تحدثنا أنا سنأتي البيت فنطوف به قال: بلى فأخبرتك أنا نأتيه العام قال قلت: لا قال: فإنك آتيه ومطوف به قال: فأتيت أبا بكر فقلت: يا أبا بكر أليس هذا نبي الله حقا قال: بلى قلت: ألسنا على الحق وعدونا على الباطل قال: بلى قلت: فلم نعطي الدنية في ديننا إذا قال: أيها الرجل إنه لرسول الله ﷺ وليس يعصي ربه وهو ناصره فاستمسك بغرزه فوالله إنه على الحق قلت: أليس كان يحدثنا أنا سنأتي البيت

ونطوف به قال: بلى أفأخبرك أنك تأتيه العام قلت: لا قال: فإنك آتيه ومطوف به قال الزهري قال عمر: فعملت لذلك أعمالا قال: فلما فرغ من قضية الكتاب قال رسول الله ﷺ لأصحابه: قوموا فانحروا ثم احلقوا قال: فوالله ما قام منهم رجل حتى قال ذلك ثلاث مرات فلما لم يقم منهم أحد دخل على أم سلمة فذكر لها ما لقي من الناس فقالت أم سلمة: يا نبي الله أتحب ذلك اخرج لا تكلم أحدا منهم كلمة حتى تنحر بدنك وتدعو حالقك فيحلقك فخرج فلم يكلم أحدا منهم حتى فعل ذلك نحر بدنه ودعا حالقه فحلقه فلما رأوا ذلك قاموا فنحروا وجعل بعضهم يحلق بعضا حتى كاد بعضهم يقتل بعضا غما ثم جاء نسوة مؤمنات فأنزل الله تعالى: (يَٰٓأَيُّهَا ٱلَّذِينَ ءَامَنُوٓا۟ إِذَا جَآءَكُمُ ٱلْمُؤْمِنَٰتُ مُهَٰجِرَٰتٍ فَٱمْتَحِنُوهُنَّ) حتى بلغ: (بِعِصَمِ ٱلْكَوَافِرِ) فطلق عمر يومئذ امرأتين كانتا له في الشرك فتزوج إحداهما معاوية بن أبي سفيان والأخرى صفوان بن أمية ثم رجع النبي ﷺ إلى المدينة فجاءه أبو بصير رجل من قريش وهو مسلم فأرسلوا في طلبه رجلين فقالوا: العهد الذي جعلت لنا فدفعه إلى الرجلين فخرجا به حتى بلغا ذا الحليفة فنزلوا يأكلون من تمر لهم فقال أبو بصير لأحد الرجلين: والله إني لأرى سيفك هذا يا فلان جيدا فاستله الآخر فقال: أجل والله إنه لجيد لقد جربت به ثم جربت فقال أبو بصير: أرني أنظر إليه فأمكنه منه فضربه حتى برد وفر الآخر حتى أتى المدينة فدخل المسجد يعدو فقال رسول الله ﷺ حين رآه: لقد رأى هذا ذعرا فلما انتهى إلى النبي ﷺ قال: قتل والله صاحبي وإني لمقتول فجاء أبو بصير فقال: يا نبي الله قد والله أوفى الله ذمتك قد رددتني إليهم ثم أنجاني الله منهم قال النبي ﷺ: ويل أمه مسعر حرب لو كان له أحد فلما سمع ذلك عرف أنه سيرده إليهم فخرج حتى أتى سيف البحر قال: وينفلت منهم أبو جندل بن سهيل فلحق بأبي بصير فجعل لا يخرج من قريش رجل قد أسلم إلا لحق بأبي بصير حتى اجتمعت منهم عصابة فوالله ما يسمعون بعير خرجت لقريش إلى الشام إلا اعترضوا لها فقتلوهم وأخذوا أموالهم فأرسلت قريش إلى النبي ﷺ تناشده بالله والرحم لما أرسل فمن أتاه فهو آمن فأرسل النبي ﷺ إليهم فأنزل الله تعالى: (وَهُوَ ٱلَّذِى كَفَّ أَيْدِيَهُمْ عَنكُمْ وَأَيْدِيَكُمْ عَنْهُم بِبَطْنِ مَكَّةَ مِنۢ بَعْدِ أَنْ أَظْفَرَكُمْ عَلَيْهِمْ) حتى بلغ: (ٱلْحَمِيَّةَ حَمِيَّةَ ٱلْجَٰهِلِيَّةِ) وكانت حميتهم أنهم لم يقروا أنه نبي الله ولم يقروا ببسم الله الرحمن الرحيم وحالوا بينهم وبين البيت.

قال أبو عبد الله: معرةُ العرِّ: الجرب. تزيلوا: تميزوا. حميت القوم: منعتهم حماية. وأحميت الحمى: جعلته حمى لا يدخل. وأحميت الرجل: إذا أغضبته إحماء.

Al-Miswar ibn Makhramah ؓ and Marwaan both said, "The Messenger of Allaah ﷺ set out during the time of the incident at Al-Hudaibiyah (a town close to Makkah). Then while they were on the path, the Prophet ﷺ said, 'Verily Khaalid ibn Al-Waleed is at Al-Ghameem (a place between Raabigh and Juhfah) with a cavalry for Quraish in the forefront of an army so take the path on the right.'[123] By Allaah, Khaalid did not notice them until they had reached the dust trail of the army so he quickly galloped back to warn Quraish while the Prophet ﷺ continued to travel on. Then when he reached the mountain pass where he would descend upon them, his riding camel knelt down to the ground. The people then said, "*Hal*! *Hal*! (An expression used to urge on the camel)" ; however, it continued to kneel . They then said, "Al-Qaswaa (the name of the Prophet's camel) has been obstinate." The Prophet ﷺ replied, 'Al-Qaswaa has not been obstinate, nor is not her character; rather, the one who halted the elephant has halted her. By the one who has my soul is in His hand, they will not ask from me a course of action which they thereby magnify the Sacred Precincts of Allaah except that I will comply with it.'

He then urged her to get up and she sprung up. He then moved away from them (the polytheists) and wound up stopping to rest at the furthest tip of Al-Hudaibiyah at a small well that had little water. The people started to take it (the water) little by little not ceasing until it was left dry. [The people] complained to the Messenger of Allaah ﷺ of thirst so he took an arrow out of his quiver and ordered them to put it inside of the well. By Allaah, the well then gushed with drinking water until they departed from it. Then while they were preoccupied with the water, Budail ibn Warqaa Al-Khuzaa'ee suddenly arrived with a group of his people who were loyal to the Messenger of Allaah ﷺ from Khuzaa'ah, who were from the people of Tihaamah. Budail said, "I have left Ka'b ibn Lu'aiy and 'Amr ibn Lu'aiy. They have stopped to rest at the copious waters of Al-Hudaibiyah. They have their women with them and she-camels containing milk. They intend to fight you and prevent you from the Sacred House." The Messenger of Allaah ﷺ replied by saying, 'Verily we have not come to fight anyone; instead, we have only come to perform '*umrah* (the minor pilgrimage). The war has weakened Quraish and has affected them negatively. If they wish, I will make a truce with them for an appointed time in which they will refrain from interfering between myself and the people (meaning the disbelievers); And if I gain victory over them and they (Quraish) wish to embrace Islam as the people have done, they can do so and if not, they will have regained strength by the time the truce ends. Moreover, if they refuse, by the one who has my soul in His hand, I will certainly fight them for my cause until I die, and indeed Allaah will continue to support His cause.'

Budail said, "I will inform them of what you are saying," then he left. When he arrived at Quraish he said, 'Verily we have come from this man after hearing what he had to say. If you wish that I present his statements to you I will do so.' The foolish ones amongst them said, "We are in no need for you to tell us anything about him." However, the intellectuals amongst them said, 'Convey what you heard him say.' He said, "I heard him say such-and-such,"

---

[123] Khaalid ibn Al-Waleed at this time had not yet embraced Islaam.

informing them of what the Prophet ﷺ said. 'Urwah ibn Mas'ood then stood up and said, 'O my people, are you not the father?' They said, "Certainly." He said, 'Am I not the son?' They said, "Certainly." He said, 'Do you doubt me?' They replied, "No." He continued, 'Are you not aware that once I called the people of 'Ukaadh to come out and fight and they refused, I came to you with my family, children and others who obeyed me?' They said, "Certainly." He replied, 'In reality, this person has proposed to you a good course of action so accept it and allow me to go speak to him.' They agreed and said, "Go to him." So he went and spoke to the Prophet ﷺ and the Prophet ﷺ then said something similar to what he said to Budail. 'Urwah then responded to the statement, "O Muhammad tell me, if you annihilate your people, have you heard of anyone from the Arabs who has annihilated his people before you? And if the opposite occurs, which seems likely since, by Allaah, I do not see with you dignified faces, I certainly see an array of people that are prone to flee and leave you by yourself."

'Suck the clitoris of *Al-laat* (one of the idols of Quraish),' Abu Baker replied, in defense of the Messenger. 'Are you implying that we flee from him and leave him alone!?' He asked, "Who is this (speaking)?" 'Abu Bakr,' they replied. He said, "were it not for a favor you've done for me that I have yet to repay, I would have responded to you." He then began speaking to the Prophet ﷺ and every time he would say something he would touch the Prophet's beard. Standing above the Prophet ﷺ was Al-Mugheerah ibn Shu'bah who would hit Urwah's hand with the bottom part of the sheath of his sword and say, 'Get your hand off the beard of the Messenger of Allaah ﷺ.' 'Urwah then raised his head and inquired, "Who is this?" , 'Al-Mugheerah ibn Shu'bah' they said. He said, "O treacherous one, am I not already busy trying to repair the damage of your treachery?" During the days of pre-Islamic ignorance, Al-Mugheerah accompanied a group of people which he killed and robbed of their money. Thereafter he came (to Madeenah) and embraced Islaam. In this regard the Prophet ﷺ said, 'As for his Islaam then I accept it to be valid, but as for the money that was taken, I will have no part in it.'

'Urwah then started to look at the Companions of the Prophet ﷺ. By Allaah, the Messenger of Allaah ﷺ did not spit a single time except that it fell into the palm of one of their hands, then he would wipe his face and skin with it. Whenever he ordered them to do something they would rush to carry out his command. When he made *wudoo* (ablution) they would nearly fight for the remaining water from his ablution. Whenever they spoke in his presence, they would lower their voices and would avoid staring at him out of respect. 'Urwah then returned to his comrades and exclaimed, "O my people, by Allaah, I have gone to kings, I have visited Caesar (the king of Rome), Kisraa (the king of Persia) and An-Najaashee (the king of Abysinnia). By Allaah, I have never seen a king who has been more exalted and respected than the way the Companions of Muhammad magnify and exalt him. By Allaah, he never spat once except that it fell into the palm of one of their hands and he would then wipe his face and skin with it. When he commanded them to do something they would rush to carry out his command. When he made ablution they would almost fight for the remaining water from his ablution. When they spoke they would lower their voices in his presence and would refrain from staring at him out of respect. He (Muhammad) has certainly proposed to you a good course of action, so accept it."

A man from the Banee Kinaanah tribe said, 'Let me go have a word with him,' and they replied affirmatively. When he approached the Prophet ﷺ and his Companions, the Messenger of Allaah ﷺ said, 'This is so-and-so. He comes from a people who honor the sacrificial animals so send the sacrificial animals to him.' They were sent to him as the people received him while making *talbiyah* (the pilgrim's chant). When he saw that he said, "*Subhaanallaah* (Glorified be Allaah)! It is not appropriate that these people be prevented from the Sacred House." When he returned to his comrades he said, 'I saw the sacrificial animals. They were adorned and marked for sacrifice so I do not believe they should be prevented from the Sacred House.' A man named Mikraz ibn Hafs stood up and said, "Let me go to him." When he approached them the Prophet ﷺ said, 'This is Mikraz. He is a deceitful man.' He then began speaking to the Prophet ﷺ when suddenly, Suhail ibn 'Amr came. Ma'mar (a narrator in the chain) said, "Ayyoob informed me by way of 'Ikrimah that when Suhail ibn 'Amr came, the Prophet ﷺ said, 'Indeed, He (Allaah) has facilitated some of the situation for you.' Suhail ibn 'Amr came and said, "Write a treaty between us and yourself." The Prophet then called ﷺ for the scribe and once the scribe arrived he said ﷺ said, '*Bismillaah Ar-Rahmaan Ar-Raheem* (In the name of Allaah, the Most Beneficent, the Most Merciful).'[124] Suhail replied, "As for *Ar-Rahmaan* (the Most Beneficent), by Allaah, I do not know what that is. Instead write

---

[124] NOTE: *Ar-Rahmaan* and *Ar-Raheem* are from the beautiful names of Allaah ﷻ and they both contain the attribute of mercy so what is the difference between them? Ibnul-Qayyim ﷺ explained in *Badaa'i Al-Fawaa'id*, volume 1, page 24, that *Ar-Rahmaan* is the one described with mercy and *Ar-Raheem* is the one who shows His mercy to His creation. So based on this *Ar-Rahmaan* contains a *Sifah Dhaatiyah* (an attribute of the being) and *Ar-Raheem* contains a *Sifah Fi'liyah* (an action). Also, Ibn Katheer ﷺ explained in the beginning of his *Tafseer* that these two nouns contain *mubaalaghah* (exaggeration or emphasis etc.) and that *Ar-Rahmaan* has more *mubaalaghah* than *Ar-Raheem*. So based upon this we understand that *Ar-Rahmaan* is the Possessor of the utmost mercy and *Ar-Raheem* is the one who is Most Merciful towards His creation. Another difference is that *Ar-Rahmaan* is a name that is specific for Allaah while the name *Raheem*, it is possible that other than Allaah be called *Raheem*. Allaah ﷻ said about His Messenger ﷺ:

لَقَدْ جَآءَكُمْ رَسُولٌ مِّنْ أَنفُسِكُمْ عَزِيزٌ عَلَيْهِ مَا عَنِتُّمْ حَرِيصٌ عَلَيْكُم بِٱلْمُؤْمِنِينَ رَءُوفٌ رَّحِيمٌ

"Verily there has come unto you a messenger from amongst yourselves. It grieves him that you should receive any injury or difficulty. He is anxious over you and he is for the believers full of kindness and merciful." (*At-Tawbah*: 128).

"*Bismikallaahumma* (In your name O Allaah), as you used to write." 'By Allaah, we will not write anything other than "In the name of Allaah, the Most Beneficent, the Most Merciful,' the Muslims retorted. The Prophet ﷺ then said, "write 'In your name O Allaah this is what Muhammad the Messenger of Allaah has rendered as a treaty.' Suhail rebutted, "By Allaah, if we knew you to be the Messenger of Allaah we would not have prevented you from the Sacred House nor would we have fought you. Instead write 'Muhammad ibn 'Abdillaah." The Prophet ﷺ said, 'By Allaah, indeed I am the Messenger of Allaah even if you deny me. Write, "Muhammad ibn 'Abdillaah.' The Prophet ﷺ then said to him, "[This treaty is contingent] On you allowing us to visit the Sacred House and make *tawaaf*." Suhail said, 'By Allaah, we do not want the Arabs to say that we were pressured, however, that is for you in the coming year.'

Then Suhail said, "On condition that not a single man of ours comes to you, even if he has embraced your religion except that you must send him back to us." '*Subhaanallaah!* (Glorified be Allaah), the Muslims replied. How can he be sent back to the polytheists after he has embraced Islaam?' While they were engrossed in that issue, Abu Jandal, the son of Suhail ibn 'Amr arrived walking slowly in his shackles. He had escaped by leaving from the southern region of Makkah; once he arrived he joined the Muslims. "This, O Muhammad, is the first one that I demand you send back to me," Suhail said. The Prophet ﷺ replied, 'We have not yet completed the treaty.' He said, "By Allaah, in that case I will never make any compromise with you." The Prophet ﷺ said, 'Let me have him.' He refused saying, "I won't let you have him." He said, 'No (in disagreement), do it!' He said, "I won't do it!" Mikraz said finally, 'Rather, we give him to you.' Abu Jandal exclaimed, "O community of Muslims, am I to be sent back to the polytheists after I have embraced Islam? Do you not see what I have encountered (he had been severely tortured for Allah's sake)?"

'Umar ibn Al-Khattaab commented about this occurrence saying, 'I then went to the Prophet of Allaah ﷺ and said, "Are you not truly the Prophet of Allaah?" He replied, 'Certainly.' I continued, "Are we not followers of the truth and are not our enemies followers of falsehood?" 'Certainly,' he said. I then asked, "In that case why do we display weakness in our religion?" He said, 'Verily I am the Messenger of Allaah and I am not going to disobey Him; and He is my helper.' I said, "Did you not tell us that we would soon go to the Sacred House and perform *tawaaf*?" He said, 'Certainly, but did I tell you it would be this year?' "No," I said. He said, 'Verily, you will soon go and make *tawaaf*.'

I then went to Abu Bakr and said, "O Abaa Bakr, is this not truly the Prophet of Allaah?" He said, 'Certainly.' I said, "Are we not followers of the truth, while our enemies are followers of falsehood?" He said, 'Certainly.' I said, "In that case why do we display weakness in our religion?" 'O man, verily he is the Messenger of Allaah ﷺ and he will not disobey his Lord. Furthermore, his lord is his helper so stick by his orders; by Allaah, he is upon the truth,' he said." I said, "Did he not tell us that we would soon go to the Sacred House and perform *tawaaf*?" He replied, 'Certainly; however, did he tell you that it would take place this year?' I said, "No." He said, 'Verily you will go and perform *tawaaf* [shortly].'

Az-Zuhree (a narrator in the chain) mentioned that 'Umar said, "I later performed righteous deeds (as atonement)."

Once the writing of the treaty was complete, the Messenger of Allaah ﷺ said to his Companions, 'Go and slaughter (the sacrificial animals), then shave (your heads).' By Allaah, none of them got up immediately causing him to say it three times. Finally when none of them got up, he went to Umm Salamah and mentioned to her what [difficulty] he encountered from the people so Umm Salamah advised him saying, "O Prophet of Allaah, do you really want [what you have requested] to be done? Then go out there without saying a word to them until you slaughter your sacrificial camel and order your barber to shave your head." He then went out without saying a word to any of them until he did what she had advised. When they saw that, they began slaughtering their animals and shaving each other's, almost killing each other out of grief. Then when the believing women arrived (for *hijrah*) Allaah ﷻ sent down,

$$\text{يَٰٓأَيُّهَا ٱلَّذِينَ ءَامَنُوٓا۟ إِذَا جَآءَكُمُ ٱلْمُؤْمِنَٰتُ مُهَٰجِرَٰتٍ فَٱمْتَحِنُوهُنَّ}$$

'O you who believe, when believing women come to you as emigrants examine them…'
Including,

$$\text{بِعِصَمِ ٱلْكَوَافِرِ}$$

"…and do not hold on to the disbelieving women as wives (*Al-Mumtahanah*: 10)."

So on that day, 'Umar divorced two women he had married from days of polytheism. Mu'aawiyah ibn Abee Sufyaan then married one of them and Safwaan ibn Umaiyah married the other.

The Prophet ﷺ then returned to Madeenah. During this time Abu Baseer, a man from Quraish, came to him having embraced Islam and the polytheists sent two men requesting to have him sent back. They asserted, "Remember the promise you gave us." So he handed him over, fulfilling his promise. They departed with him and started traveling until they reached Dhaa Al-Hulaifah where they stopped to rest and eat some dates they had with them. It was at that time Abu Baseer said to one of them, 'By Allaah, O so-and-so, I find this sword of yours to be of good quality.' The other man unsheathed it and said, "Yes, by Allaah, it is good. I put it to use, then I put it to use, then I put it to use." Abu Baseer said, 'Let me have a look at it.' The man showed it to him enabling him to grab it and Abu Baseer struck him with it, taking his life. The other man fled until he finally reached Madeenah and ran into the *masjid*. The Messenger of Allaah ﷺ said when he saw him, "Indeed this one has seen something frightening." When he reached the Prophet ﷺ he said, "By Allaah, my companion has been killed and I am soon to be killed!" Abu Baseer then reached the masjid and said, 'O Prophet of Allaah, indeed Allaah has given you full protection. You sent me back to them and Allaah saved me from them.' "Woe to his mother. A starter of a war, if only he had someone to help him," the Prophet ﷺ said. When Abu Baseer heard that he knew that he was going to be sent back to the disbelievers so he fled until he reached the coastline of the sea. After some time, Abu Jandal escaped and joined Abu Baseer. From that point on, there was no man who embraced Islaam and escaped from Quraish except that he joined Abu Baseer. This continued until a large group of them had assembled together. By Allaah, they did not catch word of a caravan belonging to Quraish going to Shaam except that they intercepted the caravan, killing the people and taking their wealth. Quraish then sent a message to the Prophet ﷺ imploring him by Allaah and the ties of the womb to send for them promising that whoever goes to him (the Prophet) will be secure. So the Prophet ﷺ sent for them and Allaah ﷻ revealed:

$$وَهُوَ ٱلَّذِى كَفَّ أَيْدِيَهُمْ عَنكُمْ وَأَيْدِيَكُمْ عَنْهُم بِبَطْنِ مَكَّةَ مِنۢ بَعْدِ أَنْ أَظْفَرَكُمْ عَلَيْهِمْ$$

'And He is the one who has withheld their hands from you and your hands from them in the midst of Makkah after He had given you victory over them…"
Including,

$$ٱلْحَمِيَّةَ حَمِيَّةَ ٱلْجَٰهِلِيَّةِ$$

"…the pride, the pride of *Jaahiliyah*."

Their pride was their refusal to acknowledge that he was the Prophet of Allaah as well as their opposition to having 'In the name of Allaah, the Most Beneficent, the Most Merciful, written on the treaty, and hindering the Muslims from the Sacred."

Al-Bukhaaree transmitted this *hadeeth* in his *Saheeh* (2731, 2732).)

قال الإمام مسلم رحمه الله (1808): حدثني عمرو بن محمد الناقد حدثنا يزيد بن هارون أخبرنا حماد بن سلمة عن ثابت عن أنس بن مالك رضي الله عنه أن ثمانين رجلا من أهل مكة هبطوا على رسول الله ﷺ من جبل التنعيم متسلحين يريدون غرة النبي ﷺ وأصحابه فأخذهم سلما فاستحياهم فأنزل الله عز وجل: (وَهُوَ ٱلَّذِى كَفَّ أَيْدِيَهُمْ عَنكُمْ وَأَيْدِيَكُمْ عَنْهُم بِبَطْنِ مَكَّةَ مِنۢ بَعْدِ أَنْ أَظْفَرَكُمْ عَلَيْهِمْ).

Anas ibn Maalik ؓ narrated that eighty men from the people of Makkah descended from the mountain At-Tan'eem with arms, intending to attach the Messenger of Allaah ﷺ. They wanted to take the Prophet ﷺ and his Companions by surprise, however, he wound up capturing them once they surrendered and then he let them go. In this regard Allaah ﷻ sent down the following:

$$\text{وَهُوَ ٱلَّذِى كَفَّ أَيْدِيَهُمْ عَنكُمْ وَأَيْدِيَكُمْ عَنْهُم بِبَطْنِ مَكَّةَ مِنۢ بَعْدِ أَنْ أَظْفَرَكُمْ عَلَيْهِمْ}$$

"And He is the one who has withheld their hands from you and your hands from them in the midst of Makkah after He had given you victory over them…"

This *hadeeth* has been transmitted by Muslim in his *Saheeh* (1808).

قال الإمام مسلم ؓ (1807): حدثنا أبو بكر بن أبي شيبة حدثنا هاشم بن القاسم ح وحدثنا إسحاق بن إبراهيم أخبرنا أبو عامر العقدي كلاهما عن عكرمة بن عمار ح وحدثنا عبد الله بن عبد الرحمن الدارمي وهذا حديثه أخبرنا أبو علي الحنفي عبيد الله بن عبد المجيد حدثنا عكرمة وهو ابن عمار حدثني إياس بن سلمة حدثني أبي ﷺ قال: قدمنا الحديبية مع رسول الله ﷺ ونحن أربع عشرة مائة وعليها خمسون شاة لا ترويها قال: فقعد رسول الله ﷺ على جبا الركية فإما دعا وإما بسق فيها قال: فجاشت فسقينا واستقينا قال: ثم إن رسول الله ﷺ دعانا للبيعة في أصل الشجرة قال: فبايعته أول الناس ثم بايع وبايع حتى إذا كان في وسط من الناس قال: بايع يا سلمة قال قلت: قد بايعتك يا رسول الله في أول الناس قال: وأيضا قال: ورآني رسول الله ﷺ عزلا يعني ليس معه سلاح قال: فأعطاني رسول الله ﷺ حجفة أو درقة ثم بايع حتى إذا كان في آخر الناس قال: ألا تبايعني يا سلمة قال قلت: قد بايعتك يا رسول الله في أول الناس وفي أوسط الناس قال: وأيضا قال: فبايعته الثالثة ثم قال لي: يا سلمة أين حجفتك أو درقتك التي أعطيتك قال قلت: يا رسول الله لقيني عمي عامر عزلا فأعطيته إياها قال: فضحك رسول الله ﷺ وقال: إنك كالذي قال الأول: اللهم أبغني حبيبا هو أحب إلي من نفسي ثم إن المشركين راسلونا الصلح حتى مشى بعضنا في بعض واصطلحنا قال: وكنت تبيعا لطلحة بن عبيد الله أسقي فرسه وأحسه وأخدمه وآكل من طعامه وتركت أهلي ومالي مهاجرا إلى الله ورسوله ﷺ قال: فلما اصطلحنا نحن وأهل مكة واختلط بعضنا ببعض أتيت شجرة فكسحت شوكها فاضطجعت في أصلها قال: فأتاني أربعة من المشركين من أهل مكة فجعلوا يقعون في رسول الله ﷺ فأبغضتهم فتحولت إلى شجرة أخرى وعلقوا سلاحهم واضطجعوا فبينما هم كذلك إذ نادى مناد من أسفل الوادي: يا للمهاجرين قتل ابن زنيم قال: فاخترطت سيفي ثم شددت على أولئك الأربعة وهم رقود فأخذت سلاحهم فجعلته ضغثا في يدي قال: ثم قلت: والذي كرم وجه محمد لا يرفع أحد منكم رأسه إلا ضربت الذي فيه عيناه قال: ثم جئت بهم أسوقهم إلى رسول الله ﷺ قال: وجاء عمي عامر

برجل من العَبَلات يقال له مِكرَز يقوده إلى رسول الله ﷺ على فرس مجفف في سبعين من المشركين فنظر إليهم رسول الله ﷺ فقال: دعوهم يكن لهم بدء الفجور وثناه فعفا عنهم رسول الله ﷺ وأنزل الله: (وَهُوَ ٱلَّذِى كَفَّ أَيْدِيَهُمْ عَنكُمْ وَأَيْدِيَكُمْ عَنْهُم بِبَطْنِ مَكَّةَ مِنْ بَعْدِ أَنْ أَظْفَرَكُمْ عَلَيْهِمْ) الآية كلها قال: ثم خرجنا راجعين إلى المدينة فنزلنا منزلا بيننا وبين بنى لِحيان جبل وهم المشركون فاستغفر رسول الله ﷺ لمن رقى هذا الجبل الليلة كأنه طليعة للنبي ﷺ وأصحابه قال سلمة: فرقيت تلك الليلة مرتين أو ثلاثا ثم قدمنا المدينة فبعث رسول الله ﷺ بظهره مع رباح غلام رسول الله ﷺ ومعه وخرجت معه بفرس طلحة أُنديّه مع الظهر فلما أصبحنا إذا عبد الرحمن الفزاري قد أغار على ظهر رسول الله ﷺ فاستاقه أجمع وقتل راعيه قال فقلت: يا رباح خذ هذا الفرس فأبلغه طلحة بن عبيد الله وأخبر رسول الله ﷺ أن المشركين قد أغاروا على سرحه قال: ثم قمت على أكمة فاستقبلت المدينة فناديت ثلاثا: يا صباحاه ثم خرجت في آثار القوم أرميهم بالنبل وأرتجز أقول:

واليوم يوم الرُضَّع   أنا ابن الأكوع

فألحق رجلا منهم فأصك سهما في رحله حتى خَلَصَ نصل السهم إلى كتفه قال قلت: خذها

واليوم يوم الرضَّع   وأنا ابن الأكوع

قال: فوالله ما زلت أرميهم وأعقر بهم فإذا رجع إلي فارس أتيت شجرة فجلست في أصلها ثم رميته فعقرت به حتى إذا تضايق الجبل فدخلوا في تضايقه علوت الجبل فجعلت أُردّيهم بالحجارة قال: فما زلت كذلك أتبعهم حتى ما خلق الله من بعير من ظهر رسول الله ﷺ إلا خلفته وراء ظهري وخلوا بيني وبينه ثم اتبعتهم أرميهم حتى ألقوا أكثر من ثلاثين بردة وثلاثين رمحا يستخفون ولا يطرحون شيئا إلا جعلت عليه آراما من الحجارة يعرفها

رسول الله ﷺ وأصحابه حتى أتوا متضايقا من ثنية فإذا هم قد أتاهم فلان بن بدر الفزاري فجلسوا يتضحون يعني يتغدون وجلست على رأس قرن قال الفزاري: ما هذا الذي أرى قالوا: لقينا من هذا البَرْح والله ما فارقنا منذ غلس يرمينا حتى انتزع كل شيء في أيدينا قال: فليقم إليه نفر منكم أربعة قال: فصعد إلي منهم أربعة في الجبل قال: فلما أمكنوني من الكلام قال قلت: هل تعرفوني قالوا: لا ومن أنت قال قلت: أنا سلمة بن الأكوع والذي كرم وجه محمد ﷺ لا أطلب رجلا منكم إلا أدركته ولا يطلبني رجل منكم فيدركني قال أحدهم: أنا أظن قال: فرجعوا فما برحت مكاني حتى رأيت فوارس رسول الله ﷺ يتخللون الشجر قال: فإذا أولهم الأخرم الأسدي على إثره أبو قتادة الأنصاري وعلى إثره المقداد بن الأسود الكندي قال: فأخذت بعنان الأخرم قال: فولوا مدبرين قلت: يا أخرم احذرهم لا يقتطعوك حتى يلحق

263

رسول الله ﷺ وأصحابه قال: يا سلمة إن كنت تؤمن بالله واليوم الآخر وتعلم أن الجنة حق والنار حق فلا تحل بيني وبين الشهادة قال: فخليته فالتقى هو وعبد الرحمن قال: فعقر عبد الرحمن فرسه وطعنه عبد الرحمن فقتله وتحول على فرسه ولحق أبو قتادة فارس رسول الله ﷺ بعبد الرحمن فطعنه فقتله فوالذي كرم وجه محمد ﷺ لتبعتهم أعدو على رجلي حتى ما أرى ورائي من أصحاب محمد ﷺ ولا غبارهم شيئا حتى يعدلوا قبل غروب الشمس إلى شعب فيه ماء يقال له ذا قَرَد ليشربوا منه وهم عطاش قال: فنظروا إلي أعدو وراءهم فحليتهم عنه يعني أجليتهم عنه فما ذاقوا منه قطرة قال: ويخرجون فيشتدون في ثنية قال: فأعدو فألحق رجلا منهم فأصكه بسهم في نغض كتفه قال قلت: خذها

وأنا ابن الأكوع   واليوم يوم الرضّع

قال: يا ثكلته أمه أكوعُه بُكرة قال قلت: نعم يا عدو نفسه أكوعك بكرة قال: وأردَوا فرسين على ثنية قال: فجئت بهما أسوقهما إلى رسول الله ﷺ قال: ولحقني عامر بسَطيحة فيها مَذْقة من لبن وسطيحة فيها ماء فتوضأت وشربت ثم أتيت رسول الله ﷺ وهو على الماء الذي حلأتهم عنه فإذا رسول الله ﷺ قد أخذ تلك الإبل وكل شيء استقذته من المشركين وكل رمح وبردة وإذا بلال نحر ناقة من الإبل الذي استقذت من القوم وإذا هو يشوي لرسول الله ﷺ من كبدها وسنامها قال قلت: يا رسول الله خلني فأنتخب من القوم مائة رجل فأتبع القوم فلا يبقى منهم مخبر إلا قتلته قال: فضحك رسول الله ﷺ حتى بدت نواجذه في ضوء النار فقال: يا سلمة أتراك كنت فاعلا قلت: نعم والذي أكرمك فقال: إنهم الآن ليُقرَون في أرض غطفان قال: فجاء رجل من غطفان فقال: نحر لهم فلان جزورا فلما كشفوا جلدها رأوا غبارا فقالوا: أتاكم القوم فخرجوا هاربين فلما أصبحنا قال رسول الله ﷺ: كان خير فرساننا اليوم أبو قتادة وخير رَجَّالتنا سلمة قال ثم أعطاني رسول الله ﷺ سهمين سهم الفارس وسهم الراجل فجمعهما لي جميعا ثم أردفني رسول الله ﷺ وراءه على العضباء راجعين إلى المدينة قال: فبينما نحن نسير قال: وكان رجل من الأنصار لا يُسبق شدًّا قال: فجعل يقول: ألا مسابق إلى المدينة هل من مسابق فجعل يعيد ذلك قال: فلما سمعت كلامه قلت: أما تكرم كريما ولا تهاب شريفا قال: لا إلا أن يكون رسول الله ﷺ قال قلت: يا رسول الله بأبي وأمي ذرني فلأسابق الرجل قال: إن شئت قال قلت: اذهب إليك وثنيت رجلي فطفرت فعدوت قال: فربطت عليه شرفا أو شرفين أستبقي نفسي ثم عدوت في إثره فربطت عليه شرفا أو شرفين ثم إني رفعت حتى ألحقه قال: فأصكه بين كتفيه قال قلت: قد سُبقت والله قال: أنا أظن قال: فسبقته إلى المدينة قال: فوالله ما لبثنا إلا ثلاث ليال حتى خرجنا إلى خيبر مع رسول الله ﷺ قال: فجعل عمي عامر يرتجز بالقوم:

تالله لولا الله ما اهتدينا   ولا تصدقنا ولا صلينا

ونحن عن فضلك ما استغنينا   فثبت الأقدام إن لاقينا

وأنزلن سكينة علينا

فقال رسول الله ﷺ: من هذا قال: أنا عامر قال: غفر لك ربك قال: وما استغفر رسول الله ﷺ لإنسان يخصه إلا استشهد قال: فنادى عمر بن الخطاب وهو على جمل له: يا نبي الله لولا ما متعتنا بعامر قال: فلما قدمنا خيبر قال: خرج ملِكهم مَرحَب يخطر بسيفه ويقول:

قد علمت خيبر أني مرحب   شاكي السلاح بطل مجرب

إذا الحروب أقبلت تلهب

قال: وبرز له عمي عامر فقال:

قد علمت خيبر أني عامر   شاكي السلاح بطل مغامر

قال: فاختلفا ضربتين فوقع سيف مرحب في ترس عامر وذهب عامر يَسفُل له فرجع سيفه على نفسه فقطع أكحَله فكانت فيها نفسه قال سلمة: فخرجت فإذا نفر من أصحاب النبي ﷺ يقولون: بطل عمل عامر قتل نفسه قال: فأتيت النبي ﷺ وأنا أبكي فقلت: يا رسول الله بطل عمل عامر قال رسول الله ﷺ: من قال ذلك قلت: ناس من أصحابك قال: كذب من قال ذلك بل له أجره مرتين ثم أرسلني إلى علي وهو أرمد فقال: لأعطين الراية رجلا يحب الله ورسوله ويحبه الله ورسوله قال: فأتيت عليا فجئت به أقوده وهو أرمد حتى أتيت به رسول الله ﷺ فبسق في عينيه فبرأ وأعطاه الراية وخرج مرحب فقال:

قد علمت خيبر أني مرحب   شاكي السلاح بطل مجرب

إذا الحروب أقبلت تلهب

فقال علي:

أنا الذي سمتني أمي حيدره   كليث غابات كريه المنظرة

أوفيهم بالصاع كيل السندرة

قال: فضرب رأس مرحب فقتله ثم كان الفتح على يديه رضوان الله عليه.
قال إبراهيم حدثنا محمد بن يحيى حدثنا عبد الصمد بن عبد الوارث عن عكرمة بن عمار بهذا الحديث بطوله.

Salamah ibn Al-Akwa' ﷺ stated, "We arrived at Al-Hudaibiyah with the Messenger of Allaah ﷺ numbering one thousand four hundred. We had fifty sheep with us that were in need of water however, Al-Hudaibiyah offered no water for them to drink. In an effort ameliorate this problem, the Messenger of Allaah ﷺ sat at the edge of the well either supplicated or spit in it. The water then started to rise so we gave [the animals] water to drink and we ourselves drank. The Messenger of Allaah ﷺ then summoned us to give a pledge of allegiance at the trunk of the tree and I was the first of the people to give him the pledge of allegiance. He took the pledges one after another until he reached the middle group of people he said, 'Give your pledge, O Salamah.' I said, "I have already given you the pledge, O Messenger of Allaah, with the first group of people." He said, 'And again.' Seeing that I did not have a weapon the Messenger of Allaah ﷺ gave me a shield and continued taking pledges. When he reached the last group of people he said, "Will you not give your pledge, O Salamah?" I said, 'I have given you my pledge, O Messenger of Allaah, along with the first group of people as well as the middle group of people.' He replied, "And again." So I gave him my pledge a third time then he stated, 'O Salamah, where is the shield that I gave you?' I said, "O Messenger of Allaah, I saw that my uncle 'Aamir did not have a weapon so I gave it to him." 'Verily you are similar the one who initially said, "O Allaah give me a beloved friend who is more beloved to me than myself.'

The polytheists then sent a message requesting a peace treaty so both parties walked towards one another and made a peace treaty. At that time I was a servant for Talhah ibn 'Ubaidillaah. I would give his horse water to drink, groom it, serve him (Talhah) and eat some of his food. My situation was such because I had left my family and wealth during *hijrah* to Allaah and His Messenger ﷺ. When we intermingled with the people of Makkah for the purpose of the treaty, I went to a tree, swept away its fallen thorns and began to lie down at its trunk. Four polytheists from the people of Makkah then came towards me and started to revile the Messenger of Allaah ﷺ. For this I despised them and moved to another tree; so they hung their weapons from the tree and began lying down. While they were reclining under the tree a caller cried out from the lower part of the valley saying, "Help, O *Muhaajireen*! Ibn Zunaim has been killed!" I pulled out my sword and headed for those four while they were lying down. I took their weapons, wrapped them in my hand and then I said, 'By the one who has honored the face of Muhammad, let not one of you raise his or I'll strike (with my sword) what is holding his two eyes.'

I then took them to the Messenger of Allaah ﷺ while walking behind them. My uncle 'Aamir also brought in a man from the tribe Al-'Abalaat named Mikraz, leading him on an armored horse to the Messenger of Allaah ﷺ along with seventy polytheists. "Let them go, the start of treachery and its repetition is for them," the Messenger of Allaah stated as he ﷺ looked at them. He had chosen to pardon them ﷺ and Allaah ﷻ sent down:

وَهُوَ ٱلَّذِى كَفَّ أَيْدِيَهُمْ عَنكُمْ وَأَيْدِيَكُمْ عَنْهُم بِبَطْنِ مَكَّةَ مِنۢ بَعْدِ أَنْ أَظْفَرَكُمْ عَلَيْهِمْ

"And He is the one who has withheld their hands from you and your hands from them in the midst of Makkah after He had given you victory over them…".

Then when we left heading back to Madeenah, stopping to rest at a place near the tribe of Banee Lihyaan with a mountain serving as a partition between us and the people of this tribe who were polytheists. The Messenger of Allaah ﷺ then supplicated asking Allah to forgive whoever ascended the mountain that night. It was the front line for the Prophet ﷺ and his Companions, so I climbed it that night two or three times. [The next day] we arrived in Madeenah. The Messenger of Allaah ﷺ sent his riding camels with Rabaah (so he could give them water), his boy servant, as well as myself. I left with Talha's horse so I could let it drink and graze along with the riding camels. However, Once morning came, to our surprise 'Abdur-Rahmaan Al-Fazaaree had raided the riding camels of the Messenger of Allaah ﷺ driving all of them away, and he also killed the herder. 'O Rabaah, take this horse and give it to Talhah ibn 'Ubaidillaah and inform the Messenger of Allaah ﷺ that the polytheists have raided his livestock,' I said. I then stood up on a hill, faced Madeenah and shouted three times '*Yaa Sabaahaah*!'[125] I then followed their tracks shooting them with arrows while saying my rhyme,

أنا ابن الأكوع   واليوم يوم الرضّع

"I am the son of Al-Akwa', and today is the day the misers get destroyed."

I caught up to one of their men and shot an arrow through his saddle. The tip of the arrow wound up his shoulder and I exclaimed, 'Take that! I am the son of Al-Akwa', and today is the day the misers get destroyed.' By Allaah, I continued shooting them and injuring their horses. When a horseman would turn around to chase me down I would retreat to a tree and sit behind its trunk, then I would shoot him and injure his horse. Eventually they entered the narrow passes of the mountain and I climbed the mountain and began to knock them down with rocks. I continued doing this, hunting them down to such and extent that every camel that Allaah had created that belonged to the Messenger of Allaah ﷺ was in my possession and they (the polytheists) would leave me to have it. I continued hunting them down and shooting them to the point that they had thrown away over thirty garments and thirty spears to lighten the loads carried by their riding animals. I placed a stone marker next to every thing they had thrown away so the Messenger of Allaah ﷺ and his Companions would recognize it.

---

[125] Ibn Al-Atheer said in *An-Nihaayah*, "This is a phrase that the one who calls for help says. It was originally used when they would shout due to a raid because most of their raids would occur in the morning (*sabaah*)… it is as if he is saying: The enemy has come!"

Surprisingly, when they reached a narrow mountain pass so-and-so, the son of Badr Al-Fazaaree had come to them. They sat down and ate while I sat on a small mountain peak. Al-Fazaaree said, "What is this I see?" They replied, 'We have encountered hardship from this one. By Allaah, he has not stopped shooting us since the darkness of early morning to the point that he has snatched away everything in our hands.' "Four of you must go after him," he said. Four of them then climbed up the mountain after me. When they got close enough for me to talk to them I said, 'Do you know me?' They replied, "No. Who are you?" 'I am Salamah ibn Al-Akwa'. By the one who has honored the face of Muhammad, I will not chase after any of your men without catching him; and there is not a man amongst you who will chase after me and succeed in catching me,' I said. One of them replied, "I think your right." They then retreated and I remained in my position until I spotted the horsemen of the Messenger of Allaah ﷺ passing between the trees. The first of them was Al-Ashram Al-Aside and trailing him was Abu Qattara who was trailed by Al-Misdeed ibn Al-Assad Al-Kinder. As I grabbed the reins of Al-Ashram's horse they (the polytheists) began to retreat. I said, 'O Ashram, beware of them. Do not let them catch you out there by yourself. Wait until the Messenger of Allaah ﷺ and his Companions catch up.' He said, "O Salamah, if you believe in Allaah and the last day and you know that paradise is true and the fire is true, then do not come between myself and martyrdom." I let him go and he and 'Abdur-Rahmaan (Al-Fazaaree, the polytheist) encountered one another. He injured 'Abdur-Rahmaan's horse then 'Abdur-Rahmaan stabbed him, killing him and taking his horse.

Abu Qataadah, the horseman of the Messenger of Allaah ﷺ caught up with 'Abdur-Rahmaan and stabbed him to death. By the one who has honored the face of Muhammad, I continued pursuing them running on foot to the point that I could not see any of the Companions of Muhammad ﷺ, behind me, not even their trails of dust. Before sunset, the polytheists turned onto a mountain pass called Dhaa Qarad, which contained water, so they could drink and quench their thirsts. They spotted me running behind them which caused them to depart from the water without tasting a single drop of it. They dashed into a mountain pass and I ran and caught up with one of their men shooting an arrow into his shoulder bone. "Take that! I am the son of Al-Akwa', and today is the day the misers get destroyed," I said. He rebutted, 'O may your mother be bereaved of you. Are you the same Akwa' of this morning?' I said, "Yes, O enemy to himself, I am the same Akwa' you encountered this morning."

They had left behind two horses at a mountain pass so I took them and guided them to the Messenger of Allaah ﷺ. 'Aamir caught up to me with water-skin containing milk lightly mixed with water, and water-skin containing water. I made ablution, drank some water, then went to the Messenger of Allaah ﷺ at the water spot that I had chased the disbelievers away from. I found that the Messenger of Allaah ﷺ had gathered the camels and everything else that I salvaged from the polytheists including every spear and garment. I also found that Bilaal had slaughtered a camel from the herd that I recovered from those people and was roasting a part of its liver and its hump for the Messenger of Allaah ﷺ. I said, 'O Messenger of Allaah, allow me to choose one hundred men so I can hunt down those people until I kill every one of them that has a story to tell.' The Messenger of Allaah ﷺ then laughed to the point that his back molars appeared in the light of the fire. He said, "O Salamah, do you think you can do that?" I said, 'Yes, by the one who has honored you." Indeed, they are now being received as guests in the land of the tribe Ghanaian," He said.

Later a man from the tribe arrived saying, 'So-and-so slaughtered a camel for them. When they removed its skin they noticed a dust trail and said, "The people have come for you (Meaning Salamah with a cavalry)!" They then left fleeing. When morning came the Messenger of Allaah ﷺ said, 'The best of our horsemen today was Abu Qataadah, and the best foot soldiers was Salamah.' The Messenger of Allaah ﷺ then gave me two shares of the booty: the horseman's share and the share of a foot soldier. The Messenger of Allaah ﷺ placed me behind him on Al-'Adbaa (his camel) as we traveled back to Madeenah. As we were traveling, a man from the *Ansaar* who would always win footraces said, "Is there someone daring enough to race me back to Madeenah? Is there a racer among you" he said repeatedly? When I heard what he was saying I replied, 'Will you not honor a noble person? Do you not fear and have awe of a highbred?' He said, "No, unless he is the Messenger of Allaah ﷺ." 'O Messenger of Allaah, I give my father and mother as ransom for you. Let me go race this man,' I said. "If you wish," he replied. I said 'Go!,' while opening my legs (in the starter's stance) then thrusting forward. I refrained from running full speed initially so that I wouldn't lose my breathe, then I ran behind him holding back for one or two more phases before turning up the speed and finally catching up to him as I hit him between the shoulders. I said, "You've been beaten, by Allaah." 'I think so,' he replied. I had one the race to Madeenah. By Allaah, we only remained in Madeenah for three nights before heading to Khaibar with the Messenger of Allaah ﷺ. My uncle 'Aamir started chanting a rhyme along with the people saying:

| و لا تصدقنا و لا صلينا | تالله لو لا الله ما اهتدينا |
| فثبّت الأقدام إن لاقينا | ونحن عن فضلك ما استغنينا |

و أنزلن سكينة علينا

"By Allaah, if it were not for Allaah, we would not have been guided
Nor would we have given charity nor would we have prayed
And we can not do without your grace
So make us stand firmly if we meet (the enemy)
And send tranquility upon us."

The Messenger of Allaah ﷺ said, 'Who is this?' "I am 'Aamir," he replied. The Messenger of Allah stated, 'May your Lord forgive you.' The Messenger of Allaah ﷺ never sought forgiveness for a person specifically except that he died as a martyr. Then 'Umar ibn Al-Khattaab ؓ called out while on his camel, "O Prophet of Allaah, if only you had let us enjoy the benefit of 'Aamir."

When we reached Khaibar their king Marhab stepped forward flashing his sword saying:

قد علمت خيبر أني مرحب   شاكي السلاح بطل مجرّب

إذا الحروب أقبلت تلهّب

'Khaibar knows I am Marhab
Fully armed, brave, experienced
When the battles approach they get burned.'

My uncle 'Aamir stepped forward to duel with him saying:

قد علمت خيبر أني عامر   شاكي السلاح بطل مغامر

"Khaibar knows I am 'Aamir
Fully armed and brave, one that ventures the thick of the battle."

They exchanged two blows. Marhab's sword got stuck in 'Aamir's shield while 'Aamir went low in an attempt to swipe him but missed, and his sword came back around striking himself cutting his medial arm vein. He died from that blow. I went (to get him), then to my surprise I heard a group of the Companions of the Prophet ﷺ saying, 'The deeds of 'Aamir have been nullified. He has killed himself.' I went to the Prophet ﷺ in tears and said, "O Messenger of Allaah, have the deeds of 'Aamir been nullified?" The Messenger of Allaah ﷺ asked, 'Who said that?' "A group of your Companions," I said. He replied, 'Whoever said that has lied. In fact, he gets his reward twofold.'

He then sent me to 'Ali ؓ, who was suffering from eye sores, and then said, "I will certainly give the banner to a man who loves Allaah and His Messenger, and Allaah and His Messenger love him." I went to 'Ali and guided him because of his eye condition bringing him to the Messenger of Allaah ﷺ. He then spit in his eyes which resulted in his cure and he gave him the banner (to lead the army in battle). Marhab then stepped forward saying:

قد علمت خيبر أني مرحب   شاكي السلاح بطل مجرّب

إذا الحروب أقبلت تلهّب

'Khaibar knows I am Marhab

Fully armed, brave and experienced
When the battles approach they get burned.'

Then 'Ali said:

أنا الذي سمتني أمي حَيدَره   كليث غابات كريه المنظره

أوفيهم بالصاع كيل السَندَره

"I am the one my mother has named Haidarah[126]
Like a lion of the jungles, an unpleasant sight
I kill them (the enemy) quickly in large numbers."

He then struck the head of Marhab killing him. The victory came through his leadership, may Allaah be pleased with him."

Muslim transmitted this *hadeeth* in his *Saheeh* (1807).

قال الإمام أحمد رَحِمَهُ اللهُ (ج 4 ص 86): ثنا زيد بن الحباب قال حدثني حسين بن واقد قال حدثني ثابت البناني عن عبد الله بن مغفل المزني رَضِيَ اللهُ عَنهُ قال: كنا مع رسول الله ﷺ بالحديبية في أصل الشجرة التي قال الله تعالى في القرآن وكان يقع من أغصان تلك الشجرة على ظهر رسول الله ﷺ وعلي بن أبي طالب وسهيل بن عمرو بين يديه فقال رسول الله ﷺ لعلي رَضِيَ اللهُ عَنهُ: اكتب بسم الله الرحمن الرحيم فأخذ سهيل بن عمرو بيده فقال: ما نعرف بسم الله الرحمن الرحيم اكتب في قضيتنا ما نعرف قال: اكتب باسمك اللهم فكتب: هذا ما صالح عليه محمد رسول الله ﷺ أهل مكة فأمسك سهيل بن عمرو بيده وقال: لقد ظلمناك إن كنت رسوله اكتب في قضيتنا ما نعرف فقال: اكتب هذا ما صالح عليه محمد بن عبد الله بن عبد المطلب وأنا رسول الله فكتب فبينا نحن كذلك إذ خرج علينا ثلاثون شابا عليهم السلاح فثاروا في وجوهنا فدعا عليهم رسول الله ﷺ فأخذ الله عز وجل بأبصارهم فقدمنا إليهم فأخذناهم فقال رسول الله ﷺ: هل جئتم في عهد أحد أو هل جعل لكم أحد أمانا فقالوا: لا فخلى سبيلهم فأنزل الله عز وجل: (وَهُوَ ٱلَّذِى كَفَّ أَيْدِيَهُمْ عَنكُمْ وَأَيْدِيَكُمْ عَنْهُم بِبَطْنِ مَكَّةَ مِنۢ بَعْدِ أَنْ أَظْفَرَكُمْ عَلَيْهِمْ ۚ وَكَانَ ٱللَّهُ بِمَا تَعْمَلُونَ بَصِيرًا).

قال أبو عبد الرحمن[127]: قال حماد بن سلمة في هذا الحديث عن ثابت عن أنس وقال حسين بن واقد عن عبد الله بن مغفل وهذا الصواب عندي إن شاء الله.

'Abdullaah ibn Mughaffal ؓ said, "We were with the Messenger of Allaah ﷺ at Al-Hudaibiyah, at the trunk of the tree that Allaah ﷻ mentioned in the

---

[126] *Haidarah* is one of the names of the lion.

[127] أبو عبد الرحمن هو عبد الله بن أحمد بن حنبل

Qur'aan. [During this time] Some of the branches of that tree had fallen on the back of the Messenger of Allaah ﷺ while 'Ali ibn Abee Ta'Alib and Suhail ibn 'Amr were in front of him. [When the time for writing the treated had commenced] The Messenger of Allaah ﷺ said to 'Ali ؓ, 'Write: *Bismillaah Ar-Rahmaan Ar-Raheem* (In the name of Allaah, the Most Beneficent, the Most Merciful).' Suhail ibn 'Amr grabbed his hand and rebutted, "We are unfamiliar with '*Bismillaah Ar-Rahmaan Ar-Raheem* (In the name of Allaah, the Most Beneficent, the Most Merciful),' [instead] write the treaty in accordance with what we know. Write, in your name, O Allaah." He then wrote, 'This is the peace treaty that Muhammad, the Messenger of Allaah, has made with the people of Makkah.' Suhail ibn 'Amr then grabbed his hand a second time and said, "We have oppressed you if you are His Messenger. Write the treaty in accordance with what we know. Instead, write: This is the peace treaty that Muhammad ibn 'Abdillaah ibn 'Abdil-Muttalib, and I am the Messenger of Allaah..." he said. So he wrote it. While this was occurring, thirty young armed men suddenly headed in our direction to attack us, so the Messenger of Allaah ﷺ supplicated against them and Allaah blinded them allowing us to go over and capture hem. The Messenger of Allaah ﷺ said, 'Has anyone commissioned you to come, or has anyone given you an assurance of protection?' "No," They said. So he let them go and Allaah ﷻ sent down the following verse:

$$\text{وَهُوَ ٱلَّذِى كَفَّ أَيْدِيَهُمْ عَنكُمْ وَأَيْدِيَكُمْ عَنْهُم بِبَطْنِ مَكَّةَ مِنۢ بَعْدِ أَنْ أَظْفَرَكُمْ عَلَيْهِمْ وَكَانَ ٱللَّهُ بِمَا تَعْمَلُونَ بَصِيرًا ۝}$$

'And He is the one who has withheld their hands from you and your hands from them in the midst of Makkah after He had given you victory over them. And Allaah is ever All-Seer over what you do.'

Al-Imaam Ahmad transmitted this *hadeeth* in his *Musnad*, volume 4, page 86. There is some doubt whether or not Thaabit, a narrator in the chain, has actually heard from 'Abdullaah ibn Mughaffal. In this regard Ash-Sheikh Muqbil ؒ has stated, "...and the *hadeeth* we have here is mentioned in a supporting role as you see, even though Al-Haafidh Al-Mizzee mentioned in *Tuhfah Al-Alashraaf* that Abu Bakr ibn Abee Daawud narrated it on Muhammad ibn 'Aqeel with this chain by way of Thaabit who has said, 'Abdullaah ibn Mughaffal narrated to me,' and Allaah knows best. And in *Jaami' At-Tahseel* it reads, "...and Al-Husain ibn Waaqid has narrated on Thaabit on 'Abdullaah ibn Mughaffal, and we do not know whether or not he met him."

NOTE: Al-Haafidh Ibn Hajar has said, commenting on the *hadeeth* of Al-Miswar ibn Makhramah in *Fathul-Baaree* in the explanation of *hadeeth* number 2731, "[As for] His statement, 'Then Allaah ﷻ sent down the following verse:

$$\text{وَهُوَ ٱلَّذِى كَفَّ أَيْدِيَهُمْ عَنكُمْ وَأَيْدِيَكُمْ}$$

"And He is the one who has withheld their hands from you…"

That is the way it is [stated] here and it appears that it descended because of the story of Abu Baseer; however, there is some speculation about that since it is well known that the reason for its revelation is what Muslim has transmitted from the *hadeeth* of Salamah ibn Al-Akwa', as well as the *hadeeth* of Anas ibn Maalik, and what Ahmad and An-Nasaa'ee transmitted from the *hadeeth* of 'Abdullaah ibn Mughaffal with a chain that is *saheeh*. It descended because of those people from Quraish who wanted to ambush the Muslims but instead were defeated by the Muslims the Prophet ﷺ pardoned them. The verse descended in this regard, and it has been said that it descended for other reasons."

Ash-Sheikh Muqbil ﷺ commented, "I say, what Al-Haafidh has said, may Allaah have mercy upon him, is supported by the fact that the verse itself reads:

$$\text{بِبَطْنِ مَكَّةَ}$$

'…in the midst of Makkah…'

and Abu Baseer and his group were not in the midst of Makkah, and Allaah knows best."

سورة الحجرات

Sooratul-Hujuraat

His, the Exalted One's statement:

$$\text{يَٰٓأَيُّهَا ٱلَّذِينَ ءَامَنُوا۟ لَا تُقَدِّمُوا۟ بَيْنَ يَدَىِ ٱللَّهِ وَرَسُولِهِۦ}$$

"O you who believe, do not hasten (in affairs) before Allaah and His Messenger…" (verse: 1).

قال الإمام البخاري رَحِمَهُ اللهُ (4367): حدثني إبراهيم بن موسى حدثنا هشام بن يوسف أن ابن جريج أخبرهم عن ابن أبي مليكة أن عبد الله بن الزبير رَضِيَ اللهُ عَنْهُ أخبرهم أنه قدم ركب من بني تميم على النبي ﷺ فقال أبو بكر: أمّر القعقاع بن معبد بن زرارة قال عمر: بل أمّر الأقرع ابن حابس قال أبو بكر: ما أردت إلا خلافي قال عمر: ما أردت خلافك فتماريا حتى ارتفعت أصواتهما فنزل في ذلك: (يَٰٓأَيُّهَا ٱلَّذِينَ ءَامَنُوا۟ لَا تُقَدِّمُوا۟ بَيْنَ يَدَىِ ٱللَّهِ وَرَسُولِهِۦ) حتى انقضت.

'Abdullaah ibn Az-Zubair ؓ narrated that a group of travelers from the tribe Banee Tameem came to the Prophet ﷺ, and Abu Bakr said, "Appoint Al-Qa'qaa' ibn Ma'bad ibn Zuraarah to be the one in charge." 'Umar commented, 'Instead, appoint Al-Aqra' ibn Haabis to be the one in charge.' "You only wanted to differ with me," Abu Bakr said. 'Umar replied, 'I did not want to differ with you.' They began to argue and raise their voices. The descending of the following verse ensued,

$$\text{يَٰٓأَيُّهَا ٱلَّذِينَ ءَامَنُوا۟ لَا تُقَدِّمُوا۟ بَيْنَ يَدَىِ ٱللَّهِ وَرَسُولِهِۦ}$$

"O you who believe, do not hasten (in affairs) before Allaah and His Messenger…".

Al-Bukhaaree has transmitted this hadeeth in his *Saheeh* (4367).

His, the Exalted One's statement:

$$\text{يَٰٓأَيُّهَا ٱلَّذِينَ ءَامَنُوا۟ لَا تَرْفَعُوٓا۟ أَصْوَٰتَكُمْ فَوْقَ صَوْتِ ٱلنَّبِىِّ}$$

"O you who believe, raise not your voices above the voice of the Prophet…" (verse 2).

قال الإمام البخاري رَحِمَهُ اللهُ (4845): حدثنا يسرة بن صفوان بن جميل اللخمي حدثنا نافع بن عمر عن ابن أبي مليكة قال: كاد الخيران أن يهلكا أبو بكر وعمر رَضِيَ اللهُ عَنْهُمَا رفعا أصواتهما عند النبي ﷺ حين قدم

عليه ركب بني تميم فأشار أحدهما بالأقرع بن حابس أخي بني مجاشع وأشار الآخر برجل آخر قال نافع: لا أحفظ اسمه فقال أبو بكر لعمر: ما أردت إلا خلافي قال: ما أردت خلافك فارتفعت أصواتهما في ذلك فأنزل الله: (يَٰٓأَيُّهَا ٱلَّذِينَ ءَامَنُوا۟ لَا تَرْفَعُوٓا۟ أَصْوَٰتَكُمْ) الآية. قال ابن الزبير ﷺ: فما كان عمر يسمع رسول الله ﷺ بعد هذه الآية حتى يستفهمه ولم يذكر ذلك عن أبيه يعني أبا بكر.

Ibn Abee Mulaikah said, "The two outstanding ones were almost ruined: Abu Bakr and 'Umar ﷺ. They raised their voices in the presence of the Prophet ﷺ when a group of travelers from the Banee Tameem tribe came to him. One of them suggested that Al-Aqra' ibn Haabis, the brother of the Banee Mujaashi' tribe, be put in charge while the other one suggested that another man be put in charge." Naafi' (a narrator in the chain) said, "I can not remember his name." "So Abu Bakr said to 'Umar, 'You only wanted to differ with me." He replied, 'I did not want to differ with you.' They raised their voices because of this and Allaah sent down:

$$\text{يَٰٓأَيُّهَا ٱلَّذِينَ ءَامَنُوا۟ لَا تَرْفَعُوٓا۟ أَصْوَٰتَكُمْ}$$

"O you who believe, raise not your voices…".

Ibn Az-Zubair ﷺ said, "After this verse, 'Umar would not let the Messenger of Allaah ﷺ hear his voice such that he ﷺ would have to put forth effort understand him properly." He (Ibn Az-Zubair) did not mention this about his father, meaning Abu Bakr.

Al-Bukhaaree transmitted this *hadeeth* in his *Saheeh* (4845) as well as Ahmad in his *Musnad*, volume 4, page 6. In this hadeeth Ibn Abee Mulaikah, a *Taabi'ee*, narrated this *hadeeth* on Ibn Az-Zubair, the *Sahaabee*. Ash-Sheikh Muqbil ﷺ said, "So it is known that the *hadeeth* is connected as Al-Haafidh pointed out in *Fathul-Baaree*."

His, the Exalted One's statement:

$$\text{وَإِن طَآئِفَتَانِ مِنَ ٱلْمُؤْمِنِينَ ٱقْتَتَلُوا۟ فَأَصْلِحُوا۟ بَيْنَهُمَا}$$

"And if two groups of the believers fall into fighting, make peace between them…" (verse 9).

قال الإمام البخاري ﷺ (2691): حدثنا مسدد حدثنا معتمر قال سمعت أبي أن أنسا ﷺ قال: قيل للنبي ﷺ: لو أتيت عبد الله بن أبي فانطلق إليه النبي ﷺ وركب حمارا فانطلق المسلمون يمشون معه وهي أرض سبخة فلما أتاه النبي ﷺ قال: إليك عني والله لقد آذاني نتن حمارك فقال رجل من الأنصار منهم: والله لحمار رسول الله ﷺ أطيب ريحا منك فغضب لعبد الله رجل من قومه فشتمه

فغضب لكل واحد منهما أصحابه فكان بينهما ضرب بالجريد والأيدي والنعال فبلغنا أنها أنزلت: (وَإِن طَآئِفَتَانِ مِنَ ٱلْمُؤْمِنِينَ ٱقْتَتَلُوا۟ فَأَصْلِحُوا۟ بَيْنَهُمَا).

Anas said, "It was said to the Prophet, 'If only you were to go to 'Abdullaah ibn Ubay," so the Prophet went to him riding on a donkey. The Muslims walked along with him as the ground was covered with salt marshes. Then when the Prophet reached him he said, "Get away from me. By Allaah, the stench of your donkey has offended me." A man from the *Ansaar* said, 'By Allaah, the odor of the donkey of the Messenger of Allaah smells better than you.' One of the men from 'Abdullaah's people got upset, so the two started insulting one another. Then each one's companions would get upset on behalf of the one being insulted until they started hitting one another with palm leaves and their hands and shoes. It has reached us that this verse was sent down because of that:

وَإِن طَآئِفَتَانِ مِنَ ٱلْمُؤْمِنِينَ ٱقْتَتَلُوا۟ فَأَصْلِحُوا۟ بَيْنَهُمَا

"And if two groups of the believers fall into fighting, make peace between them…".

Al-Bukhaaree transmitted This *hadeeth* in his *Saheeh* (2691) and Muslim in his *Saheeh* (1799).

His, the Exalted One's statement:

وَلَا تَنَابَزُوا۟ بِٱلْأَلْقَٰبِ

"And do not insult one another by nicknames…" (verse 11).

قال الإمام الترمذي رَحِمَهُ اللهُ (3268): حدثنا عبد الله بن إسحاق الجوهري البصري حدثنا أبو زيد عن شعبة عن داود بن أبي هند قال سمعت الشعبي يحدث عن أبي جبيرة بن الضحاك قال: كان الرجل منا يكون له الاسمان والثلاثة فيدعى ببعضها فعسى أن يكره قال: فنزلت: (وَلَا تَنَابَزُوا۟ بِٱلْأَلْقَٰبِ).

قال أبو عيسى: هذا حديث حسن صحيح أبو جبيرة هو أخو ثابت بن الضحاك بن خليفة أنصاري وأبو زيد سعيد ابن الربيع صاحب الهروي بصري ثقة حدثنا أبو سلمة يحيى بن خلف حدثنا بشر بن المفضل عن داود بن أبي هند عن الشعبي عن أبي جبيرة بن الضحاك نحوه. قال أبو عيسى: هذا حديث حسن صحيح.

Abu Jubairah ibn Ad-Dahhaak stated, "One of us would have two or three names that he may be called by and perhaps at times he would detest that. Then this verse revealed in respect to that,

وَلَا تَنَابَزُوا بِٱلْأَلْقَٰبِ

"And do not insult one another by nicknames…".

This *hadeeth* has been transmitted by At-Tirmidhee in his *Jaami'* (3268) and he has classified it to be *hasan saheeh*.

NOTE: There is a difference of opinion about whether Abu Jubairah is a *Sahaabee* or not. Ibn Hajar said in *Al-Isaabah*, "I say, Al-Bukhaaree transmitted his *hadeeth* in *Al-Adab Al-Mufrad* and as well as the people of *As-Sunan*. Also, Al-Haakim declared it to be authentic, and At-Tirmidhee declared it to be *hasan*…". Ash-Sheikh Muqbil commented, "I say, it appears that he is a *Sahaabee* because if he were a *Taabi'ee*, those people who transmitted his *hadeeth* would have pointed out that it is *mursal* and the person who knows is a proof against the person who does not know regarding the fact that this *hadeeth* has been transmitted as found in the *Musnad* of Ahmad, volume 4, page 69, and volume 5, page 380, on some of his uncles, that the Prophet arrived when there was not one of us who did not have one or two nicknames. Al-Haithamee stated (in *Majma' Az-Zawaa'id*) volume 7, page 111, "Its people are people of the *Saheeh* (Al-Bukhaaree and/or Muslim)." In conclusion, the *hadeeth* is authentic, and all praise is due to Allaah."

A SECOND NOTE: In *Tahdheeb At-Tahdheeb*: Abu Ahmad Al-'Askaree said that Ash-Sha'bee (the narrator in this chain) on Abu Jubairah is *mursal*.[128]

---

[128] Meaning Ash-Sha'bee did not hear from Abu Jubairah. However, in some of the chains of this *hadeeth* it was made clear that Ash-Sha'bee did hear from Abu Jubairah. Refer to the *Musnad* of Al-Imaam Ahmad, volume 4, page 260 and *As-Sunan* by Abu Daawud (4962), and Allaah knows best.

سورة القمر

Sooratul-Qamar

<u>His, the Exalted One's statement:</u>

$$\text{اقْتَرَبَتِ السَّاعَةُ وَانشَقَّ الْقَمَرُ}$$

"The hour has drawn near and the moon has been cleft asunder…" (verses 1-2)

قال الإمام الطبراني ﷺ في المعجم الكبير (ج11 ص 250): حدثنا أحمد بن عمرو البزار ثنا محمد بن يحيى القطعي ثنا محمد بن بكر ثنا ابن جريج عن عمرو بن دينار عن عكرمة عن ابن عباس ﷺ قال: كسف القمر على عهد رسول الله ﷺ فقالوا: سحر القمر فنزلت: (اقْتَرَبَتِ السَّاعَةُ وَانشَقَّ الْقَمَرُ) إلى قوله: (سِحْرٌ مُسْتَمِرٌّ).

Ibn 'Abbaas ؓ said, "The moon eclipsed in the era of the Messenger of Allaah ﷺ so they (the polytheists) said, 'He has performed magic on the moon.' Then the verse descended:

$$\text{اقْتَرَبَتِ السَّاعَةُ وَانشَقَّ الْقَمَرُ}$$

"The hour has drawn near and the moon has been cleft asunder" including His statement,

$$\text{سِحْرٌ مُسْتَمِرٌّ}$$

…this is continuous magic."

At-Tabaraanee transmitted this *hadeeth* in *Al-Mu'jam Al-Kabeer*, volume 11, page 250. Ibn Katheer said in *Al-Bidaayah wa An-Nihaayah*, "Its chain is *jayyid*."

قال الحاكم ﷺ (ج 2 ص 471): أخبرنا أبو زكريا العنبري حدثنا محمد بن عبد السلام حدثنا إسحاق أنبأ عبد الرزاق أنبأ ابن عيينة ومحمد بن مسلم عن ابن أبي نجيح عن مجاهد عن أبي معمر عن عبد الله بن مسعود ﷺ قال: رأيت القمر منشقا بشقتين مرتين بمكة قبل مخرج النبي ﷺ شقة على أبي قبيس وشقة على السويداء فقالوا: سحر القمر فنزلت: (اقْتَرَبَتِ السَّاعَةُ وَانشَقَّ الْقَمَرُ) يقول كما رأيتم القمر منشقا فإن الذي أخبرتكم عن اقتراب الساعة حق.

هذا حديث صحيح على شرط الشيخين ولم يخرجاه بهذه السياقة إنما اتفقا على حديث أبي معمر عن عبد الله مختصرا.

'Abdullaah ibn Mas'ood ؓ said, "I saw the moon split into two-halves twice in Makkah before the Prophet ﷺ had left (for Madeenah). One half was over the mountain Abee Qabees and other half was over As-Suwaidaa (an area outside Makkah that has a mountain). So they said, "He performed magic on the moon." Then it descended:

$$ ٱقْتَرَبَتِ ٱلسَّاعَةُ وَٱنشَقَّ ٱلْقَمَرُ ﴿١﴾ $$

"The hour has drawn near and the moon has been cleft asunder."

He is saying, as you saw the moon split, indeed, what I have told about the about the hour drawing near is true."

Al-Haakim transmitted this *hadeeth* in *Al-Mustadrak*, volume 2, page 471, and he ruled it to be authentic according to standards of the two Sheikhs (Al-Bukhaaree and Muslim). Ash-Sheikh Muqbil ؒ commented saying, "It is as Al-Haakim said."

His, the Exalted One's statement:

$$ يَوْمَ يُسْحَبُونَ فِى ٱلنَّارِ عَلَىٰ وُجُوهِهِمْ ذُوقُوا۟ مَسَّ سَقَرَ ﴿٤٨﴾ إِنَّا كُلَّ شَىْءٍ خَلَقْنَـٰهُ بِقَدَرٍ ﴿٤٩﴾ $$

"The day they will be dragged in the fire on their faces. Taste the touch of hell. Verily We have created all things with divine decree." (verses 48-49)

قال الإمام مسلم ؒ (2656): حدثنا أبو بكر بن أبي شيبة وأبو كريب قالا حدثنا وكيع عن سفيان عن زياد بن إسماعيل عن محمد بن عباد بن جعفر المخزومي عن أبي هريرة ؓ قال: جاء مشركو قريش يخاصمون رسول الله ﷺ في القدر فنزلت: (يَوْمَ يُسْحَبُونَ فِى ٱلنَّارِ عَلَىٰ وُجُوهِهِمْ ذُوقُوا۟ مَسَّ سَقَرَ) (إِنَّا كُلَّ شَىْءٍ خَلَقْنَـٰهُ بِقَدَرٍ).

Abu Hurairah ؓ said, "The polytheists of Quraish came to the Messenger of Allaah ﷺ disputing with him about divine decree. Then the verse descended:

$$\text{يَوْمَ يُسْحَبُونَ فِي ٱلنَّارِ عَلَىٰ وُجُوهِهِمْ ذُوقُوا۟ مَسَّ سَقَرَ ﴿٤٨﴾}$$

"The day they will be dragged in the fire on their faces. Taste the touch of hell."

$$\text{إِنَّا كُلَّ شَيْءٍ خَلَقْنَٰهُ بِقَدَرٍ ﴿٤٩﴾}$$

"Verily We have created all things with divine decree."

Muslim has transmitted this *hadeeth* in his *Saheeh* (2656). In the chain is Ziyaad ibn Ismaa'eel who is a weak narrator; however, Ash-Sheikh Muqbil ﷺ said, "The *hadeeth* is strengthened by the supporting *ahaadeeth* that I mentioned, and Allaah knows best."

قال الإمام البخاري ﷺ في خلق أفعال العباد ص (19): حدثنا محمد بن يوسف حدثنا يونس ابن الحارث حدثنا عمرو بن شعيب عن أبيه عن جده ﷺ قال: نزلت هذه الآية:

(إِنَّ ٱلْمُجْرِمِينَ فِي ضَلَٰلٍ وَسُعُرٍ) في أهل القدر.

ويروى فيه عن ابن عباس ومعاذ بن أنس رضي الله عنهم.

'Abdullaah ibn 'Amr ﷺ said, "This verse descended:

$$\text{إِنَّ ٱلْمُجْرِمِينَ فِي ضَلَٰلٍ وَسُعُرٍ ﴿٤٧﴾}$$

"Verily the criminals are in error and distress" (verse 47),

because of the people who deny divine decree."

Al-Bukhaaree transmitted this *hadeeth* in *Khalq Af'aal Al-'Ibaad*, page 19, and said, "And it has been narrated on Ibn 'Abbaas and Mu'aadh ibn Anas, may Allaah be pleased with them." And At-Tabaraanee transmitted a similar *hadeeth* on Zuraarah in *Al-Mu'jam Al-Kabeer*, volume 5, page 276. Ash-Sheikh Muqbil ﷺ said commented, "In its chain is the son of Zuraarah who is *mubham* (his name is not known)."

سورة الواقعة

Sooratul-Waaqi'ah

<u>His, the Exalted One's statement:</u>

$$وَتَجْعَلُونَ رِزْقَكُمْ أَنَّكُمْ تُكَذِّبُونَ$$

"And you turn your provision (from Allaah) into your denial…"(verse 82).

قال الإمام مسلم ﷺ (73): وحدثني عباس بن عبد العظيم العنبري حدثنا النضر بن محمد حدثنا عكرمة وهو ابن عمار حدثنا أبو زميل قال حدثني ابن عباس ﷺ قال: مطر الناس على عهد النبي ﷺ فقال النبي ﷺ: أصبح من الناس شاكر ومنهم كافر قالوا: هذه رحمة الله وقال بعضهم: لقد صدق نوء كذا وكذا قال فنزلت هذه الآية: (فَلَا أُقْسِمُ بِمَوَاقِعِ ٱلنُّجُومِ) حتى بلغ: (وَتَجْعَلُونَ رِزْقَكُمْ أَنَّكُمْ تُكَذِّبُونَ).

Ibn 'Abbaas ﷺ said, "It rained during the time of the Prophet ﷺ and he said, "Some of the people have awaken thankfully and some of them have awaken as disbelievers. They (the thankful) said, 'This [rain] is mercy from Allaah.' While some of them (the disbelievers) said, "Such-and-such star proved to be true."[129] Then this verse descended:

$$فَلَا أُقْسِمُ بِمَوَاقِعِ ٱلنُّجُومِ$$

"So I swear by the setting positions of the stars…,"

Reaching,

$$وَتَجْعَلُونَ رِزْقَكُمْ أَنَّكُمْ تُكَذِّبُونَ$$

"…And you turn your provision (from Allaah) into your denial…".

This *hadeeth* has been transmitted by Muslim in his *Saheeh* (73). An-Nawawee said in his explanation of *Saheeh Muslim*, "Ash-Sheikh Abu 'Amr ﷺ said, 'He does not mean that all of this descended because of their

---

[129] Ash-Sheikh Ibnul-'Uthaimeen ﷺ said in *Al-Qawl Al-Mufeed 'Alaa Kitaab At-Tawheed*, volume 2, page, 157, "Attributing the rain to a star is of three types:
1- Attributing the creation (of rain to a star). This is major *shirk*.
2- Attributing the causing factor (of rain to a star). This is minor *shirk*.
3- Attributing the time (of rain to a star). This is permissible… meaning the rain came at the time of this star."

statement about the stars, for verily the matter concerning that and its explanation oppose that. Rather, the only thing that descended because of that was His ﷻ statement:

$$\text{وَتَجْعَلُونَ رِزْقَكُمْ أَنَّكُمْ تُكَذِّبُونَ}$$

"And you turn your provision (from Allaah) into your denial…,"

while the rest descended because of something else; however, they were joined together during the time of revelation so they all were mentioned because of that." Ash-Sheikh Abu 'Amr ؒ then said, "And what supports this is the fact that in some narrations of this *hadeeth* on Ibn 'Abbaas ؓ this small portion was only mentioned.

سورة المجادلة

Sooratul-Mujaadilah

His, the Exalted One's statement:

قَدْ سَمِعَ ٱللَّهُ قَوْلَ ٱلَّتِى تُجَٰدِلُكَ فِى زَوْجِهَا

"Indeed Allaah has heard the statement of she who disputes with you concerning her husband…" (verse 1).

قال الإمام أحمد ﵁ (ج 6 ص 46): ثنا أبو معاوية ثنا الأعمش عن تميم بن سلمة عن عروة عن عائشة ﵂ قالت: الحمد لله الذي وسع سمعه الأصوات لقد جاءت المجادلة إلى النبي ﷺ تكلمه وأنا في ناحية البيت ما أسمع ما تقول فأنزل الله عز وجل: (قَدْ سَمِعَ ٱللَّهُ قَوْلَ ٱلَّتِى تُجَٰدِلُكَ فِى زَوْجِهَا) إلى آخر الآية.

'Aishah said, "All praise is due to Allaah, the one who His hearing encompasses all voices. Indeed the woman who disputed about her husband came to the Prophet and spoke to him while I was in a section of the house where I could not hear what she said. Then Allaah sent down the following verse,

قَدْ سَمِعَ ٱللَّهُ قَوْلَ ٱلَّتِى تُجَٰدِلُكَ فِى زَوْجِهَا

'Indeed Allaah has heard the statement of she who disputes with you concerning her husband…'.

This *hadeeth* has been transmitted by Al-Imaam Ahmad in his *Musnad*, volume 6, page 46, as well as Al-Haakim in *Al-Mustadrak*, volume 2, page 481; he considered it to have an authentic chain and Adh-Dhahabee did not oppose his view.

His, the Exalted One's statement:

وَإِذَا جَآءُوكَ حَيَّوْكَ بِمَا لَمْ يُحَيِّكَ بِهِ ٱللَّهُ

"And when they come to you they greet you with a greeting which Allaah greets you not…" (verse 8).

قال الإمام أحمد ﵀ (ج 2 ص 170): ثنا عبد الصمد ثنا حماد عن عطاء بن السائب عن أبيه عن عبد الله بن عمرو ﵁ أن اليهود كانوا يقولون لرسول الله ﷺ: سام عليك ثم يقولون في أنفسهم لولا يعذبنا الله بما نقول فنزلت هذه الآية: (وَإِذَا جَاءُوكَ حَيَّوْكَ بِمَا لَمْ يُحَيِّكَ بِهِ ٱللَّهُ) إلى آخر الآية.

'Abdullaah ibn 'Amr ﵁ narrated that the Jews used to say "*Saam 'alaik* (May death be upon you)" to the Messenger of Allaah ﷺ. Then they would say to themselves, "If only Allaah would punish us for what we say." Then this verse descended,

$$وَإِذَا جَاءُوكَ حَيَّوْكَ بِمَا لَمْ يُحَيِّكَ بِهِ ٱللَّهُ$$

"And when they come to you they greet you with a greeting which Allaah greets you not…".

Al-Imaam Ahmad transmitted this *hadeeth* in his *Musnad*, volume 2, page 170. Al-Haithamee said in *Majma' Az-Zawaa'id*, volume 7, page 122, "Its chain is *jayyid* because Hammaad has heard from 'Ataa ibn As-Saa'ib while he was in a state of good health (before his memory deteriorated)."

قال الإمام مسلم ﵀ (2165 / 11): حدثنا أبو كريب حدثنا أبو معاوية عن الأعمش عن مسلم عن مسروق عن عائشة ﵂ قالت: أتى النبي ﷺ أناس من اليهود فقالوا: السام عليك يا أبا القاسم قال: وعليكم قالت عائشة قلت: بل عليكم السام والذام فقال رسول الله ﷺ: يا عائشة لا تكوني فاحشة فقالت: ما سمعت ما قالوا فقال: أو ليس قد رددت عليهم الذي قالوا قلت: وعليكم. حدثناه إسحاق بن إبراهيم أخبرنا يعلى بن عبيد حدثنا الأعمش بهذا الإسناد غير أنه قال: ففطنت بهم عائشة فسبتهم فقال رسول الله ﷺ: مه يا عائشة فإن الله لا يحب الفحش والتفحش. وزاد فأنزل الله عز وجل: (وَإِذَا جَاءُوكَ حَيَّوْكَ بِمَا لَمْ يُحَيِّكَ بِهِ ٱللَّهُ) إلى آخر الآية.

'Aishah ﵂ said, "A group of people from the Jews came to the Prophet ﷺ and said, '*As-Saam 'alaik* (May death be upon you), O Abaa Al-Qaasim.' He said, "And upon you." I replied, 'Rather, may death and disgrace be upon you!' The Messenger of Allaah ﷺ said, "O 'Aishah, do not be a foul mouth." She said, 'Did you not hear what they said?' He said, "Did I not reply to what they said? I said, 'And upon you."

In another narration of this *hadeeth* it reads, "'Aishah caught on to what they said and she threw insults at them. The Messenger of Allaah ﷺ said to her, 'Restrain yourself O 'Aishah, for verily Allaah does not love indecency or obscenity." Then Allaah ﷻ revealed the following,

$$\text{وَإِذَا جَاءُوكَ حَيَّوْكَ بِمَا لَمْ يُحَيِّكَ بِهِ ٱللَّهُ}$$

"And when they come to you they greet you with a greeting which Allaah greets you not…".

This *hadeeth* has been transmitted by Muslim in his *Saheeh* (2165/11).

His, the Exalted One's statement:

$$\text{وَيَحْلِفُونَ عَلَى ٱلْكَذِبِ وَهُمْ يَعْلَمُونَ}$$

"And they swear on a lie while they know."

قال الإمام أحمد ﷺ (ج 1 ص 240): ثنا محمد بن جعفر ثنا شعبة عن سماك بن حرب عن سعيد بن جبير عن ابن عباس ﷺ قال: قال رسول الله ﷺ: يدخل عليكم رجل ينظر بعين شيطان أو بعيني شيطان قال: فدخل رجل أزرق فقال: يا محمد علام سببتني أو شتمتني أو نحو هذا قال: وجعل يحلف قال: فنزلت هذه الآية في المجادلة: (وَيَحْلِفُونَ عَلَى ٱلْكَذِبِ وَهُمْ يَعْلَمُونَ) والآية الأخرى.

Ibn 'Abbaas ﷺ said, "The Messenger of Allaah ﷺ said, "A man will come to you looking with the eye of a devil," or, "the two eyes of a devil." A blue-eyed man then entered and said, 'O Muhammad, why do you revile me or abuse me?,' or something similar to that.[130] So the man then started to swear and thereafter this verse in *Sooratul-Mujaadilah* descended,

$$\text{وَيَحْلِفُونَ عَلَى ٱلْكَذِبِ وَهُمْ يَعْلَمُونَ}$$

"And they swear on a lie while they know," along with the other verse."[131]

Al-Imaam Ahmad transmitted this *hadeeth* in his *Musnad*, volume 1, page 240. In some narrations of this *hadeeth*, verse 74 of *Sooratut-Tawbah* was mentioned:

---

[130] In this narration of the *hadeeth* it was the man who said to the Prophet ﷺ, "Why do you revile me?" Ash-Sheikh Ahmad Shaakir explained in his footnotes on the *Musnad* of Al-Imaam Ahmad, volume 4, page 16, that this is a mistake and what is correct from other narrations is that the Prophet ﷺ said to the man, "Why do you and your comrades revile me."

[131] In other narrations of this *hadeeth* in the *Musnad* of Al-Imaam Ahmad verse 18 of *Sooratul-Mujaadilah* was mentioned:

$$\text{فَيَحْلِفُونَ لَهُ كَمَا يَحْلِفُونَ لَكُمْ}$$

"…then they will swear to Him as they swear to you…"

$$\text{يَحْلِفُونَ بِٱللَّهِ مَا قَالُواْ}$$

"They swear by Allaah that they said nothing (bad)…"

Ash-Sheikh Muqbil ﷺ said about this, "Either the two verses were revealed for one reason or Simaak ibn Harb (a narrator in the chain) was inconsistent in it (this *hadeeth*). Indeed he is known to be inconsistent in *hadeeth* especially after he grew old, and Allaah knows best. Also, it is more likely that the verse in *Sooratul-Mujaadilah* was the verse that descended because the one who narrates on him is Shu'bah, who heard from him earlier before his old age, as is mentioned in *Tahdheeb At-Tahdheeb*."

سورة الحشر

Sooratul-Hashr

قال الإمام البخاري رَحِمَهُ اللهُ (4882): حدثنا محمد بن عبد الرحيم حدثنا سعيد بن سليمان حدثنا هشيم أخبرنا أبو بشر عن سعيد بن جبير قال قلت لابن عباس رَضِيَ اللهُ عَنْهُ: سورة التوبة قال: التوبة هي الفاضحة ما زالت تنزل ومنهم ومنهم حتى ظنوا أنها لن تبقي أحدا منهم إلا ذكر فيها قلت قال: سورة الأنفال قال: نزلت في بدر قال قلت: سورة الحشر قال: نزلت في بني النضير.

Sa'eed ibn Jubair said, "I said to Ibn 'Abbaas ؓ, 'Sooratut-Tawbah?' He said, "At-Tawbah is Al-Faadihah (the exposing chapter). It continued to descend stating, "And amongst them, and amongst them," until they (the hypocrites) thought it would not let a single one of them go unmentioned." I said, 'Sooratul-Anfaal?' "It descended because of Badr," He replied. I continued, 'Sooratul-Hashr?' He said, "It descended because of the tribe Banee An-Nadeer (a tribe of the Jews)."

Al-Bukhaaree transmitted this *hadeeth* in his *Saheeh* (4882), as well as Muslim in his *Saheeh* (3031).

قال الحاكم رَحِمَهُ اللهُ (ج 2 ص 483): أخبرني أبو عبد الله محمد بن علي الصنعاني بمكة حدثنا علي بن المبارك الصنعاني حدثنا زيد بن المبارك الصنعاني حدثنا محمد بن ثور عن معمر عن الزهري عن عروة عن عائشة رَضِيَ اللهُ عَنْها قالت: كانت غزوة بني النضير وهم طائفة من اليهود على رأس ستة أشهر من وقعة بدر وكان منزلهم ونخلهم بناحية المدينة فحاصرهم رسول الله ﷺ حتى نزلوا على الجلاء وعلى أن لهم ما أقلت الإبل من الأمتعة والأموال إلا الحلقة يعني السلاح فأنزل الله فيهم: (سَبَّحَ لِلَّهِ مَا فِي ٱلسَّمَٰوَٰتِ وَمَا فِي ٱلۡأَرۡضِ) إلى قوله: (لِأَوَّلِ ٱلۡحَشۡرِۚ مَا ظَنَنتُمۡ أَن يَخۡرُجُواْ) فقاتلهم النبي ﷺ حتى صالحهم على الجلاء فأجلاهم إلى الشام وكانوا من سبط لم يصبهم جلاء خلا ما كان الله قد كتب عليهم ذلك ولولا ذلك لعذبهم في الدنيا بالقتل والسبي وأما قوله: (لِأَوَّلِ ٱلۡحَشۡرِ) فكان جلاؤهم ذلك أول حشر في الدنيا إلى الشام.

هذا حديث صحيح على شرط الشيخين ولم يخرجاه.

'Aishah ؓ stated, "The battle of the tribe Banee An-Nadeer, a group of Jews, occurred six months after the battle of Badr. Their houses and date palm groves were located in a section of Madeenah. The Messenger of Allaah ﷺ surrounded them until they finally conceded to being dislodged on condition that they could keep whatever wealth and belongings their camels could carry except for weapons. Then Allaah sent down the following because of them,

$$\text{سَبَّحَ لِلَّهِ مَا فِى ٱلسَّمَٰوَٰتِ وَمَا فِى ٱلْأَرْضِ}$$

'Whatsoever is in the heavens and whatsoever is on earth glorifies Allaah…,'
Including His statement,

$$\text{لِأَوَّلِ ٱلْحَشْرِ ۚ مَا ظَنَنتُمْ أَن يَخْرُجُوا}$$

"…at the first gathering. You did not think that they would leave…"

The Prophet ﷺ fought them until finally making a treaty with them that they be dislodged and ousted to Shaam. They were from a tribe of the Jews that had never previously been ousted. Allaah ordained that for them and if it were not for that He would have punished them in this world with killing and capture. As for His statement,

$$\text{لِأَوَّلِ ٱلْحَشْرِ}$$

"…at the first gathering…,"

Their dislodgement was the first gathering in this world, when they were ousted to Shaam."

This *hadeeth* has been transmitted by Al-Haakim in *Al-Mustadrak*, volume 2, page 483, and he classified it to be authentic according to the standards of the two Sheikhs (Al-Bukhaaree and Muslim). Ash-Sheikh Muqbil ﷺ commented, "That is what Al-Haakim ﷺ has said and the *hadeeth* is authentic; however, it does not meet the standards of the two Shieks because they did not transmit (the *ahaadeeth*) of Zaid ibn Al-Mubaarak and Muhammad ibn Thawr."

His, the Exalted One's statement:

$$\text{مَا قَطَعْتُم مِّن لِّينَةٍ أَوْ تَرَكْتُمُوهَا قَآئِمَةً عَلَىٰ أُصُولِهَا فَبِإِذْنِ ٱللَّهِ}$$

"What you cut down of the palm trees or left standing on their trunks, it was by the permission of Allaah…" (verse 5).

قال الإمام البخاري رَحِمَهُ اللهُ (4031): حدثنا آدم حدثنا الليث عن نافع عن ابن عمر ﷺ قال: حرق رسول الله ﷺ نخل بني النضير وقطع وهي البويرة فنزلت: (مَا قَطَعْتُم مِّن لِّينَةٍ أَوْ تَرَكْتُمُوهَا قَآئِمَةً عَلَىٰ أُصُولِهَا فَبِإِذْنِ ٱللَّهِ).

Ibn 'Umar said, "The Messenger of Allaah burned the date palms that belonged to the tribe of Banee An-Nadeer and cut them down. That was at Al-Buwairah.[132] Then the following verse descended:

$$\text{مَا قَطَعْتُم مِّن لِّينَةٍ أَوْ تَرَكْتُمُوهَا قَآئِمَةً عَلَىٰ أُصُولِهَا فَبِإِذْنِ ٱللَّهِ}$$

"What you cut down of the palm trees or left standing on their trunks, it was by the permission of Allaah…".

This *hadeeth* has been transmitted by Al-Bukhaaree in his *Saheeh* (4031) as well as Muslim in his *Saheeh* (1746).

قال الإمام الترمذي (3303): حدثنا الحسن بن محمد الزعفراني حدثنا عفان بن مسلم حدثنا حفص ابن غياث حدثني حبيب بن أبي عمرة عن سعيد بن جبير عن ابن عباس في قول الله عز وجل: (مَا قَطَعْتُم مِّن لِّينَةٍ أَوْ تَرَكْتُمُوهَا قَآئِمَةً عَلَىٰ أُصُولِهَا) قال: اللينة النخلة: (وَلِيُخْزِيَ ٱلْفَاسِقِينَ) قال: استنزلوهم من حصونهم قال: وأمروا بقطع النخل فحك في صدورهم فقال المسلمون: قد قطعنا بعضا وتركنا بعضا فلنسألن رسول الله: هل لنا فيما قطعنا من أجر وهل علينا فيما تركنا من وزر فأنزل الله تعالى: (مَا قَطَعْتُم مِّن لِّينَةٍ أَوْ تَرَكْتُمُوهَا قَآئِمَةً عَلَىٰ أُصُولِهَا) الآية.

قال أبو عيسى: هذا حديث حسن غريب وروى بعضهم هذا الحديث عن حفص بن غياث عن حبيب بن أبي عمرة عن سعيد بن جبير مرسلا ولم يذكر فيه عن ابن عباس حدثني بذلك عبد الله بن عبد الرحمن حدثنا مروان بن معاوية عن حفص بن غياث عن حبيب بن أبي عمرة عن سعيد بن جبير عن النبي صلى الله عليه وسلم مرسلا.

On Ibn 'Abbaas concerning the statement of Allaah:

$$\text{مَا قَطَعْتُم مِّن لِّينَةٍ أَوْ تَرَكْتُمُوهَا قَآئِمَةً عَلَىٰ أُصُولِهَا}$$

"What you cut down of the palm trees or left standing on their trunks…"

He said, "*Al-leenah* is the date palm."

$$\text{وَلِيُخْزِيَ ٱلْفَاسِقِينَ}$$

"…that He may disgrace the disobedient."

He stated, "They forced them out of their fortresses and they were ordered to cut down the date palms which had a deep effect on them. The Muslims said,

---

[132] Al-Buwairah is a place located between Madeenah and Teemaa.

"We have cut down some and left others standing. Indeed we will ask the Messenger of Allaah ﷺ if there is any reward for us for what we cut down and any sin on us for what we left standing." Then Allaah sent down:

$$\text{مَا قَطَعْتُم مِّن لِّينَةٍ أَوْ تَرَكْتُمُوهَا قَائِمَةً عَلَىٰ أُصُولِهَا}$$

"What you cut down of the palm trees or left standing on their trunks…".

At-Tirmidhee transmitted this *hadeeth* it in his *Jaami'* (3303) and classified it to be *hasan ghareeb*.

<u>His, the Exalted One's statement:</u>

$$\text{وَيُؤْثِرُونَ عَلَىٰ أَنفُسِهِمْ وَلَوْ كَانَ بِهِمْ خَصَاصَةٌ}$$

"And they give them preference over themselves even though they are in need…" (verse 9).

قال الإمام البخاري رحمه الله (3798): حدثنا مسدد حدثنا عبد الله بن داود عن فضيل بن غزوان عن أبي حازم عن أبي هريرة رضي الله عنه أن رجلا أتى النبي ﷺ فبعث إلى نسائه فقلن: ما معنا إلا الماء فقال رسول الله ﷺ: من يضم أو يضيف هذا فقال رجل من الأنصار: أنا فانطلق به إلى امرأته فقال: أكرمي ضيف رسول الله ﷺ فقالت: ما عندنا إلا قوت صبياني فقال: هيئي طعامك وأصبحي سراجك ونومي صبيانك إذا أرادوا عشاء فهيأت طعامها وأصبحت سراجها ونومت صبيانها ثم قامت كأنها تصلح سراجها فأطفأته فجعلا يريانه أنهما يأكلان فباتا طاويين فلما أصبح غدا إلى رسول الله ﷺ فقال: ضحك الله الليلة أو عجب من فعالكما فأنزل الله: (وَيُؤْثِرُونَ عَلَىٰ أَنفُسِهِمْ وَلَوْ كَانَ بِهِمْ خَصَاصَةٌ وَمَن يُوقَ شُحَّ نَفْسِهِ فَأُولَٰئِكَ هُمُ الْمُفْلِحُونَ).

Abu Hurairah ؓ narrated that a man came to the Prophet ﷺ, so he sent (someone) to his wives [requesting food]. They replied, "We have nothing but water." The Messenger of Allaah ﷺ then asked, "Who will take in" or "receive this person as a guest?" A man from the *Ansaar* said, "I." So he brought the man with him to his wife and said, "Be hospitable to the guest of the Messenger of Allaah ﷺ." She said, "We have nothing except the food for my children." He said, "Prepare your food and light your lamp and put your children to sleep when they want dinner." She then prepared her food, lit her lamp and put her children to sleep. Then she stood and acted as if she was fixing her lamp and put it out. Then the two (the husband and wife) acted as if they were eating and spent the night in hunger. When he (the husband) woke up in the morning, he went to the Messenger of Allaah ﷺ and he (The

Prophet ﷺ) said, "Allaah laughed" or "was amazed[133] last night at what you two did." Then Allaah sent down:

$$\text{وَيُؤْثِرُونَ عَلَىٰ أَنفُسِهِمْ وَلَوْ كَانَ بِهِمْ خَصَاصَةٌ ۚ وَمَن يُوقَ شُحَّ نَفْسِهِ فَأُولَٰئِكَ هُمُ ٱلْمُفْلِحُونَ}$$

"And they give them preference over themselves even though they are in need. And whoever is saved from the stinginess of his own soul, they are the successful [ones]."

Al-Bukhaaree transmitted *this hadeeth* in his *Saheeh* (3798) as well as Muslim in his *Saheeh* (2054).

---

[133] Ash-Sheikh Ibnul-'Uthaimeen ﷺ explained in his explanation of *Al-'Aqeedah Al-Waasitiyah*, volume 2, page 27, that amazement can have two different reasons. He said, "The first reason: (When) the causes for the thing being amazed at are not known to the one being amazed whereas it comes to him unexpectedly without notice. This is not possible to be ascribed to Allaah ﷻ because Allaah knows everything. Nothing on earth or in the heavens is hidden to him. The second: When the reason for that is this thing goes against its peers and against the norm without any deficiency on part of the one being amazed whereas he (the one being amazed at) does something strange that does not normally happen from the likes of him. This is an affirmed attribute of Allaah."

سورة الممتحنة

Sooratul-Mumtahanah

His, the Exalted One's statement:

يَٰٓأَيُّهَا ٱلَّذِينَ ءَامَنُوٓا۟ إِذَا جَآءَكُمُ ٱلْمُؤْمِنَٰتُ مُهَٰجِرَٰتٍ فَٱمْتَحِنُوهُنَّ

"O you who believe, when believing women come to you as emigrants examine them…" (verse 10).

قال الإمام البخاري ﷺ (2711) (2712): حدثنا يحيى بن بكير حدثنا الليث عن عقيل عن ابن شهاب قال أخبرني عروة بن الزبير أنه سمع مروان والمسور بن مخرمة ﷺ يخبران عن أصحاب رسول الله ﷺ قال: لما كاتب سهيل بن عمرو يومئذ كان فيما اشترط سهيل بن عمرو على النبي ﷺ أنه لا يأتيك منا أحد وإن كان على دينك إلا رددته إلينا وخليت بيننا وبينه فكره المؤمنون ذلك وامتعضوا منه وأبى سهيل إلا ذلك فكاتبه النبي ﷺ على ذلك فرد يومئذ أبا جندل إلى أبيه سهيل بن عمرو ولم يأته أحد من الرجال إلا رده في تلك المدة وإن كان مسلما وجاء المؤمنات مهاجرات وكانت أم كلثوم بنت عقبة بن أبي معيط ممن خرج إلى رسول الله ﷺ يومئذ وهي عاتق فجاء أهلها يسألون النبي ﷺ أن يرجعها إليهم فلم يرجعها إليهم لما أنزل الله فيهن: (إِذَا جَآءَكُمُ ٱلْمُؤْمِنَٰتُ مُهَٰجِرَٰتٍ فَٱمْتَحِنُوهُنَّ ٱللَّهُ أَعْلَمُ بِإِيمَٰنِهِنَّ) إلى قوله: (وَلَا هُمْ يَحِلُّونَ لَهُنَّ).

(2713): قال عروة: فأخبرتني عائشة ﷺ أن رسول الله ﷺ كان يمتحنهن بهذه الآية: (يَٰٓأَيُّهَا ٱلَّذِينَ ءَامَنُوٓا۟ إِذَا جَآءَكُمُ ٱلْمُؤْمِنَٰتُ مُهَٰجِرَٰتٍ فَٱمْتَحِنُوهُنَّ) إلى: (غَفُورٌ رَّحِيمٌ) قال عروة: قالت عائشة: فمن أقر بهذا الشرط منهن قال لها رسول الله ﷺ: قد بايعتك كلاما يكلمها به والله ما مست يده يد امرأة قط في المبايعة وما بايعهن إلا بقوله.

Marwaan and Al-Miswar ibn Makhramah ﷺ narrated about the Companions of the Messenger of Allaah ﷺ saying, "On that day when Suhail ibn 'Amr made the treaty, one of the conditions that Suhail ibn 'Amr proposed to the Prophet ﷺ was that not a single one of us be would be permitted to go the Prophet, even as a Muslim, except that he would be required to send him back to the disbelievers. The believers disliked and resented this proposal but Suhail insisted, so the Prophet ﷺ made a treaty with him [based] on that (condition). That same day he sent back Abu Jandal to his father Suhail ibn 'Amr. Not a single man came to him during that time except that he sent him back, even if he was Muslim.

On one occasion, the believing women came to make *hijrah*. Umm Kulthoom bint 'Uqbah ibn Abee Mu'ait was one of those who went to the Messenger of Allaah ﷺ on that day [as an emigrant]. During this time she was a young lady. Her family came to the Prophet ﷺ requesting that her send her back to them but he refused after Allaah sent down the following in their regard:

$$إِذَا جَاءَكُمُ ٱلْمُؤْمِنَاتُ مُهَاجِرَاتٍ فَٱمْتَحِنُوهُنَّ ٱللَّهُ أَعْلَمُ بِإِيمَانِهِنَّ$$

"When believing women come to you as emigrants examine them. Allaah knows best as to their faith…," including,

$$وَلَا هُمْ يَحِلُّونَ لَهُنَّ$$

"…nor are they (the disbelievers) lawful for them (the believing women)."

'Urwah stated, "'Aishah narrated to me that the Messenger of Allaah ﷺ used to examine them with this verse,

$$يَٰٓأَيُّهَا ٱلَّذِينَ ءَامَنُوٓاْ إِذَا جَاءَكُمُ ٱلْمُؤْمِنَاتُ مُهَاجِرَاتٍ فَٱمْتَحِنُوهُنَّ$$

'O you who believe, when believing women come to you as emigrants examine them…,' including

$$غَفُورٌ رَّحِيمٌ$$

"…Oft-Forgiving Most Merciful" (verses 10-12).

'Urwah continued, "Aishah said, "the Messenger of Allaah ﷺ would say to any of them who accepted this condition, 'I accept your pledge of allegiance,' a simple statement. By Allaah, his hand never touched the hand of a woman when taking their pledge of allegiance. He would only accept their pledges through verbal confirmation."

Al-Bukhaaree transmitted this *hadeeth* in his *Saheeh* (2711, 2712, and 2713).

سورة الصف

Sooratus-Saff

قال الإمام الدارمي رَحِمَهُ اللهُ (ج 2 ص 200): أخبرنا محمد بن كثير عن الأوزاعي عن يحيى بن أبي كثير عن أبي سلمة عن عبد الله بن سلام رَضِيَ اللهُ عَنْهُ قال: قعدنا نفر من أصحاب رسول الله ﷺ فتذاكرنا فقلنا: لو نعلم أي الأعمال أحب إلى الله تعالى لعملناه فأنزل الله تعالى: (سَبَّحَ لِلَّهِ مَا فِى ٱلسَّمَـٰوَٰتِ وَمَا فِى ٱلْأَرْضِ ۖ وَهُوَ ٱلْعَزِيزُ ٱلْحَكِيمُ ۝ يَـٰٓأَيُّهَا ٱلَّذِينَ ءَامَنُوا۟ لِمَ تَقُولُونَ مَا لَا تَفْعَلُونَ ۝ كَبُرَ مَقْتًا) حتى ختمها.

قال عبد الله: فقرأها علينا رسول الله ﷺ حتى ختمها قال أبو سلمة: فقرأها علينا ابن سلام قال يحيى: فقرأها علينا أبو سلمة وقرأها علينا يحيى وقرأها علينا الأوزاعي وقرأها علينا محمد.

Ad-Daarimee stated in his *Musnad*, volume 2, page 200, "Muhammad ibn Katheer narrated to us on Al-Awzaa'ee, on Yahyaa ibn Abee Katheer, on Abee Salamah, on 'Abdillaah ibn Salaam ؓ that he said, 'We, a group of Companions of the Messenger of Allaah ﷺ sat down and began talking to one another. We said, "If only we knew which deed is most beloved to Allaah ﷻ we would perform it." Then Allaah ﷻ sent down:

سَبَّحَ لِلَّهِ مَا فِى ٱلسَّمَـٰوَٰتِ وَمَا فِى ٱلْأَرْضِ ۖ وَهُوَ ٱلْعَزِيزُ ٱلْحَكِيمُ ۝ يَـٰٓأَيُّهَا ٱلَّذِينَ ءَامَنُوا۟ لِمَ تَقُولُونَ مَا لَا تَفْعَلُونَ ۝ كَبُرَ مَقْتًا

"Whatsoever is in the heavens and whatsoever is on earth glorifies Allaah, and He is the All-Mighty the All-Wise. O you who believe, why do you say that which you do not do. Most hateful it is…" (verse 1-2).

'Abdullaah said, "The Messenger of Allaah ﷺ recited it to us completely." Abu Salamah said, "Ibn Salaam recited it to us." Yahyaa said, "Abu Salamah recited it to us." (Al-Awzaa'ee) said, "Yahyaa recited it to us." (Muhammad said), "Al-Awzaa'ee recited it to us." (Ad-Daarimee said), "Muhammad recited it to us."[134]

Al-Imaam Ahmad has also transmitted this *hadeeth* in his *Musnad*, volume 5, page 452, and others. Al-Haafidh Ibn Hajar said in his explanation of

---

[134] In the science of *hadeeth*, this *hadeeth* is called *Musalsal*. *Musalsal* is a type of *hadeeth* in which the people of the chain follow one another in sequence in a particular characteristic or in a manner of narrating. In this *hadeeth* each Sheikh recited to his student *Sooratus-Saff*.

Nukhbah Al-Fikar, "Indeed it is the most authentic of the *Musalsalaat* (plural of *Musalsal*)."

سورة الجمعة

Sooratul-Jumu'ah

His, the Exalted One's statement:

$$\text{وَإِذَا رَأَوْاْ تِجَٰرَةً أَوْ لَهْوًا ٱنفَضُّوٓاْ إِلَيْهَا وَتَرَكُوكَ قَآئِمًا}$$

"And when they see some trade or some amusement they disperse to it and leave you standing…" (verse 11).

قال الإمام البخاري ﷺ (936): حدثنا معاوية بن عمرو قال حدثنا زائدة عن حصين عن سالم ابن أبي الجعد قال حدثنا جابر بن عبد الله ﷺ قال: بينما نحن نصلي مع النبي ﷺ إذ أقبلت عير تحمل طعاما فالتفتوا إليها حتى ما بقي مع النبي ﷺ إلا اثنا عشر رجلا فنزلت هذه الآية: (وَإِذَا رَأَوْاْ تِجَٰرَةً أَوْ لَهْوًا ٱنفَضُّوٓاْ إِلَيْهَا وَتَرَكُوكَ قَآئِمًا).

Jaabir ibn 'Abdillaah ﷺ stated, "While we were praying[135] with the Prophet ﷺ a caravan carrying food suddenly arrived. Consequently a bunch of them headed for it such that only twelve men remained with the Prophet ﷺ. The verse in question descended as a result:

$$\text{وَإِذَا رَأَوْاْ تِجَٰرَةً أَوْ لَهْوًا ٱنفَضُّوٓاْ إِلَيْهَا وَتَرَكُوكَ قَآئِمًا}$$

"And when they see some trade or some amusement they disperse to it and leave you standing…".

Al-Bukhaaree transmitted this *hadeeth* in his *Saheeh* (936) as well as Muslim in his *Saheeh* (863).

قال الإمام ابن جرير ﷺ (ج 23 ص 388): حدثنا محمد بن سهل بن عسكر قال ثنا يحيى بن صالح قال ثنا سليمان بن بلال عن جعفر بن محمد عن أبيه عن جابر بن عبد الله ﷺ قال: كان الجواري إذا نكحوا كانوا يمرون بالكبر والمزامير ويتركون النبي ﷺ قائما على المنبر وينفضون إليها فأنزل الله: (وَإِذَا رَأَوْاْ تِجَٰرَةً أَوْ لَهْوًا ٱنفَضُّوٓاْ إِلَيْهَا).

---

[135] In another narration of this *hadeeth* in *Muslim* the wording was: "While the Messenger of Allaah ﷺ was giving the sermon." Al-Haafidh Ibn Hajar said in *Fathul-Baaree* in the explanation of *hadeeth* (936), "So due to this, his statement: 'While we were praying,' means while we were waiting for the prayer."

قال السيوطي ﷺ في الدر المنثور (ج 6 ص 221): وأخرج ابن جرير وابن المنذر عن جابر ابن عبد الله ﷺ أن النبي ﷺ كان يخطب الناس يوم الجمعة فإذا كان نكاح لعب أهله وعزفوا ومروا باللهو على المسجد وإذا نزل بالبطحاء جلب قال وكانت البطحاء مجلسا بفناء المسجد الذي يلي بقيع الغرقد وكانت الأعراب إذا جلبوا الخيل والإبل والغنم وبضائع الأعراب نزلوا البطحاء فإذا سمع ذلك من يقعد للخطبة قاموا للهو والتجارة وتركوه قائما فعاتب الله المؤمنين لنبيه ﷺ فقال: (وَإِذَا رَأَوْا تِجَٰرَةً أَوْ لَهْوًا ٱنفَضُّوٓا۟ إِلَيْهَا وَتَرَكُوكَ قَآئِمًا).

Jaabir ibn 'Abdillaah ؓ narrated that the Prophet ﷺ used to deliver a sermon to the people on the day of *Jumu'ah* and whenever there was a wedding taking place, the family of the newlyweds would play music and pass by the *masjid* with their entertainment. Moreover, when an import would arrive at Al-Bathaa, which was a sitting area in the open space on the side of the *masjid* next to the graveyard Baqee' Al-Gharqad, where the desert Arabs would bring camels, sheep, and other merchandise of the Bedouin Arabs for sale, the people sitting in the *Jumu'ah* sermon would go to the amusement and trade and leave him (the Prophet) standing. As a result, Allaah censured the believers on behalf of His Prophet ﷺ saying:

وَإِذَا رَأَوْا تِجَٰرَةً أَوْ لَهْوًا ٱنفَضُّوٓا۟ إِلَيْهَا وَتَرَكُوكَ قَآئِمًا

"And when they see some trade or some amusement they disperse to it and leave you standing…".

As-Suyootee mentioned this *hadeeth* in *Ad-Durr Al-Manthoor*, volume 6, page 221, and stated that it has been transmitted by Ibn Jareer and Ibn Al-Mundhir. Furthermore, in the *Tafseer* of Ibn Jareer, volume 23, page 388 a small portion of this *hadeeth* was mentioned. Ash-Sheikh Muqbil ؒ commented on the chain of Ibn Jareer saying, "The people of its chain are people of the *Saheeh* (Al-Bukhaaree and/or Muslim)." The Sheikh also stated in the footnote of the latest edition, "I only quoted it from *Ad-Durr Al-Manthoor* because the wording of At-Tabaree (Ibn Jareer) is not clear and because in it, two reasons were mentioned together."

سورة المنافقون

Sooratul-Munaafiqoon

قال الإمام البخاري رَحِمَهُ اللَّه (4900): حدثنا عبد الله بن رجاء حدثنا إسرائيل عن أبي إسحاق عن زيد بن أرقم رَضِيَ اللَّهُ عَنْهُ قال: كنت في غزاة فسمعت عبد الله بن أبي يقول: لا تنفقوا على من عند رسول الله حتى ينفضوا من حوله ولئن رجعنا من عنده ليخرجن الأعز منها الأذل فذكرت ذلك لعمي أو لعمر فذكره للنبي ﷺ فدعاني فحدثته فأرسل رسول الله ﷺ إلى عبد الله بن أبي وأصحابه فحلفوا ما قالوا فكذبني رسول الله ﷺ وصدقه فأصابني هم لم يصبني مثله قط فجلست في البيت فقال لي عمي: ما أردت إلى أن كذبك رسول الله ﷺ ومقتك فأنزل الله تعالى: (إِذَا جَآءَكَ ٱلۡمُنَٰفِقُونَ) فبعث إليّ النبي ﷺ فقرأ فقال: إن الله قد صدقك يا زيد.

Zaid ibn Arqam ؓ said, "I was on a military expedition when I heard 'Abdullaah ibn Ubay say, 'Do not financially support those who are with the Messenger of Allaah so that they may disperse from him' and, "If we return after being with him, then indeed the mightier one will expel the lowliest one from that place." So I mentioned that to my uncle or to 'Umar, who mentioned it to the Prophet ﷺ. He then summonsed me so I went and told him about that. The Messenger of Allaah ﷺ then sent for 'Abdullaah ibn Ubay and his companions. They swore they did not say [what I had told the Messenger of Allah] and he did not believe me but instead believed him. I was stricken with grief, the likes of which I have never experienced so I sat in the house. My uncle said to me, 'What where you trying to do that led the Messenger of Allaah ﷺ to disbelieve [in what you have said] and detest you?' Then Allaah ﷻ sent down:

$$\text{إِذَا جَآءَكَ ٱلۡمُنَٰفِقُونَ}$$

"When the hypocrites come to you…"

The Prophet ﷺ sent for me, recited it and said, 'Verily Allaah has confirmed your truthfulness, O Zaid.'

Al-Bukhaaree transmitted this *hadeeth* in his *Saheeh* (4900) and likewise Muslim in his *Saheeh* (2772).

قال الإمام البخاري رَحِمَهُ اللَّه (4902): حدثنا آدم حدثنا شعبة عن الحكم قال سمعت محمد بن كعب القرظي قال سمعت زيد بن أرقم ﷺ قال: لما قال عبد الله بن أبي: لا تنفقوا على من عند رسول الله وقال أيضا: لئن رجعنا إلى المدينة أخبرت به النبي ﷺ فلامني الأنصار وحلف عبد الله بن أبي ما قال

ذلك فرجعت إلى المنزل فنمت فدعاني رسول الله ﷺ فأتيته فقال: إن الله قد صدقك ونزل: (هُمُ ٱلَّذِينَ يَقُولُونَ لَا تُنفِقُوا) الآية.

وقال ابن أبي زائدة عن الأعمش عن عمرو عن ابن أبي ليلى عن زيد عن النبي ﷺ.

Zaid ibn Arqam ؓ said, "When 'Abdullaah ibn Ubay said, 'Do not financially support those who are with the Messenger of Allaah,' and he also stated, "If we return to Madeenah…". I informed the Prophet about his statement which caused the *Ansaar* to criticize me and 'Abdullaah ibn Ubay swore that he did not say that. I returned to the house and fell asleep. Then the Messenger of Allaah ﷺ summonsed me so I went to him. 'Verily Allaah has confirmed your truthfulness, he said.' Thereafter the following verse descended:

$$هُمُ ٱلَّذِينَ يَقُولُونَ لَا تُنفِقُوا$$

"They are the ones who say: 'do not financially support …'".

This *hadeeth* has been transmitted by Al-Bukhaaree in his *Saheeh* (4902).

سورة التحريم

Sooratut-Tahreem

قال الإمام البخاري ﷺ (5267): حدثني الحسن بن محمد بن صباح حدثنا حجاج عن ابن جريج قال زعم عطاء أنه سمع عبيد بن عمير يقول سمعت عائشة ﷺ أن النبي ﷺ كان يمكث عند زينب بنت جحش ويشرب عندها عسلاً فتواصيت أنا وحفصة أن أيتنا دخل عليها النبي ﷺ فلتقل: إني أجد منك ريح مغافير أكلت مغافير فدخل على إحداهما فقالت له ذلك فقال: لا بل شربت عسلاً عند زينب بنت جحش ولن أعود له فنزلت: (يَا أَيُّهَا ٱلنَّبِيُّ لِمَ تُحَرِّمُ مَا أَحَلَّ ٱللَّهُ لَكَ) إلى: (إِن تَتُوبَا إِلَى ٱللَّهِ) لعائشة وحفصة: (وَإِذْ أَسَرَّ ٱلنَّبِيُّ إِلَىٰ بَعْضِ أَزْوَٰجِهِۦ) لقوله: بل شربت عسلاً.

'Aishah ﷺ narrated that the Prophet ﷺ was staying with Zainab bint Jahsh to drink honey with her. So Hafsah and I agreed that whichever of us the Prophet ﷺ was to come to [after being with Zainab] she would say, 'Indeed I smell the aroma of sweet gum [emanating from you]. Have you eaten sweet gum?' He then came to one of them and she said what they had agreed to say so he said, "No, rather I drank honey with Zainab bint Jahsh and I will not do it again." Then this verse descended:

$$\text{يَا أَيُّهَا ٱلنَّبِيُّ لِمَ تُحَرِّمُ مَا أَحَلَّ ٱللَّهُ لَكَ}$$

"O Prophet, why do you forbid what Allaah has made permissible for you…" including,

$$\text{إِن تَتُوبَا إِلَى ٱللَّهِ}$$

'If you two turn in repentance to Allaah…,' because of 'Aishah and Hafsah.

$$\text{وَإِذْ أَسَرَّ ٱلنَّبِيُّ إِلَىٰ بَعْضِ أَزْوَٰجِهِۦ}$$

"And (remember) when the Prophet confidentially mentioned an issue to one of his wives," [descended] because of his statement," Rather I drank honey."

This *hadeeth* has been transmitted by Al-Bukhaaree in his *Saheeh* (5267) and by Muslim in his *Saheeh* (1474/20).

قال الإمام النسائي ﷺ في التفسير (627): أخبرني إبراهيم بن يونس بن محمد نا أبي نا حماد ابن سلمة عن ثابت عن أنس ﷺ أن رسول الله ﷺ كانت له أمة يطؤها فلم تزل به عائشة وحفصة حتى

حرمها فأنزل الله عز وجل: (يَٰٓأَيُّهَا ٱلنَّبِىُّ لِمَ تُحَرِّمُ مَآ أَحَلَّ ٱللَّهُ لَكَ تَبْتَغِى مَرْضَاتَ أَزْوَٰجِكَ) إلى آخر الآية.

Anas narrated that the Messenger of Allaah used to have a slave girl that he would have sexual relations with. So 'Aishah and Hafsah kept on nagging him about her until he finally made her forbidden for himself. Then Allaah sent down:

يَٰٓأَيُّهَا ٱلنَّبِىُّ لِمَ تُحَرِّمُ مَآ أَحَلَّ ٱللَّهُ لَكَ تَبْتَغِى مَرْضَاتَ أَزْوَٰجِكَ

"O Prophet, why do you forbid that which Allaah has made permissible for you seeking to please your wives…".

This *hadeeth* has been transmitted by An-Nasaa'ee in his *Tafseer* (627) and Al-Haakim in *Al-Mustadrak*, volume 2, page 393, who classified it to be authentic according to the standards of Muslim, although they (Al-Bukhaaree and Muslim) did not transmit it. Adh-Dhahabee was silent in this regard (he did not oppose that classification). Ash-Sheikh Muqbil commented saying, "In it (the chain of Al-Haakim) is Muhammad ibn Bukair Al-Hadramee who is not from the people of Muslim and he has been marked in *Tahdheeb At-Tahdheeb*, in accordance to what is in *Al-Kamaal*, to be from the people of Al-Bukhaaree; however, Al-Mizzee stated, 'I have not found his narration on him, not in the *Saheeh* or in another collection.' Based upon this, it is said that the *hadeeth* is authentic but not according to the standards of Muslim. Al-Haafidh Ibn Hajar said in *Fathul-Baaree* after ascribing it to An-Nasaa'ee, "Its chain is *saheeh*."

قال الإمام البزار كما في كشف الأستار (ج 3 ص 76-77): حدثنا بشر ثنا ابن رجاء عن إسرائيل عن مسلم عن مجاهد عن ابن عباس: (يَٰٓأَيُّهَا ٱلنَّبِىُّ لِمَ تُحَرِّمُ مَآ أَحَلَّ ٱللَّهُ لَكَ) قال: نزلت هذه الآية في سُرِّيته.

حدثنا محمد بن موسى القطان الواسطي ثنا عاصم بن علي ثنا قيس بن سالم الأفطس عن سعيد ابن جبير عن ابن عباس قال بنحوه.

قال البزار: لا نعلمه متصلا عن ابن عباس إلا من هذين الوجهين.

Ibn 'Abbaas said:

يَٰٓأَيُّهَا ٱلنَّبِىُّ لِمَ تُحَرِّمُ مَآ أَحَلَّ ٱللَّهُ لَكَ

"O Prophet, why do you forbid what Allaah has made permissible for you…", descended because of his concubine."

Al-Bazzaar transmitted this *hadeeth* as mentioned in *Kashf Al-Astaar*, volume 3, page 76. Ash-Sheikh Muqbil ﷺ stated, "The chain that Al-Bazzaar has which includes Bishr ibn Aadam is *matrook* (abandoned) and the chain that comes after it is *hasan*."

قال الضياء المقدسي ﵀ في المختارة (189): أخبرنا أبو أحمد عبد الباقي بن عبد الجبار بن عبد الباقي الحرضي الهروي قراءة عليه ونحن نسمع ببغداد قيل له أخبركم أبو شجاع عمر ابن محمد بن عبد الله البسطامي قراءة عليه وأنت تسمع أنا أبو القاسم أحمد بن محمد بن محمد الخليلي أنا أبو القاسم علي بن أحمد بن محمد بن الحسن الخزاعي أنا أبو سعيد الهيثم بن كليب الشاشي ثنا أبو قلابة عبد الملك بن محمد الرقاشي ثنا مسلم بن إبراهيم ثنا جرير بن حازم عن أيوب عن نافع عن ابن عمر عن عمر ﷺ قال: قال: النبي ﷺ لحفصة لا تحدثي أحدا وإن أم إبراهيم علي حرام فقالت: أتحرم ما أحل الله لك قال: فوالله لا أقربها قال: فلم يقربها حتى أخبرت عائشة فأنزل الله عز وجل: (قَدْ فَرَضَ ٱللَّهُ لَكُمْ تَحِلَّةَ أَيْمَـٰنِكُمْ). إسناده صحيح

'Umar ﷺ said, "The Prophet ﷺ said to Hafsah, 'Do not tell anyone. Indeed Umm Ibraaheem is forbidden to me.' She said, "Do you make forbidden what Allaah has made permissible for you?" He said, 'By Allaah, I will not go near her.' He refrained from her until Hafsah told 'Aishah. Then Allaah ﷻ sent down:

$$قَدْ فَرَضَ ٱللَّهُ لَكُمْ تَحِلَّةَ أَيْمَـٰنِكُمْ$$

"Allaah has already ordained for you the absolution of your oaths…" (verse 2).

Al-Maqdisee transmitted this *hadeeth* in *Al-Ahaadeeth Al-Mukhtaarah* (189) and Al-Haafidh Ibn Katheer classified its chain to be *saheeh*.

Al-Haafidh Ibn Hajar said in *Fathul-Baaree* in the explanation of *hadeeth* number 4912, "It is possible that the verse was revealed because of both reasons." Ash-Sheikh Muqbil ﷺ explained by saying, "Meaning his forbiddance of the honey and his female slave." However, Ash-Shawkaanee said in his *Tafseer, Fath Al-Qadeer*, volume 5, page 252, "These are two authentic reasons for the revelation of the verse. It is possible to harmonize them by saying that both incidences occurred, the story of the honey as well as the story of Maariyah (Umm Ibraaheem), causing Qur'aan to descend in both situations and in both stories he spoke confidentially to one of his wives."

His, the Exalted One's statement:

$$عَسَىٰ رَبُّهُۥٓ إِن طَلَّقَكُنَّ أَن يُبْدِلَهُۥٓ أَزْوَٰجًا خَيْرًا مِّنكُنَّ$$

"Perhaps his Lord, if he were to divorce you, will give him better wives than you…" (verse 5).

قال الإمام مسلم رحمه الله (30/1479): حدثني زهير بن حرب حدثنا عمر بن يونس الحنفي حدثنا عكرمة بن عمار عن سماك أبي زُميل حدثني عبد الله بن عباس رضي الله عنهما حدثني عمر بن الخطاب رضي الله عنه قال: لما اعتزل نبي الله ﷺ نساءه قال: دخلت المسجد فإذا الناس ينكتون بالحصى ويقولون: طلق رسول الله ﷺ نساءه وذلك قبل أن يُؤمرن بالحجاب فقال عمر: لأعلمن ذلك اليوم قال: فدخلت على عائشة فقلت: يا بنت أبي بكر أقد بلغ من شأنك أن تؤذي رسول الله ﷺ فقالت: ما لي وما لك يابن الخطاب عليك بعيبتك قال: فدخلت على حفصة بنت عمر فقلت لها: يا حفصة أقد بلغ من شأنك أن تؤذي رسول الله ﷺ والله لقد علمت أن رسول الله ﷺ لا يحبك ولولا أنا لطلقك رسول الله ﷺ فبكت أشد البكاء فقلت لها: أين رسول الله ﷺ قالت: هو في خزانته في المشربة فدخلت فإذا أنا برباح غلام رسول الله ﷺ قاعدا على أُسكُفّة المشربة مدلٍّ رجليه على نقير من خشب وهو جذع يرقى عليه

رسول الله ﷺ وينحدر فناديت: يا رباح استأذن لي عندك على رسول الله ﷺ فنظر رباح إلى الغرفة ثم نظر إليّ فلم يقل شيئا ثم قلت: يا رباح استأذن لي عندك على رسول الله ﷺ فنظر رباح إلى الغرفة ثم نظر إليّ فلم يقل شيئا ثم رفعت صوتي فقلت: يا رباح استأذن لي عندك على رسول الله ﷺ فإني أظن أن رسول الله ﷺ ظن أني جئت من أجل حفصة والله لئن أمرني رسول الله ﷺ بضرب عنقها لأضربن عنقها ورفعت صوتي فأومأ إليّ أن ارقه فدخلت على رسول الله ﷺ وهو مضطجع على حصير فجلست فأدنى عليه إزاره وليس عليه غيره وإذا الحصير قد أثر في جنبه فنظرت ببصري في خزانة رسول الله ﷺ فإذا أنا بقبضة من شعير نحو الصاع ومثلها قرظا في ناحية الغرفة وإذا أفيق معلق قال: فابتدرت عينايَ قال: ما يبكيك يابن الخطاب قلت يا نبي الله وما لي لا أبكي وهذا الحصير قد أثر في جنبك وهذه خزانتك لا أرى فيها إلا ما أرى وذاك قيصر وكسرى في الثمار والأنهار وأنت رسول الله ﷺ وصفوته وهذه خزانتك فقال: يابن الخطاب ألا ترضى أن تكون لنا الآخرة ولهم الدنيا قلت: بلى قال: ودخلت عليه حين دخلت وأنا أرى الغضب في وجهه فقلت: يا رسول الله ما يشق عليك من شأن النساء فإن كنت طلقتهن فإن الله تعالى معك وملائكته وجبريل وميكائيل وأنا وأبو بكر والمؤمنون معك وقلما تكلمت وأحمد الله بكلام إلا رجوت أن يكون الله يُصدّق قولي الذي أقول ونزلت هذه الآية آية التخيير: (عَسَىٰ رَبُّهُۥٓ إِن طَلَّقَكُنَّ أَن يُبْدِلَهُۥٓ أَزْوَٰجًا خَيْرًا مِّنكُنَّ) (وَإِن تَظَٰهَرَا عَلَيْهِ فَإِنَّ ٱللَّهَ هُوَ مَوْلَىٰهُ وَجِبْرِيلُ وَصَٰلِحُ ٱلْمُؤْمِنِينَ ۖ وَٱلْمَلَٰٓئِكَةُ بَعْدَ ذَٰلِكَ ظَهِيرٌ) وكانت عائشة بنت أبي بكر وحفصة تظاهران على سائر نساء النبي ﷺ فقالت: يا رسول الله أطلقتهن قال: لا قلت: يا رسول الله إني دخلت المسجد والمسلمون ينكتون بالحصى يقولون طلق رسول الله ﷺ نساءه أفأنزل فأخبرهم أنك لم تطلقهن قال: نعم إن شئت فلم أزل أحدثه حتى تحسر الغضب عن وجهه وحتى كشر فضحك وكان من أحسن الناس ثغرا ثم نزل نبي الله ﷺ ونزلت ونزلت أتشبث بالجذع

303

ونزل رسول الله ﷺ كأنما يمشي على الأرض ما يمسه بيده فقلت: يا رسول الله إنما كنت في الغرفة تسعة وعشرين قال: إن الشهر يكون تسعا وعشرين فقمت على باب المسجد فناديت بأعلى صوتي: لم يطلق رسول الله ﷺ نساءه ونزلت هذه الآية: (وَإِذَا جَاءَهُمْ أَمْرٌ مِّنَ ٱلْأَمْنِ أَوِ ٱلْخَوْفِ أَذَاعُوا۟ بِهِۦ ۖ وَلَوْ رَدُّوهُ إِلَى ٱلرَّسُولِ وَإِلَىٰٓ أُو۟لِى ٱلْأَمْرِ مِنْهُمْ لَعَلِمَهُ ٱلَّذِينَ يَسْتَنۢبِطُونَهُۥ مِنْهُمْ) فكنت أنا استنبطت ذلك الأمر وأنزل الله عز وجل آية التخيير.

'Umar ibn Al-Khattaab ﷺ narrated about when the Prophet of Allaah ﷺ cut off relations with his wives saying, "I entered the *masjid* and found the people scratching up the ground with pebbles (out of grief) saying, 'The Messenger of Allaah ﷺ has divorced his wives,' and this was before the women were ordered to wear the veil.[136] 'Umar said, "Today I will come to know what happened." So I went to 'Aishah and asked, "O daughter of Abu Bakr, have you gone so far as to annoy the Messenger of Allaah ﷺ!" She replied, 'What business do I have with you, O son of Al-Khattaab? Go advise your daughter.' So I went to Hafsah bint 'Umar and said to her, "O Hafsah, have you gone so far as to annoy the Messenger of Allaah ﷺ! By Allaah, you know very well that the Messenger of Allaah ﷺ does not love you, and if it were not for me the Messenger of Allaah ﷺ would have divorced you." She then began crying very intensely. I said to her, 'Where is the Messenger of Allaah ﷺ?' "He is in his storage room in the attic," she said. I went to the storage room and found Rabaah, the boy servant of the Messenger of Allaah ﷺ, sitting at the doorstep of the attic with his legs hanging down from the wooden stairs made from a tree trunk that the Messenger of Allaah ﷺ used in order to climb up and down. I called out, 'O Rabaah, ask permission for me to enter the Messenger of Allaah's ﷺ storage room!' Rabaah looked towards the room, then he looked towards me without saying anything so I repeated, "O Rabaah, ask permission for me to enter the storage room of the Messenger of Allaah ﷺ!" Again, Rabaah then looked towards the room, then he looked towards me and did not say anything so I raised my voice saying, 'O Rabaah, ask permission for me to enter the storage room of the Messenger of Allaah ﷺ; Indeed I think that the Messenger of Allaah ﷺ thinks that I have come because of Hafsah! By Allaah, if the Messenger of Allaah ﷺ orders me to strike her neck (chopping off her head), I will indeed strike her neck!'

He then signaled for me to come up. I entered the Messenger of Allaah's ﷺ room while he was lying down on his side on a mat. I sat down and he tucked in his *Izaar* (lower garment) [and I noticed that] he was not wearing anything else. To my surprise, I found that the mat had left an imprint in his side and I began to look around the storage room of the Messenger of Allaah ﷺ. I saw

---

[136] Refer to footnote number 58.

some barley that measured about one *Saa'* (four double handfuls) and the same measurement of pods of the sant tree in the corner. I also saw a poor quality water-skin hanging (on the wall). My eyes began flowing with tears. He asked, "What makes you cry, O son of Al-Khattaab?" I replied, 'O Prophet of Allaah, why should I not cry while this mat has left an imprint in your side and I see nothing in you storage room but this [little amount of food] while Caesar (the emperor of Rome) and Kisraa (the emperor of Persia) have fruits and rivers; and you are the Messenger of Allaah ﷺ and His chosen one, yet, this is your storage room.' He said, "O son of Al-Khattaab, are you not pleased that we have the hereafter and they have this life?" I said, 'Certainly!'

He ('Umar) said, "When I entered his room I saw the anger in his face so I said, 'O Messenger of Allaah, what, in regards to the women has distressed you? Verily if you have divorced them then indeed Allaah ﷻ is with you, as well as His angels, Jibreel, Mikaa'eel, and Abu Bakr and I and the believers are with you.' Rarely, and I praise Allaah I and, did I make a statement without hoping that Allaah approves of what I have said. Thereafter this verse, the verse of the choice, descended:

عَسَىٰ رَبُّهُۥ إِن طَلَّقَكُنَّ أَن يُبْدِلَهُۥٓ أَزْوَٰجًا خَيْرًا مِّنكُنَّ

"Perhaps his Lord, if he were to divorce you, will give him better wives than you…"

وَإِن تَظَٰهَرَا عَلَيْهِ فَإِنَّ ٱللَّهَ هُوَ مَوْلَىٰهُ وَجِبْرِيلُ وَصَٰلِحُ ٱلْمُؤْمِنِينَ ۖ وَٱلْمَلَٰٓئِكَةُ بَعْدَ ذَٰلِكَ ظَهِيرٌ

"And if you help one another against him then verily Allaah is his protector and Jibreel and the righteous among the believers, and furthermore, the angels are his helpers" (*At-Tahreem*: 4).

'Aishah, the daughter of Abu Bakr, and Hafsah were helping one another against the rest of the wives of the Prophet ﷺ. I asked, 'O Messenger of Allaah, did you divorce them?' "No, he replied. I said, 'O Messenger of Allaah, verily I entered the *masjid* and found the Muslims scratching up the ground with pebbles saying, "The Messenger of Allaah ﷺ has divorced his wives.' Should I go down and tell them that you have not divorced them?" He said, "Yes, if you wish." I continued to talk with him until the signs of anger disappeared from his face and he began smiling and laughing. He had the best looking gap between his two front teeth that I have ever seen.

The Prophet of Allaah ﷺ and I went down the stairs. I went down the steps hanging on to the trunk while the Messenger of Allaah ﷺ descended without touching it as if he were walking on the ground. I then said to him, 'O Messenger of Allaah, you were only in the room for twenty nine days.' "A month can be twenty nine days," he said. I then went and stood at the door of the *masjid* and shouted with my loudest voice, 'The Messenger of Allaah ﷺ did not divorce his wives!' And this verse descended in this regard:

$$\text{وَإِذَا جَآءَهُمْ أَمْرٌ مِّنَ ٱلْأَمْنِ أَوِ ٱلْخَوْفِ أَذَاعُواْ بِهِۦ ۖ وَلَوْ رَدُّوهُ إِلَى ٱلرَّسُولِ وَإِلَىٰٓ أُوْلِى ٱلْأَمْرِ مِنْهُمْ لَعَلِمَهُ ٱلَّذِينَ يَسْتَنۢبِطُونَهُۥ مِنْهُمْ}$$

"And when there comes to them a matter concerning safety or fear they publicize it. And if only they had referred it to the Messenger or to those of authority amongst them, those who investigate it would come to know about it directly from them" (*An-Nisei*: 83). I investigated that situation and in consequence, Allaah ﷻ sent down the verse of the choice."

Muslim transmitted this *hadeeth* in his *Saheeh* (1479/30). As for the hadeeth of 'Umar which reads, "I (my opinion) was in agreement with my Lord in three situations…" has already been mentioned in *Sooratul-Baqarah*, verse 125.

سورة الـجـن

Sooratul-Jinn

قال الإمام البخاري رحمه الله (4921): حدثنا موسى بن إسماعيل حدثنا أبو عوانة عن أبي بشر عن سعيد بن جبير عن ابن عباس رضي الله عنهما قال: انطلق رسول الله ﷺ في طائفة من أصحابه عامدين إلى سوق عكاظ وقد حيل بين الشياطين وبين خبر السماء وأرسلت عليهم الشهب فرجعت الشياطين فقالوا: ما لكم فقالوا: حيل بيننا وبين خبر السماء وأرسلت علينا الشهب قال: ما حال بينكم وبين خبر السماء إلا ما حدث فاضربوا مشارق الأرض ومغاربها فانظروا ما هذا الأمر الذي حدث فانطلقوا فضربوا مشارق الأرض ومغاربها ينظرون ما هذا الأمر الذي بينهم وبين خبر السماء قال فانطلق الذين توجهوا نحو تهامة إلى رسول الله ﷺ بنخلة وهو عامد إلى سوق عكاظ وهو يصلي بأصحابه صلاة الفجر فلما سمعوا القرآن تسمعوا له فقالوا: هذا الذي حال بينكم وبين خبر السماء فهنالك رجعوا إلى قومهم فقالوا: يا قومنا إنا سمعنا قرآنا عجبا يهدي إلى الرشد فآمنا به ولن نشرك بربنا أحدا وأنزل الله عز وجل على نبيه ﷺ: ﴿قُلْ أُوحِيَ إِلَيَّ أَنَّهُ ٱسْتَمَعَ نَفَرٌ مِّنَ ٱلْجِنِّ﴾ وإنما أوحي إليه قول الجن.

Ibn 'Abbaas said, "The Messenger of Allaah set out with a group of his Companions to the market 'Ukaadh. [During this time] The devils had been obstructed from listening to the news of the heavens and shooting stars were rained down on them. The devils returned [without any news from the heavens] so they (their comrades) said to them, 'What's with you all?' They said, "We have been obstructed from listening to the news of the heavens and shooting stars were sent down on us." He (the devil) said, 'Nothing would obstruct you from the news of the heavens except the occurrence of a major event. Travel to the eastern and western corners of the earth and see what event has taken place." So they left traveling to the eastern and western corners of the earth to find out about this event that had obstructed them from the news of the heavens. Those who headed towards Tihaamah went to the Messenger of Allaah while he was at a date palm tree where he stopped to pray *Fajr* with his Companions on their way to the market 'Ukaadh. When they heard the Qur'aan they listened to it closely and said, 'This is what has obstructed us from the news of the heavens.' At that point they returned to their people and said to them, "O our people, verily we have heard a wonderful recitation. It guides to the right path and we have believed it in and we shall never join anything in worship with our Lord." And Allaah sent down the following to His Prophet:

﴿قُلْ أُوحِيَ إِلَيَّ أَنَّهُ ٱسْتَمَعَ نَفَرٌ مِّنَ ٱلْجِنِّ﴾

"Say, 'It has been revealed to me that a group of *Jinn* listened…'".

Only the statement of the *Jinn* was revealed to him."

Al-Bukhaaree transmitted this *hadeeth* in his *Saheeh* (4921) and likewise Muslim in his *Saheeh* (449).

سورة المزمل

Sooratul-Muzzammil

قال الإمام أبو داود ﵀ (1305): حدثنا أحمد بن محمد يعني المروزي ثنا وكيع عن مسعر عن سماك الحنفي عن ابن عباس ﵄ قال: لما نزلت أول المزمل كانوا يقومون نحوا من قيامهم في شهر رمضان حتى نزل آخرها وكان بين أولها وآخرها سنة.

Ibn 'Abbaas said, "When the first part of *Sooratul-Muzzammil* descended, they used to stand in night prayer similar to how they would stand during the month of Ramadaan until the last part of it descended. Between the first and last part of it was one year."[137]

This *hadeeth* has been transmitted by Abu Daawud in *As-Sunan* (1305). Ash-Sheikh Muqbil said, "the people of the *hadeeth*'s chain are people of the *Saheeh* (Al-Bukhaaree and/or Muslim) except for Ahmad ibn Muhammad Al-Marwazee Abul-Hasan ibn Shabbuwaih, however, he is trustworthy…".

---

[137] A similar *hadeeth* to this has been narrated by 'Aishah in a portion of a long *hadeeth* in *Saheeh Muslim* (746/139) the highlight is: "…So she said, "Do you not read:

يَٰٓأَيُّهَا ٱلْمُزَّمِّلُ

"O you wrapped in garments."
I said, "Certainly!" She said, "Verily Allaah ﷻ made the night prayer obligatory in the first part of this *Soorah*. So the Prophet of Allaah ﷺ and his Companions prayed it for a year and Allaah had withheld its last part for twelve months in the heavens until Allaah sent down in the end of this *Soorah* the relief. Then the night prayer became voluntary after being obligatory…"

سورة المـدثـر

Sooratul-Muddath'thir

قال الإمام البخاري رَحِمَهُ اللهُ (4922): حدثنا يحيى حدثنا وكيع عن علي بن المبارك عن يحيى بن أبي كثير سألت أبا سلمة بن عبد الرحمن عن أول ما نزل من القرآن قال: (يَٰٓأَيُّهَا ٱلۡمُدَّثِّرُ) قلت: يقولون:

(ٱقۡرَأۡ بِٱسۡمِ رَبِّكَ ٱلَّذِى خَلَقَ) فقال أبو سلمة: سألت جابر بن عبد الله رَضِيَ اللَّهُ عَنْهُ عن ذلك وقلت له مثل الذي قلت فقال جابر: لا أحدثك إلا ما حدثنا رسول الله ﷺ قال: جاورت بحراء فلما قضيت جواري هبطت فنوديت فنظرت عن يميني فلم أر شيئا ونظرت عن شمالي فلم أر شيئا ونظرت أمامي فلم أر شيئا ونظرت خلفي فلم أر شيئا فرفعت رأسي فرأيت شيئا فأتيت خديجة فقلت: دثروني وصبوا علي ماء باردا قال: فدثروني وصبوا علي ماء باردا قال: فنزلت: (يَٰٓأَيُّهَا ٱلۡمُدَّثِّرُ ۝ قُمۡ فَأَنذِرۡ ۝ وَرَبَّكَ فَكَبِّرۡ ۝).

Yahyaa ibn Abee Katheer said, "I asked Abu Salamah ibn 'Abdir-Rahmaan about the first part of the Qur'aan to descend. He replied [by reciting],

يَٰٓأَيُّهَا ٱلۡمُدَّثِّرُ

'O you enveloped in garments.'

I said, "They say [it was],

ٱقۡرَأۡ بِٱسۡمِ رَبِّكَ ٱلَّذِى خَلَقَ

'Read in the name of your Lord who has created.'

Abu Salamah said, "I asked Jaabir ibn 'Abdillaah ﷺ about that and I said to him similar to what you said and he replied by saying, "I will only tell you what the Messenger of Allaah has ﷺ told us. He said, "I [used] to worship in seclusion at the cave Hiraa. [On one occasion] when I finished my worship in seclusion, I came down [from the cave] and I was called so I looked to my right but I did not see anything. I then looked to my left but I did not see anything. I looked in front of me but I did not see anything and I looked in back of me but I did not see anything. Then I raised my head I saw something. Because of this, I went to Khadeejah and said, 'Cover me and pour cold water over me!' So they covered me and poured cold water over me, then the verse descended:

$$\text{يَٰٓأَيُّهَا ٱلْمُدَّثِّرُ ۝ قُمْ فَأَنذِرْ ۝ وَرَبَّكَ فَكَبِّرْ ۝}$$

"O you enveloped in garments. Arise and warn. And magnify your Lord."

Al-Bukhaaree transmitted this *hadeeth* in his *Saheeh* (4922) as well as Muslim in his *Saheeh* (161/257).

NOTE: Al-Haafidh Ibn Katheer explained in his *Tafseer*, volume 4, page 440 that Jaabir ibn 'Abdillaah went against the majority of Scholars when he asserted that "the first part of the Qur'aan to be revealed was *Al-Muddath'thir*," because they took the position that the first part of the Qur'aan to descend was His statement,

$$\text{ٱقْرَأْ بِٱسْمِ رَبِّكَ ٱلَّذِى خَلَقَ}$$

"Read in the name of your Lord who has created."

Ibn Katheer then went on to mention the previously mentioned *hadeeth* of the two Saheehs, "And Muslim transmitted by way of the chain of 'Aqeel on Ibn Shihaab on Abee Salamah that he said, 'Jaabir ibn 'Abdillaah narrated to me that he heard the Messenger of Allaah talk about the period when the revelation was delayed." In this regard he mentioned the following in his narration: "Then while I was walking I suddenly heard a voice from the heavens so I looked towards the heavens and found the angel that came to me at Hiraa sitting on a throne between the heavens and the earth. I was so frightened by him that I fell to the ground. Then I went to my family and said, "Cover me! Cover me!" Then Allaah sent down:

$$\text{يَٰٓأَيُّهَا ٱلْمُدَّثِّرُ ۝ قُمْ فَأَنذِرْ ۝}$$

"O you enveloped in garments. Arise and warn," including

$$\text{فَٱهْجُرْ}$$

'And keep away from *Ar-Rujz*.'

Abu Salamah said, "*Ar-Rujz* is the idols." After this the revelation increased and came consistently."

This is the text of Al-Bukhaaree and this wording is what has been correctly memorized and it necessitates that revelation had already descended before this because of his statement, "...And found the angel that was at Hiraa." That was Jibreel when he came to him with His statement,

ٱقۡرَأۡ بِٱسۡمِ رَبِّكَ ٱلَّذِي خَلَقَ ۝ خَلَقَ ٱلۡإِنسَـٰنَ مِنۡ عَلَقٍ ۝ ٱقۡرَأۡ وَرَبُّكَ ٱلۡأَكۡرَمُ ۝ ٱلَّذِي عَلَّمَ بِٱلۡقَلَمِ ۝ عَلَّمَ ٱلۡإِنسَـٰنَ مَا لَمۡ يَعۡلَمۡ ۝

"Read in the name of your Lord who has created. He has created man from a clot. Read, and your Lord is the Most Generous. He who has taught by the pen. He has taught man that which he knew not." After this initial revelation there was a delay and eventually the angel returned. The way to harmonize (these narrations) is (to say) that the first thing revealed after the delay of the revelation was this *Soorah*." Then he (Ibn Katheer) mentioned the proofs for that. Al-Haafidh Ibn Hajar also mentioned something similar to this in *Fathul-Baaree* in the explanation of *hadeeth* (4) and *hadeeth* (4924).

سورة القيامة

Sooratul-Qiyaamah

His, the Exalted One's statement:

لَا تُحَرِّكْ بِهِ لِسَانَكَ لِتَعْجَلَ بِهِ ۝ إِنَّ عَلَيْنَا جَمْعَهُ وَقُرْآنَهُ ۝

"Move not your tongue with it (the Qur'aan) to make haste therewith. Indeed, its collection and recitation is upon Us" (verses 16-17).

قال الإمام البخاري رحمه الله (5): حدثنا موسى بن إسماعيل قال حدثنا أبو عوانة قال حدثنا موسى ابن أبي عائشة قال حدثنا سعيد بن جبير عن ابن عباس ﷺ في قوله تعالى: (لَا تُحَرِّكْ بِهِ لِسَانَكَ لِتَعْجَلَ بِهِ) قال كان رسول الله ﷺ يعالج من التنزيل شدة وكان مما يحرك شفتيه فقال ابن عباس: فأنا أحركهما لكم كما كان رسول الله ﷺ يحركهما وقال سعيد: أنا أحركهما كما رأيت ابن عباس يحركهما فحرك شفتيه فأنزل الله تعالى: (لَا تُحَرِّكْ بِهِ لِسَانَكَ لِتَعْجَلَ بِهِ ۝ إِنَّ عَلَيْنَا جَمْعَهُ وَقُرْآنَهُ ۝) قال: جمعه لك في صدرك وتقرأه: (فَإِذَا قَرَأْنَاهُ فَاتَّبِعْ قُرْآنَهُ) قال: فاستمع له وأنصت: (ثُمَّ إِنَّ عَلَيْنَا بَيَانَهُ) ثم إن علينا أن تقرأه فكان رسول الله ﷺ بعد ذلك إذا أتاه جبريل استمع فإذا انطلق جبريل قرأه النبي ﷺ كما قرأه.

Sa'eed ibn Jubair narrated on Ibn 'Abbaas ﷺ about His ﷻ statement:

لَا تُحَرِّكْ بِهِ لِسَانَكَ لِتَعْجَلَ بِهِ

"Move not your tongue with it (the Qur'aan) to make haste therewith."

He said, "The Messenger of Allaah ﷺ used to undergo hardship from the revelation and he would often move his lips." Ibn 'Abbaas said, "I am now moving them for you the way the Messenger of Allaah ﷺ used to move them." Sa'eed said, "I am now moving them the way I saw Ibn 'Abbaas move them," and he began moving his lips. "Then Allaah ﷻ sent down the following:

لَا تُحَرِّكْ بِهِ لِسَانَكَ لِتَعْجَلَ بِهِ ۝ إِنَّ عَلَيْنَا جَمْعَهُ وَقُرْآنَهُ ۝

'Move not your tongue with it (the Qur'aan) to make haste therewith. Indeed, its collection and recitation is upon Us.'

He (Ibn 'Abbaas) said, "Collecting it for you in your chest and your recitation of it."

فَإِذَا قَرَأْنَاهُ فَاتَّبِعْ قُرْءَانَهُ

"So when We recite it, follow its recitation."

He (Ibn 'Abbaas) said [it means], "Listen to it and remain silent."

ثُمَّ إِنَّ عَلَيْنَا بَيَانَهُ

"Then its exposition is upon Us."

[Meaning] "Then your recitation of it is upon Us."
After that, when Jibreel would come to the Messenger of Allaah ﷺ he would listen. Then when Jibreel would leave, the Prophet ﷺ would recite it as he had recited it."

Al-Bukhaaree transmitted this *hadeeth* in his *Saheeh* (5) as well as Muslim in his *Saheeh* (448).

His, the Exalted One's statement:

أَوْلَىٰ لَكَ فَأَوْلَىٰ ۝ ثُمَّ أَوْلَىٰ لَكَ فَأَوْلَىٰ ۝

"You are close (to destruction), you are close. Again, you are close (to destruction), you are close" (verses 34-35).

قال الإمام النسائي رحمه الله في التفسير (658): أخبرني إبراهيم بن يعقوب نا أبو النعمان نا أبو عوانة، وأنا أبو داود نا محمد بن سليمان نا أبو عوانة عن موسى بن أبي عائشة عن سعيد بن جبير قال قلت لابن عباس ﷺ: (أَوْلَىٰ لَكَ فَأَوْلَىٰ) قاله رسول الله ﷺ وأنزله الله عز وجل قال: قاله رسول الله ﷺ ثم أنزله الله.

اللفظ لإبراهيم.

Sa'eed ibn Jubair said, "I said to Ibn 'Abbaas:

أَوْلَىٰ لَكَ فَأَوْلَىٰ

'You are close (to destruction), you are close.'

Did the Messenger of Allaah ﷺ say it initially and then Allaah ﷻ sent it down?' He replied, "The Messenger of Allaah ﷺ said it, then Allaah sent it down."[138]

An-Nasaa'ee transmitted this *hadeeth* in his *Tafseer* (658) with an authentic chain.

---

[138] Ibn Katheer mentioned in his *Tafseer* that Ibn Abee Haatim transmitted on Sa'eed ibn Jubair that the Prophet ﷺ said it to Abu Jahl and then Qur'aan descended with it.

سورة النازعات

Sooratun-Naazi'aat

<u>His, the Exalted One's statement:</u>

يَسْـَٔلُونَكَ عَنِ ٱلسَّاعَةِ أَيَّانَ مُرْسَىٰهَا ۝ فِيمَ أَنتَ مِن ذِكْرَىٰهَآ ۝ إِلَىٰ رَبِّكَ مُنتَهَىٰهَآ ۝ إِنَّمَآ أَنتَ مُنذِرُ مَن يَخْشَىٰهَا ۝

"They ask you about the hour [saying], 'When is it going to take place?" In what (position) are you to mention [when] it [will occur]? (Knowledge of it) ultimately goes to your Lord. You are only a warner for those who fear it" (verses 42-45).

قال الإمام ابن جرير ﵀ (ج 24 ص 213): حدثنا أبو كريب قال ثنا وكيع عن إسماعيل عن طارق بن شهاب ﵁ قال: كان النبي ﷺ لا يزال يذكر شأن الساعة حتى نزلت: (يَسْـَٔلُونَكَ عَنِ ٱلسَّاعَةِ أَيَّانَ مُرْسَىٰهَا) إلى قوله: (مَن يَخْشَىٰهَا).

Taariq ibn Shihaab ﵁ said, "The Prophet ﷺ used to constantly mention the hour until this verse descended:

يَسْـَٔلُونَكَ عَنِ ٱلسَّاعَةِ أَيَّانَ مُرْسَىٰهَا

"They ask you about the hour [saying], 'When is it going to take place?," up to His statement,

مَن يَخْشَىٰهَا

"... for those who fear it."

Ibn Jareer transmitted this *hadeeth* in his *Tafseer*, volume 24, page 213. Al-Haithamee said in *Majma' Az-Zawaa'id*, volume 7, page 133, "Al-Bazzaar has transmitted it and the people of its chain are people of the *Saheeh* (Al-Bukhaaree and/or Muslim)." Ibn Katheer said in his *Tafseer*, volume 2, page 273, "This is a chain that is *jayyid awe*."

سورة عبس

Sooratu 'Abasa

قال الحافظ ابن كثير ﷺ في التفسير (ج 4 ص 470): قال الإمام أبو يعلى في مسنده حدثنا محمد بن مهدي حدثنا عبد الرزاق أخبرنا معمر عن قتادة عن أنس ﷺ في قوله تعالى: (عَبَسَ وَتَوَلَّىٰ) جاء ابن أم مكتوم إلى النبي ﷺ وهو يكلم أبي بن خلف فأعرض عنه فأنزل الله عز وجل: (عَبَسَ وَتَوَلَّىٰ ۝ أَن جَآءَهُ ٱلْأَعْمَىٰ ۝) فكان النبي ﷺ بعد ذلك يكرمه.

Anas ﷺ said about His ﷻ statement,

عَبَسَ وَتَوَلَّىٰ

"He frowned and turned away,"

"Ibn Umm Mattoon went to the Prophet ﷺ while he was speaking to Ubay ibn Khalid and he turned away from him. Then Allaah ﷻ revealed,

عَبَسَ وَتَوَلَّىٰ ۝ أَن جَآءَهُ ٱلْأَعْمَىٰ ۝

'He frowned and turned away. Because there came to him the blind man.' After that [occurrence] the Prophet ﷺ used to honor him."

Abu Ya'laa transmitted this *hadeeth* as mentioned in *Tafseer Ibn Katheer*, volume 4, page 470. Ash-Shawkaanee mentioned in his *Tafseer* that 'Abdur-Razzaaq and 'Abd ibn Humaid and Abu Ya'laa have transmitted it as well. Ash-Sheikh Muqbil ﷺ commented saying, "The people of its chain are from the *Saheeh collection* (Al-Bukhaaree and/or Muslim) except for Muhammad ibn Mahdee the Sheikh of Abu Ya'laa and I was unable to find his biography. In any case it, does not effect the *hadeeth*. As long as 'Abdur-Razzaaq has transmitted it then its people are people of the *Saheeh*…".

سورة المطففين

Sooratul-Mutaffifeen

قال الإمام ابن ماجه رَحِمَهُ اللهُ (2223): حدثنا عبد الرحمن بن بشر بن الحكم ومحمد بن عقيل بن خويلد قالا ثنا علي بن الحسين بن واقد حدثني أبي حدثني يزيد النحوي أن عكرمة حدثه عن ابن عباس رَضِيَ اللهُ عَنْهُ قال: لما قدم النبي ﷺ المدينة كانوا من أخبث الناس كيلا فأنزل الله سبحانه: (وَيْلٌ لِّلْمُطَفِّفِينَ) فأحسنوا الكيل بعد ذلك.

Ibn 'Abbaas said, "When the Prophet ﷺ arrived at Madeenah they (the inhabitants of Madeenah) were the worst people [when it came] to measuring. Then Allaah sent down the following:

$$\text{وَيْلٌ لِّلْمُطَفِّفِينَ}$$

'Woe to those who give less in measure and weight.' After this they began measuring correctly.

Ibn Maajah transmitted this *hadeeth* in *As-Sunan* (2223) as well as Ibn Jareer in his *Tafseer*, volume 24, page 277. Similarly Al-Haakim transmitted it in *Al-Mustadrak*, volume 2, page 33. Ash-Sheikh Muqbil added, "These chains combined substantiate the authenticity of the *hadeeth*, and Allaah knows best."

سورة الـضحى

Sooratud-Duhaa

قال الإمام البخاري رحمه الله (4950): حدثنا أحمد بن يونس حدثنا زهير حدثنا الأسود بن قيس قال سمعت جندب بن سفيان ﷺ قال: اشتكى رسول الله ﷺ فلم يقم ليلتين أو ثلاثا فجاءت امرأة فقالت: يا محمد إني لأرجو أن يكون شيطانك قد تركك لم أره قربك منذ ليلتين أو ثلاثا فأنزل الله عز وجل: (وَٱلضُّحَىٰ ۝ وَٱلَّيْلِ إِذَا سَجَىٰ ۝ مَا وَدَّعَكَ رَبُّكَ وَمَا قَلَىٰ ۝).

Jundub ibn Sufyaan ﷺ said, "The Messenger of Allaah ﷺ was sick and in consequence, he did not stand (at night for prayer) for two or three nights. A woman came and said, 'O Muhammad, indeed I hope that your devil has abandoned you. I have not seen him approach you for two or three nights.' Then Allaah ﷻ sent down:

وَٱلضُّحَىٰ ۝ وَٱلَّيْلِ إِذَا سَجَىٰ ۝ مَا وَدَّعَكَ رَبُّكَ وَمَا قَلَىٰ ۝

"By the forenoon. And the night when it is still. Your Lord has neither forsaken you nor hated you."

This *hadeeth* has been transmitted by Al-Bukhaaree in his *Saheeh* (4950), and by Muslim in his *Saheeh* (1797/115).

His, the Exalted One's statement:

وَلَسَوْفَ يُعْطِيكَ رَبُّكَ فَتَرْضَىٰ

"And indeed your Lord is going to give to you so that you will be well pleased" (verse 5).

قال الحافظ ابن كثير رحمه الله في التفسير (ج 4 ص 522): وقال الإمام أبو عمرو الأوزاعي عن إسماعيل بن عبد الله بن أبي المهاجر المخزومي عن علي بن عبد الله بن عباس عن أبيه رضي الله عنهما قال: عرض على رسول الله ﷺ ما هو مفتوح على أمته من بعده كنزا كنزا فسر بذلك فأنزل الله: (وَلَسَوْفَ يُعْطِيكَ رَبُّكَ فَتَرْضَىٰ) فأعطاه في الجنة ألف قصر في كل قصر ما ينبغي له من الأزواج والخدم.

رواه ابن جرير وابن أبي حاتم من طريقه وهذا إسناد صحيح إلى ابن عباس ومثل هذا ما يقال إلا عن توقيف.

Ibn 'Abbaas ؓ said, "The Messenger of Allaah ﷺ was shown what his nation would be granted through victory, treasure after treasure and he was pleased by [what he saw]. Then Allaah sent down:

$$\text{وَلَسَوْفَ يُعْطِيكَ رَبُّكَ فَتَرْضَىٰ}$$

'And indeed your Lord is going to give to you so that you will be well pleased.' So he gave him one thousand palaces in paradise, every palace [containing] what suits it of wives and servants."

Ibn Katheer mentioned this *hadeeth* and its chain in his *Tafseer*, volume 4, page 522, and classified it to be *saheeh* Ibn 'Abbaas. The *hadeeth* was also transmitted by Ibn Jareer in his *Tafseer*, volume 24, page 487, and At-Tabaraanee in *Al-Mu'jam Al-Kabeer*, volume 10, page 277, and in *Al-Mu'jam Al-Awsat* (526), and Al-Haakim in *Al-Mustadrak*, volume 2, page 526.

سورة العلق

Sooratul-'Alaq

His, the Exalted One's statement:

$$كَلَّآ إِنَّ ٱلْإِنسَـٰنَ لَيَطْغَىٰٓ$$

"Nay, verily man does transgress…" (verse 6-19).

قال الإمام مسلم ﵀ (2797): حدثنا عبيد الله بن معاذ ومحمد بن عبد الأعلى القيسي قالا حدثنا المعتمر عن أبيه حدثني نعيم بن أبي هند عن أبي حازم عن أبي هريرة ﵁ قال: قال أبو جهل: هل يعفر محمد وجهه بين أظهركم قال فقيل: نعم فقال: واللات والعزى لئن رأيته يفعل ذلك لأطأن على رقبته أو لأعفرن وجهه في التراب قال فأتى رسول الله ﷺ وهو يصلي زعم ليطأ على رقبته قال: فما فجئهم منه إلا وهو ينكص على عقبيه ويتقي بيديه قال فقيل له: ما لك فقال: إن بيني وبينه لخندقا من نار وهولا وأجنحة فقال رسول الله ﷺ: لو دنا مني لاختطفته الملائكة عضوا عضوا قال: فأنزل الله عز وجل لا ندري في حديث أبي هريرة أو شيء بلغه: (كَلَّآ إِنَّ ٱلْإِنسَـٰنَ لَيَطْغَىٰٓ ۝ أَن رَّءَاهُ ٱسْتَغْنَىٰٓ ۝ إِنَّ إِلَىٰ رَبِّكَ ٱلرُّجْعَىٰٓ ۝ أَرَءَيْتَ ٱلَّذِى يَنْهَىٰ ۝ عَبْدًا إِذَا صَلَّىٰٓ ۝ أَرَءَيْتَ إِن كَانَ عَلَى ٱلْهُدَىٰٓ ۝ أَوْ أَمَرَ بِٱلتَّقْوَىٰٓ ۝ أَرَءَيْتَ إِن كَذَّبَ وَتَوَلَّىٰٓ ۝) يعني أبا جهل (أَلَمْ يَعْلَم بِأَنَّ ٱللَّهَ يَرَىٰ ۝ كَلَّا لَئِن لَّمْ يَنتَهِ لَنَسْفَعًۢا بِٱلنَّاصِيَةِ ۝ نَاصِيَةٍ كَـٰذِبَةٍ خَاطِئَةٍ ۝ فَلْيَدْعُ نَادِيَهُۥ ۝ سَنَدْعُ ٱلزَّبَانِيَةَ ۝ كَلَّا لَا تُطِعْهُ). زاد عبيد الله في حديثه قال: وأمره بما أمره به وزاد بن عبد الأعلى: (فَلْيَدْعُ نَادِيَهُۥ) يعني قومه.

Abu Hurairah ﵁ said, "Abu Jahl said, 'Does Muhammad dirty his face (by prostrating in prayer) in your presence?' It was said, "Yes." He said, 'By Al-laat and Al-'Uzzaa, if I see him doing that I will certainly step on his neck' or "shove his face in the dirt." He then went to the Messenger of Allaah ﷺ while he was praying claiming that he was going to step on his neck. Then they (the onlookers) were taken by surprise when they saw none other than him (Abu Jahl) walking backwards on his heels holding his arms up to guard himself. It was said to him, 'What's with you?' "Verily there was between myself and him a ditch of fire and a terrifying sight and wings," He replied. The Messenger of Allaah ﷺ said, 'If he were to have come close to me, the angels would have snatched him [ripping him apart] limb by limb.' Then

Allaah ﷻ sent down the following, and I am not sure if this is the *hadeeth* of Abu Hurairah or something that has reached him:[139]

$$ كَلَّآ إِنَّ ٱلْإِنسَٰنَ لَيَطْغَىٰٓ ۞ أَن رَّءَاهُ ٱسْتَغْنَىٰٓ ۞ إِنَّ إِلَىٰ رَبِّكَ ٱلرُّجْعَىٰٓ ۞ أَرَءَيْتَ ٱلَّذِى يَنْهَىٰ ۞ عَبْدًا إِذَا صَلَّىٰٓ ۞ أَرَءَيْتَ إِن كَانَ عَلَى ٱلْهُدَىٰٓ ۞ أَوْ أَمَرَ بِٱلتَّقْوَىٰٓ ۞ أَرَءَيْتَ إِن كَذَّبَ وَتَوَلَّىٰٓ ۞ $$

"Nay, verily man does transgress. Because he considers himself self-sufficient. Surely unto your Lord is the return. Tell me, the one who prevents a slave when he prays. Tell me, if he is on the guidance, or enjoins piety. Tell me, if he denies and turns away." He, refers to Abu Jahl.

$$ أَلَمْ يَعْلَم بِأَنَّ ٱللَّهَ يَرَىٰ ۞ كَلَّا لَئِن لَّمْ يَنتَهِ لَنَسْفَعًۢا بِٱلنَّاصِيَةِ ۞ نَاصِيَةٍ كَٰذِبَةٍ خَاطِئَةٍ ۞ فَلْيَدْعُ نَادِيَهُۥ ۞ سَنَدْعُ ٱلزَّبَانِيَةَ ۞ كَلَّا لَا تُطِعْهُ ۞ $$

"Does he not know that Allaah sees. Nay, if he ceases not We will snatch him be the forelock. A lying, sinful forelock. Then let him call upon his council. We will call out the angels of hell. Nay, Do not obey him...".

This *hadeeth* has been transmitted by Muslim in his *Saheeh* (2797).

قال الإمام الترمذي ﵁ (3349): حدثنا أبو سعيد الأشج حدثنا أبو خالد عن داود بن أبي هند عن عكرمة عن ابن عباس ﵁ قال: كان النبي ﷺ يصلي فجاء أبو جهل فقال: ألم أنهك عن هذا ألم أنهك عن هذا فانصرف النبي ﷺ فزبره فقال أبو جهل: إنك لتعلم ما بها ناد أكثر مني فأنزل الله: (فَلْيَدْعُ نَادِيَهُۥ ۞ سَنَدْعُ ٱلزَّبَانِيَةَ ۞) فقال ابن عباس: فوالله لو دعا ناديه لأخذته زبانية الله.

قال: هذا حديث حسن غريب صحيح وفيه عن أبي هريرة رضي الله عنه.

Ibn 'Abbaas ﵁ said, "The Prophet ﷺ was praying when Abu Jahl came and said, 'Did I not forbid you from doing this! Did I not forbid you from doing this!' The Prophet ﷺ then turned away and began giving him a harsh word causing Abu Jahl to say (in response), "Indeed you know that there is no council here that is bigger than mine." Then Allaah sent down the following in this regard:

---

[139] This doubt is from one of the narrators in the chain. Ash-Sheikh Muqbil ﵀ said, "This doubt effects the authenticity of the reason for the revelation, however, I wrote it down because of the many supporting narrations it has."

$$\text{فَلْيَدْعُ نَادِيَهُ ۝ سَنَدْعُ ٱلزَّبَانِيَةَ ۝}$$

'Then let him call upon his council. We will call out the angels of hell.'

Ibn 'Abbaas said, "By Allaah, if he would have called his council, Allaah's angels would have snatched him [away]."

This *hadeeth* has been transmitted by At-Tirmidhee it in his *Jaami'* (3349) and he classified it to be *hasan ghareeb saheeh*.

سورة المسد

Sooratul-Masad

قال الإمام البخاري رحمه الله (4770): حدثنا عمر بن حفص بن غياث حدثنا أبي حدثنا الأعمش قال حدثني عمرو بن مرة عن سعيد بن جبير عن ابن عباس رضي الله عنهما قال: لما نزلت: (وَأَنذِرْ عَشِيرَتَكَ ٱلْأَقْرَبِينَ) صعد النبي ﷺ على الصفا فجعل ينادي: يا بني فهر يا بني عدي لبطون قريش حتى اجتمعوا فجعل الرجل إذا لم يستطع أن يخرج أرسل رسولا لينظر ما هو فجاء أبو لهب وقريش فقال: أرأيتكم لو أخبرتكم أن خيلا بالوادي تريد أن تغير عليكم أكنتم مصدقي قالوا: نعم ما جربنا عليك إلا صدقا قال: فإني نذير لكم بين يدي عذاب شديد فقال أبو لهب: تبا لك سائر اليوم ألهذا جمعتنا فنزلت: (تَبَّتْ يَدَآ أَبِي لَهَبٍ وَتَبَّ ۝ مَآ أَغْنَىٰ عَنْهُ مَالُهُۥ وَمَا كَسَبَ ۝).

Ibn 'Abbaas رضي الله عنه said, "When this verse descended,

$$\text{وَأَنذِرْ عَشِيرَتَكَ ٱلْأَقْرَبِينَ ۝}$$

'And warn your closest kindred (Ash-Shu'araa: 214),'

The Prophet ﷺ climbed onto the mountain As-Safaa and started to call out saying, "O tribe Banee Fihr! O tribe Banee Adee!" He called all the tribes of Quraish until they gathered and if someone was unable to come, he would send a messenger to see what was going on. So Abu Lahab and [members] of Quraish came and then the Prophet said, 'Tell me, if I were to inform you that a cavalry was at the valley waiting to attack you, would you believe me?' "Yes, we have only known you to be truthful," They replied. He said, 'Certainly I am a warner to you before the coming of a severe punishment.' Abu Lahab said, "May you perish in the remainder of this day! Did you gather us for this?" Then this descended:

$$\text{تَبَّتْ يَدَآ أَبِي لَهَبٍ وَتَبَّ ۝ مَآ أَغْنَىٰ عَنْهُ مَالُهُۥ وَمَا كَسَبَ ۝}$$

'Perish the two hands of Abee Lahab and perish he. His wealth and his children will not benefit him."

Al-Bukhaaree transmitted this *hadeeth* in his *Saheeh* (4770) as well as Muslim in his *Saheeh* (208).

All praise is due to Allaah, Lord of all that exists.